C.Smith

Rand Morimoto, Ph.D.,
MCSE, CISSP
Jeff Guillet, MCITP,
MCSE, CISSP

Windows® Server 2008 Hyper-V

UNLEASHED

SAMS | 800 East 96th Street, Indianapolis, Indiana 46240 USA

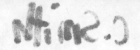

Windows® Server 2008 Hyper-V Unleashed

Copyright © 2009 by Sams Publishing

ISBN-13: 978-0-672-33028-5
ISBN-10: 0-672-33028-8

Library of Congress Cataloging-in-Publication Data

Morimoto, Rand.

  Windows server 2008 Hyper-V unleashed / Rand Morimoto, Jeff Guillet.

       p. cm.

  ISBN 978-0-672-33028-5

 1. Microsoft Windows server Hyper-V. 2. Virtual computer systems. I. Guillet, Jeff. II. Title.

  QA76.9.V5M656 2008

  005.4'476–dc22

                             2008031823

Printed in the United States of America

First Printing: September 2008

Trademarks

All terms mentioned in this book that are known to be trademarks or service marks have been appropriately capitalized. Sams Publishing cannot attest to the accuracy of this information. Use of a term in this book should not be regarded as affecting the validity of any trademark or service mark.

Warning and Disclaimer

Every effort has been made to make this book as complete and as accurate as possible, but no warranty or fitness is implied. The information provided is on an "as is" basis. The authors and the publisher shall have neither liability nor responsibility to any person or entity with respect to any loss or damages arising from the information contained in this book.

Bulk Sales

Sams Publishing offers excellent discounts on this book when ordered in quantity for bulk purchases or special sales. For more information, please contact

U.S. Corporate and Government Sales
1-800-382-3419
corpsales@pearsontechgroup.com

For sales outside of the U.S., please contact

International Sales
international@pearsoned.com

Editor-in-Chief
Karen Gettman

Executive Editor
Neil Rowe

Development Editor
Mark Renfrow

Managing Editor
Patrick Kanouse

Project Editor
Jennifer Gallant

Copy Editor
Keith Cline

Indexer
Brad Herriman

Proofreader
Water Crest
Publishing, Inc.

Technical Editor
Scott Rose, MCSE

Publishing Coordinator
Cindy Teeters

Book Designer
Gary Adair

Contents at a Glance

Table of Contents

Part II   Windows 2008 Hyper-V Host and Guest Installation

4   Installing Windows 2008 Server and the Hyper-V Role   101

About the Authors

Rand Morimoto, Ph.D., MCSE, CISSP, has been in the computer industry for more than 30 years and has authored, co-authored, or been a contributing writer for dozens of best-selling books on Windows 2008, Exchange 2007, Security, BizTalk Server, and remote and mobile computing. Rand is the president of Convergent Computing, an IT consulting firm in the San Francisco Bay Area that was one of the key early adopter program partners with Microsoft implementing beta versions of Windows Server 2008 in production environments over 3 years before the product release. Rand has spoken at more than 50 conferences and conventions around the world in the past year on tips, tricks, and best practices on planning, migrating, and implementing Windows 2008 Hyper-V and System Center Virtual Machine Manager 2008.

Jeff Guillet, MCITP, MCSE, CISSP, has been in the computer industry for more than 25 years and has been a contributing writer and technical editor for several books on Windows Server 2008, Windows Server 2003, Exchange 2007, and Exchange 2003. Jeff is a senior consultant for Convergent Computing and participates in many early adopter beta programs. Jeff holds Charter MCITP: Enterprise Administrator and MCITP: Enterprise Messaging Administrator certifications for Windows Server 2008 and has maintained MCSE certifications since 1999. He maintains a popular technical blog at www.expta.com.

Dedication

I dedicate this book to Kelly and Chip, whose lives will hopefully be made better by efforts we do today in virtualizing our computer data centers as our part to make a greener IT environment!

—Rand Morimoto

I dedicate this book to my wife, Amy. It is only through her love, patience, and encouragement, even when I'm working long hours on weekends and late nights after coming home from my "real" job, that I enjoy my small successes.

—Jeff Guillet

Acknowledgments

Rand Morimoto   I would like to thank all the consultants at Convergent Computing who have worked with Hyper-V and System Center Virtual Machine Manager 2008 for many, many months before the product release and have built up the knowledge and best practices found in the pages of this book.

I also want to thank Kevin Lane and Ken Spann at Microsoft for including us in the early adopter program on Hyper-V and giving us the opportunity to work with customers willing to put a beta product into their production environments.

Thanks go out to the various Windows Server 2008 contributors whose knowledge and content are leveraged in this Hyper-V book, including Chris Amaris, Chris Wallace, Kim Amaris, Omar Droubi, Ross Mistry, and Scott Chimner.

And as always, a thank you to my mother, Vickie, whom I'm grateful to for all the lessons you taught me about hard work, dedication, and determination that I put to use in everything I do!

Jeff Guillet   I would like to thank Rand Morimoto for all his help and coaching through the development of this book. His drive and quest for excellence fuels the excitement that I have for technology and providing solutions for our clients. It is an honor to work with him.

I also want to acknowledge the application developers and program managers at Microsoft for their hard work and for making such a great suite of software products. It's amazing to see the products progress and mature so quickly between beta releases.

I would very much like to thank my parents, Art and Joan, for their support, love, and encouragement. They taught me the honor of good work, integrity, respect, and most of all, how to be a good human being. My dearest wish is to be as good a parent as both of them are to me.

We Want to Hear from You!

As the reader of this book, you are our most important critic and commentator. We value your opinion and want to know what we're doing right, what we could do better, what areas you'd like to see us publish in, and any other words of wisdom you're willing to pass our way.

As a Senior Acquisitions Editor for Sams Publishing, I welcome your comments. You can email or write me directly to let me know what you did or didn't like about this book—as well as what we can do to make our books better.

Please note that I cannot help you with technical problems related to the topic of this book. We do have a User Services group, however, where I will forward specific technical questions related to the book.

When you write, please be sure to include this book's title and author as well as your name, email address, and phone number. I will carefully review your comments and share them with the author and editors who worked on the book.

Email: feedback@samspublishing.com

Mail: Neil Rowe
           Executive Editor
           Sams Publishing
           800 East 96th Street
           Indianapolis, IN 46240 USA

For more information about this book or another Sams Publishing title, visit our website at www.samspublishing.com. Enter the ISBN (excluding hyphens) or the title of a book into the Search field to find the page you're looking for.

Reader Services

Visit our website and register this book at www.samspublishing.com/register for convenient access to any updates, downloads, or errata that might be available for this book.

Introduction

Windows Server 2008 shipped with several server roles that provide application services such as Active Directory, web services, thin client Terminal Services, video streaming media services, server virtualization services, and many others. This book focuses on the services specific to server virtualization called Hyper-V.

Hyper-V enables an organization to consolidate several physical server systems into a single host server while still providing isolation between virtual guest session application operations. With an interest to decrease costs in managing their information technology (IT) infrastructure, organizations are virtualizing servers. Bringing multiple physical servers into a single host server decreases the cost of purchasing and maintaining multiple physical server systems, decreases the cost of electricity and air-cooling systems to maintain the physical servers, and enables an organization to go "green" (by decreasing the use of natural resources in the operation of physical server systems).

In addition to covering Hyper-V virtualization in this book, the System Center Virtual Machine Manager 2008 (VMM 2008) product is also covered. VMM 2008 adds management capabilities to Hyper-V. VMM 2008 enables an administrator view and administer virtual guest sessions more easily, delegate administrative rights to others in the management of guest sessions, and use helpful tools to perform specific functions and tasks. Specific functions and tasks supported in VMM 2008 include the ability to take a production server and convert the server to a virtual guest image. In addition, VMM 2008 will take an existing virtual session and convert the image into a Hyper-V virtual guest session. These tools make managing, administering, and supporting a Hyper-V session much easier for the administrator.

The authors of this book had the opportunity to work with Windows Server 2008 for more than three years before it was released, and have been involved in the development and deployment of Hyper-V in production environments since the product inception.

It is our hope that we can provide you, the reader of our book, with a lot of really valuable information—not basic marketing fluff that talks about features and functions in Hyper-V and System Center Virtual Machine Manager 2008, but to really dig down into the products and share with you best practices for planning, preparing, implementing, and supporting a Windows 2008 Hyper-V-based virtual environment.

The thing about being involved with a product so early on is that our first experiences with Hyper-V and VMM were without any documentation, without help files that provided guidance, and without any shared experiences from others. We had to learn the technologies from experience, usually the hard way, but that has given us a distinct advantage of knowing the products forward and backward, better than anyone could ever imagine.

So, the pages of this book are filled with years of experience with Hyper-V and VMM 2008, live production environment best practices, and tips and tricks that we hope will help you design, plan, prototype, implement, administer, and support a Windows 2008-based server virtualization environment!

This book is organized into five parts, each part focusing on key Hyper-V and VMM areas, with chapters making up each part. The parts of this book are as follows:

▶ **Part I: Windows 2008 Hyper-V Overview**—This part provides an introduction to Hyper-V not only from the perspective of a general technology overview, but also to note what is truly new in Hyper-V that made it compelling enough for organizations to implement the technology in beta in a production environments. We also cover basic planning, prototype testing, and migration techniques. This part also covers running tools to assess physical servers for consolidation to virtual guest sessions and the process of architecting an enterprise virtual host environment.

▶ **Part II: Windows 2008 Hyper-V Host and Guest Installation**—This part covers the installation of Hyper-V from the perspective of both the host server and the guest virtual sessions. The server installation includes the setup and configuration of Windows Server 2008 and the specific versions that support Hyper-V virtualization. The guest session installation covers the installation of both Microsoft Windows and non-Windows guests that are supported as virtual server sessions within a Hyper-V host environment.

▶ **Part III: Administering and Maintaining Hyper-V Host Services**—This part covers the management, administration, optimization, and maintenance of the Hyper-V host with the tools that come out of the box with Windows Server 2008. As with any application, Hyper-V is best run when the system is properly installed and configured with specific focus on optimizing the memory, disk storage, and processing capabilities of the underlying hardware. Hyper-V distributes resources of a host server across guest sessions, and thus it is important to have the right hardware and system optimization in place.

- ▶ **Part IV: System Center Virtual Machine Manager in a Hyper-V Environment**— Hyper-V and Windows Server 2008 provide administrative tools for Hyper-V, but the addition of the System Center Virtual Machine Manager 2008 product on top of Hyper-V provides significant enhancements for the management and operations of virtual guest sessions and host-level configuration options. VMM 2008 allows for the extraction of physical server configurations down to virtual guest sessions and for the management of virtual guest templates and ISO disc image files and the provisioning of guest session.

- ▶ **Part V: Maintaining Guest Session Uptime in a Hyper-V Environment**—This last part of the book covers guest session uptime, debugging, and problem solving intended to help administrators maintain a reliable host and guest virtual environment. Disaster recovery and high availability of guest applications are addressed with regard to the clustering of hosts and guest sessions. In addition, this part addresses application-level high-availability and disaster-recovery technologics built in to common applications in use today.

We hope that our real-world experience with Windows Server 2008 Hyper-V virtualization and our commitment to share that planning, implementation, and support of Hyper-V information will help get you up-to-speed on the latest in virtual server software!

PART I

Windows 2008 Hyper-V Overview

IN THIS PART

1

Windows Server 2008 Hyper-V Technology Primer

Hyper-V is a long-awaited technology that has been anticipated to help Microsoft leap past rival virtual server technologies such as VMware and XenServer. Although Microsoft has had a virtual server technology for a few years, the features and capabilities have always lagged behind its competitors. Windows Server 2008 was written to provide enhanced virtualization technologies through a rewrite of the Windows kernel itself to support virtual server capabilities equal to, if not better than, other options on the market. This chapter introduces the Hyper-V server role in Windows Server 2008 and provides best practices that organizations can follow to leverage the capabilities of server virtualization to lower costs and improve the manageability of an organization's network server environment.

What Is Server Virtualization and Microsoft Hyper-V?

Server virtualization is the ability for a single system to host multiple guest operating system sessions, effectively taking advantage of the processing capabilities of very powerful servers. Most servers in data centers run under 5% to 10% processor utilization, meaning that excess capacity on the servers goes unused. By combining the workloads of multiple servers onto a single system, an organization can better utilize the processing power available in its networking environment.

Virtualization as an IT Organization Strategy

Just 2 to 3 years ago, virtualization was used primarily as a test environment solution for information technology (IT) departments. If an IT administrator wanted to test new software, rather than building up a full physical server and loading software on that system, the administrator would install the software on a virtual server system and fiddle with the software off the virtual server. A virtual server enabled the IT administrator to load up several different test systems without purchasing or setting up separate computer systems. However, virtual servers were not considered reliable or robust enough to handle the day-to-day demands of an organization's IT needs. Much of that belief stemmed from the limitations of computer hardware capacity that existed just half a decade ago; server systems were underutilized but still taking up 20% to 30% of system capacity.

Virtualization Driven by Hardware Capabilities

Only recently, with the release of dual-core or quad-core processors and 64-bit operating systems, have servers gone from having 2 or 4 core processors to easily 8 to 16 core processors, and from 4GB of RAM to 16, 32, or 64GB of RAM. Now instead of running at 20% to 30% capacity, servers are running at 2% to 3% capacity.

Virtualization Driven by the Desire to Go "Green"

Whereas hardware provided significant excess capacity to consolidate server processes into fewer server systems, the social interest to go "green" has driven organizations to decrease their power consumption and improve their resource utilization. Virtualization enables an organization to decrease the number of physical computers they need to purchase, and in doing so also decreases the power and air-conditioning cooling demands that physical computer systems require. An organization that can decrease the physical number of its servers by 50% to 75% can decrease their electrical power requirements by a similar percentage.

Virtualization also decreases the computer data center "sprawl," whereas the increase of physical servers in the recent past caused organizations to continue to increase the square footage of their data centers. With virtualization physical server systems, an organization can decrease the size of their data centers and decrease the overall footprint required to host their information systems.

Virtualization Driven by Lower Costs

Many organizations now realize that fewer server systems and lower demands on electrical power, air-conditioning costs, and the decrease in data center space are lowering the cost of IT operations. To increase profitability, or just to manage overhead costs, virtualization enables organizations to decrease costs and better utilize IT resources.

Microsoft Hyper-V Server as a Role in Windows Server 2008

Microsoft has simplified the process of adding virtualization into a network environment by including Hyper-V virtualization in the x64-bit version of Windows Server 2008. As organizations install Windows Server 2008 into their environment, they can just run the Server Manager tool in Windows 2008 and choose to install the Hyper-V role, shown in

Figure 1.1 (along with a system reboot); the Windows 2008 server is then ready to start adding virtual guests to the system.

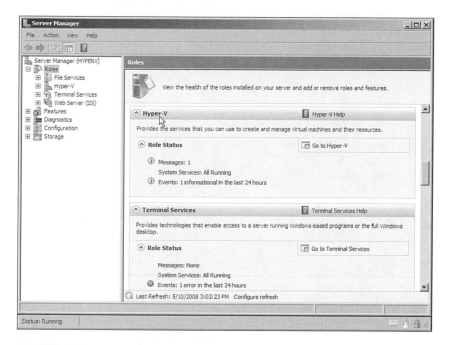

FIGURE 1.1   Hyper-V as a Windows 2008 role.

Hyper-V on a Familiar Operating System

Unlike some other server virtualization systems that are hosted on the Linux operating system (VMware ESX) or proprietary host systems, Hyper-V runs right on a familiar Microsoft Windows Server operating system. Network administrators do not need to learn a new operating system, management system, or specialized tools. Early adopters of Hyper-V, even without documentation or training, have been able to install the Hyper-V server role, finding it just like installing any other server role (such as installing domain name service [DNS], media services, Internet Information Services [IIS] web services, and the like).

The administrative tools for Hyper-V, shown in Figure 1.2, are also just like any other administrative tool in Windows. Therefore, the creation of virtual guest sessions, the monitoring of those sessions, and the administration of guest sessions is a familiar process for IT administrators.

The ease of learning, using, and supporting Hyper-V has been a huge factor in organizations adopting Hyper-V for their virtual server environments.

Microsoft Applications on a Microsoft Virtual Server

A concern for organizations relative to virtualization in a production environment is the support they will receive from their software vendors (Microsoft, Oracle, IBM, and the

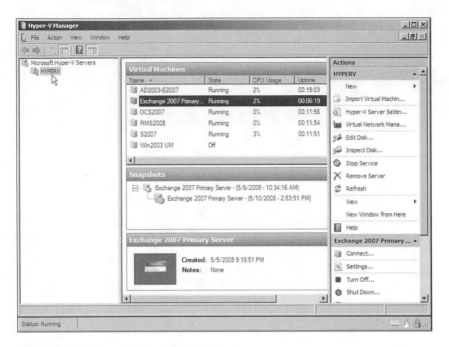

FIGURE 1.2   Hyper-V administrative tools.

like). Whereas software vendors readily support their applications on physical hardware systems, they have not necessarily fully supported their applications on virtualized systems.

With the release of Hyper-V virtualization from Microsoft, however, Microsoft has openly announced full support for their current versions of applications running in a Hyper-V virtualized environment. So, products such as Exchange Server 2007 with Service Pack 1 and Microsoft Office SharePoint Server 2007 with Service Pack 1 are all directly supported. No longer will IT administrators have to worry about finger pointing resulting from server software not being supported by their vendor because the application was installed on a virtualized server rather than a physical server.

A single phone call to Microsoft tech support can provide an IT administrator support for both their Microsoft application and their Microsoft virtual server environment.

Hyper-V Support More Than Just Windows Guest Sessions

With the release of Hyper-V, Microsoft made a concerted effort to ensure that Hyper-V not only supports Windows guest sessions (like Windows 2003 and Windows 2008), but also non-Windows guest sessions running Linux. By providing support for a variety of guest sessions, Microsoft is enabling organizations to consolidate both their Windows and non-Windows server systems onto fewer Hyper-V host servers.

Choosing to Virtualize Servers

The section "Virtualization as an IT Organization Strategy" identified basic reasons why organizations have chosen to virtualize their physical servers into virtual guest sessions. However, organizations also benefit from server virtualization in several areas. Organizations can use virtualization in test and development environments. They can also use virtualization to minimize the number of physical servers in an environment, and to leverage the capabilities of simplified virtual server images in high-availability and disaster-recovery scenarios.

Virtualization for Test and Development Environments

Server virtualization got its start in test and development environments in IT organizations. The simplicity of adding a single host server and loading up multiple guest virtual sessions to test applications or develop multiserver scenarios without having to buy and manage multiple physical servers was extremely attractive. Today, with physical servers with 4, 8, or 16 core processors in a single system with significant performance capacity, organizations can host dozens of test and development virtual server sessions just by setting up 1 or 2 host servers.

With administrative tools built in to the virtual server host systems, the guest sessions can be connected together or completely isolated from one another, providing virtual local area networks (LANs) that simulate a production environment. In addition, an administrator can create a single base virtual image with, for example, Windows Server 2003 Enterprise Edition on it, and can save that base image as a template. To create a "new server" whenever desired, the administrator just has to make a duplicate copy of the base template image and boot that new image. Creating a server system takes 5 minutes in a virtual environment. In the past, the administrator would have to acquire hardware, configure the hardware, shove in the Windows Server CD, and wait 20 to 30 minutes before the base configuration was installed. And then after the base configuration was installed, it was usually another 30 to 60 minutes to download and install the latest service packs and patches before the system was ready.

With the addition of provisioning tools, such as Microsoft System Center Virtual Machine Manager 2008 (VMM), covered in Chapter 11, "Using Virtual Machine Manager 2008 for Provisioning," the process of creating new guest images from templates and the ability to delegate the provisioning process to others greatly simplifies the process of making virtual guest sessions available for test and development purposes.

Virtualization for Server Consolidation

Another common use of server virtualization is consolidating physical servers, as covered in the section "What Is Server Virtualization and Microsoft Hyper-V?" Organizations that have undertaken concerted server consolidation efforts have been able to decrease the number of physical servers by upward of 60% to 80%. It's usually very simple for an organization to decrease the number of physical servers by at least 25% to 35% simply by identifying low-usage, single-task systems.

Servers such as domain controllers, Dynamic Host Configuration Protocol (DHCP) servers, web servers, and the like are prime candidates for virtualization because they are typically running on simple "pizza box" servers (thin 1 unit high rack-mounted systems). Chapter 3, "Planning, Sizing, and Architecting a Hyper-V Environment," shows you how to identify servers that are prime candidates for virtualization and server consolidation.

Beyond just taking physical servers and doing a one-for-one replacement as virtual servers in an environment, many organizations are realizing they just have too many servers doing the same thing and underutilized because of lack of demand or capacity. The excess capacity may have been projected based on organizational growth expectations that never materialized or has since been reduced due to organization consolidation.

Server consolidation also means that organizations can now decrease their number of sites and data centers to fewer, centralized data centers. When wide area network (WAN) connections were extremely expensive and not completely reliable, organizations distributed servers to branch offices and remote locations. Today, however, the need for a fully distributed data environment has greatly diminished because the cost of Internet connectivity has decreased, WAN performance has increased, WAN reliability has drastically improved, and applications now support full-feature robust web capabilities.

Don't think of server consolidation as just taking every physical server and making it a virtual server. Instead, spend a few moments to think about how to decrease the number of physical (and virtual) systems in general, and then virtualize only the number of systems required. Because it is easy to provision a new virtual server, if additional capacity is required, it doesn't take long to spin up a new virtual server image to meet the demands of the organization. This ease contrasts starkly with requirements in the past: purchasing hardware and spending the better part of a day configuring the hardware and installing the base Windows operating system on the physical use system.

Virtualization as a Strategy for Disaster Recovery and High Availability

Most use organizations realize a positive spillover effect from virtualizing their environments: They create higher availability and enhance their disaster-recovery potential, and thus fulfill other IT initiatives. Disaster recovery and business continuity is on the minds of most IT professionals, effectively how to quickly bring back online servers and systems in the event of a server failure or in the case of a disaster (natural disaster or other). Without virtualization, disaster-recovery plans generally require the addition (to a physical data center perhaps already bloated with too many servers) of even more servers to create redundancy (both in the data center and in a remote location).

Virtualization has greatly improved an organization's ability to actually implement a disaster-recovery plan. As physical servers are virtualized and the organization begins to decrease physical server count by 25%, 50%, or more, the organization can then repurpose spare systems as redundant servers or as hosts for redundant virtual images both within the data center and in remote locations for redundant data sites. Many organizations have found their effort to consolidate servers is negated because even though they virtualized half their servers, they went back and added twice as many servers to get redundancy and fault tolerance. However, the net of the effort is that the organization has been able to get disaster recovery in place without adding additional physical servers to the network.

After virtualizing servers as guest images, organizations are finding that a virtualized image is *very* simple to replicate; after all, it's typically nothing more than a single file sitting on a server. In its simplest form, an organization can just "pause" the guest session temporarily, "copy" the virtual guest session image, and then "resume" the guest session to bring it back online. The copy of the image has all the information of the server. The image can be used to re-create a scenario in a test lab environment; or it can be saved so that in the event that the primary image fails, the copy can be booted and bring the server immediately back up and running. There are more elegant ways to replicate an image file, as covered in the section "Using Guest Clustering to Protect a Virtual Guest Session" in Chapter 12, "Application-Level Failover and Disaster Recovery in a Hyper-V Environment." However, the ability for an IT department to bring up a failed server within a data center or remotely has been greatly simplified though virtualization technologies.

Understanding Microsoft's Virtualization Strategy

Microsoft jumped into the virtualization market several years behind its competitors. Being relatively new to the virtualization space, Microsoft had some catching up to do.

Acquisition of Virtual PC

Microsoft jumped into the virtualization market through the acquisition of a company called Connectix in 2003. At the time of the acquisition, Virtual PC provided a virtual session of Windows on either a Windows system or on a Macintosh computer system. Virtual PC was used largely by organizations testing server software or performing demos of Windows systems on desktop and laptop systems. Virtual PC for the Mac enabled Macintosh users to run Windows on their Macintosh computers.

Microsoft later dropped the development of Virtual PC for the Mac. However, they continued to develop virtualization for Windows systems with the release of Virtual PC 2007. Virtual PC 2007 enables users running Windows XP or Windows Vista to install, configure, and run virtual guest sessions of Windows Server or even non-Windows operating systems.

Microsoft Virtual Server

Virtual PC is targeted at those operating under an operating system that is typically optimized for personal or individual applications. It does not scale for a data center wanting to run four, eight, or more sessions on a single system. At the time of the acquisition of Connectix, Connectix was developing a virtual server solution to allow for the operation of virtualization technologies on a Windows 2003 host server system.

Because a Windows Server 2003 system provides more RAM availability, supports multiple processors, and generally has more capacity and capabilities than a desktop client system, Microsoft Virtual Server provided organizations with more capabilities for server-based virtualization in a production environment.

Virtual Server 2005

Although the initial Virtual Server acquired through the Connectix acquisition provided basic server virtualization capabilities, it wasn't until Virtual Server 2005 that Microsoft had its first internally developed product. Virtual Server 2005 provided better support and integration into a Windows 2003 environment, better support for multiprocessor systems and systems with more RAM, and better integration and support with other Microsoft server products.

In just two years, Microsoft went from having no virtual server technologies to a second-generation virtual server product; however, even with Virtual Server 2005, Microsoft was still far behind its competitors.

Virtual Server 2005 R2

Over the subsequent two years, Microsoft released two major updates to Virtual Server 2005 with the release of an R2 edition of the Virtual Server 2005 product and a service pack for the R2 edition. Virtual Server 2005 R2 Service Pack 1 provides the following capabilities:

- ▶ **Virtual Server host clustering**—This technology allows an organization to cluster host systems to one another, thus allowing guest sessions to have higher redundancy and reliability.

- ▶ **x64 host support**—x64 host support means that organizations had the capability to use the 64-bit version of Windows 2003 as the host operating system, thus providing better support for more memory and system capacity found in x64-bit systems. Guest operating systems, however, are still limited to x86 platforms.

- ▶ **Hardware-assisted virtualization**—New to processors released from Intel (Intel VT) and AMD (AMD-V) are processors that provide better distribution of processor resources to virtual guest sessions.

- ▶ **iSCSI support**—This technology allows virtual guest sessions to connect to iSCSI storage systems, thus providing better storage management and storage access for the guest sessions running on a virtual server host.

- ▶ **Support for more than 16GB virtual disk sizes**—Virtual disk sizes can reach 2TB in size, thus enabling organizations to have guest sessions with extremely large storage capacity.

These capabilities—among other capabilities of the latest Virtual Server 2005 product—brought Microsoft closer to its competition in the area of server virtualization.

Integration of Hypervisor Technology in Windows Server 2008

To leap beyond its competition in the area of server virtualization, Microsoft had to make some significant changes to the operating system that hosted its next-generation virtual server technology. With Windows 2008 in development, Microsoft took the opportunity to add in a core technology to Windows 2008 that provided the basis of Microsoft's future dominance in server virtualization. The core technology is called hypervisor, which effectively is a layer within the host operating system that provides better support for guest operating systems. Microsoft calls their hypervisor-based technology Hyper-V.

Before the inclusion of Hyper-V in Windows 2008, the Virtual Server application sat on top of the host operating system and effectively required all guest operating systems to share system resources, such as network communications, video-processing capabilities, and memory allocation. In the event that the host operating system has a system failure of something like the host network adapter driver, all guest sessions fail to communicate on the network. This monolithic approach is similar to how most server virtualization technologies operate.

Technologies such as VMware ESX and Hyper-V leverage a hypervisor-based technology that allows the guest operating systems to effectively communicate directly with system resources without having to pass through the host operating system. In some instances, the hypervisor manages shared guest session resources, and in other cases passes guest session requests directly to the hardware layer of the system. By ensuring better independence of systems' communications, the hypervisor-supported environment provides organizations better scalability, better performance, and ultimately, better reliability of the core virtual host environment.

Hyper-V is available in Windows 2008 Standard, Enterprise, and Datacenter editions. Each of these SKUs is available with and without Hyper-V; so from product launch in February 2008, Windows 2008 has been ready to be a virtual server host system.

> **NOTE**
>
> Hyper-V in Windows 2008 is supported only on x64-bit systems that have hardware-assisted virtualization support. Therefore, an organization cannot load up the 32-bit version of Windows 2008 and try to set up virtual guest sessions on the 32-bit host version of Windows.

What's New in Hyper-V

Many long-awaited features and technologies are built in to Hyper-V. These enable Microsoft to compete with other server virtualization products on the market and provide incremental capabilities requested by IT organizations. These Hyper-V capabilities provide better support for host functionality, administration support, guest session support, and improvements in server reliability.

New Features That Provide Better Virtual Host Capabilities

The broadest improvements made by Microsoft to the virtual host capabilities of Hyper-V are the core functions added in to Windows Server 2008 that relate to security, performance, and reliability. However, the addition of a new virtual switch capability in Hyper-V provides greater flexibility in managing network communications among guest images, and between guest images and an organization's internetworking infrastructure.

Effectively, Windows Server 2008 and Hyper-V leverage the built-in capabilities of Windows 2008 along with specific Hyper-V components to improve overall support, administration, management, and operations of a Hyper-V host server. When Hyper-V host server is joined to a Microsoft Active Directory environment, the host server can be managed and administered just like any other application server in the Active Directory environment. Security is centralized and managed through the use of Active Directory organizational units, groups, and user administrators. Monitoring of the Hyper-V host server and its guest sessions is done through the same tools organizations use to monitor and manage their existing Windows server systems.

Security policies, patch management policies, backup procedures, and the corresponding tools and utilities used to support other Windows server systems can be used to support the Hyper-V host server system. The Hyper-V host server becomes just another managed Windows server on the network.

Also important is the requirement for the Hyper-V host server to run on a 64-bit system, to not only take advantage of hardware-assisted virtualization processors like the AMD64 and Intel IA-32E and EM64T (x64) but also to provide more memory in the host server to distribute among guest sessions. When a 32-bit host server was limited to about 4GB of RAM memory, there weren't too many ways to divide that memory among guest sessions in which guests could run any business application. With 64-bit host servers supporting 8GB, 16GB, 32GB, or more, however, guest sessions can easily take 4GB or 8GB of memory each and still leave room for other guest sessions, tasks, and functions.

Unlike multiple physical servers that might be connected to different network switches, the guest sessions on a Hyper-V host all reside within a single server. Therefore, the virtual switch capability built in to the Hyper-V Administration tool and shown in Figure 1.3 enables the Hyper-V administrator to create special network segments and associate virtual guest sessions to specific network adapters in the host server to ensure that virtual guests can be connected to network segments that meet the needs of the organization.

New Features That Provide Better Administration Support

Hyper-V guest sessions can be administered by two separate tools. One tool, the Hyper-V Administration tool, comes free out of the box with Windows Server 2008. The other tool, System Center VMM, can be purchased separately. Some overlap exists between what the Hyper-V Administration tool and the VMM tool do. For the most part, however, the built-in tool enables you to start and stop guest sessions and to take snapshots of the sessions for image backup and recovery. The VMM tool provides all those capabilities, too. But, it also enables an administrator to organize images across different administrative groups, as shown in Figure 1.4. Thus, the VMM tool allows for the creation and management of

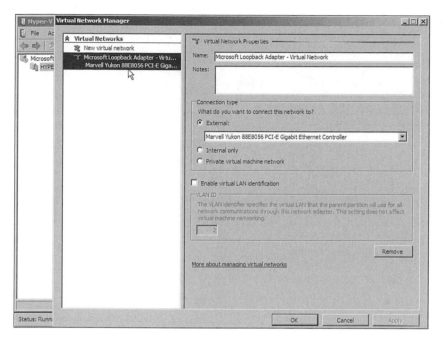

FIGURE 1.3   Virtual switch capability in Hyper-V.

template images for faster and easier image provisioning, provides a way to create a virtual image from existing physical or running virtual sessions, and provides clustering of virtual images across multiple VMM manage host servers.

New Features That Provide Better Guest Support

Hyper-V added several new features that provide better support for guest sessions, such as 64-bit guest support, support for non-Windows guest sessions, and support for dedicated processors in guest sessions.

Hyper-V added the ability to support not only 32-bit guest sessions as earlier versions of Microsoft's Virtual Server 2005 product provided, but also 64-bit guest sessions. This improvement allows guest sessions to run some of the latest 64-bit-only application software from Microsoft and other vendors, such as Exchange Server 2007. And although some applications will run in either 32-bit or 64-bit versions, for organizations looking for faster information processing, or support for more than 4GB of RAM, the 64-bit guest session provides the same capabilities as if the organization were running the application on a dedicated physical 64-bit server system.

With Hyper-V, you can also dedicate one, two, or four processor cores to a virtual guest session. Instead of aggregating the performance of all the Hyper-V host server's processors and dividing the processing performance for the guest images somewhat equally, an administrator can dedicate processors to guest images to ensure higher performance for the guest session. With hardware supporting two or four quad-core processors in a single

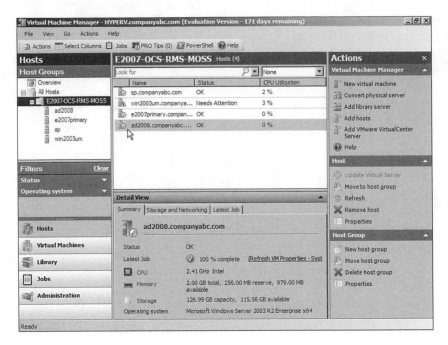

FIGURE 1.4   System Center Virtual Machine Manager 2008 administration organization.

server system, there are plenty of processors in servers these days to appropriately allocate processing speed to the server guests that require more performance.

Support for non-Windows guests, such as Linux, was an indication from Microsoft that they are serious about providing multiplatform support within their Hyper-V host servers. Linux servers are not only supported to run as guest sessions on Hyper-V, but Microsoft has developed integration tools to better support Linux guest integration into a managed Hyper-V host environment.

More on guest session support and the implementation of virtual guest server sessions in Chapter 5, "Installing a Guest Session on Hyper-V."

New Features That Provide Better Reliability Capabilities

Another critical area of improvement in Hyper-V is its support for capabilities that improve reliability and recoverability of the Hyper-V host and guest environments. The technologies added to Windows 2008 and Hyper-V are clustering technologies as well as server snapshot technologies.

Clustering is supported on Hyper-V both for host clustering and guest clustering. The clustering capabilities allow redundancy both at the host server level and the Hyper-V guest level, with both areas of clustering greatly improving the uptime that can be created for applications. More on clustering in Chapter 12 in the section, "Application-Level Failover and Disaster Recovery in a Hyper-V Environment."

Another capability added to Hyper-V for better reliability is the ability to take snapshots of virtual guest sessions, as shown in Figure 1.5. A snapshot allows the state of a guest image to be retained so that at any time an administrator wants to roll back to the state of the image at the time of the snapshot, the information all exists. This capability is used frequently to take a snapshot before a patch or update is applied so that the organization can, if need be, quickly and easily roll back to that image. Snapshots are also used for general recovery purposes. If a database becomes corrupted or an image no longer works, the network administrator can roll back the image to a point before the corruption or system problems started to occur.

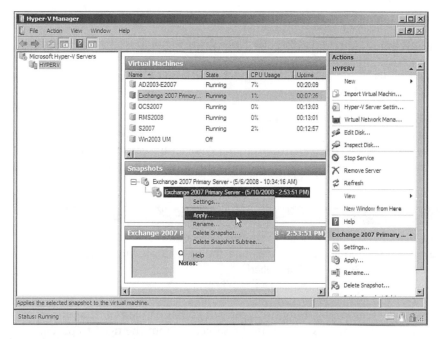

FIGURE 1.5   Snapshots in the Hyper-V Administration tool.

Determining What Is Needed to Virtualize Servers

Hyper-V is supported on both the host server side and the guest image side. Hyper-V runs on a Windows Server 2008 system, but not all versions of Windows 2008 allow installation of the Hyper-V role. Likewise, Microsoft does not support all operating systems as guest images. So, you want to ensure that both host and guest images are supported. This section covers what is needed to support virtual hosts and guest sessions.

Versions of Windows Server 2008 That Host Hyper-V

Windows 2008 comes in several versions: Web Server, Standard, Enterprise, and Datacenter. It also comes in a version called Server Core, which is a version of Windows 2008 that provides a lighter, GUI-less version of Windows 2008. Hyper-V runs only on the

Standard, Enterprise, and Datacenter versions of Windows 2008 (not on Web Server), and it runs only on the x64-bit version of Windows.

> **NOTE**
>
> Technically, Hyper-V also runs on the Itanium version of Windows 2008 and provides the ability to run 32-bit Itanium guest sessions. From the experience of the authors of this book, however, Itanium-based virtualization is rarely implemented. Most organizations implement the x64-bit version of Hyper-V to support standard 32-bit and 64-bit applications. Therefore, this book makes very little reference to and spends very little time addressing the Itanium version of Hyper-V.

From a licensing standpoint, Microsoft allows organizations to purchase and use Windows 2008 at a lower cost with a version of Windows 2008 x64-bit that does not support Hyper-V. This version is more likely purchased by an organization using a virtualization product from a third-party vendor and not planning to use the Hyper-V capabilities.

Windows Server 2008 x64-bit, Enterprise Edition
Windows Server 2008 x64-bit Enterprise Edition is the most common version of Windows purchased for a Hyper-V host server for virtualization. The x64-bit version is needed to support both 32-bit and 64-bit guest sessions and provides the ability to support up to 2TB of RAM.

> **NOTE**
>
> A Hyper-V host cannot run on the 32-bit (x86) version of Windows Server 2008. For the Hyper-V role to show up on the server for installation, the host server must have the x64-bit version of Windows Server 2008 installed.

Microsoft is licensing the Enterprise Edition of Windows 2008 in a manner that allows an organization to run up to four guest sessions on the server without the need to purchase additional Windows server licenses. So effectively, an organization can purchase one Enterprise Edition of Windows 2008 and run four Windows 2008 Enterprise Edition guest sessions for free.

> **NOTE**
>
> The Windows 2008 Enterprise Edition provides licensing support for four guest sessions under the single cost of the purchase of the Enterprise Edition server software. However, an organization can run more than four guest sessions on the Enterprise server system. Each Hyper-V guest session beyond the first four systems requires the purchase of the appropriate server license, whether that be a Standard Edition license or Enterprise Edition license. So, an organization running seven guest sessions would purchase a copy of Windows 2008 Enterprise Edition for the host, run the first four guest sessions for free, and be required to purchase three additional server licenses to support all seven guest sessions running on the system.

As an Enterprise Windows 2008 server, the host system and any of the Enterprise guest sessions are capable of extremely large-scale processing and memory functions, clustering, and Active Directory Federation Services.

The Enterprise Edition, with support for server clustering, can provide organizations with true 24×7, 99.999% uptime capabilities required in high-availability environments. Windows Server 2008, Enterprise Edition supports a wide variety of regularly available server systems, thus allowing an organization its choice of hardware vendor systems to host its Windows 2008 application needs.

Windows Server 2008 x64-bit, Standard Edition

While the Windows Server 2008, Standard Edition is a common server version of the operating system for basic server functions (domain controllers, DNS servers, DHCP servers, and the like), and while the x64-bit version of the Standard Edition of Windows 2008 supports Hyper-V virtualization, most organizations still purchase the Enterprise Edition of Windows 2008 for their Hyper-V hosts. They do so because the Standard Edition of Windows 2008 provides licensing support for the host server plus one additional guest session. Each guest session beyond the first session requires the organization to buy additional server licenses. By the time the organization adds two or three guest sessions to a Standard Edition host, the organization would have been better off buying the Enterprise Edition host and run up to four additional sessions at no additional cost.

> **NOTE**
>
> If a Windows 2008 server host is running Hyper-V on a Standard Edition of Windows, the guest sessions under the host can be Enterprise Edition guests. However, the one additional free guest session running under the Standard Edition host is for a Standard Edition guest. So, to run Enterprise guests under a Standard host, all the guest sessions much run under purchased licenses of the Windows Enterprise Edition of the software.

The Standard Edition of Windows 2008 x64-bit provides support for up to 32GB of memory, which is plenty of memory to run several guest sessions within the 32GB host limit. The Standard Edition of Windows is a good version of the operating system to support domain controllers, utility servers (such as DNS or DHCP), file servers, print servers, media servers, SharePoint servers, Network Policy and Access Services systems, and so on. Most organizations, large and small, find the capabilities of the Standard Edition sufficient for most network services.

Windows Server 2008, Datacenter Edition

Windows Server 2008, Datacenter Edition is a high-end hardware version of the operating system that supports very large-scale data center operations. The Datacenter Edition supports organizations that need more than 16-way symmetric multiprocessing, or memory up to 2TB, or clustering beyond 8 nodes. The Datacenter Edition is focused at organizations that need scale-up server technology to support a large centralized data warehouse on one or limited numbers of server clusters.

Based on Microsoft's licensing of the Datacenter Edition, an organization that properly licenses Datacenter based on the number of processors of the Datacenter host server has the right to install an unlimited number of guest sessions at no additional cost for Windows server licensing for the guest sessions.

As noted in Chapter 7, "Optimizing the Hyper-V Host Server and Guest Sessions," on performance and capacity analysis, an organization can scale out or scale up its server applications. Scale out refers to an application that performs better when it is distributed across multiple servers, whereas scale up refers to an application that performs better when more processors are added to a single system. Typical scale-out applications include web server services, electronic messaging systems, and file and print servers. In those cases, organizations are better off distributing the application server functions to multiple Windows Server 2008, Standard Edition or Enterprise Edition systems. However, applications that scale up, such as e-commerce, data warehousing applications, or potentially server virtualization, benefit from having all the data and processing on a single server cluster. For these applications, Windows Server 2008, Datacenter Edition provides better centralized scaled performance and the added benefit of fault tolerance and failover capabilities.

Windows Server 2008 Server Core
New to Windows 2008 is a Server Core version of the operating system. Windows 2008 Server Core, shown in Figure 1.6, is a GUI-less version of the Windows 2008 operating system. When a system boots with Server Core installed on it, the system does not load the normal Windows GUI. Instead, the Server Core system boots to a logon prompt, and from the logon prompt the system drops to a DOS command prompt. There is no Start button, no menu, no GUI at all.

FIGURE 1.6   Windows 2008 Server Core.

Server Core is not sold as a separate edition, but rather as an install option that comes with the Standard, Enterprise, Datacenter, and Web Server editions of the operating system. So, when you purchase a license of Windows Server 2008, Enterprise Edition, for example, the DVD has both the normal Enterprise Edition code plus a Windows 2008 Enterprise Edition Server Core version.

The operating system capabilities are limited to the edition of Server Core being installed, so a Windows Server 2008, Enterprise Edition Server Core server has the same memory and processor limits as the regular Enterprise Edition of Windows 2008.

Server Core has proven to be a great version of Windows for utility servers such as domain controllers, DHCP servers, DNS servers, and IIS web servers. The limited overhead provides more resources to the applications running on the server, and by removing the GUI and associated applications, there's less of a security attack footprint on the Server Core system. Because most administrators don't play Solitaire or use Media Player on a domain controller, those applications don't need to be patched, updated, or maintained on the GUI-less version of Windows. With fewer applications to be patched, the system requires less maintenance and management to remain operational.

With the lighter "footprint," Server Core has proven to be an excellent edition of Windows to run Hyper-V host services. The Hyper-V host can be centrally administered from a different server or workstation, and all the guest sessions are virtually managed and administered anyway. So, minimizing the attack surface and administration surface of a host server using Server Core has proven to make a lot of sense. Chapter 4, "Installing Windows 2008 Server and the Hyper-V Role," covers how to install the Server Core and how to install the Hyper-V application from a command prompt of the Server Core host system.

Versions of Guest Sessions Supported Under Hyper-V

Microsoft has specific support for certain versions of operating systems as guest sessions within Hyper-V. Although you can effectively boot and try to install any operating system on Hyper-V and can frequently get to the point where the operating system will work under Hyper-V, Microsoft officially supports only specific versions of operating systems as guest sessions.

NOTE

When attempting to install an operating system that may not be officially supported by Microsoft, you might find that a network adapter driver, hard drive driver, audio/sound driver, or the like is not supported, and either the operating system will fail to complete the installation or it will appear to install correctly. However, the guest session has no support to communicate externally, because a network driver was not available to support the guest session. Many times, legacy drivers will work, and a guest image will work fine. Again, however, Microsoft technically only supports the operating systems they state that they support for guest sessions.

Windows Server 2008 x86 and x64

Microsoft provides full support for running the Web Server, Standard, and Enterprise editions of Windows Server 2008 as a guest session under Hyper-V. In addition, the support extends to both the 32-bit x86 version and the 64-bit x64 versions of the Windows Server software. A guest session has the same limitation as the operating system has in running on a physical server. So, a 32-bit version of Windows 2008 Standard Edition will support a maximum of 4GB of RAM, whereas an Enterprise Edition of x86 will support up to 32GB of RAM, and the x64-bit version of Windows 2008 Enterprise will support the maximum amount of memory available in the host server.

In addition, symmetrical multiprocessing support (SMP) is limited to the maximum capability of the operating system being installed. So, support for one-, two-, or four-way SMP for each guest session up to the available number of processors in the host system is available for guest sharing.

Specific support for Windows 2008 guest sessions are as follows:

Microsoft Windows Server 2008 x64 (VMs configured with 1, 2, or 4 virtual processors)

- ▶ Windows Server 2008 Standard
- ▶ Windows Server 2008 Enterprise
- ▶ Windows Server 2008 Datacenter
- ▶ Windows HPC Server 2008
- ▶ Windows Web Server 2008
- ▶ Windows Server 2008 Standard without Hyper-V
- ▶ Windows Server 2008 Enterprise without Hyper-V
- ▶ Windows Server 2008 Datacenter without Hyper-V

Microsoft Windows Server 2008 x86 (VMs configured with 1, 2, or 4 virtual processors)

- ▶ Windows Server 2008 Standard (x86 Edition)
- ▶ Windows Server 2008 Enterprise (x86 Edition)
- ▶ Windows Server 2008 Datacenter (x86 Edition)
- ▶ Windows Web Server 2008 (x86 Edition)
- ▶ Windows Server 2008 Standard without Hyper-V (x86 Edition)
- ▶ Windows Server 2008 Enterprise without Hyper-V (x86 Edition)
- ▶ Windows Server 2008 Datacenter without Hyper-V (x86 Edition)

Windows Server 2003 x86 and x64
Windows Server 2003 guest sessions are also supported for Service Pack 2 and later. As with Windows 2008 guest sessions, the guest sessions of Windows Server 2003 are limited to the maximum support for the core Windows 2003 operating system itself, or in some cases less than the maximum support of the core operating system itself.

As a Hyper-V guest session, Windows 2003 x86 and Windows 2003 x64-bit support up to two-way SMP. The specific support is as follows:

Microsoft Windows Server 2003 x86 (VMs configured with 1 or 2 virtual processors)

▶ Windows Server 2003 R2 Standard x86 Edition with Service Pack 2

▶ Windows Server 2003 R2 Enterprise x86 Edition with Service Pack 2

▶ Windows Server 2003 R2 Datacenter x86 Edition with Service Pack 2

▶ Windows Server 2003 Standard x86 Edition with Service Pack 2

▶ Windows Server 2003 Enterprise x86 Edition with Service Pack 2

▶ Windows Server 2003 Datacenter x86 Edition with Service Pack 2

▶ Windows Server 2003 Web Edition with Service Pack 2

Microsoft Windows Server 2003 x64 (VMs configured with 1 or 2 virtual processors)

▶ Windows Server 2003 R2 Standard x64 Edition with Service Pack 2

▶ Windows Server 2003 R2 Enterprise x64 Edition with Service Pack 2

▶ Windows Server 2003 R2 Datacenter x64 Edition with Service Pack 2

▶ Windows Server 2003 Standard x64 Edition with Service Pack 2

▶ Windows Server 2003 Enterprise x64 Edition with Service Pack 2

▶ Windows Server 2003 Datacenter x64 Edition with Service Pack 2

Windows 2000 Server SP4

Microsoft also released Hyper-V to support Windows 2000 Server guest sessions for organizations that need to support a guest session with an older server operating system. Both Windows 2000 Server and Windows 2000 Advanced Server editions are supported. The specific support is as follows:

Microsoft Windows 2000 Server (VMs configured with 1 virtual processor)

▶ Windows 2000 Server with Service Pack 4

▶ Windows 2000 Advanced Server with Service Pack 4

Windows Vista x86 and x64-bit

Windows Vista is supported with Service Pack 1 in both the 32-bit and x64-bit versions of Vista and with support for one or two processors per guest session. Hyper-V supports a broad range of support for Windows Vista guest sessions for an administrator to install a guest session on the host server for application testing or to simulate user-access host services from within Hyper-V.

Specific support for Windows Vista is as follows:

Microsoft Windows Vista x86 (VMs configured with 1 or 2 virtual processors)

- ▶ Windows Vista Business x86 with Service Pack 1
- ▶ Windows Vista Enterprise x86 with Service Pack 1
- ▶ Windows Vista Ultimate x86 with Service Pack 1

Microsoft Windows Vista x64 (VMs configured with 1 or 2 virtual processors)

- ▶ Windows Vista Business x64 with Service Pack 1
- ▶ Windows Vista Enterprise x64 with Service Pack 1
- ▶ Windows Vista Ultimate x64 with Service Pack 1

Windows XP x86 and x64-bit

Similarly, Windows XP is rarely installed on a Hyper-V system for anything more than to test applications running in guest sessions on the Hyper-V host server. Windows XP with Service Pack 2 and Service Pack 3 are supported, with the ability to support one (SP2 or SP3) or two processors (SP3) for the guest session.

The specific support for a guest session running Windows XP is as follows:

Microsoft Windows XP Professional x86

- ▶ Windows XP Professional x86 with Service Pack 3 (VMs configured with 1 or 2 virtual processors)
- ▶ Windows XP Professional x86 with Service Pack 2 (VMs configured with 1 virtual processor)

Microsoft Windows XP Professional x64 (VMs configured with 1 or 2 virtual processors)

- ▶ Windows XP Professional x64 with Service Pack 2

SUSE Linux Enterprise Server 10 x86 and x64

Because of its partnership with Novell, Microsoft came out with support for SUSE Linux Enterprise Server running Service Pack 1 or Service Pack 2 (the first Linux operating system to receive such support). A SUSE Linux session can support one processor and up to the maximum amount of RAM memory supported by the x86 or the x64 versions of the operating system.

The support for Linux as a guest session under Hyper-V is as follows:

Linux Distributions (VMs configured with 1 virtual processor)

- ▶ Suse Linux Enterprise Server 10 with Service Pack 2 x86 Edition
- ▶ Suse Linux Enterprise Server 10 with Service Pack 2 x64 Edition
- ▶ Suse Linux Enterprise Server 10 with Service Pack 1 x86 Edition
- ▶ Suse Linux Enterprise Server 10 with Service Pack 1 x64 Edition

Guest Session Integration Support Tools

Key to the support of a guest operating system is not just whether Microsoft officially supports the guest operating system under Hyper-V, but also whether the integration support tools are available for the given operating system. This is where the version of operating system is critical. If you install Windows 2003 SP1 and want to install the Windows 2003 integration support tools, for instance, you will get an error saying that the integration tools will install only on Windows 2003 with Service Pack 2 installed.

> **NOTE**
>
> The Installation Wizard for integration support tools will typically fail to complete on a version of the operating system not directly supported by Microsoft. However, it has been found that a Windows 2003 server that was installed initially as the RTM or SP1 version of operating system can be upgraded to Service Pack 2, and then have the Hyper-V integration support tools installed. Then, the Service Pack 2 update can be uninstalled, returning the server back to RTM or SP1 but with the integration support tools still running. Be aware, however, Microsoft does not support workarounds of this type; therefore, if you ever need to reinstall the integration support tools, you'll have to upgrade the server temporarily to SP2 again, reinstall the support tools, and then drop the server back off SP2.

The integration support tools have key network drivers, sound drivers, disk drivers, and the like optimized to support a guest session within Windows 2008 Hyper-V. The integration support tools also enable seamless use of the mouse and keyboard between host and guest that allows the administrator to simply switch between administering the host and the guest sessions. If the guest session doesn't have the integration tools installed, however, the administrator must "release" the keyboard and mouse from a guest session before the host has access and control of the keyboard and mouse on the system.

The integration support tools are installed on the host system when the Hyper-V role is installed on the host. The integration support tools can be installed onto the guest sessions, as shown in Figure 1.7, from within the Hyper-V Administration tool. You can find more information about the Hyper-V integration support tools in Chapter 5.

The Right Time to Implement Hyper-V

Hyper-V has had an interesting release cycle. It was bundled into the release of Windows 2008 as a beta component when Windows 2008 shipped in February 2008. And over the first few months of 2008 as Windows Server 2008 was gaining momentum in organizations as a solid server operating system, organizations were installing the beta version of Hyper-V and giving it a try. Early adopters found Hyper-V to be extremely stable and reliable, and because the images use the same Virtual Hard Disk (VHD) file format used in Microsoft Virtual Server 2005, the adoption of Hyper-V since its formal release has been brisk.

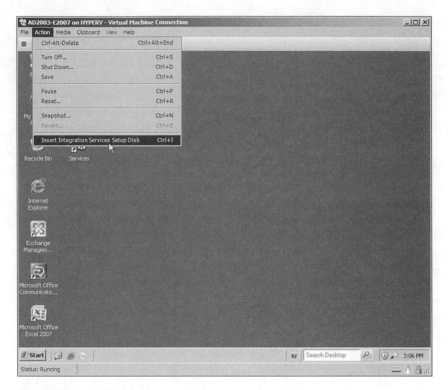

FIGURE 1.7   Hyper-V integration support tools add-in.

So, the decision of when to implement Hyper-V has come down to the same decision on implementing any technology: Identify the value received by implementing Hyper-V virtualization, test the solution in a limited environment, and roll out Hyper-V when you are comfortable that the product meets the needs of your organization.

Adding a Hyper-V Host Server in an Existing Active Directory 2000/2003 Environment

The Hyper-V server is nothing more than any other application server in a Windows environment. You can join the Windows 2008 Hyper-V host to an existing Active Directory 2000 or Active Directory 2003 environment. The Hyper-V host will operate just like any member server in the environment. If you want to remove the server, just "unjoin" the member server from Active Directory. Because it is so easy to add and remove a Hyper-V host to Active Directory and being that it requires *no* schema updates to Active Directory, the choice to add or remove Hyper-V from Active Directory is pretty simple and self-contained.

In addition, the fact that the Hyper-V host is or is not joined to the domain has no effect on whether the Hyper-V guest sessions need to join or can choose to not be joined to the domain. The guest sessions run completely independently of the host server. In fact, while

Hyper-V is joined to one domain, the guest sessions of a Hyper-V host can easily be joined to a different domain or to a completely different forest. Again, the guest sessions run independently of the host server.

Waiting to Fully Implement Windows 2008 in the Environment

Although an administrator may choose to wait until more Windows 2008 servers are added to the network before adding Hyper-V to the network, or wait until Active Directory is upgraded to an Active Directory 2008 level, it is not necessary. In fact, there are no benefits in joining Hyper-V to a Windows 2008 versus Windows 2000 or 2003 Active Directory. In the early-adopter community, Hyper-V has been one of the first Windows 2008 servers added to an existing Active Directory 2000 or 2003 domain; after all, it is so easy to just join or remove the Hyper-V server from the domain. And the benefits gained from using virtualization (as discussed throughout this chapter) have been compelling reasons for organizations to add Hyper-V to a network.

Migrating from Microsoft Virtual Server 2005 and VMware

Many organizations have already implemented Microsoft Virtual Server 2005 or VMware in their environments and wonder what it takes to migrate to Hyper-V, or whether there are ways to centrally manage and administer a dual virtualization platform environment. The simple answer is that there are several ways to migrate, integrate, and support Virtual Server 2005 and VMware images in a Hyper-V environment.

Mounting Existing Virtual Guest Images on Hyper-V

Hyper-V can mount and run both Microsoft Virtual Server 2005 VHD images and VMware guest images directly as guests within Hyper-V. Because Hyper-V has this ability to mount other virtual images, some organizations use Hyper-V as a disaster-recovery host for existing images. In such a scenario, if a VS/2005 server or VMware server fails, the images can be copied over to Hyper-V, and Hyper-V can easily boot and mount the images onto the network backbone.

However, despite Hyper-V's ability to mount VMware images natively within Hyper-V, a VMware image does not have the same administration, management, snapshotting, backup, and support capabilities as a native Hyper-V guest image. So the long-term plan should be to migrate images from VMware to Hyper-V using a virtual to virtual image-migration tool like what is available in System Center Virtual Machine Manager 2008. When you migrate the VMware to a native Hyper-V image, all the capabilities built in to support Hyper-V images are supported.

For Virtual Server 2005 images mounted on Hyper-V, those images work fine as long as you install the Hyper-V integration tools onto the image that update the drivers of the image itself.

Performing a Virtual to Virtual Migration of Guest Images

A strategy for migrating older images to Hyper-V is to do a virtual to virtual image migration. Via VMM, an administrator can select a running virtual machine (running VMware, XenServer, Virtual Server 2005, or the like) and choose to migrate the image to Hyper-V. This process extracts all the pertinent server image information, applications, data, Registry settings, user settings, and the like and moves the information over to a target Hyper-V host server. Once migrated, the Hyper-V integration tools can be installed, and the image is now clear and ready to be supported by Hyper-V or VMM.

Using VMM to Manage VMware Virtual Infrastructure 3

For organizations that have a fairly substantial investment in VMware and the VMware Infrastructure 3 (VI3) management environment, Microsoft System Center VMM has a built-in configuration setting, shown in Figure 1.8, that allows for the support, monitoring, and consolidation of information between VI3 and VMM. This integration between management tools is vital for organizations that want to keep both the VMware and a new Hyper-V environment running in parallel, and for organizations that are migrating to Hyper-V but still want to have integrated support for the old VMware environment while the migration process is performed.

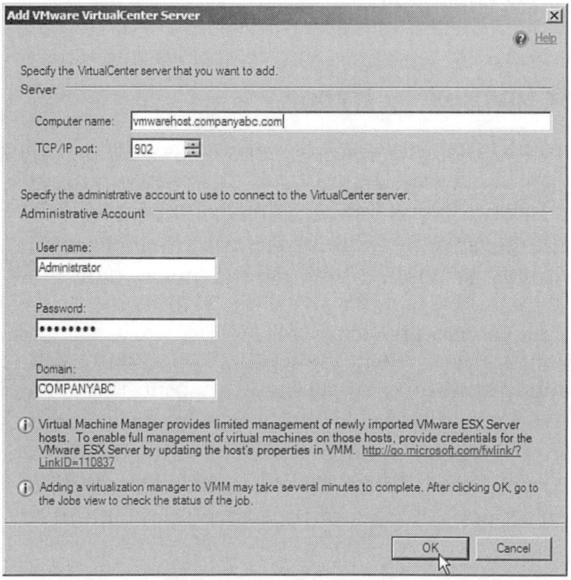

FIGURE 1.8   VMware Infrastructure 3 integration support.

Understanding the Administration of Virtual Guest Sessions

One question that comes up frequently from administrators implementing virtual environments for the first time is how one administers a virtual server. For years, we have just walked up to a server that has a keyboard, mouse, and monitor and worked on "that system." Having a different mouse, keyboard, and monitor for each system is simple; we know which devices go to which server that is running a specific application. With virtualization, however, guest sessions do not have their own mouse, keyboard, or monitor. So, how do you administer the system?

Many organizations have already been working off of centralized mice, keyboards, and monitors by using switchboxes that allow 4, 8, 16, or more servers to all plug into a single physical mouse, keyboard, and monitor. Simply by pushing a button on the switchbox, or using a command sequence, the administrator "toggles" between the servers.

Administration of virtual servers works the exact same way. An administrator utility is loaded, and that utility enables administrators to open multiple virtual server sessions on their screen. Various tools and strategies, including the following, enable you to administer virtual systems:

- ▶ Using the Hyper-V Administration tool
- ▶ Using the System Center VMM tool
- ▶ Using Terminal Services for remote administration

The various administration options provide different levels of support to the management of the virtual guest sessions on Hyper-V.

Management Using the Hyper-V Administration Tool

The built-in Hyper-V Administration tool provides basic functions such as starting and stopping guest images, pausing guest images, forcing a shutdown of guest images, immediately turning off guest images, and the ability to snapshot images for a configuration state at a given time.

In most environments, the administrator would set a guest image to automatically start as soon as the host server itself has been started. That way, if the server is rebooted, the appropriate guest images are also started (but like if a physical server lost power and rebooted when the power came back on).

For images that have been set to be off after the host server reboot, those images can be manually started from the Hyper-V Administration tool. The manual start of images is common for servers that are hosting test images, images used for demonstration purposes, and copies of images that can be manually started when a specific server is required (that is, cold standby server startup).

You can find more information about the built-in Hyper-V Administration tool in Chapter 6, "Managing, Administering, and Maintaining a Hyper-V Host Server."

Management Using the Virtual Machine Manager 2008 Tool

Organizations that want more than just starting and stopping guest images should consider buying and implementing the System Center Virtual Machine Manager 2008 (VMM) tool. VMM provides basic information about whether a guest image has been started or not, and it provides more information than the built-in Hyper-V Administration tool in terms of how much memory and disk space each image is taking on the host server. The VMM 2008 tool has several wizards and functions that allow an administrator to capture physical server information and bring the server configuration into a virtual image. VMM 2008 can also extract an image from another virtual server and bring that information into a new Hyper-V guest image.

Another feature built in to VMM 2008 is the ability to create a library where template images, ISO application images, snapshot libraries, and the like are stored. With a central-ized library, administrators have at their fingertips the images, tools, and resources to build new images, to recover from failed images, and to deploy new images more easily. In addition, VMM 2008 provides delegation and provisioning capabilities so that administra-tors can issue rights to other users to self-provision and self-manage specific images without depending on the IT department to manage images or manually build out config-urations.

You can find more information about System Center Virtual Machine Manager in the four chapters included in Part IV of this book, "System Center Virtual Machine Manager 2008 in a Hyper-V Environment."

Management Using Thin Client Terminal Services

Aside from using the centralized Hyper-V Administration tool to manage guest images, administrators can still use Terminal Services to remotely administer servers on the network, whether that's physical servers or images running as virtual sessions in a Hyper-V environment.

An administrator may choose to gain remote access into the Hyper-V host server, and then control all the guest images on that host server, or the administrator could gain remote access one by one to each of the guest sessions. The latter, which is the ability to individually administer a remote system, is a good solution to provide to an individual who needs access to a single server or a limited number of servers, such as a web adminis-trator or a database administrator.

> **NOTE**
>
> If an administrator needs to manage and control several servers, such as all the Exchange servers or all the SharePoint servers in an organization, it may be better to use the VMM 2008 tool, create a administration delegation policy, and provide the administrator access to a group of servers through VMM. That way, security and access control is centralized in the VMM tool. If the administrator no longer needs rights access to the group of servers (changes departments, roles, or is terminated) or if the administrator needs rights to new servers, VMM can manage security access privileges from a central console.

Improvements in Windows 2008 Terminal Services

Windows 2008 incorporates significant improvements in Terminal Services capabilities for thin client access for remote managed users to access servers in an environment. What used to require third-party add-ons to make the basic Windows 2000 or 2003 Terminal Services functional, Microsoft has included in Windows 2008. These technologies include things such as the ability to access Terminal Services using a standard port 443 Secure Sockets Layer (SSL) rather than the proprietary port 3389; and the ability to publish just specific programs rather than the entire desktop; and improvements in allowing a client to have a larger remote-access screen, multiple screens, and to more easily print to remote print devices.

These improvements to Windows 2008 Terminal Services make it a component that's easy to add to an existing Windows 2003 Active Directory to test out the new Windows 2008 capabilities. The installation of a Windows 2008 Terminal Services system requires just the addition of a member server to the domain, and that can be removed at any time (similar to the addition and removal of a Hyper-V host server).

You can find more information about using Terminal Services for remote administration in Chapter 6.

Improvements in RDP 6.x for Better Client Capabilities

One area of significant improvement in Windows 2008 Terminal Services can be seen in the update to the Remote Desktop Protocol (RDP) 6.x client, shown in Figure 1.9.

FIGURE 1.9   Remote Desktop Protocol client for Terminal Services.

The new RDP client provides the following:

▶ **Video support up to 4,096 x 2,048**—Administrators can now use very large monitors across an RDP connection to view data off a Windows 2008 Terminal Services system, providing a view to many virtual guest sessions from a single Hyper-V cost connection.

▶ **Multimonitor support**—Administrators can also have multiple monitors supported off a single RDP connection. For help desk and operations staff monitoring multiple servers in the environment, having different monitors display different remote servers or configurations can help simplify remote administration tasks.

▶ **Secured connections**—The new RDP client now provides for a highly encrypted remote connection to a Terminal Services system through the use of Windows 2008 security. When remote administration of key servers is required, the new RDP security ensures that server access is protected and information privacy is ensured through a highly secured encrypted connection between a Windows 2008 Terminal Services system and the remote client.

Terminal Services Web Access

Also new to Windows 2008 Terminal Services is a new role called Terminal Services Web Access, or TSWA. TSWA enables a remote administrator to access a Terminal Services session without having to launch the RDP 6.x client. The administrator instead connects to a web page that then allows the administrator to log on and access the session off the web page. This simplifies the access method for administrators. They can just set a browser favorite to link them to a URL that provides them Terminal Services access to the specific servers they need to manage.

> **NOTE**
>
> Terminal Services Web Access still requires the client system to be a Windows XP, Windows Vista, Windows 2003, or Windows 2008 server system to connect to a Terminal Services session. A browser user cannot be running from an Apple Macintosh or Linux system and access TSWA. For non-Windows-based web clients, third-party vendors such as Citrix Systems provide connector support for these types of devices.

Terminal Services Gateway

Terminal Services Gateway (TS Gateway) is a new addition to Windows 2008 Terminal Services and provides the connectivity to a Terminal Services session over a standard port 443 SSL connection. In the past, administrators could only connect to Windows Terminal Services using a proprietary port 3389 connection. Unfortunately, most organizations block nonstandard port connections for security purposes, and therefore if an administrator was connected to an Internet connection at a hotel, airport, coffee shop, or other location that blocked nonstandard ports, the administrator could not access Terminal Services.

Now with TS Gateway, the remote connection to the TS Gateway goes over port 443, just like surfing a secure web page. This provides better support for a remote administrator working from home or remotely who needs access to a server for remote administration.

Ensuring High Availability of a Hyper-V Host Server

One of the concerns expressed by many IT administrators when consolidating and central-izing their physical servers into fewer virtual host systems is "what happens when the host server fails," because a single host server failure can now impact several network servers simultaneously. Instead of just having 1 server down, the organization can have 4, 8, or 10 systems all down at the same time. The good and bad of centralized servers is that although it is bad that all these server systems are offline, because there is so much riding on a single server, it becomes easier to justify the high availability of a server that is hosting so many business applications. Instead of clustering 10 physical servers, an organi-zation may choose to just cluster the virtual host server that will then protect the guest sessions under the host. Or in an environment where redundancy and disaster recovery is part of the IT strategy, the organization would split server resources across multiple Hyper-V host systems.

In the SQL world, split server resources means mirroring databases across two or more servers; and with virtualization, that means putting one SQL server on one host server and a mirror copy of the SQL server on a second host server. In the event that either of the guest SQL sessions fails or even if either of the virtual host server sessions fails, the SQL mirroring will provide redundant resource storage and access from more than one system.

Significant improvements in Windows Server 2008 clustering and support for both host and guest session clustering provides reliability and improved uptime for virtualized hosts and guest sessions. Because IT administrators are tasked with the responsibility of keeping the network operational 24 hours a day, 7 days a week, it becomes even more important that clustering works. Fortunately, the cost of hardware that supports clustering has gotten significantly less expensive; in fact, any server that meets the required specifica-tions to run Windows Server 2008, Enterprise Edition can typically support Windows clus-tering. The basic standard for a server that is used for enterprise networking has the technologies built in to the system for high availability. Windows Server 2008, Enterprise Edition or Datacenter Edition is required to run Windows 2008 clustering services.

No Single Point of Failure in Clustering

Clustering by definition should provide redundancy and high availability of server systems; however, in previous versions of Windows clustering, a "quorum drive" was required for the cluster systems to connect to as the point of validation for cluster opera-tions. If at any point the quorum drive failed, the cluster would not be able to fail over from one system to another. Windows 2008 clustering removed this requirement of a static quorum drive. Two major technologies facilitate this elimination of a single or central point of failure: majority-based cluster membership verification and witness-based quorum validation.

The majority-based cluster membership allows the IT administrator to define which devices in the cluster get a vote to determine whether a cluster node is in a failed state (and so the cluster needs to fail over to another node). Instead of assuming the disk will always be available as in the previous quorum disk model, now nodes of the cluster and shared storage devices participate in the new enhanced quorum model in Windows 2008.

Effectively, Windows 2008 server clusters have better information to determine whether it is appropriate to fail over a cluster in the event of a system or device failure.

The witness-based quorum eliminates the single quorum disk from the cluster-operation validation model. Instead, a completely separate node or file share can be set as the file share witness. In the case of a GeoCluster, where cluster nodes are in completely different locations, the ability to place the file share in a third site and even enable that file share to serve as the witness for multiple clusters becomes a benefit for organizations with distributed data centers and also provides more resiliency in the cluster-operation components.

The elimination of points of failure in clustering plus the ability to cluster across geographic distances allows the administrators of an organization to put one cluster server on one host system and another cluster server on another host system and have guest session redundancy without single points of failure.

Stretched Clusters for Hyper-V Hosts and Guests Across Sites

Windows 2008 also introduced the concept of stretched clusters to provide better server and site server redundancy. Effectively, Microsoft has eliminated the need to have cluster servers remain on the same subnet, as has been the case in Windows clustering in the past. Although organizations have used virtual local area networks (VLANs) to stretch a subnet across multiple locations, this was not always easy to do and, in many cases, technologically not the right thing to do in IP networking design.

By allowing cluster nodes to reside on different subnets, plus with the addition of a configurable heartbeat timeout, clusters can now be set up in ways that match an organization's disaster-failover and -recovery strategy. In the case of multiple host environments, one host with a cluster guest session can sit in one site, and another host with a cluster guest session can sit in another site. In the event that either the guest session fails or the entire site becomes available, the virtualized cluster spanning multiple physical sites can provide extremely high-level redundancy in a Windows 2008 Hyper-V environment.

Leveraging Storage Area Networks for Virtual Hosts and Guests

Windows 2008 has also improved its support for storage area networks (SANs) by providing enhanced mechanisms for connecting to SANs and switching between SAN nodes. In the past, a connection to a SAN was a static connection, meaning that a server was connected to a SAN just as if the server was physically connected to a direct attached storage system. However, the concept of a SAN is that if a SAN fails, the server should reconnect to a SAN device that is now online. This could not be easily done with Windows 2003 or earlier. SCSI bus resets were required to disconnect a server from one SAN device to another.

With Windows 2008, a server can be associated with a SAN with a persistent reservation to access a specific shared disk; however, in the event that the SAN fails, the server session can be logically connected to another SAN target system without having to script device resets that have been complicated and disruptive in disaster-recovery scenarios.

All the SAN connect and disconnect associations, failover, and recovery are translated back to the Windows 2008 Hyper-V host server and to any of the guest sessions running on Hyper-V that are Windows 2008 server guests. With the inclusion of clustering along with SAN storage replication, an organization can design and implement a highly available network environment based on Hyper-V virtualization.

Summary

This introductory chapter was intended to highlight what Windows Server 2008 Hyper-V is, generally how it works, where it fits in to an organization, and how virtualization can greatly decrease the cost, management, and administration of network server systems. In addition, through the implementation of failover technologies, a virtualized environment can leverage host clustering, guest clustering, stretch clusters, and SAN technologies to greatly improve the reliability of network and server system operations.

The inclusion of Hyper-V into an existing Windows 2000 or 2003 Active Directory requires just attaching a member server to an existing domain. The built-in administration tools in the form of the Hyper-V Administration tool or the purchase of the System Center VMM 2008 tool provides extensive capabilities to an organization for virtual guest image support.

In just a few short years, server virtualization has shifted from being a technology that was good to fiddle with for test and development lab purposes. Drastic improvements in server technologies and initiatives to decrease costs and provide better environment conscious business practices have driven server virtualization out of the test labs and into main-stream production environments. It's no longer whether an organization will virtualize part or all of its IT environment, it's a matter of when and how virtualization will be implemented.

The balance of this book covers planning, testing, implementing, administering, managing, and supporting the Windows Server 2008 Hyper-V virtualization technology in production environments.

Best Practices

The following are best practices from this chapter:

- ▶ Consolidate physical servers down to virtual guest sessions to decrease the number of physical servers in an organization, and thus ultimately lower electrical costs, server management costs, and rack-space costs associated with sprawling physical server systems.

- ▶ Although server consolidation will decrease the number of servers in the environment, take the opportunity to repurpose servers and implement high-availability and disaster-recovery strategies within the environment.

▶ Consider using the native high-availability and disaster-recovery technologies built in to applications (such as Exchange 2007 Cluster Continuous Replication and SQL 2005 Mirror) to establish reliable application servers in a networking environment.

▶ Use the built-in virtual switch technology in Hyper-V to segment guest servers and associate segments to specific network adapters on the host server for better internet-working communications.

▶ Dedicate core processors to virtual guest sessions to guarantee processing performance to virtual sessions that require high processing capabilities.

▶ Consider using Windows 2008 Server Core for the basis of the Hyper-V host server to minimize the attack surface of a host server by removing the GUI from the host system.

▶ Install the guest integration support tools after installing the guest operating system to take advantage of optimized drivers and session administration functions.

▶ Use the System Center Virtual Machine Manager 2008 tool to migrate physical and virtual servers into native Hyper-V virtual guest images.

▶ When considering adding a Windows 2008 server to an existing Windows 2000/2003 Active Directory environment, consider implementing Hyper-V virtualization, which has proven to be pretty easy to implement and provides a lot of value to organizations.

▶ Consider using the snapshot capabilities built in to the Hyper-V Administration tool before patching or upgrading a virtual server system. That way, if you need to roll back, you can roll back to a copy of the virtual image right before the update was applied.

▶ Use Terminal Services in Windows 2008 to provide administrators direct access to a limited number of servers they need to remotely access.

▶ Use System Center Virtual Machine Manager 2008 to create administration and delegation groups for the centralized administration management of server systems.

▶ Leverage the capabilities of stretch clustering in Windows Server 2008 to provide redundancy across a WAN link for virtual guest sessions clustered between multiple host servers.

2

Best Practices at Planning, Prototyping, Migrating, and Deploying Windows Server 2008 Hyper-V

The technical process to implement or to migrate physical or virtual servers to a Windows Server 2008 Hyper-V virtual environment is similar to the migration processes of any IT migration project. However, the requirements and expectations of organizations to ensure the virtual environment is just as dependable as a physical environment have made it important for IT professionals to do better planning, preparation, and testing before merely running tools to convert physical to virtual server sessions. Organizations are extremely dependent on the reliability of their network server systems and less tolerant of downtime, such that the migration process needs to be planned and executed with great attention paid to minimizing user impact and system downtime.

This chapter examines how a structured multistep process for migrating physical servers to Windows 2008 virtual server sessions can enhance the success of the project. Consisting of discovery, design, testing, and implementation phases, this methodology can be scaled to meet the needs of the wide variety of organizations and businesses that use Microsoft technologies. The results of this methodology are three important documents created to map out the implementation process: the design document, the migration document, and the migration plan.

The examples used in this chapter assume that the physical and virtual servers being migrated are primarily Windows-based systems, but the concepts and process can certainly apply to the migration of non-Windows systems to Hyper-V, too.

Determining the Scope of Your Project

This chapter provides guidance and best practices that can assist with the process of migrating servers and assist organizations in creating a well thought-out and structured implementation plan.

Instead of forging ahead with no plan or goals and simply converting servers and inserting them back into an existing network environment, a more organized process will control the risks involved and define in detail what the end state will look like.

The first steps involve getting a better sense of the scope of the project, in essence writing the executive summary of your design document. The scope should define from a high level what the project consists of and why the organization is devoting time, energy, and resources to its completion. This might seem like a drawn-out process to migrate servers to virtual systems, but there's a big difference in doing a flat-out one for one migration of all physical servers to virtual servers versus the better plan of choosing which servers to migrate and the smartest way to consolidate servers so that there's more than a one-to-one conversation.

Creating this scope of work requires an understanding of the different goals of the organization, and recognizing the pieces of the puzzle that need to fit together to meet the company's stated goals for the project. For Hyper-V virtualization, the primary pieces are servers that handle key network functionality, servers that handle and manage the data, servers that control or provide access to the information, and servers that handle specific applications.

Identifying the Business Goals and Objectives to Implement Hyper-V Virtualization

It is important to establish a thorough understanding of the goals and objectives of a company that guide and direct the efforts of the different components of the organization, to help ensure the success of the Hyper-V virtualization project. It might seem counterintuitive to start at this high level and keep away from the bits- and bytes-level details, but time spent in this area will clarify the purposes of the project and start to generate productive discussions.

As an example of the value of setting high-level business goals and objectives, an organization can identify the desire for zero downtime on file access; this downtime could be facilitated through the implementation of Windows Clustering at either the Hyper-V host or guest level to improve high availability and system reliability. Starting with the broad goals and objectives will create an outline for a technical solution that will meet all the criteria the organization wants, at a lower cost and with an easier-managed solution.

In every organization, a variety of different goals and objectives need to be identified and met for a project to be considered successful. These goals and objectives represent a snap-shot of the end state that the company or organization is seeking to create. For a smaller company, this process might be completed in a few brainstorming sessions, whereas larger companies might require more extensive discussions and assistance from external resources or firms.

High-Level Business Goals

To start the organizational process, it is helpful to break up business goals and objectives into different levels, or vantage points. Most organizations have high-level business goals, often referred to as the "vision of the company," which is typically shaped by the key decision makers in the organization (such as the CEO, CFO, CIO, and so on). These goals are commonly called the "50,000-foot view." Business unit or departmental goals, or the "10,000-foot view," are typically shaped by the key executives and managers in the organi-zation (such as the VP of sales, HR director, site facilities manager, and so on). Most orga-nizations also have well-defined "1,000-foot view" goals that are typically tactical in nature, implemented by IT staff and technical specialists.

It is well worth the time to perform some research and ask the right questions to help ensure that the virtualization strategy meets business goals and not just technical IT goals. To get specific information and clarification of the objectives of the different business units, make sure the goals of a technology implementation or upgrade are in line with these business goals.

Although most organizations have stated company visions and goals, and a quick visit to the company's website or intranet can provide this information, it is worth taking the time to gather more information about what the key stakeholders believe to be their primary objectives. Often, this task starts with asking the right questions of the right people and then opening discussion groups on the topic. Of course, it also matters who asks the questions because the answers will vary accordingly, and employees might be more forthcoming when speaking with external consultants as opposed to co-workers. Often, the publicly stated vision and goals are "the tip of the iceberg" and might even be in contrast to internal company goals, ambitions, or initiatives.

High-level business goals and visions can vary greatly among different organizations, but generally they bracket and guide the goals of the units that make up the company. For example, a corporation might be interested in offering the "best" product in its class, and this requires corresponding goals for the sales, engineering, marketing, finance, and manufacturing departments. Additional concepts to look for are whether the highest-level goals embrace change and new ideas and processes, or want to refine the existing practices and methods.

High-level business goals of a company can also change rapidly, whether in response to changing economic conditions or as affected by a new key stakeholder or leader in the company. So, it is also important to get a sense of the timeline involved for meeting these high-level goals.

> **NOTE**
>
> High-level business goal examples include a desire to have no downtime, access to the network from any of the organization's offices around the world, and lowering the cost of IT operations from both hardware and licensing perspectives, but also from electrical power consumption and data center facilities perspective.

Business Unit or Departmental Goals

When the vision or 50,000-foot view is defined, additional discussions should reveal the goals of the different departments and the executives who run them. Theoretically, they should "add up" to the highest-level goals, but the findings might be surprising. Whatever the case turns out to be, the results will start to reveal the complexity of the organization and the primary concerns of the different stakeholders.

The high-level goals of the organization also start to paint the picture of which departments carry the most weight in the organization, and will most likely get budgets approved, which will assist in the design process. Logically, the goals of the IT department will play a very important role in a server virtualization project, but the other key departments shouldn't be forgotten.

As an example of the business unit or departmental goals for an organization, the CFO may want to decrease IT costs with thoughts in mind of eliminating all IT upgrade projects. Or a legal department may influence security access projects with a focus on information storage rights and storage retention.

If the department's goals are not aligned with the overall vision of the company, or don't take into account the needs of the key stakeholders, the result of the project might not be appreciated. "Technology for technology's sake" does not always fulfill the needs of the organization and in the long run is viewed as a wasteful expenditure of organizational funds.

In the process of clarifying these goals, the initiatives to consolidate servers or to increase server availability and disaster recovery are most important to the different departments and executives should become apparent. It is safe to assume that access to company data in the form of documents or database information; to communications tools, such as email, faxing, and Internet access; and to vertical market software applications that the company relies upon will affect the company's ability to meet its various business goals.

It is also worth looking for the "holes" in the goals and objectives presented. Some of the less-glamorous objectives, such as a stable network, data-recovery abilities, or protection from the hostile outside world, are often neglected.

A by-product of these discussions will ideally be a sense of excitement about the possibilities of reducing the number of servers to manage and reducing the hard costs of electrical power and cooling while improving overall systems reliability and availability. These discussions will also convey to the executives and key stakeholders that they are involved in helping to define and craft a solution that takes into account the varied needs of the company. Many executives look for this high-level strategy, thinking, and discussions to reveal the maturity of the planning and implementation process in action.

> **NOTE**
>
> Departmental goal examples include a desire to have secured storage of human resource and personnel information, 30-minute response time to help desk questions during business hours, 24-hour support for sales executives when they are traveling, and easy lookup of files stored on servers throughout the organization.

Identifying the Technical Goals and Objectives to Implement Hyper-V

Although the consolidation of physical servers into virtual guest images might not initially seem integral to the highest-level company goals, its importance will become clearer as the goals get close to the 1,000-foot view. When the business goals are sketched out and the cost savings are identified, the technical goals should fall into place quite naturally.

At this point in the process, questions should focus on which components and capabilities of the network are most important, and how they contribute to or hinder the goals expressed by the different units.

As with business goals, the technical goals of the project should be clarified on different levels (50,000-foot, 10,000-foot, 1,000-foot, and so on). At the highest level, the technical goals might be quite vague, such as "no downtime" or "no degradation in performance." But as the goals are clarified on a departmental and individual level, they should become specific and measurable. For example, instead of identifying a goal as "no downtime," ferreting out the details might result in a more specific goal of "99.99% uptime during business hours, and no more than 4-hour downtime during nonbusiness hours scheduled at least 2 days in advance." Instead of stating a goal of "no degradation in performance," a more specific goal of "providing equal or better end-user performance" can more reasonably be attained.

Part of the art of defining technical goals and objectives also resides in limiting them. System performance can be assessed in many different ways, and the complexity of the variables can boggle even the veteran IT manager's mind.

Departmental technical goals can include 10,000-foot items—for example, adding more storage capacity and making data available to all users in the organization worldwide, or protecting data so that there's no more than 30 minutes of lost data even in the worst-case scenario.

Defining the Scope of the Work

By now, the list of goals and objectives might be getting quite long. But when the myriad business and technical objectives and the overall priorities start to become clear, the scope of work starts to take shape. A key question to ask at this point, to hone in on the scope of the project, is whether the migration is primarily an exercise to consolidate servers or a project that commits to a direct decrease in operational costs (that is, electricity savings, hardware maintenance cost savings, software license savings, and so on). Often, the answer to this question seems clear at first but becomes more complex as the different goals of the business units are discussed, so the scope of work that is created might be quite different from how it appeared at first.

Specifically, a decision needs to be made whether all physical servers need to be virtualized, or only a subset of it, and what other infrastructure components need to be changed or replaced in the process. This section focuses on the server components, and later sections focus on other hardware and software areas that should be reviewed.

Migrating physical servers to virtual servers does not necessarily require server applications to be upgraded at the same time. Just migrating physical servers to virtual servers in one-to-one conversations can minimize taking on too many migrations and upgrades at the same time. If an application must be accessed, organizations must consider whether the vendor supports the running of the application on a virtualized server and weigh factors such as time, effort, and cost savings. Consider just migrating the applications that can easily be migrated and are widely known to be compatible and supported in virtual environments first. Keep the more difficult/complicated systems on the schedule to be migrated at a much later date.

It is important to also examine how the business and technology goals fit into this plan. If one of the goals of the organization is improve system availability and disaster recovery at the same time as virtualizing the server infrastructure, either sequential projects or parallel projects relative to server consolidation and disaster recovery need to be accounted for.

Questions raised at this point might require further discussion and even research. The section "The Discovery Phase: Understanding the Existing Environment" later in this chapter examines some areas that generally need review. With a solid understanding of the different departmental and companywide goals for the project, however, you can sketch out a basic outline of the required configuration.

You need to get answers to these sample questions:

- ▶ How many servers will be migrated from physical to virtual?

- ▶ How many servers will be migrated from virtual to virtual?

- ▶ Where do these servers reside?

- ▶ Do core business applications need to be upgraded at this time?

- ▶ What additional applications and devices need to be upgraded or modified to support the new virtualized environment?

Based on the goals and objectives for the project and the answers to these types of questions, the high-level scope of the work begins to take shape. Here are some general rules to consider:

▶ Keep it as simple as possible.

▶ Break up the project into logical segments.

▶ Don't forget that server administrators will need to familiarize themselves with the new way of administering servers.

It often makes sense to virtualize utility servers (domain controllers, Dynamic Host Control Protocol [DHCP] servers, domain name service [DNS] servers) first, and then virtualize application servers (file and print, messaging, web) after that. When an initial group of servers has been successfully migrated and the new process of administering the servers and managing the servers is well understood, other applications can be migrated to the virtual environment. In other cases, the installation of new application can be done on virtual servers so that during the course of a normal migration (for example, Exchange 2003 to Exchange 2007) or for a new installation of servers (for instance, new install of Windows 2008 Rights Management Services), the new servers can be built on Hyper-V virtual guest sessions.

As noted, the implementation of the latest version of Exchange is a good time to add virtualized servers. This implementation requires the installation of new servers (x64-bit Client Access servers, x64-bit Hub Transport servers) that are perfect for virtualized guests, and mailboxes can be dragged and dropped from the old Exchange 2003 servers to the new Exchange 2007 servers.

Often, an application-focused upgrade will introduce a limited number of new servers that can be built in virtual sessions rather than on physical server hardware. This can be an effective way to get virtualization implemented in the environment in a faster method than purchasing all new physical servers, mounting the servers into racks, installing individual operating systems on the new servers, and adding applications to the new systems. The cost savings of virtualizing the new application instead of buying all new hardware may in itself pay for the cost of a handful of Hyper-V host server systems that can be used for other applications than the initial set of applications installed on the host systems.

Again, the answers might not be obvious at this point in the design process. But by asking the questions and engaging in what-if discussions and speculations, you can identify the primary pieces of the puzzle. The next step is to determine how best to fit those pieces together.

Determining the Time Frame for Implementation or Migration

An equally important component of the migration is the time frame, and this component will affect the path and process that needs to be followed to create the results desired. Often, the goals for the project will dictate the timeline, and the technology upgrade can drastically affect other critical business project dependencies. Other upgrades might not have strict timelines, and it is more important that the process be a smooth one than a quick one.

Dependent on the scope of the project, a time frame of 2 to 4 weeks could be considered to be a short time frame, with 4 to 6 weeks offering a more comfortable window for testing applications and training time. Within these time constraints, several days are available for discovery and design, a similar amount of time is available for the testing process, and then the implementation can proceed.

A fundamental point to remember is that change will bring with it a learning curve for the administrative staff managing the Hyper-V host environment and the administrators managing the applications. Because many administrators merely use Terminal Services to access a server to manage it, or use a centralized tool to see all of their servers, there might be little or no training required because the process might be no different when the servers are running on Hyper-V. The greater the amount of change that is made to the applications themselves (for example, Exchange 2003 migration to Exchange 2007), the more support and training will be required specific to the application change, but not so much for the implementation of the applications on Hyper-V.

A safe strategy to follow when sketching out the timeline is to start by setting a completion date and then working backward from it, to get a sense for the time available to each component of the process. As this chapter discusses, the project has several key phases—discovery, design, prototype, and implementation—and sufficient time should be allowed for each one of them. Although there are no hard-and-fast rules of how the time should be split up among each of these phases, each phase tends to take longer than its predecessor, and the discovery and design phases typically take as long, combined, as the testing phase (that is, discovery + design = prototype time frame).

The implementation phase will vary tremendously based on the scope of the project. For simpler projects, where the implementation consists only of a new server housing a new application, the implementation might be as simple as "flipping a switch" over a weekend (assuming the solution has been thoroughly tested in the lab environment). At the other end of the spectrum, a full migration of an application that requires a network operating system upgrade, application upgrade, and client software upgrade may take several weeks or months, not from the Hyper-V perspective, but from the migration of the application and any related client desktop software install that the application itself might require. Again, the virtualization piece is relatively simple in the whole process.

Even when the deadline for the completion of the project is the infamous "by yesterday," time should be allocated for the design and planning process. If time and energy are not invested at this point, the prototype testing process might be missing the mark because it might not be clear exactly what is being tested, and the implementation might not be smooth or even successful. A good analogy here is that of the explorer who sets off on an adventure without planning what should go in his or her backpack or bringing a map along.

Faster migrations typically occur when the existing environment is fairly mature and stable and the vertical applications are fairly current and meet the company's needs.

Slower time frames should allow a period of days or weeks for the staff to fully understand the goals of the project and requirements of the key stakeholders, review the existing environment, and document the design. Time will also be available to choose appropriate hardware and any outside consulting partners for the project, train the internal resources who will assist in (or lead) the process, and prototype the migration in a safe lab environment. Assuming the testing is successful, a phased implementation can further limit the risks of the project, and a pilot phase (with a limited subset of servers migrated first) will allow the staff to get familiar with the tools used in managing virtual server guest sessions.

Milestones should be set for the completion of the phases, even if they aren't essential to the project's success, to keep momentum going and to avoid the "never-ending project." Projects without periodic dates set as interim milestone points will almost certainly not meet an expected completion date. Projects that extend too far beyond the allotted time frame add costs and risks such as employee turnover, changing business conditions, and new revisions of hardware and software products.

Naturally, projects with shorter timelines bring their own challenges, and typically, some compromises need to be made to successfully complete a large project in a limited amount of time. However, it is important not to abandon the basic principles of discovery, design, and testing. If these steps are skipped and an upgrade is kicked off without planning or a clear understanding of the desired results, the result will often be flawed. In fact, the result might never even be reached because "showstoppers" can suddenly appear in the middle of the project.

It is usually possible to meet a quick timeline (a number of days at the very least) and have the results make the stakeholders happy. The real key is to understand the risks involved in the tight time frame and define the scope of the project so that the risks are controlled. This might include putting off some of the functionality that is not essential, or contracting outside assistance to speed up the process and to leverage the experience of a firm that has performed similar upgrades many times.

Hardware and software procurement can also pose delays. For shorter time frames, therefore, they should be procured as soon as possible after the ideal configuration has been defined. Note that often the "latest and greatest" hardware—that is, the fastest processors and largest-capacity drives—might take longer to arrive than those a step down. The new equipment should still be tested, or "burned in," and fine-tuned in a lab environment, but can often be moved right into production with the pilot implementation. For most medium and large organizations, it is recommended that a permanent lab be set up. This step is discussed in more depth in the section "The Prototype Phase: Creating and Testing the Plan," later in this chapter.

Defining the Participants of the Design and Deployment Teams

Division of labor is a key component of the implementation process. Organizations should evaluate the capabilities of their internal staff and consider hiring an outside firm for assistance in the appropriate areas. If the organization understands and defines the roles that internal staff can play, and defines the areas where professional assistance is needed, the project will flow more smoothly.

The experience levels of the existing resources should be assessed, as should the bandwidth that they have available for learning new technologies or participating in a new project. If the staff is fully occupied on a daily basis supporting the user base, it is unlikely that they will be able to "make more time" to design and plan the new implementation, even with outside assistance. The track record of the existing staff often reveals how the next project will turn out; and if there are existing half-finished or unsuccessful projects, those can interfere with a new project.

Although classroom-style training and manufacturer-sponsored training do not guarantee expertise, they do indicate the IT staff's willingness to learn and illustrate that they are willing to dedicate time to learning new technologies. A new implementation can be a great opportunity to test the commitment levels of the existing staff and to encourage them to update their skills.

Consider also how the changes to the environment (one with fewer physical servers, and potentially servers that are hosted in an offsite data center and not even in the local data center) will affect how personnel will perceive their role in managing and administering all servers "remotely." For example, an upgrade off old hardware to new virtual guest sessions might enable a company to consolidate and reduce the number of servers on the network and replace "flaky" applications with more stable ones. An upgrade might also introduce brand-new tools that can add support duties in unfamiliar areas to the existing staff.

After the organization takes an inventory of resources at this level and determines roughly what percentage of the project can be handled internally, an external partner should be considered. Even a smaller organization faced with a relatively simple project of, say, installing Windows 2008 Hyper-V for the first time can benefit from outside assistance. Some tight time frames necessitate delegating 90% of the tasks to outside resources, whereas other, more leisurely projects might require only 10% assistance levels.

A key distinction to make at this point is between the design resources and the deployment resources. The company or individuals in charge of the design work must have significant experience with the technologies to be implemented and be able to educate and lead the other members of the project team. For projects of moderate or greater complexity, these resources should be dedicated to the design process to ensure that the details are fully sketched out and that the solution designed is as well thought out as possible. Often, the design team has the challenging task of negotiating with the key stakeholders concerning the final design, because not all the staff will get everything they want and wish for in the project. The deployment team can contain members of the design team, and these individuals should have training and hands-on experience with the technologies involved and will have more end-user interaction.

Look for certain prerequisites when choosing an independent consultant or solution provider organization as a partner. The individual or firm should have proven experience with the exact technologies to be implemented, have a flexible approach to implementing the solution, and have specialized resources to handle the different components of the project. No one person can "do it all," especially if he gets sick or goes on vacation, so breadth and depth of experience should be considered. Obviously, the hourly fees charged are important, but the overall costs and whether a firm is willing to commit to a price cap can be more important. In the current business environment, it makes sense to invest your time wisely in choosing a firm that is good at what it does, and one that will be around in future months when your project reaches its critical phases.

Soft skills of the partner are also important because many projects are judged not only by whether the project is completed on time, on scope, and on budget, but also by the response of the stakeholders and user community. Communications skills, reliability, and willingness to educate and share knowledge along the way bring great value in the long run.

The Discovery Phase: Understanding the Existing Environment

If you complete the previously discussed steps, the high-level picture of the implementation of Windows 2008 Hyper-V should be clear by now. It should be clear what the business and technology goals are from a 50,000-foot view business standpoint all the way down to the 1,000-foot staff level. The components of the upgrade, or the scope of the work, and priorities of these components should also be identified, as should the time constraints and who will be on the design and implementation teams.

The picture of the end state (or scope of work) and goals of the project should start becoming more clear. Before the final design is agreed upon and documented, however, it is essential to review and evaluate the existing environment to make sure the network foundation in place will support the new virtualized environment.

It is an important time to make sure the existing environment is configured the way you think it is and to identify existing areas of exposure or weakness in the network. The level of effort required will vary greatly here, depending on the complexity and sheer scope of the network. Organizations with fewer than 200 users and a single or small number of locations that use off-the-shelf software applications and standard hardware products (for example, Hewlett-Packard, IBM, Cisco) will typically have relatively simple configurations. In contrast, larger companies, with multiple locations and vertical-market, custom software and hardware will be more complex. Companies that have grown through the acquisition of other organizations might also have mystery devices on the network that play unknown roles.

Another important variable to define is the somewhat intangible element of network stability and performance. What is considered acceptable performance for one company might be unacceptable for another, depending on the importance of the infrastructure and type of business. Some organizations lose thousands of dollars of revenue per minute of downtime, whereas others can go back to paper for a day or more without noticeable impact.

The discovery work needs to involve the design team and internal resources. External partners can often produce more thorough results because they have extensive experience with network reviews and analysis and predicting the problems that can emerge midway through a project and become showstoppers. The discovery process will typically start with onsite interviews, with the IT resources responsible for the different areas of the network, and proceed with hands-on review of the network configuration.

Standard questionnaires can prove helpful when collecting data about the various applications on servers and their specific configurations. These also prove useful for recording input about areas of concern related to the application (known "quirks" of the application relative to specific service packs not supported, or hard-coded IP addresses in the application, or the like). Key end users can reveal needs that their managers or directors aren't aware of, especially in organizations with less-effective IT management or unstable infrastructures. Special attention should be paid to ferreting out the problem areas and technologies that never worked right or have proven to be unstable. After all, they likely won't mysteriously be fixed when migrating them from physical to virtual configurations.

For the most part, the bigger the project, the more thorough the discovery should be. For projects involving a complete upgrade or system replacement, every affected device and application should to be reviewed and evaluated to help determine its role in the new environment.

If network diagrams exist, they should be reviewed to make sure they are current and contain enough information (such as server names, roles, applications managed, switches, routers, firewalls, and so on) to fully define the location and function of each infrastructure device.

If additional documentation exists on the detailed configuration of key infrastructure devices, such as "as-built" server documents with details about the server hardware and software configurations, or details about router configurations or firewalls, they should be dusted off and reviewed. Information such as whether patches and fixes have been applied to servers and software applications becomes important in the design process. In some cases, the desktop configurations need to be inventoried if client changes are required by an application upgrade. Software inventory tools can save many hours of work in these cases.

Certain documented company policies and procedures that are in place need to be reviewed. Some, such as disaster-recovery plans or service-level agreements (SLAs), can be vital to the IT department's ability to meet the needs of the user community.

The discovery process can also shed light on constraints to the implementation process that weren't considered previously, such as time restrictions that would affect the window of opportunity for change. These restrictions can include seasonal businesses and company budgeting cycles and even vacation schedules.

Ultimately, although the amount of time spent in the discovery process will vary greatly, the goals are the same: to really understand the technology infrastructure in place and the risks involved in the project, and to limit the surprises that might occur during the testing and implementation phases.

Understanding the Geographical Depth and Breadth

At the same time that data is being gathered and verified pertaining to what is in place and what it does, connectivity among devices should also be reviewed, to review the logical and the physical components of the network. This information might be available from existing diagrams and documentation, or might need to be gathered in the field.

Important items to understand include answering the following questions: How are DNS, WINS, and DHCP being handled? Are there VPNs or VLANs in place? How are the routers configured? What protocols are in use? What types of circuits connect the offices: DSL, T1, fiber? What is the guaranteed throughput or the SLAs that are in place?

Has connectivity failure been planned for through a partially or fully meshed environment? Connections to the outside world and other organizations need to be reviewed and fully understood at the same level, especially with an eye toward the security features in place. The best security design in the world can be defeated by a modem plugged in a plain old telephone line and a disgruntled ex-employee.

Along the same lines, remote-access needs, such as access to email, network file and print resources, and the support needs for PDAs and other mobile devices, should be reviewed.

Frequently during a server consolidation project that involves virtualization of servers, servers that appear to be redundant are not virtualized and are eliminated. If the server is running a specific utility or was hard-coded as a point of connection for users, however, the removal of the system can impact operations of key processes or tasks.

Geographically diverse companies bring added challenges to the table. As much as possible, the same level of information should be gathered on all the sites that will be involved in and affected by the migration and conversion of servers. Is the IT environment centralized, where one location manages the whole environment, or decentralized, where each office is its own "fiefdom"? The consolidation of servers out of a remote location to a centralized location may make good business sense, but may face severe resistance from an IT administrator who has been managing the server for years (and unfortunately may be the only person who really knows how the application works). So, understanding more than just the devices and the applications, but also the personnel behind the devices and applications, is very important. Therefore, the distribution of personnel should be reviewed and clarified.

How many support personnel are in each location, what key hardware and software are they tasked with supporting, and how many end users are there? Often, different offices have specific functions that require a different combination of support personnel. Some smaller, remote offices might have no dedicated staff at all, and this can make it difficult to gather updated information. Accordingly, is expansion or contraction likely in the near future, or will office consolidations change the user distribution?

Review problems and challenges that the wide area network (WAN) design has presented in the past. How is directory information replicated between sites, and what domain design is in place? If the company already has Active Directory in place, is a single domain with a simple organizational unit (OU) structure in place, or are there multiple domains with a complex OU structure? Global catalog placement should also be clarified.

How is the Internet accessed? Does each office have its own Internet connection, firewall, router, and so on, or is it accessed through one location?

The answers to these questions will directly shape the design of the solution, and will affect the testing and rollout processes.

Managing Information Overload

Another area that can dramatically affect the design of the Windows 2008 solution to be implemented is the place where the company's data lives and how it is managed.

At this point, you should know what the key network software applications are, so it is worth having some numbers on the amount of data being managed and where it lives on the network (1 server? 10 servers?). The total number of individual user files should be reviewed, and if available, statistics on the growth of this data should be reviewed.

Database information is often critical to an organization, whether it pertains to the services and products the company offers to the outside world or enables the employees to perform their jobs. Databases also require regular maintenance to avoid corruption and optimize performance, so it is useful to know whether maintenance occurs on a regular basis.

Mail databases pose their own challenges. Older mail systems typically were quite limited in the size of their databases, and many organizations were forced to come up with interesting ways of handling large amounts of data. As email has grown in importance and become a primary tool for many companies, the Inbox and personal folders have become the primary storage place for many email users. If the organization uses Microsoft Exchange for its email system, users might have personal stores or offline stores that might need to be taken into account.

In addition, review how data is backed up and stored. Some organizations have extremely complex enterprise storage systems and use clustering, storage area networks, or a distributed file system to ensure that data is always available to the user community. Sometimes, hierarchical storage processes are in place to move old data to optical media or even to tape.

An overall goal of this sleuthing is to determine where the data is, what file stores and databases are out there, how the data is maintained, and whether it is safe. It might also become clear that the data can be consolidated, or needs to be better protected through clustering or fault-tolerance disk solutions. Also discuss the costs to the company of data loss or temporary unavailability.

Assessing Applications for Resource Requirements

Chapter 3, "Planning, Sizing, and Architecting a Hyper-V Environment," provides more information about specific tools you can use to assess the current operational requirements of existing servers. By running these tools on existing systems, you can generate a report that notes how much RAM is being used by the server systems, how much processing performance is demanded by the applications, the network and disk I/O generated by the traffic and demands of the application, and other key information that helps administrators assess the requirements of existing servers.

For those responsible for performance assessment of applications and services and for designing scalability demands that recognize potential future server hardware needs, take a look at Chapter 3. The understanding you gain by examining the performance-assessment tools in that chapter will help frame the technical information gathering needed at this point of the project plan. Return back to this chapter to continue with the project management portion of the virtualization project.

The Design Phase: Documenting the Vision and the Plan

With the completion of the discovery process and documentation of the results, it should now be clear what you have to work with in terms of which servers or applications are available to be virtualized. Essentially, the research is all done, and many decisions now need to be made and documented.

By now, a dozen documents could be written; however, the most important document that needs to be created is the design document. This document is a log of the salient points of the discussions that have taken place to date. It should make clear why the project is being invested in, describe the scope of the project, and provide details about what the results will look like. A second document that needs to be created is the migration document, which provides the road map showing how this end state will be reached.

Companies often strive for an all-in-one document, but as explained in the next section, there are specific advantages to breaking up this information into two key components. A simple analogy is that you want to agree on what the floor plan for a house will look like (the design) and what the function of each room will be before deciding on how to build it (the migration/implementation).

Collaboration Sessions: Making the Design Decisions

The design team is most likely not ready to make all the decisions yet, even though quite a bit of homework has already been done. A more formal collaborative and educational process should follow to ensure that the end state of the project is defined in detail and that the design team members fully understand the new technologies to be introduced. The collaborative process involves interactive brainstorming and knowledge-sharing sessions, in which the stakeholders work with facilitators who have expertise with the technologies in question.

Ideally, a consultant with hands-on experience designing and consolidating physical to virtual servers with Hyper-V will provide leadership through this process. Well thought-out agendas can lead the design team through a logical process that educates them about the key decisions to be made and helps with the decisions.

Whiteboards can be used to illustrate the new physical layout of the virtualized environment, and to explain how the data will be managed and protected on the network. Take notes about decisions made in these sessions. If the sessions are effectively planned and executed, a relatively small number of collaboration sessions will provide the key decisions required for the implementation.

With effective leadership, these sessions can also help establish positive team dynamics and excitement for the project itself. Employees might feel negative about a major upgrade that will eliminate physical servers they have been managing "forever." Their attitudes may change, however, if they feel they are contributing to the design, learning about the technologies to be implemented, and better understanding their own roles in the process.

Through these sessions, the details of the end state should become crystal clear. Specifics can be discussed, such as how many host servers are needed in which locations, which guest severs will be hosted on each system, and how each host server will be backed up and maintained. Other design decisions and logistical concerns will come up and should be discussed, such as whether to repurpose existing server and network infrastructure hardware or to buy new equipment. Decisions also need to be made concerning secondary applications to support the upgraded environment, such as tape backup software, antivirus solutions, firewall protection, and network management software.

Ideally, some of the details about the actual migration process will start to become clear. For instance, the members of the testing and deployment teams, the training they will require, and the level of involvement from outside resources can be discussed.

Organizing Information for a Structured Design Document

The complexity of the project will affect the size of the document and the effort required to create it. As mentioned previously, this document summarizes the goals and objectives that were gathered in the initial discovery phase and describes how the project's result will meet them. It should represent a detailed picture of the end state when the new technologies and devices have been implemented. The amount of detail can vary, but it should include key design decisions made in the discovery process and collaboration sessions.

The following is a sample table of contents and brief description of the design document:

- ▶ **Executive Summary**—Provides a brief discussion about the scope of the Hyper-V virtual server implementation (the pieces of the puzzle).

- ▶ **Goals and Objectives**—Includes the 50,000-foot view business objectives, down to the 1,000-foot view staff-level tasks that will be met by the project.

- ▶ **Background**—Provides a high-level summary of the current state of the network and applications, focusing on problem areas, as clarified in the discovery process, and summary decisions made in the collaboration sessions.

- ▶ **Approach**—Outlines the high-level phases and tasks required to virtualize physical and existing virtual servers. (The details of each task will be determined in the migration document.)

- ▶ **End State**—Defines the details of the new technology configurations. For example, this section describes the number, placement, and functions of virtual host servers.

- ▶ **Budget Estimate**—Provides an estimate of basic costs involved in the project. Whereas a detailed cost estimate requires the creation of the migration document, experienced estimators can provide order of magnitude numbers at this point. Also, it should be clear what software and hardware are needed, so budgetary numbers can be provided.

The Executive Summary

The executive summary should set the stage and prepare the audience for what the document will contain, and it should be concise. It should outline, at the highest level, the scope of the work. Ideally, the executive summary also positions the document in the decision-making process and clarifies that approvals of the design are required to move forward.

The Goals and Objectives

The goals and objectives section should cover the high-level goals of the project and include the pertinent departmental goals. It's easy to go too far in the goals and objectives sections and get down to the 1,000-foot view level, but this can end up becoming very confusing. Therefore, this information might better be recorded in the migration document and the detailed project plan for the project.

The Background

The background section should summarize the results of the discovery process and the collaboration sessions, and can list specific design decisions made during the collaboration sessions. In addition, decisions made about what technologies or features not to include can be summarized here. This information should stay at a relatively high level, too, and more details can be provided in the end state section of the design document. This information is extremely useful to have as a reference to come back to later in the project when the infamous question "Who made that decision?" comes up.

The Approach

The approach section should document the implementation strategy agreed upon to this point, and will also serve to record decisions made in the discovery and design process about the timeline (end to end, and for each phase) and the team members participating in the different phases. This section should avoid going into too much detail because in many cases the end design might not yet be approved and might change after review. Also, the migration document should provide the details of the process that will be followed.

The End State

In the end state section, the specifics of the Windows 2008 implementation should be spelled out in detail, and the high-level decisions summarized in the background section should be fleshed out here. Essentially, the guest sessions to be migrated to each host server and any elimination of server roles (global catalog servers, domain controllers, DNS services, web servers) deemed redundant and not needed are spelled out here. Diagrams and tables can help explain the new concepts, and actually show what the end environment will look like, where each physical server will be virtualized to, and how the overall topology of the network will change. Often, besides a standard physical diagram of "what goes where," a logical diagram illustrating how devices communicate is needed.

The Budget Estimate

The budget section will not be exact, but should provide order of magnitude prices for the different phases of the project. If an outside consulting firm is assisting with this document, it can draw from experience with similar projects with like-sized companies. Because no two projects are ever the same, there needs to be some flexibility in these estimates. Typically, ranges for each phase should be provided.

Windows Server 2008 Hyper-V Design Decisions

As the previous section mentioned, the key Windows 2008 Hyper-V design decisions should be recorded in the design document. This is perhaps the most important section of the document because it will define how each Hyper-V host server will be configured and how it will interact with the network infrastructure.

Decisions should have been made about the hardware and software needed for the migration. They should take into account whether existing hardware will be repurposed as host servers in the migration process, used for other purposes, or retired. This decision, in turn, will determine how many server software licenses will be required, which will directly affect the costs of the project. In many cases, the software licensing will decrease as virtualization use rights, covered in Chapter 1, "Windows 2008 Hyper-V Technology Primer," notes how Windows 2008 Enterprise and Datacenter editions provide "free use" of server licenses in guest sessions.

The level of redundancy and security the solution will provide should be detailed. Again, it is important to be specific when talking about data availability and when discussing the situations that have been planned for in the design.

The server and other infrastructure hardware and software should be defined in this section. If upgrades are needed for existing hardware (more processors, RAM, hard drives, tape drives, and so on) or the existing software (upgrades from the existing network operating system licenses, server applications, and vertical market applications), they should be detailed here.

Other key technologies such as messaging applications or industry-specific applications will be included here, in as much detail as appropriate.

Agreeing on the Design

The final step in the design document process actually takes place after the document has been created. When the document is considered complete, it should be presented to the project stakeholders and reviewed to make sure that it does, in fact, meet their requirements, that they understand the contents, and to see whether any additional concerns come up that weren't addressed in the document.

It is unlikely that every goal of every stakeholder will be met (because some might conflict). This process will clarify which goals are the most important and can be met by the technologies to be implemented.

Specific decisions made in the design document that should be reviewed include any disparities between stakeholder wish lists and what the final results of the project will be. Also, the timeline and high-level budget should be discussed and confirmed. If the design document outlines a budget of $500K for hardware and software, but the stakeholders won't be able to allocate more than $250K, the changes should be made at this point, rather than after the migration document is created. A smaller budget might require drastic changes to the design document because capabilities in the solution might need to be removed, which will have ripple effects throughout the project.

If the time frame outlined in the design document needs to be modified to meet the requirements of the stakeholders, this should be identified prior to expending the effort of creating the detailed implementation plan, too.

Bear in mind, too, that the design document can be used for different purposes. Some companies want the design document to serve as an educational document to inform not only what the end state will look like, but why it should be that way. Others just need to document the decisions made and come up with budgetary information.

Having this level of detail will also make it easier to get competitive bids on the costs to implement. Many organizations make the mistake of seeking bids for solutions before they even know what the solution will consist of.

The Migration Planning Phase: Documenting the Process for Migration

Before the migration document is created, the end state of the project has been documented in detail and agreed upon by the key stakeholders in the organization. There should be no question as to exactly what the next evolution of the network will be composed of and what functionality it will offer. In addition, an estimated budget for the hardware and software required and an estimated timeline for the project have been identified. In some cases, depending on the size and complexity of the project, and whether outside consulting assistance has been contracted, a budget has also been established for the implementation services.

So, now that the end state has been clearly defined, the migration document can be created to document the details of the steps required to reach the end state with minimal risk of negative impact to the network environment.

The migration plan should not contain any major surprises.

A key component of the migration document is the project plan, or migration plan, that provides a list of the tasks required to implement the solution. It is the road map from which the migration document will be created. The migration document will also provide a narrative, where needed, of the specifics of the tasks that the project plan does not provide, and provide other details as outlined next.

Time for the Project Plan

As mentioned previously, the primary stepping stones needed to reach the endpoint have been sketched out in the discovery process, and in collaboration sessions or design discussions that have taken place. The project plan in the migration document provides a tool to complement the design document, which graphically illustrates the process of building and testing the technologies required and provides an outline of who is doing what during the project.

By using a product such as Microsoft Project, you can organize the steps in a logical, linear process. The high-level tasks should be established first. Typically, they are the phases or high-level tasks involved in the project, such as lab testing, pilot implementation, production implementation, and support. Then, you can fill in the main components of these tasks.

Dates and durations should be included in the project plan, using the basic concept of starting with the end date when everything needs to be up and running, and then working backward. It's important to include key milestones, such as acquiring new software and hardware, sending administrative resources to training classes, and provisioning new data circuits. Slack time should also be included for unexpected events or stumbling blocks that might be encountered. Each phase of the project needs to be outlined and then expanded.

A good rule of thumb is not to try to list every task that needs to take place during the phase, but to have each line represent several hours or days of work. If too much detail is put into the project plan, it quickly becomes unmanageable. For the detailed information that does not necessarily need to be placed in the project plan (Gantt chart), you can detail the information in the migration document. The migration document adds in technical and operational details that will help clarify more specific project information.

> **NOTE**
>
> The terms *project plan* and *Gantt chart* are commonly interchanged in IT organizations and might have different meanings to different individuals. In this book, the term *project plan* refers to the chronological steps needed to successfully plan, prepare, and implement Windows Server 2008 Hyper-V virtualization. The term *Gantt chart* is used to refer to the chronological steps, but also the inclusion of resource allocation, start and end dates, and cost distribution.

The plan should also assign resources to the tasks and start to define the teams that will work on the different components of the project. If an outside organization is going to assist in the process, it should be included at the appropriate points in the project. Microsoft Project offers an additional wealth of features to produce reports and graphical information from this plan; they will prove to be extremely helpful when the work starts. Also, accurate budgetary information can be extracted, which can take into account overtime and after-hours rates and easily give what-if scenario information.

Speed Versus Risk

The project plan will also enable you to test what-if scenarios. When the high-level tasks are defined, and the resources required to complete each task are also defined, you can easily plug in external contractors to certain tasks and see how the costs change. After-hours work might take place during working hours in certain places.

If the timeline still isn't acceptable, tasks can be stacked so that multiple tasks occur at the same time, instead of one after the other. Microsoft Project also offers extensive tools for resource leveling to make sure that you haven't accidentally committed a resource to, for example, 20 hours of work in 1 day.

The critical path of the project should be defined, too. Certain key events will need to take place for the project to proceed beyond a certain point. Ordering the hardware and having it arrive will be one of these steps. Getting stakeholder approval on the lab environment and proving that key network applications can be supported might be another. Administrative and end-user training might need to happen to ensure that the resulting environment can be effectively supported.

You might need to build contingency time into the project plan, too. Hardware can get delayed and take an extra week or two to arrive. Testing can take longer, especially with complex configurations and when customization of the network operating system (NOS) is required or directory information needs to be modified.

Creating the Migration Document

The migration document can now narrate the process detailed in the project plan. The project plan does not need to be 100% complete, but the order of the steps and the strategies for testing and implementing will be identified. Typically, the migration document is similar to the structure of the design document (a reason why many organizations combine the two documents), but the design document relates the design decisions made and details the end state of the upgrade, whereas the migration document details the process and steps to be taken.

The following is a sample table of contents for the migration document:

1. Executive Summary
2. Goals and Objectives of the Migration Process
3. Background
4. Risks and Assumptions
5. Roles and Responsibilities
6. Timeline and Milestones
7. Training Plan
8. Migration Process

   ▶ Hardware and Software Procurement Process

   ▶ Prototype Proof of Concept Process

   ▶ Server Configuration and Testing

   ▶ Desktop Configuration and Testing

- ▶ Documentation Required from Prototype

- ▶ Pilot Phase(s) Detailed

- ▶ Migration/Upgrade Detailed

- ▶ Support Phase Detailed

- ▶ Support Documentation Detailed

9. Budget Estimate

- ▶ Labor Costs for Prototype Phase

- ▶ Labor Costs for Pilot Phase

- ▶ Labor Costs for Migration/Upgrade Phase

- ▶ Labor Costs for Support Phase

- ▶ Costs for Training

10. Project Schedule

The Executive Summary Section

The executive summary should set the stage and prepare the audience for what the document will contain, and it should be concise. It should outline, at the highest level, the scope of the work. Ideally, the executive summary also positions the document in the decision-making process and clarifies that approvals of the design are required to move forward.

The Goals and Objectives Section

The goals and objectives section might seem redundant because the design documents documented the objectives in great detail, but it is important to consider which specific goals and objectives are important to the success of the migration project that might not have been included in the design document. For example, although the design document outlined what the final server configuration will look like, it might not have outlined the tools needed to migrate key user data or the order that physical servers will be migrated to virtual servers. So, the goals and objectives in the migration document will be very process specific.

The Background Section

A summary of the migration-specific decisions should be provided to answer questions such as "Why are we doing it that way?" because there is always a variety of ways to convert a physical server to a virtual server session, such as using tools provided by Microsoft, using third-party tools, or rebuilding a server from scratch in a virtual environment. Because a number of conversations will have taken place during the planning phase to compare the merits of one method versus another, it is worth summarizing them early in the document for anyone who wasn't involved in those conversations.

The Risks and Assumptions Section

Risks pertaining to the phases of the migration should be detailed, and typically are more specific than in the design document. For example, a risk of the prototype phase might be that the hardware available won't perform adequately and needs to be upgraded. Monitoring, virus protection, or backup software might not meet the requirements of the design document and therefore need upgrading. Custom-designed applications or applications that may direct calls to hardware devices might turn out not to work properly in a virtual environment.

The Roles and Responsibilities Section

In the roles and responsibilities section, the teams that will do the work should be identified in detail. If an outside company will be performing portions of the work, you should document which tasks it will be responsible for and which ones internal resources will take ownership of.

The Timeline and Milestones Section

Specific target dates can be listed, and should be available directly from the project schedule already created. This summary can prove very helpful to executives and managers, whereas the Gantt chart contains too much information. Constraints that were identified in the discovery process need to be kept in mind here because there might be important dates (such as the end of the fiscal year), seasonal demands on the company that black out certain date ranges, and key company events or holidays. Again, be aware of other large projects going on in your environment that might impact your timeline. There's no point trying to deploy new servers on the same weekend that the data center will be powered off for facility upgrades.

The Training Plan Section

It is useful during the planning of any upgrade to examine the skill sets of the people who will be performing the upgrade and managing the new environment to see whether any gaps need to be filled with training. Often, training will happen during the prototype testing process in a hands-on fashion for the project team with the alternate choice being classroom-style training, often provided by an outside company. Also ask yourself whether the end users will require training to use new client-side tools being installed during a parallel application upgrade process. Also pay attention to how the new environment will integrate into existing systems such as backup or monitoring. Determine whether those groups will need any training specific to interacting with the new virtual servers.

The Migration Process Section

The project schedule Gantt chart line items should be included and expanded upon so that it is clear to the resources doing the work what is expected of them. The information does not need to be on the level of step-by-step instructions, but it should clarify the process and results expected from each task. For example, the Gantt chart might indicate that a Windows 2008 server needs to be configured; and in the migration document, information would be added about how the hard drives are to be configured, how virtual network segments are to be connected to physical segments, and which additional applications (virus protection, tape backup, network management) need to be installed.

If the Gantt chart lists a task of, for example, "Configure and web services access," the migration document gives a similar level of detail: Which image should be used to configure the base system configuration, which additional applications should be loaded, how is the system to be locked down, and what testing process should be followed (is it scripted or will an administrator perform the testing)?

Documentation also should be described in more detail. The Gantt chart might simply list "Create as-built documents," with *as built* defined as "document containing key server configuration information and screenshots so that a knowledgeable resource can rebuild the system from scratch."

Sign-off conditions for the prototype phase are important and should be included. Who needs to sign off on the results of the prototype phase to indicate that the goals were all met and that the design agreed upon is ready to be created in the production environment?

Similar levels of information are included for the pilot phase and the all-important migration itself. Typically during the pilot phase, all the upgraded functionality needs to be tested, including remote access, file encryption access, and access to shared folders. Be aware that pilot testing might require external coordination. For example, if you are testing remote access through a VPN connection, you might need to acquire an additional external IP address and arrange to have an address record created in DNS to allow your external testers to reach it without having to disturb your existing remote access systems.

The migration plan should also account for support tasks that need to occur after the Hyper-V infrastructure is fully in place. If you are using an outside consulting firm for assistance in the design and implementation, make sure that they will leave staff onsite for a period of time immediately after the upgrade to be available to support user issues or to troubleshoot any technical issues that crop up.

If documentation is specified as part of the support phase, such as Windows maintenance documents, disaster-recovery plans, or procedural guides, expectations for these documents should be included to help the technical writers make sure the documents are satisfactory.

The Budget Section

With regard to the budget information, although a great amount of thought and planning has gone into the design and migration documents, and the project plan, there are still variables. No matter how detailed these documents are, the later phases of the project might change based on the results of the earlier phases. For instance, the prototype testing might go flawlessly, but during the pilot implementation, performing data migration simply takes longer than anticipated; this extra time will require modifications to the amount of time required and the associated costs. Note that changes in the opposite direction can happen, too, if tasks can occur more quickly than anticipated. Often, the implementation costs can be reduced by keeping an eye on ways to improve the process during the prototype and pilot phases.

The Project Plan Section

Whereas the project plan provides the high-level details of the steps, or tasks, required in each phase, the approach sections of the migration document can go into more detail about each step of the project plan, as needed. Certain very complex tasks are represented with one line on the project plan, such as "Configure Hyper-V Host #1," but might take several pages to describe in sufficient detail in the migration document.

Data-availability testing and disaster-recovery testing should be discussed. In the design document, you might have decided that clustering will be used, as will a particular tape backup program, but the migration plan should outline exactly which scenarios should be tested in the prototype lab environment.

Documents to be provided during the migration should be defined so that it is clear what they will contain.

The Prototype Phase: Creating and Testing the Plan

The main goal of the prototype phase is to create a lab environment in which the key elements of the design as defined in the design document can be configured and tested. Based on the results of the prototype, you can determine whether any changes are needed to the implementation and support phases as outlined in the migration document.

The prototype phase is also a training phase, in which the members of the deployment team get a chance to get their hands dirty with the new hardware and software technologies to be implemented. If an external consulting firm is assisting with the prototype testing, knowledge transfer should occur and be expected during this process. Even if the deployment team has attended classroom training, the prototype process is an environment that will more closely reflect the end state of the network that needs to be supported, and will involve technologies and processes not typically covered in classroom-style training. The deployment team can also benefit from the real-world experience of the consultants if they are assisting in this phase.

This environment should be isolated from the production network so that problems created by or encountered in the process don't affect the user community.

The design details of testing applications, confirming hardware performance, testing fault-tolerance failover, and the like should be verified in a safe lab environment. If changes are needed to the design document, make them now.

How Do You Build the Lab?

Although the details of the project will determine the specifics of exactly what will be in the prototype lab, certain common elements will be required. The migration document should clearly outline the components of the lab and which applications and processes should be tested. A typical environment will consist of an initial Windows 2008 host server required for the implementation, network switches, and sample physical servers that will be converted from the production environment. Connectivity to the outside world should be available for testing purposes.

A key decision to make is whether the lab will be implemented into the environment or stay as a lab. Some companies proceed from the prototype phase to the pilot phase with the same equipment, whereas others prefer to keep a lab set up for future use. The advantages of having a lab environment for a Windows 2008 Hyper-V environment are many, and include testing application updates, upgrades, and patches and having hardware available for replacement of failed components in the production environment.

Real data and applications should be installed and tested. Data can be copied from live production servers, or data from tape can be restored to a test server. Applications should be installed on the servers according to a manufacturer's installation instructions; in addition, however, compatibility validation with Hyper-V virtualization should be conducted.

After the software applications have been installed, representative users from the different company departments could be brought into the lab to put the applications through their paces. These users will be best able to do what they normally do in the lab environment to ensure that their requirements will be met by the new configuration. Areas that don't meet their expectations should be recorded and identified as either "showstoppers" that need to be addressed immediately or issues that won't harm the implementation plan.

Results of the Lab Testing Environment

In addition to the valuable learning that takes place, a number of other things come out of the lab testing process. If time permits, and there is room in the budget, a variety of documents can be produced to facilitate the pilot and implementation process. Another key result of the lab is hard evidence of the accuracy and completeness of the design and migration documents.

Some of the documents that can be created will assist the deployment team during the migration process. One key document is the "as-built" document, which provides a snapshot of the key configuration details of the primary servers that have been configured and tested. Whereas the design document outlines many of the key configuration details, the as-built document contains actual screenshots of the server configurations and contains the output from the Hyper-V Administration tool, which provides important details, such as physical and logical disk configuration, system memory and processor information, services installed and in use on the system, and so on.

Another important document is the disaster-recovery document (or DR document). This document should outline exactly which types of failures were tested and the process for rectifying these situations. Keep in mind that a complete disaster-recovery plan should include offsite data and application access, so the DR document that comes out of the prototype phase will, in most cases, be more of a hardware-failure document that discusses how to replace failed components, such as hard drives and power supplies, and how to restore the server configuration from tape backup or restore data sets.

If you need to implement multiple servers in the pilot and implementation phases, you can document checklists for the step-by-step processes in the prototype phase. Bear in mind that creating step-by-step documents takes a great deal of time (and paper!), and a change in process requires drastic changes to these documents. Typically, creating a step-by-step "recipe" for server builds is not worth the time unless task-focused resources need to build a large number in a short period of time.

When the testing is complete, revisit the migration plan to confirm that the timeline and milestones are still accurate. Ideally, there should be no major surprises during the prototype phase, but adjustments might be needed to the migration plan to ensure the success of the project.

Depending on the time frame for the pilot and implementation phases, the hardware and software that will be needed for the full implementation might be ordered at this point. Because the cost of server hardware has decreased over the past several years, many companies "over-spec" the hardware they think they need, and they might determine during the prototype phase that lesser amounts of RAM or fewer processors will still exceed the needs of the technologies to be implemented, so the hardware requirements might change.

The Pilot Phase: Validating the Plan on an Initial Set of Servers

Now that the prototype phase has been completed, the deployment team is raring to go and gain hands-on experience migrating servers to virtual sessions. The process documented in the migration document and migration plan will have been tested in the lab environment as completely as practical, and documentation detailing the steps to be followed during the pilot implementation will be on hand.

Although the pilot process will vary in complexity based on the extent of the changes to be made to the network infrastructure, the process should be well documented at this point.

It is important to identify the first group of servers that will be moved to the new Windows 2008 Hyper-V environment. Systems that have redundancy throughout the environment (domain controllers, DNS servers) are a better choice for initial migration than highly critical business application servers that have no existing failover or redundancy configurations.

> **NOTE**
>
> In many virtualization projects, a critical business application may be a good opera-
> tional candidate to be virtualized if the hardware the system is running on is having
> problems and evacuating the physical hardware to a virtual system can alleviate exist-
> ing physical system problems. However, be very careful in migrating a critical applica-
> tion first. Consider migrating a couple of simple servers to a virtualized state, so that
> you can get familiar with managing, monitoring, and administering the simple server
> configurations first. Then schedule the migration of the critical application server.

A rollback strategy should be clarified, just in case.

Test the disaster-recovery and redundancy capabilities thoroughly at this point with live
data but on a limited number of servers to make sure everything works as expected.

Migration processes can be fine-tuned during this process, and time estimates can be
nailed down.

The First Server in the Pilot

The pilot phase begins when the first physical server is migrated to a virtual guest session
on Windows 2008 Hyper-V and users access the application on the virtual server in the
production environment. Depending on the scope of the migration project, this first
server might be a simple web server or a SharePoint site, or the first server might be an
Active Directory domain controller.

Just as in the prototype phase, the testing to be conducted in the pilot phase is to verify
successful access to the server or application services the virtual session provides. One of
the best ways to validate functionality is to take the test sequences used in the prototype
phase and repeat the test steps in the pilot production environment.

The major difference between the prototype and pilot phases is interconnectivity and
enterprisewide compatibility. In many lab-based prototype phases, the testing is isolated to
clean system configurations or homogeneous system configurations. In a pilot production
environment, however, the virtual server session is live in a full production environment.
It is the validation that the new setup works with existing users, servers, and systems.

Rolling Out the Pilot Phase

The pilot phase is usually rolled out in subphases, with each subphase growing in number
of servers migrated and the distribution of host servers throughout the organization.

Number of Migrated Servers

The whole purpose of the pilot phase is to migrate servers one by one from physical to
virtual guest sessions to validate that prototype and test assumptions were accurate and
that they can be successful in the production environment. An initial three to five servers
are first to be migrated. These servers test basic migration processes and Hyper-V configurations.

After successful basic testing, the pilot server group can grow to 5%, then to 10%, and on to 20% of the servers planned for migration. This phased rollout will help the migration team test compatibility, connectivity, and communications with existing systems, while working with a manageable group of systems that won't overwhelm the administrators during the pilot and migration process.

The pilot phase is also a time when administrators build the knowledge base of problems that occur during the migration process. Thus, if or when problems occur again (possibly in the full rollout phase), lessons have been learned and workarounds already created to resolve stumbling blocks.

Application Complexity of Pilot Migrations

In addition to expanding the scope of the pilot phase by sheer number, selecting servers that have different application-usage requirements can provide a level of complexity across server configuration. Application compatibility and operation are critical to the administrator's experience during the migration process. Often, administrators won't mind if something runs a little slower during the migration process or that a new process takes a while to learn. However, end users will get upset if the applications they require and depend on each day to get their job done are offline, data is lost due to system instability, or the application just won't work. So, testing applications is critical in the early pilot phase of the project.

Geographical Diversity of Pilot Servers

The pilot server group should eventually include servers geographically distributed throughout the organization. It is important to start the pilot phase with servers that are local to the IT or help desk operation so that initial pilot support can be done in person or directly with the initial pilot group of systems. Before the pilot is considered complete, however, servers in remote sites should be migrated and tested to ensure remote users or branch office users still have access to migrated servers in the new virtualized networking environment.

Fixing Problems in the Pilot Phase

No matter how much planning and testing is conducted in the earlier phases of the project, problems always crop up in the pilot phase of the project. It is important to have the prototype lab still intact so that any outstanding problems can be re-created in the lab, tested, and resolved to be tested in the pilot production phase again.

Documenting the Results of the Pilot

After the pilot, it is important to document the results. Even with the extensive discovery and design work, and even though the prototype lab testing and pilot phases have taken place, problems might recur in the postpilot phases, and any documented information about how problems were resolved or configurations made to resolve problems in the pilot phase will help simplify the resolution in future phases. If you take some extra time to give attention to the pilot users, you can fine-tune the solution to make sure the full implementation succeeds.

The Migration/Implementation Phase: Conducting the Migration or Installation

By this point in the project, more than 20% of the servers flagged for migration should have been converted and tested in the pilot phase, applications thoroughly tested, administrators and support personnel trained, and common problem resolution clearly documented so that the organization can proceed with the migration of the balance of the servers identified for virtualization.

Verifying End-User Satisfaction

A critical task you can complete at this point in the project a check of end-user satisfaction. You want to make sure that users are not experiencing any problems access their applications and that server performance hasn't diminished. You also want to confirm that accessibility is not limited, questions are answered, problems are resolved, and most important, users are being made aware that IT is interested in their feedback during the backend migration of server systems. Of course, this backend migration should not negatively impact the users at all, but it's worth checking to make sure.

Not only does this phase of the project focus on the sheer rollout of the technology, it is also the key public relations and communications phase of the project. Make sure the user community gets to input their experiences in the process.

Supporting the New Virtualized Environment

Before the last servers are rolled into the new virtualized environment, besides planning the project-completion party you need to allocate time to verify the ongoing support and maintenance of the new environment. This step not only includes doing regular backups of the new servers, but also performing regular maintenance of the virtual host server and guest sessions (see Chapter 6, "Managing, Administering, and Maintaining Hyper-V Host Services").

Disaster recovery and failover should be implemented because there are now fewer servers hosting multiple application systems (covered in detail in Chapter 12, "Application-Level Failover and Disaster Recovery in a Hyper-V Environment"). You also want to tune and optimize the new Hyper-V environment (see Chapter 7, "Optimizing the Hyper-V Host Server and Guest Sessions").

Now is the time to begin planning for some of the wish list items that didn't make sense to include in the initial migration—for example, implementing new stretched clusters across a WAN, adding disk-to-disk-to-tape backup and recovery procedures, and the like.

If you have a lab still in place, use it to test these additional services.

Summary

One analogy used in this chapter is that of building a house. Although this analogy doesn't stand up to intense scrutiny, the similarities are helpful. When an organization is planning a server virtualization implementation, it is important to first understand the goals for the implementation, and not only the 50,000-foot high-level goals, but also the 10,000-foot departmental and 1,000-foot IT staff goals. Then, it is important to more fully understand the environment that will serve as the foundation for the upgrade. Whether this work is performed by external resources or by internal resources, a great deal will be learned about what is really in place, and where there might be areas of risk or exposure. Collaboration sessions with experienced and effective leadership can then educate the stakeholders and deployment resources about the technologies to be implemented and can guide the group through key decision-making areas. Now all this information needs to be documented in the design document so that the details are clear, and some initial estimates for the resources required, timeline, and budget can be set. This document serves as a blueprint of sorts, and defines in detail what the "house" will look like when it is built. When all the stakeholders agree that this is exactly what they want to see, and the timeline and budget are in line, the migration document can be produced.

The migration document includes a detailed project plan that provides the tasks that need to take place to produce the results detailed in the design document. The project plan should not go into step-by-step detail describing how to build each server, but should stick to summary tasks from 4 hours to a day or more in duration. The migration document then provides a narrative of the project plan and supplies additional information pertaining to goals, resources, risks, and deliverables, as well as budgetary information accurate in the 10% to 20% range.

Based on these documents, the organization can now proceed with building the solution in a lab environment and testing the proposed design with actual company data and resources involved. The results of the testing might require modifications to the migration document, and will prepare the deployment team for live implementation. Ideally, a pilot phase with a limited, noncritical group of users will occur to fine-tune the live implementation process and put in place key technologies and Windows Server 2008 Hyper-V. Now the remainder of the implementation process should proceed with a minimum of surprises, and the result will meet the expectations set in the design phase and verified during the prototype and pilot phases.

Even the support phase has been considered, and during this phase, the "icing on the cake" can be applied as appropriate.

Although this process might seem complex, it can be molded to fit all different sizes of projects and will yield better results.

Best Practices

The following are best practices from this chapter:

- ▶ Use a migration methodology consisting of discovery, design, testing, and implementation phases to meet the needs of your organization.

- ▶ Fully understand the business and technical goals and objectives of the upgrade and the breadth and scope of benefits the implementation will provide before implementing a new application or upgrade.

▶ Create a scope of work detailing the servers that you want to virtualize.

▶ Define high-level organizational goals.

▶ Define departmental goals.

▶ Determine which components and capabilities of the network are most important and how they contribute to or hinder the goals expressed by the different units.

▶ Clearly define the technical goals of the project on different levels (50,000-foot, 10,000-foot, 1,000-foot, and so on).

The Discovery Phase

▶ Review and evaluate the existing environment to make sure the network foundation in place will support the new virtualized environment.

▶ Make sure the existing environment is configured the way you think it is, and identify existing areas of exposure or weakness in the network.

▶ Define the current network stability and performance measurements and operation.

▶ Use external partners to produce more thorough results and predict the problems that may emerge midway through a project and become "showstoppers."

▶ Start the discovery process with onsite interviews.

▶ Review and evaluate every affected device and application to help determine its role in the new environment.

▶ Maintain and protect business-critical information.

▶ Determine where data resides, what file stores and databases are out there, how the data is maintained, and whether it is safe.

The Design Phase

▶ Create a design document including the salient points of the discussion, the reasons the project is being invested in, the scope of the project, and the details of what the results will look like.

▶ Create a migration document providing the road map showing how the end state will be reached.

▶ Use a consultant with hands-on experience designing and implementing Windows 2008 Hyper-V virtualization to provide leadership through this process.

▶ Determine what hardware and software will be needed for the migration.

▶ Determine how many server software licenses will be required.

▶ Detail the level of redundancy and security required and that the solution will ultimately provide.

▶ Present the design and migration documents to the project stakeholders for review.

The Migration Planning Phase

▶ Create a migration document containing the details of the steps required to reach the end state with minimal risk or negative impact to the network environment.

▶ Create a project plan that provides a list of the tasks, resources, and durations required to implement the solution.

The Prototype Phase

▶ Create a lab environment in which the key elements of the design as defined in the design document can be configured and tested.

▶ Isolate the lab environment from the production network so that any problems created or encountered in the process don't affect the user community.

▶ Thoroughly test all applications in a virtual environment.

The Pilot Phase

▶ Identify the first group of servers that will be moved to the new Windows 2008 Hyper-V virtual environment. Servers that are already redundant and have limited failure points should be chosen first.

▶ Clarify a rollback strategy, just in case unexpected problems occur.

▶ Test the disaster-recovery and redundancy capabilities thoroughly.

▶ Fine-tune the migration processes and nail down time estimates.

The Migration/Implementation Phase

▶ Verify that applications have been thoroughly tested, administrators and support personnel have been trained, and common problem resolution is clearly documented.

▶ Conduct a check of end-user satisfaction.

▶ Allocate time to verify ongoing support and maintenance of the new environment, before migrating the last servers into the new virtualized networking environment.

▶ Plan a project-completion party.

Planning, Sizing, and Architecting a Hyper-V Environment

Whereas Chapter 2, "Best Practices at Planning, Prototyping, Migrating, and Deploying Windows 2008 Hyper-V," focused on the project management process for a migration of physical servers to virtual servers, this chapter focuses on the technical assessment of existing physical servers and the host server sizing that is needed to prepare a virtual host environment. Instead of just randomly virtualizing physical servers onto host systems sequentially, organizations can better utilize host server hardware systems by technically assessing the server loads of existing physical servers and logically placing them on host servers to balance virtual guest sessions.

Logically Distributing Virtual Servers on Specific Host Systems

Moving physical servers to virtualized host servers is not a process that should be done randomly. A fine balance exists between the distribution of server workloads, the distribution of servers for redundancy and fault tolerance, and the distribution of servers for application performance and user connectivity.

Distributing Virtual Servers Based on Workload

Some server sessions are processor intensive (for example, index servers, transaction-analysis servers), whereas some server sessions are I/O intensive (for instance, file servers, messaging servers). Putting several processor-intensive server sessions on a single host can overload the processing capabilities of the server, whereas balancing host servers with some processor-intensive server workloads with some I/O-intensive server workloads can better extend the capabilities of a host system.

The variables and constraints of workload on a server can be technically categorized as follows:

▶ **Processor workload**—This refers to the demands a guest session places on the processor, typically from applications that do calculations or analysis of information. All applications use the processor of a server; some can get away with sharing a processor with other server sessions, whereas other server sessions require the dedication of one, two, or four processors to properly allocate processor capabilities to the guest session. Key in evaluating processor workload is to look at sustained processor workload versus burst workload. Some applications use a lot of processing speed, but only to do periodic reports or transactions, which might be an end-of-day posting of information or a month-end or quarter-end task. Differentiate between sustained workload and periodic workload so that you don't allocate two or four processors to a session when the processor transaction occurs only once a month.

▶ **Disk I/O workload**—This refers to the demands a guest session places on the disk for reading and writing of information. In the normal processing of information, a guest session may read and write information periodically to disk. For some applications, however, the guest session is constantly reading information, fetching data to place in cache, or writing transaction logs, data, or both simultaneously in the management of disk information. For guest sessions with high disk I/O workloads, you can assign dedicated disks to the virtual guest session rather than share a common disk storage system. If you dedicate the disk location, reading and writing of information should not cause an application to bottleneck (and thus you avoid degradation of performance of all other virtual guest sessions on the host server).

▶ **Network I/O workload**—This refers to the demands a guest session places on a network adapter from sending and receiving data to other servers or systems on the network. Applications that are gateways or frontend servers to backend data stores may have significant network I/O because *all* traffic passes through a specific system. Guest sessions with significant network I/O can cause all the guest sessions to slow down if all the guest sessions share a single network adapter in the host system. By identifying the guest session that has high network I/O workloads, an administrator can add an additional network adapter to the server and dedicate the network adapter for a given guest session. Doing so allows the isolation of traffic from the guest session out to a network switch, and offloads the workload data from the shared host server resource. Other strategies in managing network I/O workload is to create a dedicated virtual switch within a Hyper-V host server where communications between guest sessions is virtually dedicated in a core communication path that can be isolated from the network communications path of other guest sessions. By creating a virtual network switch between servers dependent on communicating to each other within a host server, you can greatly enhance communications between the servers, perhaps even increasing the speeds above those of traditional

Gigabyte Ethernet because the Hyper-V virtual network switch can communicate at native system bus speeds.

▶ **Guest session RAM requirements**—Some virtual guest sessions have a high demand for memory allocated to the guest session, whether that's 8GB or 16GB or 32GB for the session. Many applications use whatever available memory is given to the session to load data into RAM and cache the data to provide higher transaction fetch rates of the information when an application requires access to the information. For these applications, there appears to be no limit on how much memory the application requires; it uses whatever is available. It is important to test these applications to determine whether an optimal amount of memory can be allocated that provides a flatline return on performance. For example, an application may perform twice as fast with 4GB of memory than with 2GB of memory, but the same application gains no incremental improvement at 8GB or 16GB. These applications can then be capped at 4GB for the guest session, allowing any additional memory to be used for other guest sessions.

Distributing Virtual Servers Based on Redundancy

When choosing to distribute virtual guest sessions across virtual host servers, taking in account redundancy and high availability helps in deciding which guest server sessions to place on which host servers. As an example, placing both the primary cluster server and a passive backup cluster server on the same host system nullifies the benefits of clustering if the host server fails and both cluster nodes are brought offline. So, the placement of cluster pairs across two host servers as shown in Figure 3.1 will ensure that a guest session failure will remain operational on the second cluster pair session, and will ensure that a host server failure will also maintain operations of the second cluster pair on a separate host server system.

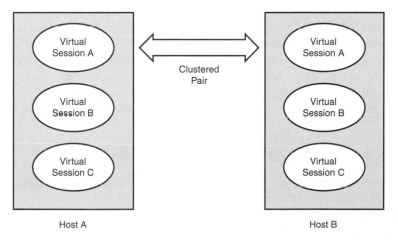

FIGURE 3.1   Distributing servers to split systems across separate hosts for reliability purposes.

Distributing Virtual Servers Based on Server Interrelationships

When analyzing servers to determine where to logically place guest server sessions, look beyond just server performance demands. Also look at how servers interact with each other. In many applications, a frontend server and a backend server make up the client connection portion and the database portion of the application (for instance, Exchange, Office Communication Server, SharePoint), as shown in Figure 3.2. The frontend and backend pair are directly associated to each other, so from a redundancy standpoint, if either is offline, the application doesn't operate. Therefore, splitting the applications across two hosts provides no benefit because the application doesn't work unless both servers in the pair are operational.

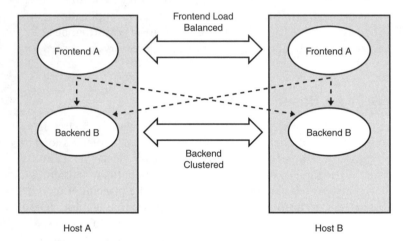

FIGURE 3.2   Frontend/backend server interrelationships.

By placing the two servers on the same virtual host system and then establishing a virtual switch that allows the two applications to communication directly with each other inside the virtual host system, you can greatly improve the communications between the frontend and the backend server. Likewise, an Exchange server communicates regularly with a global catalog server to query distribution lists, email address lists, and the like. By placing a global catalog guest session on the same host server as an Exchange server, you can greatly improve the communications between the application server and directory server.

Distributing Virtual Servers Based on User Connectivity

Other factors to consider when deciding where to place virtual guest sessions include user connectivity and where users who need access to the host servers reside. If a physical server is in a remote site close to users and is then virtualized and centralized in a data center on the other side of a WAN connection, the performance between the users and the virtualized server needs to be taken in account. Although virtualization might be a good business decision to remove servers from remote locations to simplify administration and management, performance or reliability of information access across an unreliable or slow WAN link could significantly and negatively impact users accessing the servers.

During the assessment process, identify where users are and how they interact with the servers, as illustrated in Figure 3.3. As you can see in this figure, a link is maintained between users and the data they access. Virtualize the server and centralize the system, but make sure to consider user access to the resource in the process.

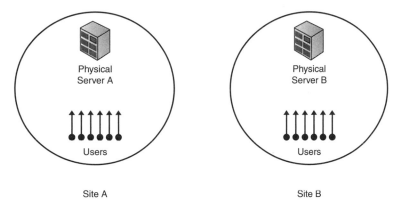

FIGURE 3.3   Maintaining links between users and user data.

Distributing Virtual Servers Across a WAN Connection

With regard to the virtualization process, many believe that migrating physical servers to virtual guest sessions in a consolidation process means that the host servers must be centralized in a single data center. However, if users are in remote locations, servers might need to be distributed closer to the remote users. Therefore, a virtual host system can be brought up in a remote location with physical servers in that remote location virtualized in the remote host system.

A remote host system can also be used as a backup to a host server in a main data center location so that stretch clusters can be established between guest sessions in host servers in separate locations. Figure 3.4 shows this distribution of host servers across WAN connections; such a distribution can provide redundancy, fault tolerance, and disaster recovery of servers and applications for the enterprise.

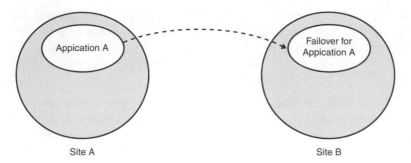

FIGURE 3.4   Distributing servers across a WAN for redundancy purposes.

Choosing Servers to Virtualize

When choosing to virtualize guest sessions, deciding which applications are the best candidates for virtualization is a key factor. Not all server applications can or should be virtualized. That's not to say, however, that an organization can't choose to virtualize 100% of their servers if desired. The key to choosing servers for virtualization is to first pick the servers that make perfect sense to virtualize, and then make the more difficult decisions about virtualizing other server systems.

Prioritizing Servers to Virtualize

As mentioned previously, some servers are prime candidates for virtualization—for example, servers that have low system resource utilization or where multiple servers exist for shear redundancy and recoverability. Other server systems that have high processor demands and excessive disk and network I/O requirements may not be the best servers to virtualize; during the physical to virtual server migration process, these servers may be the ones chosen for second-round migration.

The process of converting physical servers to virtual servers takes several days, if not weeks, depending on the number of servers an organization has. Therefore, the organization should create a priority list and stage the migration in a logical manner.

In many instances, the priority may be to virtualize a physical server that is failing. Make sure, however, that the rush to evacuate a server off faulty hardware into a virtual environment doesn't create more problems for the organization. Such a quick migration might not factor in whether the application works well in a virtualized environment, or whether the system resource demands of the application really suggest that the application should have instead been migrated off one physical server onto a new physical server.

Candidates for Immediate Virtualization to Guest Sessions

When organizations are prioritizing servers for virtualization, as noted, many server systems make perfect sense to virtualize. Server roles that are typically simple decisions to virtualize include the following:

▶ **DHCP servers**—The Dynamic Host Configuration Protocol (DHCP) server assigns IPv4/IPv6 network addresses to devices on the network. Most organizations have at least one DHCP server, if not several, for both redundancy and to associate different IP addresses to different groups of users. However, DHCP servers rarely have more than 5% utilization and are prime candidates for server virtualization.

▶ **DNS servers**—The domain name system (DNS) maintains a list of network servers and systems and their associated IP addresses. A DNS server is queried and responds with information. In general, however, DNS servers, like DHCP servers, rarely have more than 5% utilization. And because DNS servers are so critical in resolving server names and addresses, organizations generally have several DNS servers for redundancy. These systems are perfect candidates for virtualization.

▶ **Network policy servers**—Network policy servers keep track of the policies required to allow users access to certain network resources, or they may maintain a list of users authorized to access specific network resources remotely. Remote Authentication Dial-in User Service (RADIUS) servers are a form of policy server, and with Windows Server 2008, Microsoft has introduced a server called the Network Policy Server (NPS). The NPS performs centralized connection authentication, authorization, and accounting for many types of network access, including wireless and virtual private network (VPN) connections. Because these policy servers are queried only when a policy requires validation, the demands on policy servers are pretty limited; they are therefore good candidates for virtualization.

▶ **Web servers**—As more and more technologies become web aware and have web frontend interfaces for user access, enterprise web servers have proliferated. And because many Microsoft web-based frontend servers don't work well when combined together, each frontend web server needs to be on its own server session. This multitude of web frontend servers can be virtualized and hosted on a limited number of virtual host systems. In this way, you combine the web servers without forcing the web applications to share the same guest session; instead, those guest sessions share the same host server system as dedicated virtual guests.

▶ **Certificate and Rights Management servers**—As with network policy servers, certificate servers and rights management servers are queried when certificates are required or when certificate or rights management policies are requested. Other than at those limited times, the certificate server or rights management server remains idle. Hence, certificate servers and rights management servers are prime candidates for virtualization.

Secondary Candidates for Virtualization to Guest Sessions

A number of application services can be virtualized. These services will be different for every organization, and so the decision to virtualize these servers must be organization specific. In general, however, the secondary candidates for virtualization to guest sessions include the following:

▶ **File servers**—Most organizations have a lot of data stored on file servers, but the reality is that use access to the file servers is an occasional read and write of files throughout the day. Typically, a user opens a file, works on it for a while, and then saves it. Even large graphics files and computer-aided design (CAD) files are opened, worked on for a while, and then saved. So, the processing demands are relatively low. In most cases, therefore, file server systems are good candidates for virtualization. However, do consider having the actual data for file servers written to a storage area network (SAN) or other storage system that can handle large sets of data.

▶ **Print servers**—Print servers typically have bursts of data managed by the systems as users send print jobs to the print server, the job is processed, and then the job is sent to a printer. The print server then remains idle until another print job is sent. Although print servers don't fit into the category of "no-brainer for virtualization," and should be analyzed and tested, they are usually good candidates for virtualization.

▶ **Global catalog server**—The global catalog server in a Windows Active Directory environment is typically duplicated so that there are two or more servers in the environment hosting Active Directory data. However, the decision to virtualize a global catalog server is one that requires some thought and planning. Typically, a virtual host server is a member of the Active Directory domain (so that a network administrator can manage the Hyper-V host). Usually, however, you don't want your host system as a member of a domain that the host is running the global catalog for. But, as long as a physical server hosting global catalog services exists on the network that allows the Hyper-V host to authenticate to it is running on the network, having a second global catalog server within the host as a virtual guest works fine.

▶ **Domain controller**—As with the global catalog server, as long as there is a domain controller or global catalog server outside of the virtual host system, having a domain controller as a virtual guest session is fine.

▶ **Remote-access server**—Remote-access servers are frequently placed in the demilitarized zone (DMZ) and not in the primary network. For servers of this type, a virtual host system can be placed in the DMZ to host virtual guests like the remote-access server. For security reasons, however, the host systems are usually not members of the internal network domain.

▶ **Edge servers**—Just as web servers have proliferated in application server environments, so have servers in the edge (for example, the Exchange 2007 Edge server, the Office Communication Server Access proxy, ForeFront antivirus/antispam servers, and even Internet Security and Acceleration [ISA] servers). These servers in the edge can all be installed on a virtual host system as virtual guests in an organization's DMZ, thus minimizing the need to have dozens of physical servers in the DMZ.

▶ **Media servers**—With information extending beyond text-based word processing documents and spreadsheets into rich media such as video and audio, media servers have begun to pop up in organizations. Media servers typically require large storage subsystems to store video and audio content. If the data stores are placed on SANs, however, the media server managing the data and user access can be virtualized.

Servers That Need to Be Evaluated for Candidacy for Virtualization

The following server systems can be virtualized, but every organization thinking about doing so should evaluate whether their use of the application exceeds the reasonable capabilities of a virtual server guest; if so, the server should remain on a physical system. These servers are as follows:

▶ **Database servers**—Database servers include systems such as SQL servers and Exchange mailbox servers. Although many organizations want to virtualize these servers so that they can put clustering and disaster-recovery failover in place, many times the processing demands of these servers exceed the reasonable performance expectations of a virtual guest session. Performance assessment should be done before virtualizing these systems.

▶ **Cluster servers**—When fault tolerance is important to an organization, clustering provides failover from one system to another. Windows 2008 Hyper-V supports guest clustering, and it works extremely well both within a single host server or spanned across two separate host servers. Just like database servers, however, an organization needs to validate that the I/O demands of the application being clustered doesn't exceed the capabilities of a virtual guest session.

▶ **Terminal Services thin client servers**—Terminal Services provides a "many user to one server" approach for accessing applications and network resources. Because Terminal Services is already a form of virtualization (taking many sessions and running them on a single system), an administrator needs to validate that virtualization of a virtualized guest session doesn't dictate the need to maintain the Terminal Services system on a dedicated system.

▶ **Application servers**—Finally, the catchall of "other servers" is the virtualization of any other application server in a networking environment. This might be a line-of-business application like SAP, or Great Plains, or Seibel, or it might be a custom web application, portal system, or document management system. Servers must be assessed for their usage of memory, processor demands, disk I/O, and network I/O to confirm whether a server can be virtualized without taking up all the resources of the host system.

After all, the administrator wants to make sure that virtualizing a system and placing it on a host server doesn't use up all the resources of the host server. Otherwise, it is best to run the application on a dedicated physical system. In many environments where a physical server does significantly tax system resources when in full production, the offline version of the system, such as the passive node of a cluster, is not taking on a workload on a day-to-day basis. It could be argued that the secondary server can be virtualized, because the demands against that server are not utilized. The organization just needs to be aware that in the event that the primary server fails and the passive system comes online, that all the workload now gets placed on the virtualized server. This may place the Hyper-V host in an overload condition where processes across all guest sessions are slowed down a bit. If it is planned and is part of the disaster-recovery strategy to have an offline system that might run slower than the full production environment system (and so is anticipated), however, it's a strategy that can be documented and implemented in the production environment.

Capturing the Workload Demands of Existing Servers

We have now identified a list of candidate servers for virtualization. What now? The actual physical to virtual conversion and the placement of guest sessions balanced across multiple host systems require real-world assessments of the demands on the physical servers. This is best done by running tools against existing servers and testing key statistics on the servers to determine their workload demands in terms of RAM usage, processor usage, disk I/O, and network I/O throughout the day.

Introducing the Microsoft Virtualization Solution Accelerator

Microsoft has a freely downloadable tool at Microsoft.com that you can run against production servers in a Windows environment. The Microsoft Virtualization Solution Accelerator (VSA) grabs statistical information (server memory usage, CPU utilization, disk I/O, network I/O, and so on) off the servers to understand current workloads. The tool is run during the day or at times when the servers are in use to capture real-time "in-action" metrics.

VSA is part of the Microsoft Planning and Assessment Solution Accelerator series of tools. At www.microsoft.com/vsa, you can find information about the tool (including how it works and what it's capturing) and a download link. You should download it now. The rest of this section walks you through the installation of the VSA tool and explains how to capture information off your network and how to analyze VSA output.

Prerequisites for Installing the Microsoft VSA Tool

The Microsoft VSA is typically installed on a workstation system connected to the network that hosts the servers that are going to be assessed. Because of the software it installs on the system (SQL Express) and the limitation that it will work only on a 32-bit system, it is usually not installed on a network server. However, you can install it on a 32-bit utility server (DHCP server, DNS server) where an instance of SQL Express won't impact any of the other applications running on the server.

> **NOTE**
>
> The VSA does not inject any traffic or load onto the network, nor does it load any special agents on the servers. The VSA merely gathers information (using Windows Management Instrumentation, WMI) from Windows servers on the network, statistics that are commonly collected when using the Microsoft Performance Monitor (Perfmon).

The system requirements for the VSA are as follows:

- **Supported operating system**—Windows Server 2003, Windows Server 2008, Windows Vista, Windows XP Professional Edition (all 32-bit versions)

- **Hardware requirements**—1.6GHz or faster system, 1.5GB of RAM, 1GB of available hard disk space, network adapter

- **Software requirements**—Microsoft SQL Express 2005, Microsoft Word 2003 SP2 or Word 2007, Microsoft Excel 2003 SP2 or Excel 2007

During the installation process, you are prompted to allow the tool to automatically download SQL Express 2005 from the Internet and install it on your system. Alternatively, you provide the installation media to have SQL Express installed on your system.

> **NOTE**
>
> The VSA does not support the use of SQL 2000, SQL 2005, or SQL 2008 databases on other servers, nor does the Installation Wizard acknowledge that an existing copy of SQL Express 2005 is installed on the system. The Installation Wizard requires the installation of SQL Express 2005 onto the local system at the time of installation and will only use the local copy that it installs.

SQL Express is used for storing inventory and assessment data, and the reports generated by the VSA are stored in DOC and XLS formats and requires Word and Excel to be on the system prior to the Installation Wizard being launched. If Word and Excel is not on the system, the Installation Wizard will stop and you will be prompted to install a copy of Word and Excel first. After doing so, just rerun the VSA Installation Wizard.

Installing the Microsoft VSA Tool

After downloading the VSA, which is about 50MB in size, run the executable (default is Microsoft_Assessment_and_Planning_Solution_Setup.exe) to begin the installation process. The installation process is as follows:

1. At the Welcome to the Microsoft Assessment and Planning Solution Accelerator Setup Wizard screen, assuming you are connected to the Internet, select the Automatically Check for Device Compatibility check box, and then click Next.

2. Read the license agreement, and then select I Accept the Terms of the License Agreement. Click Next.

3. Click Browse to change the folder into which you want to install the VSA tool, or just click Next to accept the default folder.

4. Read the license agreement, and then select I Accept the Terms of the License Agreement. Click Next.

5. Choose to download and install SQL Express, and then click Next.

6. Read the license agreement for SQL Express, and then select I Accept the Terms of the License Agreement. Click Next.

7. Review the Ready to Install screen, which should note that it will download a copy of SQL Express, install SQL Express, and then install the Microsoft Assessment and Planning Solution Accelerator,. If this is correct, click Install.

8. After the wizard goes through the download and installation of SQL Express and installs the VSA tool, an Installation Successful screen will display. Click Finish.

Setting Up the Microsoft VSA Tool to Capture Data for the First Time

After the Microsoft VSA tool has been installed, the next step is to set up the tool to capture data for the first time. This section walks you through that process. In this example, we use just a limited number of servers for a short collection period, just to confirm the collection process is working properly. Once you know the collection process works properly, you can initiate a longer scan. To set up the collection process for the first time, follow these steps:

1. Click Start, All Program Files, Microsoft Assessment and Planning Solution Accelerator, Microsoft Assessment and Planning Solution Accelerator. You will get to a screen that look similar to the one shown in Figure 3.5.

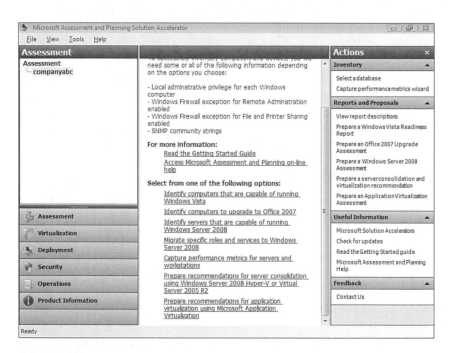

FIGURE 3.5   Main Solution Accelerator screen.

2. Click Select a Database in the middle pane, or choose File, Select a Database from the menu.

3. Assuming this is the first time you are running the VSA tool, choose Create an Inventory Database and enter the name you want to call the database. Something

like your organization name is fine (for instance, CompanyABC). If you have already run the VSA tool and have created a database already, choose Use an Existing Database and select the database you previously created. Click OK to continue.

> **NOTE**
>
> The database you create can be used for all server and site captures performed. You do not need to create a separate database every time you run the tool, nor do you need to create a separate database if you select different servers on the same network to assess. The database merely holds the statistical information. If you are a consultant going from company to company doing assessments for different organizations, you will likely want to create a new database for each company you are assessing. After all, you do want to keep the data separate for each organization you run the tool against to gather data.

4. Create a text file (TXT) using Notepad or Word or another application and enter the server names (IP address, NetBIOS name, or fully qualified DNS name) in the text file. Save the text file to the hard drive of your system that will be used in step 7. The file (for instance, servers.txt) will have contents like the following:

```
dc1.companyabc.com
dc2.companyabc.com
exchange01.companyabc.com
10.0.0.100
   10.0.0.101
```

> **TIP**
>
> When creating the server.txt file for the first time, just enter the names of a couple servers to start so that you can test the tool first before you start the VSA on a 3-day run only to find out that it wasn't capturing any information.

5. Click Prepare Recommendations for Server Consolidation Using Windows Server 2008 Hyper-V or Virtual Server 2005 R2 in the middle pane of the VSA tool.

6. When prompted that you need to capture performance metrics and to click the link specified, click the Capture Performance Metrics for Computers in the Environment.

7. Click Browse and choose the filename you created in step 4 that has the names of the servers you want to assess. Click Next.

8. Check the pop-up that tells you how many servers it identified in your text file. It should note the number of servers you entered with zero machines being ignored. Click OK to continue.

9. Enter the WMI credentials for the servers you are assessing. This is typically the administrator password for the servers. You can enter several different logons and

passwords if you have different credentials for different servers. Click New Account, and then fill in the Inventory Account with the appropriate domain name, account name, and password. If you are entering in a local account, leave the Domain Name field blank. If you know the account name and password is valid only on a specific computer, select the computer name the password is valid for so that it won't use that logon name and password on each and every system. The screen would look something like Figure 3.6. Click Save if this is the last account credentials you want to enter, or click Save and New if you need to enter in another set of account credentials

FIGURE 3.6   Inventory Account credentials screen.

10. After entering the WMI credentials for the servers in your text file list, click Next to continue.

11. For the Set Performance Collection Duration, enter the time you want the collection process to end, and then click Next.

TIP

When selecting the end time for the collection, assuming this is the first time you are testing the tool, it is recommended you choose a small amount of time to do the sampling, which can be 5 to 10 minutes. There's no reason to wait an entire day to realize you entered in the WMI credentials wrong and the tool gathered no information. And although the minimum sampling length is 5 minutes, many times when you do just 5 minutes, the system doesn't collect any information. So, run the tool on a limited number of servers with a 10-minute duration to first make sure you know how the tool works. When you know the tool is working properly, you can set the tool to run for a day, 2 days, or more to collect information.

12. Review the settings, and then click Finish to start the tool. While the collection is happening, you'll see a screen similar to Figure 3.7.

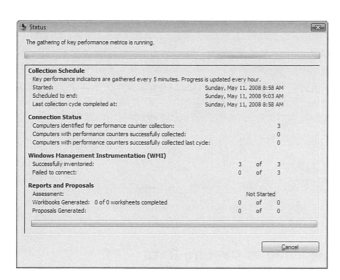

FIGURE 3.7   Collection-gathering Status screen.

After you run the tool for a 10-minute duration in a test, if the report returns that it could not sample or collect information, one of the following is likely the problem:

▶ **Wrong credentials**—Make sure you have entered the right logon name and password for the server. Usually the local administrator account is needed. On domain controllers or servers that do not have local administrator accounts, however, the domain administrator account that has access to the server typically works.

▶ **Remote Registry Service not started**—The VSA requires the Remote Registry Service to be started on all servers where data is being collected. This service is usually enabled by default because it is the service used to remotely monitor and manage servers on a network. If you need to start the Remote Registry Service, go into the Services Administrative tool and click to start the service.

▶ **No access to the server**—Make sure you have general access to the server where you can ping the server, log on to the server, map or mount drives on the server, or generally have LAN/WAN connectivity to the system and can successfully log on to the system. A quick test is to map the c$ share of the server that typically confirms you have network connectivity and administrator credentials to the server. From a command prompt, enter the following: **nct use** *x*: *servername***c$ /user:administrator**.

When you know that the tool is working and have successfully gathered information from a small subset of servers, go back to step 4 and enter all the servers you want to capture information from. Retry the tool for a 10-minute cycle to make sure the tool has successfully logged on and gathered information. Fix any credentials, Remote Registry Service, or LAN/WAN access errors until you can successfully connect to all the servers.

> **TIP**
>
> At any point during the key performance metrics gathering process that you start see-ing "Failure to Connect" counts (meaning servers are not successfully being accessed), you can click the Cancel button, have the tool generate a report, and then look at the report to determine which servers were not responding. The report also tells you whether there was a credential problem or if a server could not be reached on the net-work.

When all the servers you want to assess are accessible and responding, you are ready to move to the next step, which is to run the collection tool for a longer period of time.

Choosing the Right Time Sequence to Capture Data

When performing a full server collection, you need to run the sampling for a minimum of 2 hours. (Typically, you should run it for at least 130 minutes so that you get more than 24 samples.) The Server Consolidation Assessment Wizard needs at least 24 samples collected and stored in the SQL database before the wizard will generate a report. When you run the collection tool, it does a sample every 5 minutes; so for 24 samples, the tool needs to run for at least 120 minutes. If you run the tool for fewer than 24 samples, the Server Consolidation Assessment Wizard will continue to prompt you to run the "Capture performance metrics for computers in the environment" process first, and unfortunately it doesn't clearly tell you that you need to run the wizard for more than 2 hours, so you continue to run the tool for an hour and never get past that notice.

When choosing the 2+ hour window during which you will be doing the sampling and collection, pick a time during the middle of the day or during generally normal or peak transaction times. If you run the collection tool at night when nobody is on the system, you will get completely incorrect metrics because the servers are likely idle during those hours. It's also not recommended to run the tool for a period that extends beyond the normal server load times. Therefore, running the collection all day and all night will gather dozens of samples, but the samples at night will water down the sampling during the day, giving you less-precise metric data than you want.

For those organizations that follow the typical 8 a.m. to 5 p.m. business model, running the sampling between 7:30 a.m. and 5:30 p.m. will provide a great set of information because it will include the range of time from when employees come in at the start of the day, log on to the network, and launch their applications, to the completion of the day when employees log off and shut down their workstations.

When sampling a remote-access server that might support employees working from home, you might find that after-hours—such as in the evening after employees get home, have dinner, and then log on in the evening—are a good time to sample the remote-access servers to assess load on those systems during their peak usage times.

Preparing a Server Consolidation Recommendation Report

With the VSA successfully capturing information for all the servers you want to assess, the next step is to run the tool for more than two hours to collect enough samples so that the Prepare Recommendations for Server Consolidation Wizard works. The process is as follows:

1. Click Prepare Recommendations for Server Consolidation Using Windows Server 2008 Hyper-V or Virtual Server 2005 R2 in the middle pane of the VSA tool.

2. Assuming you have successfully run the collection for more than 2 hours and have more than 24 samplings from all the servers you entered into the text file in the section "Setting Up the Microsoft VSA Tool to Capture Data for the First Time," you will no longer get the prompt to "Capture performance metrics for computers in the environment." Instead, you will get the screen that says "Select the Microsoft Virtualization technology that you wish to use for placement recommendations." Choose Windows Server 2008 Hyper-V and click Next.

3. For the Model Host CPU, enter the configuration of your planned Hyper-V server, whether it has an Intel or AMD processor, number of core per processor, processor speed, and so on, as shown in Figure 3.8. Then click Next.

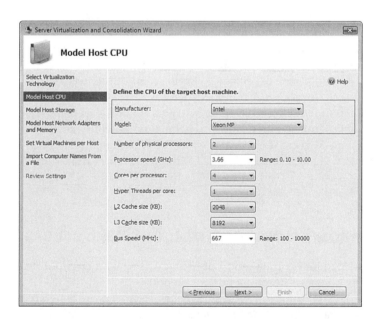

FIGURE 3.8   Defining the CPU of the target host machine.

4. For the Model Host Storage, enter the configuration of your planned Hyper-V storage in terms of type of disk, storage capacity per disk, number of disks, and so on. Then click Next.

5. For the Model Host Network Adapter and Memory, enter the configuration of your planned Hyper-V server network adapter configuration for speed of the adapters and number of adapters. Also enter the amount of RAM that will be in the server, such as 8GB or 16GB or 32GB. Then click Next.

6. If you leave Set Virtual Machines per Host unchecked, the Recommendation Wizard tells you how many of the physical servers you assessed will fit on this model configuration you have created. If you check the check box, you can note whether you want two, three, four, or more virtual sessions on the system. Typically, you'd just let the wizard recommend how many sessions you want on the server, so you would leave the check box blank. Click Next to continue.

7. Import the text file you used in step 4 in the section "Setting Up the Microsoft VSA Tool to Capture Data for the First Time" that has the names of the servers you assessed. Then click Next.

8. Review your settings, and then click Finish.

9. The wizard will go through the worksheets that were created in the data gathering process, as well as go through the data captured and stored in the SQL server for the systems that were specified in the text file. This takes a minute or two, and you will then be prompted to click the Close button.

From the Microsoft Assessment and Planning Solution Accelerator screen, choose the View Saved Reports and Proposals option. Doing so opens an Explorer window that shows the Excel spreadsheets and Word documents generated by the assessment tool. Open the ServerVirtProposal Word document that summarizes the recommendation on how many Hyper-V virtual servers would be needed, the expected CPU utilization of the servers, and the disk and network throughput of the servers. Combine the information from the Excel spreadsheet named ServerVirtRecommendation that notes a recommended split of servers between the Hyper-V host systems being acquired, and you get a good baseline recommendation on how to split the virtual guest sessions and what the anticipated workload will be on each of the host servers. Figure 3.9 shows some of the information from the reports.

Analyzing the Workload Demands of Existing Servers

Another way to review the workload and configuration of the servers in your environment other than using the Server Consolidation Recommendation Report is to open the Excel spreadsheet that is generated from the collection process. Excel spreadsheets are generated and dropped into the folder Documents\MAP\{database name}. Open the spreadsheet generated, and note the statistics about the servers being monitored.

For network utilization, the report, as shown in Figure 3.10, notes the hostname, make and model of the network adapters in the system (if multiple network adapters are in the server, each adapter is assessed separately), bytes sent and received, packets sent and received, and packet errors.

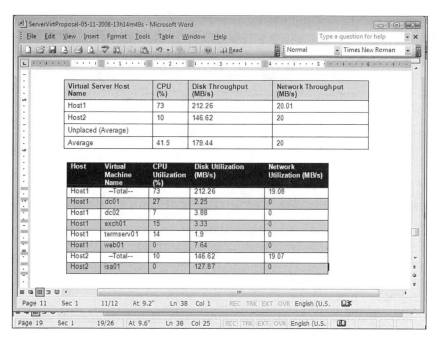

FIGURE 3.9   C Sample assessment metrics produced from the VSA tool.

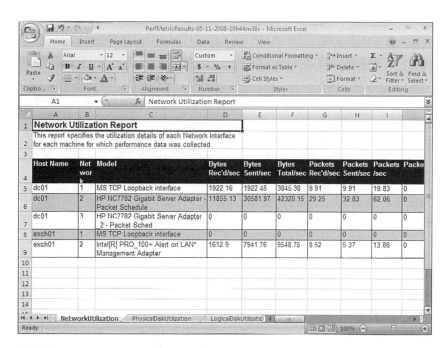

FIGURE 3.10   Sample network utilization report.

For physical disk utilization, the report notes the hostname, the type of disk configured, total capacity of the disk, % disk read and write time, % idle time, average disk bytes/read and bytes/write, average disks sec/read and sec/write, and average disk queue length.

The logical disk utilization report notes the hostname, disk volume name, total capacity of the drive, % disk read time, % disk write time, average disk sec/read and sec/write, and % free space.

The statistical information provided in the spreadsheet along with the Server Consolidation recommendation report can provide valuable information about the server demands of the systems being assessed for virtualization.

Identify Servers That Are and Are Not Virtualization Candidates

With the recommendations from the Server Consolidation report and the data in the Excel spreadsheet, you can validate certain servers as good candidates for virtualization. These servers are likely the utility servers (DHCP, DNS, domain controllers), an assumption discussed earlier in the section "Candidates for Immediate Virtualization to Guest Sessions," but are validated from the real-world statistical assessments.

Other servers that might have been iffy as to whether they would be good candidates for virtualization can be validated from the statistics. You can confirm whether the workload, disk I/O, network I/O, or other server performance metrics data indicate the server is or is not a good candidate for virtualization.

Combining Virtual Server Workloads to Create Optimized Host Servers

From the data generated, combining server workloads together to logical host server configurations is the next step. Balancing servers so that all the servers with high processor demands aren't all put on the same host server but rather distributed across different host servers is the goal.

The Server Consolidation report generated from the VSA makes suggestions on appropriate server balance. By combining the required memory statistic with disk and network I/O, the network administrator can now determine how many host servers are needed, how much memory each server should have, how many processors are recommended, and what type of disk and LAN configuration is recommended.

Choosing the Hyper-V Host System Environment

With the statistical data acquired from the Microsoft VSA analyzed and grouped together for optimum host configurations, the next task is choosing the host environment that Hyper-V will be implemented on. This is a decision whether the Hyper-V host will be implemented on a physical server or whether the Hyper-V host will be implemented on a blade server along with other physical servers or other Hyper-V host configurations.

Hyper-V on a Dedicated Host Server

For organizations consolidating physical servers to virtual servers, usually an initial server used for Hyper-V virtualization is an existing server in the environment (typically a four or eight core system with a lot of memory, 16GB to 32GB). The system may have been earmarked for a database server or messaging server, but instead has been allocated as the host virtual server. Or the organization might have purchased the server specifically with host virtualization in mind.

The dedicated physical server is like other servers on the network, with processors, memory, internal disk, and a network adapter or two. The system would be configured and have Windows Server 2008 x64-bit installed on it and have the Hyper-V role installed via the process covered in Chapter 4, "Installing Windows 2008 Server and the Hyper-V Role."

Hyper-V on a Blade Among Other Physical Servers

Some organization may choose to purchase a blade server that is a physical server system with several server processor boards in the system. So instead of having a physical server with three or four virtual guest sessions running on it, the blade server has four or eight blades in the server, with one or more of the blades running as a Hyper-V host with three or four virtual guests running on the blade. Therefore, a blade server with 8 blades can run 8 different instances of Hyper-V host, and each Hyper-V host can be running 3 or 4 virtual guest sessions, thus allowing a single chassis to run 32 simultaneous server sessions.

Blade servers can definitely consolidate servers down to a small footprint, where 32 physical servers can end up in a single-rack chassis just 6 to 10 inches high.

Sizing a Hyper-V Host System Without Existing Guest Data

Although the exercise to assess the current workload of existing physical servers using the Microsoft VSA provides great metrics to size a Hyper-V host system for existing systems, the process of sizing the Hyper-V host system is not as precise for many organizations bringing up brand-new guest sessions without historical data.

To take an educated guess at the sizing of the host system, since most servers in a data center are running less than 10% server utilization, there is typically plenty of excess server capacity available, and an administrator can take a pretty good guesstimates on server load.

Because each virtual guest session is a completely running operating system, the installation of as few as three or four high-performance guest sessions could quickly bring a server to 50% or 60% of the server performance limits. So, putting together a good educated guess is important in the process.

Sizing Your Windows Server 2008 Server to Support Virtualization

The host Windows 2008 server needs to run Windows Server 2008 x64-bit edition. Although the minimum requirements for server compatibility for Windows 2008 applies, because server virtualization is the focus of this server system, the minimum Windows 2008 server requirements will not suffice to run Windows 2008 virtualization.

In addition, although Windows 2008 theoretically has maximum processor and memory capabilities that reach into a dozen or more core processors and hundreds of gigabytes of RAM, the reality on the scaling of Windows virtualization comes down to the raw capabilities of network I/O that can be driven from a single host server. In many environments where a virtualized guest system has a relatively low system utilization and network traffic demand, a single host system can easily support a dozen, two dozen, or more guest sessions. In other environments where a virtualized guest session has an extremely high system utilization, lots of disk I/O, and significant server communications traffic I/O, the organization might find a single host server maximizes its capacity with as few as seven or eight guest sessions.

RAM for the Host Server

With the lack of any other historical information, the rule of thumb for memory of a Windows 2008 server running Hyper-V is to have 2GB of RAM for the host server plus enough memory for each guest session. Therefore, if a guest session needs to have 2GB of RAM and there are three such guest sessions running on the host system, the host system should be configured with at least 8GB of RAM. If a guest session requires 8GB of memory and three of those systems are running on the system, the server should be configured with 24GB of memory to support the three guest sessions, plus at least 2GB of memory for the host system itself.

Processors for the Host Server

The host server itself in Windows 2008 virtualization has very little processor I/O requirements. In the virtualized environment, the processor demands of each guest session dictate how much processing capacity is needed for the server. If a guest session requires 2 cores to support the processing requirements of the application, and 7 guest sessions are running on the system, the server should have at least 15 cores available in the system. With quad-core processors, the system needs four processors. With dual-core processors, the system needs at least eight processors.

With Windows 2008 virtualization, each guest session can have up to four cores dedicated to the session, or processing capacity can be distributed, either equally or as necessary to meet the performance demands of the organization. By sharing cores among several virtual machines that have low processing needs, an organization can more fully utilize their investment in hardware systems.

Disk Storage for the Host Server

A host server will typically have the base Windows 2008 operating system running on the host system itself, with additional guest sessions either sharing the same disk as the host session or the guest sessions being linked to a SAN or some form of external storage for the virtualized guest session images.

Each guest session takes up at least 4GB of disk space. For guest sessions running databases or other storage-intensive configurations, the guest image can exceed 10GB, 20GB, or more. When planning disk storage for the virtual server system, plan to have enough disk space to support the host operating system files (typically about 2GB of actual files plus space for the Pagefile) and then disk space available to support the guest sessions.

Running Other Services on the Hyper-V System

On a system running Hyper-V, an organization would usually not run other services on the host system, such as making the virtual server also a file and print server, or making the host server a SharePoint server, or so on. Typically, a server running virtualization is already going to be a system that will maximize the memory, processor, and disk storage capabilities of the system. So, instead of impacting the performance of all the guest sessions by having a system-intensive application such as SharePoint running on the host system, organizations choose to make servers running virtualization dedicated solely to the operation of virtualized guest sessions.

Of course, exceptions apply to this general recommendation. If a system will be used for demonstration purposes, frequently the host system is set up to run Active Directory Domain Services, DNS, DHCP, and other domain utility services. So, effectively, the host server is the Active Directory system. Then, the guest sessions are created to run things like Microsoft Exchange 2007, SharePoint 2007, or other applications in the guest sessions that connect back to the host for directory services.

Planning for the Use of Snapshots on the Hyper-V System

A technology built in to Hyper-V is the concept of a snapshot. A snapshot uses the Microsoft Volume Shadow Copy Service (VSS) to make a duplicate copy of a file; however, in the case of virtualization, the file is the entire virtual server guest image. The first time a snapshot is taken, the snapshot contains a compressed copy of the contents of RAM on the system along with a bitmap of the virtual disk image of the guest session. If the original guest image is 8GB in size, the snapshot will be significantly smaller in size; however, the server storage system still needs to have additional disk space to support both the original disk image plus the amount of disk space needed for the contents of the snapshot image.

Subsequent snapshots can be taken of the same guest session; however, the way VSS works, each additional snapshot just identifies the bits that differ from the original snapshot, thus limiting the required disk space for those additional snapshots to be just the same as needed for the incremental difference from the original snapshot to the current snapshot. This difference might be just megabytes in size.

Taking into account whether snapshots will be used and how they will be used is important in sizing the Hyper-V host server because this will require more disk storage for the host system as more snapshots are taken and stored.

Summary

Microsoft Hyper-V is not necessarily difficult to install. Neither is it difficult to load up guest images to the system. To properly balance applications across multiple Hyper-V host systems, however, an administrator must do some simple performance assessment and planning.

Common server images can be virtualized, such as domain controller services, DNS services, DHCP services, web services, and the like. And then there are server applications that aren't as clear-cut as to whether they are good candidates for virtualization, such as database servers and clustered application servers.

This chapter provided guidance that identifies servers that are commonly virtualized, and then provided information about the Microsoft VSA tool, which enables you to assess the performance demands of existing servers to calculate key server statistics that can be used to determine the workload of existing servers. With statistical information in hand, an administrator can analyze the information and determine how to best place virtual guest sessions across Hyper-V host systems.

Best Practices

The following are best practices from this chapter:

▶ Distribute virtual guest sessions across host servers so that a host server isn't over-loaded with too many guest sessions demanding processing speed, disk I/O demands, or network I/O demands, but instead is balanced in a logical manner.

▶ Make sure to keep cluster pairs and redundant system services on separate host systems so that a host server failure doesn't bring down both the primary and the backup image of a system. You should balance the services across separate host systems.

▶ Consider keeping links server services such as frontend and backend servers on the same host system to improve the communication link speed between the two server sessions within the same host server.

▶ Make sure to not centralize virtual guest sessions and cause remote users to have to traverse slow or unreliable WAN links to access their information. To maintain the quality of the user experience in the process, user access to information should be equal if not better than before servers were virtualized.

▶ Plan for the number of virtual guest sessions you expect to have on a server to properly size the host system with respect to memory, processor, and disk requirements.

▶ Virtualize utility servers like DHCP servers, DNS servers, policy servers, and such that typically have low utilization and are redundant throughout an enterprise.

- ▶ Evaluate whether certain servers such as file servers, print servers, global catalog servers, servers in a DMZ or edge, and media servers are good candidates for virtualization based on the organization's workload of the systems.

- ▶ Use the Microsoft VSA tool to gather server statistics on running servers during normal production hours to determine the overall usage of systems in the environment.

- ▶ Assess the information that comes out of the Microsoft VSA to determine which servers are good candidates for virtualization and which servers are not as good of candidates for virtualization.

- ▶ Combine statistical information of servers to determine the amount of memory, processor requirements, disk I/O, and network I/O of guest sessions to determine the proper size for each host system that'll be added to the network.

- ▶ Allocate enough disk space to perform snapshots of images so that the disk subsystem can handle both the required guest image and the associated snapshots of the guest session.

- ▶ Consider keeping primary servers on physical server systems, and having secondary or redundant servers virtualized so that the organization can get the fastest performance on day-to-day queries against a physical server. However, the organization can have secondary servers as virtual server systems to minimize costs and consolidate backup systems.

3

PART II

Windows 2008 Hyper-V Host and Guest Installation

IN THIS PART

4

Installing Windows 2008 Server and the Hyper-V Role

This chapter describes the step-by-step process for installing a clean version of the Windows Server 2008 operating system on a server system for the purpose of implementing the Hyper-V virtualization role on the system. Also covered in this chapter is the installation of the Server Core configuration of Windows Server 2008 to run the Hyper-V role on a GUI-less version of Windows Server.

Even though the installation process is intuitive and has been simplified, an administrator must make several key decisions to ensure that the completed installation will meet the needs of the organization. For example, based on the statistical information generated in Chapter 3, "Planning, Sizing, and Architecting a Hyper-V Environment," a Hyper-V host system needs to have enough memory and processing capabilities to handle the number of virtual guest sessions that will be hosted on the Hyper-V system.

Planning and Preparing a Server Installation

Before you begin the actual installation of Windows 2008, you must make several decisions concerning prerequisite tasks. How well you plan these steps will determine how successful your installation is—as many of these decisions cannot be changed after the installation is complete.

Verifying Minimum Hardware Requirements

Whether you are installing Windows 2008 in a lab or production environment, you need to ensure that the hardware chosen meets the minimum system requirements. In most situations, the minimum hardware requirements presented will not suffice; therefore, Table 4.1 provides not only the minimum recommendations, but also the recommended and optimal system requirements for a Hyper-V virtualization server role configuration.

TABLE 4.1   Windows Server 2008 System Requirements

Component	Minimum Requirements	Recommended Requirements
Processor	1GHZ	AMD 64 or Intel EM64T (x64) processor with at least 2 core or even 4 or 8 core 2GHz or faster
Memory	512MB of RAM	8GB of RAM, or even 16GB to 32GB, depending on the number of virtual guests
Disk space	8GB	8GB for the base installation of Windows 2008, plus enough disk space for all the virtual guest session disks

When you are designing and selecting the system specifications for a new server solution, even the recommended requirements might not suffice, and it is best to determine the required server configuration based on the metrics for virtual server host configuration identified in Chapter 2, "Best Practices at Planning, Prototyping, Migrating, and Deploying Windows Server 2008 Hyper-V."

NOTE

Windows Server 2008 supports both 32-bit and 64-bit processor architectures. However, to run the Hyper-V virtualization role, you *must* run the x64-bit version of Windows Server 2008 on a server that has hardware-assisted virtualization support (for example, AMD 64 or Intel EM64T).

Finally, the maximum amount of RAM supported on a 64-bit system for a Standard Edition server is 32GB. The Enterprise and Datacenter editions can support up to 2TB of RAM.

Choosing the Appropriate Windows Edition

There are four main editions in the Windows 2008 family of operating systems. The editions are Windows Server 2008, Standard Edition; Windows Server 2008, Enterprise Edition; Windows Server 2008, Datacenter Edition; and Windows Server 2008, Web Server

Edition. For the Hyper-V role, the Web Server Edition is not supported at all for the host server. The Standard Edition of Windows 2008 may suffice, even with its 32GB maximum memory support. However, for licensing considerations, Microsoft provides four virtual server use licenses with an Enterprise Edition of Hyper-V host, meaning that the purchase of one copy of Windows 2008 Enterprise Edition will allow the organization to run four virtual server sessions of Windows 2008 Enterprise at no additional charge.

The Standard Edition of Windows 2008 allows one virtual server session at no additional charge. Assuming that a Hyper-V server will run three to four guest sessions, the Enterprise Edition and the virtual server use license makes the Enterprise Edition a better financial choice than the Standard Edition of Windows 2008.

The Datacenter Edition allows for an unlimited number of virtual guest sessions on the system. In previous versions of Windows, the Datacenter used to run only on proprietary hardware. With Windows 2008, however, the Datacenter Edition will run on almost any server than supports the Standard or Enterprise Edition of Windows. The major difference is that the Datacenter Edition provides more license use for guest sessions.

Choosing a New Installation or an Upgrade

Although Windows 2008 enables you to install a new version of Windows 2008 on a server or upgrade an existing version of Windows on the system, for the Hyper-V role server, the organization would normally install a new copy of Windows 2008 on the system. Even if the organization is running Microsoft Virtual Server 2005 on a system running Windows Server 2003, the process usually involves installing Windows Server 2008 on a new server, and then copying over the Virtual Server 2005 VHD image files and mounting the image files on the new server.

This authors cannot think of a scenario where it would be better to upgrade an existing version of Windows to Windows 2008, so the recommendation is to always install Windows 2008 clean on a system, and then to install the Hyper-V on that system.

Full Version of Windows or Server Core Installation

When you shove in the DVD to install Windows 2008 on the server for the first time, you have the choice of choosing either a full version of Windows 2008 or installing the Server Core Edition. You must make this decision at the time of installation; you cannot switch the decision later because such a switch would require reformatting the hard drive and reinstalling the other version of Windows. The decision between full Windows versus Server Core is as follows:

- ▶ **Full Windows**—A full version of Windows provides the administrator with the normal Windows GUI interface, Start button, and all the administrative tools common in a normal Windows server installation. If the organization will be installing only one Hyper-V host system and most administration will be done on the host server itself, make the server a full version of Windows. That'll allow the administrator to install the Hyper-V Administration tool on the system, load on tape backup or other common software familiar to the administrator, and use the server for Internet downloads and other tasks commonly done on a normal Windows server.

▶ **Server Core**—The Server Core Edition of Windows does not have a GUI, but instead boots to a logon screen, and then the administrator can log on and get to a command prompt. From the command prompt, the server can be joined to a domain, the Hyper-V role can be installed, and then you can address all other administration and management from another server on the system that has the Hyper-V Administration tool. A Server Core installation minimizes the attack surface on the server because there is no GUI on the system, and thus there are no common Windows applications such as Internet Explorer, Media Player, or the like that are destinations for viruses and attacks. For an organization that will be building Hyper-V host servers and centrally administering the servers from either the Hyper-V Administration tool or the System Center Virtual Machine Manager 2008 tool, a Server Core installation provides better security and easier ongoing maintenance you.

Member Server or Standalone Server

After your Windows Server 2008 has been installed on a server system, you can join the server to an Active Directory domain to be made a member server, or the system can remain as a standalone server. Some factors to consider when deciding whether to make server a member server or standalone are as follows:

▶ **Member server**—A member server allows a server to be centrally administered with common Active Directory administrator credentials. The member server can participate in Active Directory as any other Active Directory server that might be patched, monitored, or centrally managed.

▶ **Standalone server**—A standalone server is not joined to a domain, and therefore the credentials for the server are based on the local administrator rights to the server itself. For organizations that place a Hyper-V server in their demilitarized zone (DMZ) to host several edge server systems, for security purposes the Hyper-V host may likely not be attached to a domain. The Hyper-V standalone server will be managed and administered individually, just like any other nondomain attached servers.

Gathering the Information Necessary to Proceed

During the installation of Windows 2008, you must tell the Setup Wizard how you want your server configured. The wizard takes the information you provide and configures the server settings to meet your specifications.

Taking the time to gather the information described in the following sections before starting your installation will result in a faster, smoother, and easier install.

Selecting the Computer Name

Each computer on a network must have a name that is unique within that network. Many companies have a standard naming convention for their servers and workstations. If yours does not, you can use the following information as a guideline for creating your own.

Although the computer name can contain up to 63 characters, workstations and servers that are pre–Windows 2000 recognize only the first 15 characters.

It is widely considered a best practice to use only Internet standard characters in your computer name. This includes the letters A–Z (upper- and lowercase), the numbers 0–9, and the hyphen (-).

Although it's true that implementing the Microsoft domain name system (DNS) service in your environment could allow you to use some non-Internet standard characters (such as Unicode characters and the underscore), keep in mind that this is likely to cause problems with any non-Microsoft DNS servers on your network. Think carefully and test thoroughly before straying from the standard Internet characters noted in the preceding paragraph.

Name of the Workgroup or Domain

After the server installation is complete, you need to determine the name of the workgroup or domain that the server will be joining. You can either enter the name of an existing Windows domain or workgroup to join, or create a new workgroup by entering a new name.

Users new to Microsoft networking might ask, "What is the difference between a workgroup and a domain?" Simply put, a domain is a collection of computers and supporting hardware that shares the same security database. Grouping the equipment in this manner enables you to set up centralized security and administration. Conversely, a workgroup has no centralized security or administration. Each server or workstation is configured independently and locally for all security and administration settings.

Network Protocol and IP Address of the Server

When installing Windows 2008, you must install and configure a network protocol that will allow it to communicate with other machines on the network.

Currently, the most commonly used protocol is called TCP/IP version 4, which stands for Transmission Control Protocol/Internet Protocol. This protocol allows computers throughout the Internet to communicate.

After you install TCP/IP, you need to configure an IP address for the server. You can choose one of the following three methods to assign an IP address:

▶ **Automatic Private IP Addressing (APIPA)**—APIPA can be used if you have a small network that does not have a Dynamic Host Configuration Protocol (DHCP) server, which is used for dynamic IP addresses. A unique IP address is assigned to the network adapter using the LINKLOCAL IP address space. The address always starts with 169.254 and is in the format 169.254.x.x. Note that if APIPA is in use, and a DHCP server is brought up on the network, the computer will detect this and will use the address assigned by the DHCP server instead.

▶ **Dynamic IP address**—A dynamic IP address is assigned by a DHCP server. This allows a server to assign IP addresses and configuration information to clients. Some examples of the information that is distributed include IP address, subnet mask, default gateway, DNS server address, and the Windows Internet Naming Service (WINS) server address. As the *dynamic* portion of the name suggests, this address is assigned to the computer for a configurable length of time, known as a lease. Before the lease expires, the workstation must again request an IP address from the DHCP server. It might or might not get the same address that it had previously. Although servers and workstations can both be configured to use this method of addressing, it is generally used for workstations rather than servers.

▶ **Static IP address**—Using a static IP address is the most common decision for a server configuration. By *static*, we mean that the address will not change unless you change the configuration of the server. This point is important because clients and resources that need to access the server must know the address to be able to connect to it. If the IP address were to change regularly, connecting to it would prove difficult.

NOTE

Windows Server 2008 includes the latest TCP/IP protocol suite known as the Next Generation TCP/IP stack. The legacy protocol stack was designed in the early 1990s and has been modified to accommodate for today's future growth of computers networked together. The new TCP/IP stack is known as Internet Protocol version 6 (IPv6). Organizations using IPv6 can either dynamically assign or statically assign an IPv6 address to the Hyper-V host server.

Backing Up Files

If you are performing a new installation on a previously used server, you may consider performing a complete backup of the data and operating system before you begin your new installation. This way, if there is something on the old server that somebody wants, you have a backup of the information. However, if you know the server data is not needed, skip the backup process and begin the installation of the new Windows 2008 operating system.

When performing a new installation on a previously used server, you overwrite any data stored there. In this scenario, you must use your backup tape to restore any data that you want to preserve.

NOTE

Many people back up their servers but never confirm that the data can be read from the backup media. When the time comes to recover their data, they find that the tape is unusable or unreadable, or that they do not know the proper procedures for restoring their server. You should perform backup/recovery procedures on a regular basis in a lab environment to confirm that your equipment is working properly, that you are comfortable with performing the process, and that the recovery actually works.

Installing a Clean Version of Windows Server 2008 Operating System

The setup interface for Windows 2008 is a significant departure from the blue background and white text of previous versions. After the installation software loads into memory, the configuration setup pages have a consistent look and feel. Each step outlined in the following sections also has integrated links to relevant Help topics. Many of the choices and options that were part of the pre-installation setup process in Windows 2000/2003 (such as naming the server, giving it an IP address, and so on) are now relegated to a post-installation configuration process after the base OS installation has completed. Thus, the steps required during initial installation are minimized, allowing for a more streamlined initial process and consolidating operations pertaining to settings specific to the final role of the server to the post-installation phase.

The following sections outline the preferences that must be entered during a clean installation of Windows 2008.

1. Customizing the Language, Time, Currency, and Keyboard Preferences

The first element when installing Windows 2008 is entering the Language to Install of the server. Typically, the language selected is English; however, the language selections vary based on a region. Examples of languages include English, Arabic, French, Dutch, Spanish, and many more. The next element to be specified is the Time and Currency Format. This setting dictates how the server will handle currencies, dates, and times, including daylight savings. The final element is the Keyboard or Input Method. Specify the country code, such as US, Canada, or China, and click Next to begin the installation. Figure 4.1 shows these languages and other preferences.

FIGURE 4.1   Specifying the language and other preferences.

2. The Install Now Page

The next page in the installation process prompts you with an action to Install Now. Click Install Now to commence the Windows Server 2008 installation. Alternatively, before running the installation, you can click the two operational links: the What to Know Before Installing Windows link and the Repair Your Computer link. The What to Know Before Installing Windows link provides a list of prerequisite tasks, error messages, and general information about the installation. The Repair Your Computer link should be used if you need to fix a Windows 2008 operating system that is already installed.

3. Entering the Product Key

After you select the Install Now option, you need to enter the product key. The key is validated when entered; so if you mistype the product key, the installation will halt, giving you the opportunity to reenter the key before proceeding. The key entered dictates which versions of Windows 2008 are available for install. (All versions are available on the product media; separate media is required only for 32-bit versus x64-bit versions.) You can also opt to not enter the key and then select the appropriate version of Windows 2008 for installation, including Standard, Enterprise, Datacenter, and their corresponding Server Core versions.

As with other Microsoft operating systems, Windows 2008 must be activated. Click this option to automatically activate Windows when the server comes online. Click Next to continue with the installation process.

Using a Retail Media Activation Key

When you purchase the installation media from a retail source, you will have to contact Microsoft (either online or by telephone) to activate your product key. This key is unique for each installation. Fortunately, you still can automate the installation.

Using a Volume Media Activation Key

When you purchase the installation media as part of a Microsoft volume licensing program (such as Open or Select), no activation is required. In addition, you can use a common product key across all your installations.

4. Selecting the Type of Operating System to Install

The next page is Select the Operating System You Want to Install. One of the first items that you must address on every new installation of Windows 2008 is which type of operating system will be installed. The options include a complete installation or a Server Core installation. A complete installation is a traditional installation of Windows and includes all the user interfaces and supports all the server roles. As mentioned earlier, a Server Core installation is a scaled-down installation of Windows 2008 with the intent to reduce surface attack and management. A subset of the server roles are present, and the server is managed through the command prompt; therefore, the GUI does not exist. Click Next to continue, as depicted in Figure 4.2.

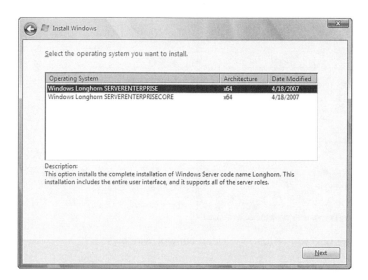

FIGURE 4.2   Specifying which operating system to install.

5. Accepting the Terms of the Windows Server 2008 License

The Please Read the License Terms page is invoked next. Review the license terms and check the I Accept the License Terms check box if you comply with these terms. Click Next to continue.

6. Selecting the Type of Windows Server 2008 Installation

On the Which Type of Installation Do You Want page, you can either select to upgrade an existing Windows server or to install a clean copy of Windows. Because this is a clean installation and a legacy operating system does not exist, the Upgrade selection is grayed out and not available. Therefore, in this scenario, the only option available is to select Custom (Advanced), to perform a client installation of Windows Server 2008. Click Next to continue, as shown in Figure 4.3.

7. Selecting the Location for the Installation

On the next page, the Install Windows Wizard asks where you want to install Windows. You need to specify where you want to install the OS and then click Next to continue, as illustrated in Figure 4.4. This section replaces the portion of both Windows 2000/2003 server installs where decisions about disk partitioning and formatting are made during the initial steps of the installation. At this point, you can supply additional disk drivers, or add, delete, extend, or format partitions in preparation for the install. It's another small change to the process for preparing a system for loading the OS, but that change simplifies and organizes the process in a logical way.

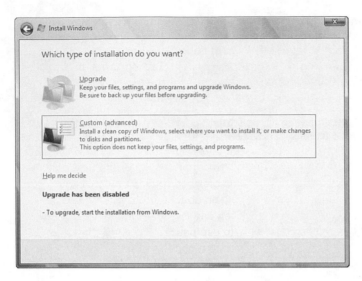

FIGURE 4.3   Specifying whether to upgrade or install a clean copy of Windows.

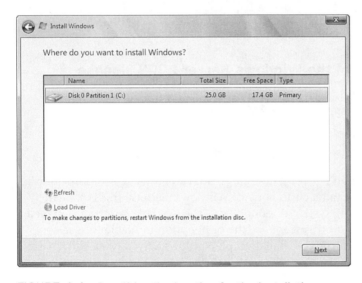

FIGURE 4.4   Specifying the location for the installation.

> **NOTE**
>
> With older versions of the Windows operating system, you had two options when partitioning the hard drive: NTFS or FAT/FAT32. When creating and formatting partitions in Windows Server 2008, FAT and FAT32 are no longer supported because NTFS is the only file system that can be sustained.

8. Finalizing the Installation and Customizing the Configuration

After the Windows Server 2008 Install Windows Wizard collects the information and installs Windows, the system prompts you to enter a password. You must key in a password that will be associated with the administrator account on the server. Once you enter in the password, you are prompted to log on to the server system.

NOTE

As a best practice, rename the administrator account after you complete the installation and assign a strong password. You must enter it twice: first in the Password text box, and then in the Confirm Password text box. As in previous Windows operating systems, the password is case sensitive and can contain up to 127 characters. In addition, a strong password should include both upper- and lowercase letters, numbers, and symbols. Many organizations choose to use passphrases that are mini-sentences instead of single words. It's harder to decode a phrase "I like my brown dOg Spot!" than a single 8- or 10-character single word.

Choose your password carefully to ensure the security of the system. You can change both the administrator account name and password in the Change Password dialog box.

When you enter the administrator name and your new password, an Initial Configuration Tasks Wizard is automatically invoked. This wizard presents the following tasks, as shown in Figure 4.5, to initially configure the server. The high-level initial configuration tasks include the following:

1. Provide Computer Information

   ▶ Set the Administrator Password

   ▶ Set Time Zone

   ▶ Configure Networking

   ▶ Provide Computer Name and Domain

2. Update This Server

   ▶ Enable Automatic Updating and Feedback

   ▶ Download and Install Updates

3. Customize This Server

   ▶ Add Roles

   ▶ Add Features

   ▶ Enable Remote Desktop

   ▶ Configure Windows Firewall

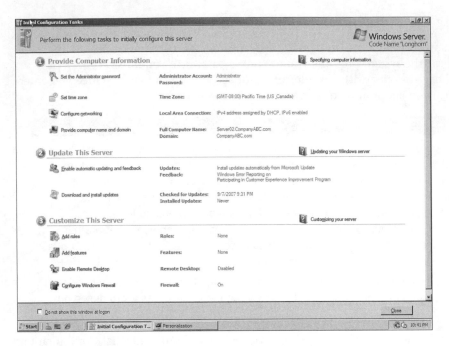

FIGURE 4.5   The Initial Configuration Tasks Wizard.

Traditionally, these configuration tasks were addressed during the initial installation of Windows; however, now these elements are configured after the initial installation of the operating system is complete. If these elements are removed from the installation, the installation process is much faster.

Setting the Time Zone

The first task that should be configured after the installation is the date and time of the server. Click the Set Time Zone link in the Initial Configuration Tasks Wizard to invoke the Date and Time dialog box. On the Date and Time tab, set the time zone where the server will operate by clicking the Change Date and Time button. In addition, click the Change Time Zone button to configure the time zone for the server. The next tab, Additional Clocks, as displayed in Figure 4.6, should be used if there is a need to display the time in another time zone. Up to two clocks can be configured on this tab. The final tab, Internet Time, is where you configure a time server for the server to synchronize its clock with. Time.windows.com is the default time server; however, other time servers can be selected by clicking the Change Settings button.

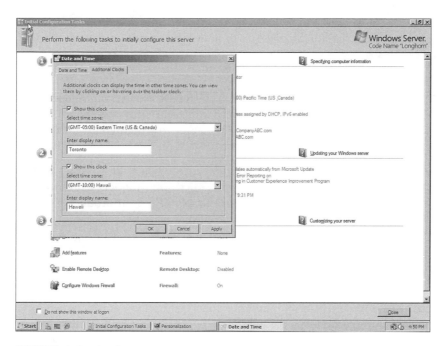

FIGURE 4.6   Configuring additional clocks for Windows.

Configuring Networking

The second setting in the Provide Computer Information section of the Initial Configuration Tasks Wizard is Configure Networking. You need to decide on network settings for the server so that it can connect to other computers, networks, and the Internet. By default, Windows 2008, as with earlier versions of Windows, installs Client for Microsoft Networks, File and Printer Sharing for Microsoft Networks, and TCP/IPv4. In addition, Windows 2008 installs QoS Packet Scheduler, Internet Protocol version 6 (TCP/IPv6), Link-Layer Topology Discover Mapper I/O Driver, and Link-Layer Topology Discover Responder.

Don't be alarmed. The default client, service, and protocols that are installed by default will meet most companies' needs and require little manual configuration. You will, however, likely want to change the TCP/IPv4 settings and assign a static address for the server.

Providing the Computer Name and Domain

Use the Provide Computer Name and Domain link to change the name of your computer and to add your computer to a domain or workgroup. If you are joining an existing domain, you need the logon name and password for a domain administrator account in that domain. Alternatively, you can have the administrator of the domain add your computer name into the domain so that your server can connect. If you do not know the name of the domain that the server will be a member of, or if you do not have the administrative rights to join the server to the domain, you can still change the computer name and you can always join the server to a domain at a later time.

Now that we configured the elements in the Provide Computer Information section of the Initial Configuration Tasks Wizard, the next step is to focus on the second configuration section called Update This Server.

Enabling Automatic Updating and Feedback

The Enable Automatic Updating and Feedback link in the Update This Server section is used to configure how your system maintains its health and security by automatically downloading and configuring software updates and the degree to which you want to participate in Microsoft's information-gathering efforts.

Although it's easy to dismiss these features, the tools do provide you with an easy way to patch your systems and contribute your experience with Microsoft products with little or no effort. Anonymous information gathered from users shapes Microsoft products and technologies, so if you don't have corporate policies around sharing technical information outside of your organization, give some thought to participating before shutting these systems down. If selected, the following options can be configured automatically, or you can manually configure the settings:

- **Automatic Updates**—Automatic Updates are not configured by default. You can leave this setting as is or configure the server to check for updates automatically on a schedule that fits your maintenance procedures. When patching large enterprise environments, it is a best practice to control software updates via a patching solution, such as System Center Operations Manager 2007 or WSUS 3.0.

- **Windows Error Reporting**—Windows Error Reporting, by default, automatically sends detailed information to Microsoft when errors occur on your server. You can turn this function off or configure it to alert a user who is logged on to the console before sending any information to Microsoft. Reports contain information that is most useful for diagnosing and solving the problem that has occurred.

- **Customer Experience Improvement Program**—The Customer Experience Improvement Program, or more benignly, CEIP, gathers anonymous information and periodically sends it to Microsoft. CEIP reports generally include information about the features and general tasks performed by a user and any problems encountered when using the Microsoft product.

Downloading and Installing Updates

Even though you might have selected the option in the previous steps to automatically configure server updates, it is still possible to download and install updates manually by selecting the Download and Install Updates link in the Update This Server section of the Initial Configuration Tasks Wizard. When selected, the server will connect to the Microsoft Windows Update site. Before configuring roles or features or making your server available to users on the network, it is a best practice to install the latest updates and patches from Microsoft. If your environment uses an automated tool such as WSUS, tested and approved patches might already be installed by your update and patching infrastructure if the system was joined to the domain and is configured to do so.

The final section on the Initial Configuration Tasks Wizard is called Customize This Server. The options are covered in the following sections.

Adding Roles

Using the Add Roles link on the Initial Configuration Tasks Wizard, you can quickly install core server roles, such as Active Directory Domain Services, DNS, and much more to your server. The process also adds dependent services and components as needed (alerting you along the way). This ensures that as you are setting up your system, all the necessary components are installed—alleviating the need to use multiple tools to install, secure, and manage a given server role—and that the roles are set up securely. Although it's critical to understand dependencies for whatever role or function the server might hold, getting the system set up quickly, efficiently, and accurately is always paramount, and these setup tools help accomplish just that. We address the addition of the Hyper-V role in the next section, "Installing the Hyper-V Server Role."

Adding Features

You can use the Add Features link to help configure useful tools and system features installed on the server. Features such as RPC over HTTP Proxy for Exchange, Terminal Services, Gateway, and SMTP Server can be installed and configured. Backup and other management tools can also be installed using this tool.

Enabling Remote Desktop

By enabling Remote Desktop, you can connect to either a remote console or an RDP session while not physically at the server. Using Remote Desktop to manage systems greatly eases administration of servers but does open another door into each system; therefore, consider restricting access via Remote Desktop to users who have a need to access those systems.

Configuring Windows Firewall

By default, Windows Firewall is turned on when the base OS is first run. Although the firewall protects the server only from outside access (as opposed to compromises from within the OS, such as a virus or other malware), this is typically adequate protection on a newly built machine until the system is patched and loaded with antivirus software or any other protective systems. Unless you configure exceptions to the firewall, users will not be able to access resources or services on the server. Exceptions to this are services or resources that are made available using the Initial Configuration Tasks Wizard or other GUI-based tools that automatically create the exceptions, enabling you to leave the firewall on while enabling access to specific functions on the server, if desired.

Installing the Hyper-V Server Role

With the background on sizing and planning for server capacity and storage covered in Chapter 3, and the basic installation of Windows Server 2008 covered so far in this chapter, this section now focuses on the installation of the Microsoft Hyper-V server role on the Windows Server 2008 system.

Running Server Manager to Add the Hyper-V Role

After the base image of Windows 2008 has been installed, some basic initial tasks should have been completed as noted in the section "Finalizing the Installation and Customizing the Configuration." The basic tasks are as follows:

1. Make sure to have changed the server name to be a name that you want the virtual server to be.
2. Configure the server to have a static IP address.
3. Join the server to an Active Directory domain (assuming the server will be part of a managed Active Directory environment with centralized administration).
4. Run Windows Update to confirm that all patches and updates have been installed and applied to the server.

After these basic tasks have been completed, the next step is to install the server virtualization software on the server and then add in the Hyper-V role to the server system. Because Windows virtualization did not ship with Windows 2008 at the time of the Windows 2008 product release, you first must download the Hyper-V role software from Microsoft and install it on the server system.

A beta version of the Hyper-V software is included on the original Windows 2008 disc and should not be installed for a production installation of the server now the Hyper-V is available. Go to www.microsoft.com/downloads and download the latest version of the Hyper-V server role onto the server system.

After the Hyper-V code has been installed on the system, do the following to add the server role to the system:

1. Make sure to be logged on to the server with local administrator or domain admin privileges.
2. Click Start, All Program Files, Administrative Tools, and choose Server Manager. This will start the Server Manager console if it is not already running on the system.
3. Right-click Roles in the left pane of the console, and select Add Roles, as shown in Figure 4.7.
4. After the Add Roles Wizard loads, click Next to continue past the Welcome screen.
5. On the Select Server Roles page, select the Hyper-V Server role, and click Next.

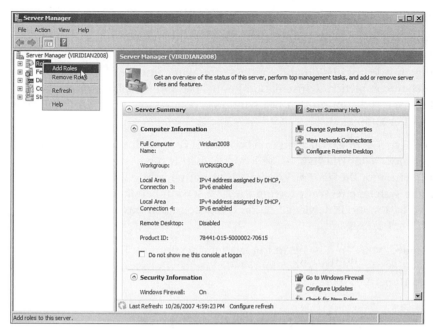

FIGURE 4.7   Adding a role to the Server Manager console.

NOTE

Hyper-V requires a system with hardware-assisted virtualization support. Both Intel EM64T and AMD64 chipsets are supported by Hyper-V. In addition, virtualization must be enabled in the BIOS. Check your server documentation for details on how to enable this setting. Although you may successfully install the Hyper-V server role software onto the server and reboot the system, if Hyper-V is not working, check your BIOS (commonly pressing the F2 key or F10 key on power up of the server to enter the "setup" of the BIOS) because hardware-assisted virtualization support is frequently not enabled by default. After making a change in the BIOS to support hardware-assisted virtualization and saving the setting, you might want to ensure the settings have successfully taken place by completely powering off the system instead of just letting the BIOS soft boot the system.

---

6. On the Hyper-V page, read the notes and information about the role, and then click Next.

7. On the Create Virtual Networks page, select the LAN adapters you want to have shared with guest sessions. Click Next to continue.

8. On the Confirm Installation Selections page, review the selections made, and then click Install.

9. On the Installation Results page, review the results, and click Close.

10. When prompted to restart the server, click Yes.

11. After the server restarts, log on to the server with local administrator or domain admin privileges.

12. After logging on, the installation and configuration will continue for a few more moments. When complete, the Installation Results page will display. Review the results in the page and confirm that the Windows Hyper-V role has been installed successfully. Click Close.

After installing the Hyper-V role, you need to reboot the server. With the Hyper-V role installed, the server now loads the HvBoot.sys loader, which is the hypervisor for the system. The continuation of the boot of Windows is actually loading Windows into the first partition on the system, effectively having the host session parallel to the guest sessions as opposed to a monolithic virtualization technology that has all guest sessions running on top of the host session.

With Hyper-V installed, you can now begin to load guest sessions on Hyper-V. See Chapter 5, "Installing a Guest Session on Hyper-V," for detailed instructions about installing virtual guest sessions onto Hyper-V.

Understanding Server Core Installation

Windows Server Core is one of the innovative and highly anticipated features of Windows 2008. The Windows Server Core installation provides a minimal environment for running a specific server role, including, but not limited to, a domain controller, web server, DHCP server, or in the context of this book, the Hyper-V role on Server Core.

With Server Core, only a subset of the Windows Server 2008 binaries is utilized. The Server Core installation is so stripped that traditional installation components, such as a desktop shell, GUI, Windows Explorer, Microsoft Internet Explorer, and the Microsoft Management Console (MMC), are not included. Therefore, the server must be fully managed and configured via the command prompt or remotely from an Administration tool running on another system.

By maintaining a minimized installation footprint by stripping out the typical components and only supporting specific roles, the Server Core installation reduces maintenance, attack surface, management, and disk space required to support the installation.

Another great feature, particularly for administrators who do not understand scripting commands and who heavily rely on the GUI tools to manage a server, is the ability to remotely manage the Server Core installation through the MMC.

Performing a Server Core Installation

When installing Windows Server 2008 Server Core, the actual installation process is similar to a regular server install, which was conducted in the earlier sections of this chapter. To recap, an administrator agrees to the licensing terms, supplies configuration responses, and the Windows Server 2008 Install Windows Wizard copies the files and configures the server. However, unlike a traditional installation of Windows, when the installation is complete and you log on, there isn't a GUI to configure the server. The server can be configured and managed only via the command prompt.

The Server Core installation will reboot your server a couple of times when device detection and the installation takes place. Eventually, you'll be presented with the logon screen.

Follow these steps to conduct a Windows Server 2008 Server Core installation:

1. Insert the Windows Server 2008 media. The Install Windows page will automatically be launched; otherwise, click Setup.exe.

2. Specify the Language to Install, Time and Currency Format, and Keyboard or Input Method, and then click Next.

3. Click Install Now to begin the installation process.

4. On the Type Your Product Key for Activation page, enter the product key included with the software. In addition, enable the option to Automatically Activate Windows When I'm Online, and then click Next.

5. On the Select the Operating System You Want to Install page, select the Windows Server 2008 Server Core, as shown in Figure 4.8. Click Next to continue.

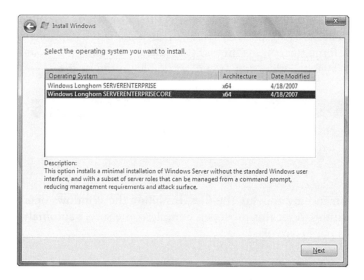

FIGURE 4.8   Selecting the Server Core installation.

6. Review the license terms and select the I Accept the License Terms option, and then click Next.

7. On the Which Type of Installation Do You Want page, select Custom (Advanced), as shown in Figure 4.9. Because you cannot upgrade a legacy Windows operating system to Server Core, the Upgrade option has been disabled.

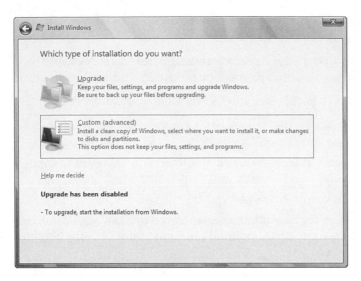

FIGURE 4.9   Selecting a custom installation.

8. On the Where Do You Want to Install Windows page, select the disk where you plan to install the Windows system files. Alternatively, you can click the Drive (Options) to create, delete, extend, or format partitions. In addition, click Load Driver to install drivers for the Windows 2008 installation that are not available on the media.

NOTE

If the only drive available is Unallocated Space, Windows Server 2008 automatically creates a partition based on the largest size and formats the partition with NTFS.

The installation process will commence by copying the files, installing the Windows operating system, and configuring features. After this process is complete, the server automatically reboots itself, and the logon page is invoked.

Performing Common Server Tasks with Server Core

When a server is installed, the administrator generally gets a configuration wizard or a familiar Start button or Control Panel where the administrator can change the server name, IP address, join a domain, or the like. Because Server Core doesn't have the Start button or GUI interface tools, however, this section covers the common tasks performed in completing the configuration of the Server Core system.

All these tasks are performed at the command prompt of the Server Core system from command-line tools included with Server Core.

Launching the Command Prompt in a Server Core Installation

Remember, the Start menu does not exist. Because of this, one of the most important tasks an administrator must understand when managing a Server Core installation is how to launch the command prompt. The following steps will assist you:

1. Click Ctrl+Alt+Delete.
2. Select Start Task Manager.
3. On the Windows Task Manager screen, select File, New Task (Run).
4. In the Create New Task dialog box, type **cmd.exe**, and then click OK.

Changing the Server Core Administrator's Password

Similar to deploying a regular Windows 2008 implementation, the administrator password is no longer assigned during the Server Core installation process. Therefore, the syntax to assign an administrator password is this:

```
Net user administrator *
```

After the command has been executed, you are prompted to type a password for the user. Enter the password, and then retype it for the confirmation process. It is a best practice to use a complex password when assigning passwords to the administrator account.

Changing the Server Core Machine Name

After the Server Core installation is complete, another common task is to change the machine name of the server. By default, Windows automatically generates and assigns a server name starting with LH and followed by a string of characters. The syntax to change the Server Core machine name follows:

```
netdom renamecomputer %computername% /newname:<NewComputerName>
```

When manipulating this syntax, replace the *<NewComputerName>* argument with the new machine name for the Server Core installation. Changing the server name to ServerCore is depicted in the following example:

```
netdom renamecomputer %computername% /newname:ServerCore
```

Assigning a Static IPV4 IP Address and DNS Settings

Another common Server Core management task is assigning an IP address, including the primary and secondary DNS settings. Before this task can be executed, you must run the following script to obtain and identify the names of the network interfaces installed on the server. This includes capturing the unique ID associated with each network interface. To display a list of network interfaces, including their respective unique IDs, run the following script:

```
netsh interface ipv4 show interfaces
```

The next step is to make a note of the network interface name and unique ID that you must change. The ID is located in the leftmost column and is referred to as Idx. This is depicted in the output of the `netsh interface ipv4 show interfaces` command, as displayed in Figure 4.10.

FIGURE 4.10   Reviewing the Idx ID for a network interface.

NOTE

If you plan to change the IP address settings on more than one interface, take note of all the interface names and Idx unique IDs.

Now that you have captured the names and IDs, use the following syntax to change the IP address for a desired interface.

```
netsh interface ipv4 set address name="<ID>" source=static address=<StaticIP>
mask=<SubnetMask> gateway=<DefaultGateway>
```

Replace the `ID` argument with the network interface name or `ID`. In addition, enter the static IP address, subnet mask, and default gateway in subsequent arguments. An example follows:

```
netsh interface ipv4 set address name="1" source=static address=192.168.115.10
mask=255.255.255.0 gateway=192.168.115.1.
```

The final step when configuring the network interface is to enter a primary and secondary DNS entry for the interface. Do this by using the following syntax:

```
netsh interface ipv4 add dnsserver name="<ID>" address=<DNSIP>index=1
```

The same command is used and repeated when entering more than one DNS entry. However, increment the index each time. When finalized, run `IP Config /all` to verify the IP address settings.

Adding the Server Core System to a Domain

The following script illustrates the basic syntax of how to add a Server Core system to a Windows domain:

```
Netdom join %computername% /domain:<domain> /userd:<domain>\<username> /passwordd:*
```

Input the domain name and supply the user account and password for an account that has permissions to add computers to the domain.

Enabling Remote Management and Remote Desktop to Server Core

Because the Server Core system can't have administration tools run directly on the system, you need to enable remote management so that the server can be remotely administered and managed. To enable remote management, enter the following:

```
netsh advfirewall firewall set rule group="Remote Admin" new enable=yes
```

If you want to enable the Remote Desktop function so that you can take control of the Hyper-V Administration console remotely, enter the following command:

```
cscript \windows\system32\scregedit.wsf /ar 0
cscript \windows\system32\scregedit.wsf /cs 0
```

Rebooting and Shutting Down a Server Core System

Even something as simple as shutting down or rebooting a Server Core system needs to be done from the command prompt because there is no Start button from which to choose to shut down or reboot the server. The command to reboot a Server Core system is as follows:

```
shutdown /r /t 0
```

The command to shut down a Server Core system is as follows:

```
shutdown /s /t 0
```

Installing Hyper-V Server Role on a Server Core System

The typical Windows server roles can be configured on a Server Core installation. Because this book is about the installation of Hyper-V, the command sequence to install the Hyper-V role on Server Core is as follows:

```
ocsetup Microsoft-Hyper-V
```

After you run this command, you are prompted to reboot the server. The server will then come up, and the Hyper-V role will have been installed. To add virtual guest sessions or administer the Hyper-V host system, you must go to another system that has the Hyper-V Administration tool on it and remotely administer the Hyper-V Server Core system.

Server Core Roles and Feature Installations

Now that the Hyper-V role installation process has been covered, this section covers the general server role installation process (for those interested in the process of adding other server roles to a Server Core system).

The following server roles are currently supported on a Server Core installation:

- ▶ Active Directory Domain Services
- ▶ Active Directory Lightweight Directory Services (AD LDS)
- ▶ Dynamic Host Configuration Protocol (DHCP) Server
- ▶ DNS Server
- ▶ File Services
- ▶ Hyper-V Virtualization
- ▶ Print Server
- ▶ Streaming Media Services
- ▶ Web Server (IIS)

The following are optional features that are also supported on a Server Core installation:

- ▶ Microsoft Failover Cluster
- ▶ Network Load Balancing
- ▶ Subsystem for UNIX-based Applications
- ▶ Windows Backup
- ▶ Multipath I/O
- ▶ Removable Storage Management
- ▶ Windows Bitlocker Drive Encryption
- ▶ Simple Network Management Protocol (SNMP)
- ▶ Windows Internet Naming Service (WINS)
- ▶ Telnet Client
- ▶ Quality of Service (QoS)

The OCSetup command-line program is responsible for setting up and configuring the server roles and features on a Server Core installation. You can configure the OCSetup command-line options using the following syntax:

```
ocsetup.exe [/?] [/h] [/help] component [/log:file] [/norestart] [/passive]
[/quiet] [/unattendfile:file] [/uninstall] [/x: parameter]
```

Use Table 4.2 to understand each of the options that are available when using the OCSetup command-line program.

TABLE 4.2   Available Command Options for OCSetup

Parameter	Description
/?, /h, /help	Explains all the options available for OCSetup
component	Represents the name of the component you plan on installing, such as DNS, DHCP, Web Server (IIS), and more
/log:file	Specifies the log file location if you do not want to take advantage of the default location
/norestart	Does not reboot the computer after the installation
/passive	Suppresses unnecessary noise and only includes progress status
/quiet	Does not require user interaction
/unattendfile:file	Requires additional configurations
/uninstall	Removes server components
/x: parameter	Supplies additional configuration parameters

Performing a Server Role Installation on a Server Core Installation

Table 4.3 outlines basic server role installation examples based on the use of the OCSetup command-line tool.

TABLE 4.3   Server Role Installation Command Lines with OCSetup

Server Role	Command
DNS Server role	start /w ocsetup DNS-Server-Core-Role
DHCP Server role	start /w ocsetup DHCPServerCore
File Server role	start /w ocsetup FRS-Infrastructure
Print Server role	Start /w ocsetup Printing-ServerCore-Role
Active Directory Lightweight Directory Server role	start /w ocsetup DirectoryServices-ADAM-ServerCore
Windows Deployment Server (Windows DS) role	start /w ocsetup Microsoft-Windows-Deployment-Services

The previous sections are a prelude to some of the common Server Core command-line arguments for installing and configuring elements on a Windows Server 2008 Server Core installation.

Summary

The Windows Server 2008 installation process is similar to those found in earlier versions of Windows. The Windows Server 2008 installation process is simpler, however, because certain things such as the server name, IP address, domain name, time zone, and so on are no longer prompted for during the installation. Instead, they are part of a post-installation process. This simplification enables administrators to start the installation process by just choosing the version of Windows 2008 they want to install on the server and selecting the disk subsystem on which to install Windows. Administrators can then come back 20 minutes later and the server will have gone through the entire installation process on its own. The administrator walks through the post-installation wizard to enter the server name, IP address, time zone, and other server specifics, and then the system is fully configured.

The new Windows Server Core installation has been an anticipated feature for the Windows 2008 family of operating systems and has been popular as the base installation for Hyper-V host servers. One reason for this is that the lack of a GUI on the virtual host means a significant decrease in the attack surface on the host system. Server Core installations meet today's administrator and organization needs by providing a way to use the Windows 2008 operating system with the fewest number of binaries, in the most highly secured fashion, while also reducing management overhead.

Best Practices

The following are best practices from this chapter:

- ▶ Verify that your hardware, devices, and drivers are supported by Windows Server 2008.

- ▶ As a Hyper-V virtualization host server, you need far more RAM, processor, and disk space than a normal "minimum requirement" server configuration. See Chapter 3 to properly size the Hyper-V server with the hardware requirements needed.

- ▶ Before beginning the installation of Windows 2008 on the server, make sure the system supports hardware-assisted virtualization through the use of an Intel EM64T or AMD64 processor.

- ▶ Only install the x64-bit version of Windows 2008 on the server; the 32-bit (x86) version of Windows 2008 does not support Hyper-V host virtualization.

- ▶ Considering installing either the Enterprise Edition or the Datacenter Edition of Windows 2008 (not the Standard Edition) if you plan to have three or more virtual guest sessions on the system (from the perspective of licensing cost under the Microsoft virtual server rights licensing policy).

- ▶ Use the Windows Server 2008 Initial Configuration Tasks Wizard to conduct post-installation tasks.

- ▶ Use Windows Server Core installations when the highest level of security is warranted.

- ▶ Use a consistent naming convention to name the servers and client machines.

- ▶ Use only Internet standard characters in your computer name. This includes the letters A–Z (upper- and lowercase), the numbers 0–9, and the hyphen (-).

- ▶ As soon as you complete the installation, rename the administrator account and assign a strong password, for the sake of security.

- ▶ Have the installation media and license keys needed for the installation of the host operating system handy when you are about to install the operating system on the server.

- ▶ Join the Hyper-V host to an Active Directory to take advantage of domain administration and management capabilities. If the Hyper-V host will be in a DMZ or nonsecure location, however, you may choose to keep the Hyper-V host as a stand-alone server.

- ▶ Enable Remote Management on a Server Core system so that you can remotely manage and administer the server.

4

Installing a Guest Session on Hyper-V

So far in this book, we have gone through the process of planning the migration of physical servers to Hyper-V virtual guests (Chapter 2, "Best Practices at Planning, Prototyping, Migrating, and Deploying Windows 2008 Hyper-V"), sized and scaled our host server to have enough memory and processing capability to support our planned virtual guest sessions (Chapter 3, "Planning, Sizing, and Architecting a Hyper-V Environment"), and we have installed the core Windows 2008 operating system and added the Hyper-V role to the server (Chapter 4, "Installing Windows 2008 Server and the Hyper-V Role"). The next step is to start building out guest sessions.

This chapter covers the creation of new guest sessions on Hyper-V. Guest sessions on Hyper-V can be both Windows images and non-Windows (Linux) images. For organizations that are looking to migrate existing physical servers or convert existing virtual server sessions to Hyper-V virtual sessions, that is covered in Chapter 10, "Creating Guest Images from Existing Production and Virtual Systems." This chapter just focuses on the creation of net new guest images from installation media.

Choosing the Guest Session Operating System

Although you can effectively boot and try to install any operating system on Hyper-V and can frequently get to the point where the operating system will work under Hyper-V, Microsoft officially supports only specific versions of operating systems as guest sessions.

The operating systems that Microsoft supports as guest sessions under Windows 2008 Hyper-V are as follows:

▶ Windows Server 2008 x86 and x64

▶ Windows Server 2003 SP2 or higher x86 and x64

▶ Windows 2000 Server with SP4 and Windows 2000 Advanced Server with SP4

▶ Windows Vista x86 and x64

▶ Windows XP SP2 or later x86 and x64

▶ SUSE Linux Enterprise Server 10 SP1 or later x86 and x64

NOTE

When attempting to install an operating system that may not be officially supported by Microsoft, you might find that a network adapter driver, hard drive driver, audio/sound driver, or the like is not supported, and either the operating system will fail to complete the installation or it will appear to install correctly, but the guest session has no support to communicate externally because a network driver was not available to support the guest session. Many times, legacy drivers will work, and a guest image will work fine. Again, however, Microsoft technically only supports the operating systems they state that they support for guest sessions.

Installing a Windows-Based Guest Operating System Session

Assuming you have a Windows 2008 server with the Hyper-V installed and running, the guest operating system installation is merely walking through the wizard-driven installation process. The Installation Wizard enables the administrator to configure settings for the guest session, and to begin the installation of the guest operating system software itself. A guest session could be a server-based session running something like Windows Server 2003 or Windows Server 2008, or a client-based session running something like Windows XP or Windows Vista. The installation of a non-Windows-based guest operating system like Linux is covered in the section "Installing a Linux-Based Guest Operating System Session" later in this chapter.

Gathering the Components Needed for a Windows-Based Guest Session

When creating a guest operating system, administrators need to make sure they have all the components required to begin the installation. The components needed are as follows:

▶ **Operating system media**—A copy of the operating system is required for the installation of the guest image. The media can be either a DVD or an ISO image of the media disc itself.

▶ **License key**—During the installation of the operating system software, if you are normally prompted to enter in the license key for the operating system, you should have a copy of the license key available.

Other things you should do before starting to install a guest operating system on the virtual server system include the following:

▶ **Guest session configuration settings**—You will be prompted to answer several core guest session configuration setting options, such as how much RAM you want to allocate for the guest session, how much disk space you want to allocate for the guest image, and so on. Either jump ahead to the next section on "Beginning the Installation of the Windows-Based Guest Session" so that you can gather the information you'll need to answer the questions you'll be asked, or be prepared to answer the questions during the installation process.

▶ **Host server readiness**—If you will be preplanning the answers to the questions that you'll be asked, make sure that the host system has enough RAM, disk space, and so on to support the addition of your guest session to the virtual server system. If your requirements exceed the physical capacity of the server, stop and add more resources (memory, disk space, and so on) to the server before beginning the installation of the guest operating system.

Beginning the Installation of the Windows-Based Guest Session

Guest session installation follow the same process whether for Windows Server 2003, Windows Server 2008, Windows XP, or Windows Vista. So, the process is covered here just once. Because the process of installing any Windows-based guest operating system is the same, the following procedures are the same for any guest session installation.

To begin the process of installing a Windows-based guest operating system, launch the Hyper-V Administration console:

1. Click Start, All Programs, Administrative Tools, and then choose Hyper-V Management for the tool to launch.

2. Click Virtualization Services to see the virtual servers to which you are connected.

3. Click the name of one of the virtual servers listed to see the virtual machines and actions available for the confirmation of the server system. By default, the Hyper-V MMC will have the local virtual server system listed, as shown in Figure 5.1.

With the Hyper-V Administration tool up on your screen, you can now begin the process of installing a guest operating system. Launch the guest operating system Installation Wizard by doing the following:

1. From the Actions pane, choose New, Virtual Machine.

2. Click Next to continue past the initial Welcome screen.

3. Give your virtual machine a name that will be descriptive of the virtual guest session you are creating, such as **AD Global Catalog Server**, or **Exchange 2007 Client Access Server 1**, or **ISA Proxy Server**.

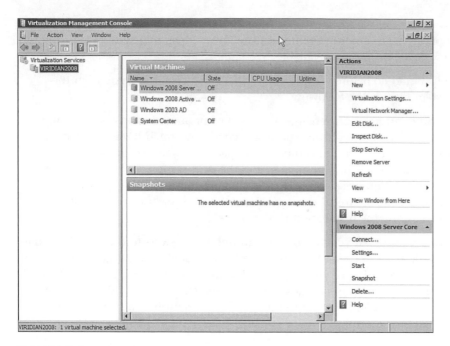

FIGURE 5.1   Virtualization Management Console.

4. If you had set the default virtual machine folder location where guest images are stored, the new image for this virtual machine will be placed in that default folder. However, if you need to select a different location where the image files should be stored, click Create a New Folder for the Virtual Machine Files, and select Browse to choose an existing disk directory or to create a new directory where the image file for this guest session should be stored. Click Next to continue.

5. Enter in the amount of RAM you want allocated to this guest image in megabytes (so 2GB should be 2048), and then click Next.

6. Choose the network segment to which you want this guest image to be initially connected. This would be an internal or external segment created in the "Managing Host Server, Virtual Switch, and Disk Settings" sections of Chapter 6. Click Next.

NOTE

You can choose Not Connected during this virtual machine creation process and change the network segment option at a later date.

7. The next option allows you to create a new virtual hard disk or use an existing virtual hard disk for the guest image file. Creating a new virtual hard disk creates a VHD disk image in the directory you choose. By default, a dynamic virtual disk image size setting is set to 127GB. The actual file itself will only be the size needed to run the image (potentially 4GB or 8GB to start) and will dynamically grow up to

the size noted in this setting. Alternatively, you can choose an existing hard disk image you might have already created (including an older image you might have created in Microsoft Virtual Server 2005), or you can choose to select a hard disk image later. The options for this configuration are shown in Figure 5.2. Click Next to continue.

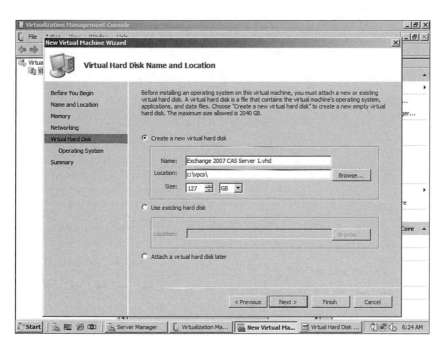

FIGURE 5.2   Virtual Hard Disk creation or selection option.

8. The next option, shown in Figure 5.3, allows for the installation of an operating system on the disk image you created in the preceding step. You can choose to install an operating system at a later time, install an operating system from a bootable CD/DVD or ISO image file, install an operating system from a floppy disk image, or install an operating system from a network-based installation server (such as Remote Installation Service [RIS]). Typically, operating system source discs are on either a physical disc or ISO image file, and choosing a CD or DVD or an associated ISO image file will allow for the operating system to be installed on the guest image. Select your option, and then click Next to continue.

9. Review the summary of the options you have selected and either click Previous to go back and make changes or click Finish if the settings you've chosen are fine. There is a Start the Virtual Machine Once This Wizard Is Finished check box that you can choose that will launch the guest session and begin the guest session installation process. If you need to make changes to the settings, you would not want to select this option yet—just click Finish so that you can make configuration setting changes and start the installation process after that.

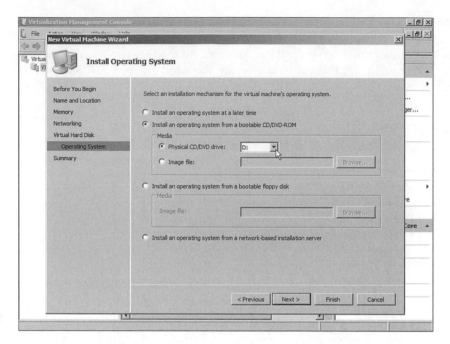

FIGURE 5.3   Choosing the installation mechanism for the guest session.

Completing the Installation of the Windows-Based Guest Session

The guest operating system installation will proceed to install just like the process of installing the operating system on a physical system. Typically, at the end of an operating system installation, the guest session restarts and brings the session to a logon prompt. Log on to the guest operating system and configure the guest operating system as you would any other server system. This typically has you do things such as the following:

1. Change the system name to a name that you want the virtual server to be. For many versions of operating systems, you will be prompted to enter the name of the system during the installation process.

2. Configure the guest session with an appropriate IP address. This might be DHCP issued; however, if you are building a server system, a static IP address is typically recommended.

3. Join the system to an Active Directory domain (assuming the system will be part of a managed Active Directory Domain Services environment with centralized administration).

4. Download and apply the latest patches and updates on the guest session to confirm that all patches and updates have been installed and applied to the system.

The installation of the guest operating system typically requires yet another reboot, and then the operating system will be installed and operational.

Installing a Linux-Based Guest Operating System Session

The installation of a Linux-based guest session is a little different from installing a Windows-based guest session in that the best way to install the Linux-based guest session is to install the Linux integration components at the time of the installation of the operating system. Although it is not imperative that you install the Linux integration components at the time of installation, if you do install the components at the time of installation, you get better integrated driver support for the guest Linux session.

Two of the main components in the Linux integration components are

1. **Driver support for network and storage controllers**—The Linux integration components include synthetic controller support for network adapters and storage adapters optimized specifically for Hyper-V. These special drivers take advantage of the VMBus in Hyper-V that provides high-speed communications and connectivity of network and storage device guest sessions.

2. **Hypercall adapter**—In addition, the Linux integration components include a hypercall adapter layer under the Linux kernel that translates Xen-specific virtualization function calls to Hyper-V hypercalls. This provides additional performance improvements for Linux-based guest sessions.

Assuming you have a Windows 2008 server with the Hyper-V installed and running, the Linux-based guest operating system installation follows a structured step-by-step installation procedure. The Installation Wizard enables the administrator to configure settings for the guest session and to begin the installation of the guest operating system software itself.

Gathering the Components Needed for a Linux-Based Guest Session

When creating a guest operating system, administrators need to make sure they have all the components required to begin the installation. The components needed are as follows:

▶ **Operating system media**—A copy of the operating system is required for the installation of the guest image. The media could be either a DVD or an ISO image of the media disc itself.

▶ **License key**—During the installation of the operating system software, if you are normally prompted to enter in the license key for the operating system, you should have a copy of the license key available.

Other things you should do before starting to install a guest operating system on the virtual server system include the following:

▶ **Guest session configuration settings**—You will be prompted to answer several core guest session configuration setting options, such as how much RAM you want to allocate for the guest session, how much disk space you want to allocate for the guest image, and so on. Either jump ahead to the next section on "Beginning the Installation of the Linux-Based Guest Session" so that you can gather up the information you'll need to answer the questions you'll be asked, or be prepared to answer the questions during the installation process.

▶ **Host server readiness**—If you will be preplanning the answers to the questions that you'll be asked, make sure that the host system has enough RAM, disk space, and so on to support the addition of your guest session to the virtual server system. If your requirements exceed the physical capacity of the server, stop and add more resources (memory, disk space, and so on) to the server before beginning the installation of the guest operating system.

Beginning the Installation of the Linux-Based Guest Session

The installation of the Linux-based guest session uses the following procedures. To begin the process of installing a Linux-based guest operating system, launch the Hyper-V Administration console:

1. Click Start, All Programs, Administrative Tools, and then choose Hyper-V Management for the tool to launch.

2. Click Virtualization Services to see the virtual servers to which you are connected.

3. Click the name of one of the virtual servers listed to see the virtual machines and actions available for the confirmation of the server system. By default, the Hyper-V MMC will have the local virtual server system listed.

With the Hyper-V Administration tool up on your screen, you can now begin the process of installing a Linux-based guest operating system. Launch the guest operating system Installation Wizard by doing the following:

1. From the Actions pane, choose New, Virtual Machine.

2. Click Next to continue past the initial Welcome screen.

3. Give your virtual machine a name that will be descriptive of the virtual guest session you are creating, such as `Apache Web Server`, or `SMTP Mailhost`, or the like.

4. If you had set the default virtual machine folder location where guest images are stored, the new image for this virtual machine will be placed in that default folder. However, if you need to select a different location where the image files should be stored, click Create a New Folder for the Virtual Machine Files, and select Browse to choose an existing disk directory or to create a new directory where the image file for this guest session should be stored. Click Next to continue.

5. Enter in the amount of RAM you want allocated to this guest image in megabytes (so 2GB should be 2048), and then click Next.

6. Choose the network segment to which you want this guest image to be initially connected. This would be an internal or external segment created the "Managing Host Server, Virtual Switch, and Disk Settings" section of Chapter 6. Click Next.

NOTE

You can choose Not Connected during this virtual machine creation process and change the network segment option at a later date.

7. The next option allows you to create a new virtual hard disk or use an existing virtual hard disk for the guest image file. Creating a new virtual hard disk creates a VHD disk image in the directory you choose. By default, a dynamic virtual disk image size setting is set to 127GB. The actual file itself will only be the size needed to run the image (potentially 4GB or 8GB to start) and will dynamically grow up to the sized noted in this setting. Alternatively, you can choose an existing hard disk image you might have already created (including an older image you might have created in Microsoft Virtual Server 2005), or you can choose to select a hard disk image later. Click Next to continue.

8. The next option allows for the installation of an operating system on the disk image you created in the preceding step. You can choose to install an operating system at a later time, install an operating system from a bootable CD/DVD or ISO image file, install an operating system from a floppy disk image, or install an operating system from a network-based installation server (such as RIS). Typically, operating system source discs are on either a physical disc or ISO image file, and choosing a CD or DVD or an associated ISO image file will allow for the operating system to be installed on the guest image. Select your option, and then click Next to continue.

9. Review the summary of the options you have selected and either click Previous to go back and make changes or click on Finish if the settings you've chosen are fine. There is a Start the Virtual Machine Once This Wizard Is Finished check box that you can choose that will launch the guest session and begin the guest session installation process. If you need to make changes to the settings, you would not want to select this option yet—just click Finish so that you can make configuration setting changes and start the installation process after that.

Completing the Installation of the Linux-Based Guest Session (x86)

The guest operating system installation will proceed to install just like the process of installing the operating system on a physical system. When installing the Linux-based guest session, make sure the development packages include the compilers necessary to install the Linux integration components.

Typically, at the end of an operating system installation, the guest session restarts and brings the session to a logon prompt. Log on to the guest operating system and configure the guest operating system as you would any other server system. From a command prompt, mount the Linux integration components media to gain access to the files on the media to complete the installation of the files. The installation process is as follows:

1. Run the rpm command to install the kernel drivers. Check the actual name of the RPM file of the installation media you are using as the version will likely vary based on when you downloaded the Linux integration components. However, for this example, the RPM filename is kernel-xen-2.6.16.46-0.12.i586.rpm for the x86 version. Therefore, run the following command:
   ```
   $  rpm -ivh /mnt/cdrom/suse/i586/kernel-xen-2.6.16.46-0.12.i586.rpm
   ```

2. Dismount the Linux integration tools media and mount the LinuxIC.iso file.

3. Copy the Linux integration components to the virtual machine using the command similar to this:

```
$ mkdir /opt/linux_ic
$ cp /mnt/cdrom/* /opt/linux_ic -R
```

4. Install the hypercall adapter driver inside the virtual guest session. Run the following command:

```
$ /opt/linux_ic/setup.pl x2v /boot/grub/menu.lst
```

5. Reboot the Linux guest session.

6. After the Linux guest session restarts, the network and storage drivers need to be installed. To install the drivers, run the following command:

```
$ /opt/linux_ic/setup.pl drivers
```

The installation of the guest operating system typically requires yet another reboot, and then the operating system will be installed and operational.

Completing the Installation of the Linux-Based Guest Session (x64)

The guest operating system installation process for an x64 system is slightly different because the x64 hypercall adapter needs to be patched, prepared, and then installed, requiring additional steps.

At the end of the x64 operating system installation, the guest session restarts and brings the session to a logon prompt. Log on to the guest operating system and configure the guest operating system as you would any other server system. From a command prompt, mount the Linux integration components media to gain access to the files on the media to complete the installation of the files. The installation process is as follows:

1. Run the rpm command to install the kernel drivers. Check the actual name of the RPM file of the installation media you are using as the version will likely vary based on when you downloaded the Linux integration components. However, for this example, the RPM filename is kernel-xen-2.6.16.46-0.12.x86_64.rpm for the x64 version. Therefore, run the following command:

```
$  rpm –ivh /mnt/cdrom/suse/i586/kernel-xen-2.6.16.46-0.12.x86_64.rpm
```

2. Dismount the Linux integration tools media and mount the LinuxIC.iso file.

3. Copy the Linux integration components to the virtual machine using the command similar to this:

```
$ mkdir /opt/linux_ic
$ cp /mnt/cdrom/* /opt/linux_ic -R
```

4. Install the Linux kernel source code by launching YaST (Control Center, Administrative Settings, Software Management).

5. In the Filter drop-down box, choose Package Groups.

6. Install the Development | Source | Kernel-Source package group.

7. Copy and apply the hypercall patch to the kernel source code by doing the following:

```
$ cd /usr/src/linux-2.6.16.46-0.12
$ cp /opt/linux_ic/patch/x2v-x64-sles.patch
```

```
$ patch -l -p1 < x2v-x64-sles.patch
$ cp /boot/config-2.6.16.46-0.12-xen ./.config
$ make oldconfig
$ make vmlinuz
$ cp vmlinuz /boot/vmlinuz-2.6.46-0.12-xen
```

8. Install the x2v hypercall adapter by doing the following:
```
$ cd /opt/linux_ic
$ perl setup.pl x2v /boot/grub/menu.lst
```

9. Reboot the Linux guest session.

10. After the Linux guest session restarts, the network and storage drivers need to be installed. To install the drivers, run the following command:
```
$ /opt/linux_ic/setup.pl drivers
```

The installation of the guest operating system typically requires yet another reboot, and then the operating system will be installed and operational.

Modifying Guest Session Configuration Settings

After a guest session has been installed, whether it is a Microsoft Windows server guest session, a Microsoft Windows client guest session, or a guest session running a non-Windows operating system, the host configuration settings for the guest session can be changed. Common changes to a guest session include things such as the following:

▶ Adding or limiting the RAM of the guest session

▶ Changing network settings of the guest session

▶ Mounting a CD/DVD image or mounting a physical CD/DVD disc

Adding or Limiting the RAM of the Guest Session

A common configuration change that is made for a guest session is to increase or decrease the amount of memory allocated to the guest session. The default memory allocated to the system frequently is fine for a basic system configuration; however, with the addition of applications to the guest session, there might be a need to increase the memory. As long as the host server system has enough memory to allocate additional memory to the guest session, adding memory to a guest session is a simple task.

To add memory to the guest session, do the following:

1. From the Server Manager console or from the Virtualization MMC snap-in, click to select the guest session for which you want to change the allocated memory.

2. Right-click the guest session name, and choose Settings.

3. Click Memory and enter in the amount of RAM you want allocated for this guest session (in megabytes).

4. Click OK when you have finished.

NOTE

You cannot change the allocated RAM on a running virtual guest session. The guest session must be shut down first, memory reallocated to the image, and then the guest image booted for the new memory allocation to take effect.

Changing Network Settings for the Guest Session

Another common configuration change made to a guest session is to change the network setting for the guest session. An administrator of a virtual server might choose to have each guest session connected directly to the network backbone just as if the guest session had a network adapter connected to the backbone, or the network administrator might choose to set up an isolated network just for the guest sessions. The configuration of the internal and external network segments that the administrator can configure the guest sessions to connect to is covered in the "Managing Host Server, Virtual Switch, and Disk Setting," section of Chapter 6.

The common configuration methods of the virtual network configurations can be broken down into two groups, as follows:

▶ **Direct addressing**—The guest sessions can connect directly to the backbone of the network to which the virtual server host system is attached. In this instance, an administrator would configure an external connection in the Virtual Network Manager and have an IP address on that external segment.

▶ **Isolated network**—If the administrator wants to keep the guest sessions isolated off of the network backbone, the administrator can set up an internal connection in the Virtual Network Manager, and the guest sessions would have an IP address of a segment common to the other guest sessions on the host system. In this case, the virtual server acts as a network switch connecting the guest sessions together.

NOTE

To connect the internal network segment with the external network segment, a guest session can be configured as a router or gateway between the internal network and external network.

Mounting a Physical CD/DVD Image or Mounting a CD/DVD Image File

When installing software on a guest session of a virtual server system, the administrator either inserts a CD or DVD into the drive of the physical server and accesses the disc from the guest session or mounts an ISO image file of the disc media.

To access a physical CD or DVD disc or to mount an image of a CD or DVD, do the following:

1. From the Server Manager console or from the Hyper-V MMC snap-in, click to select the guest session for which you want to change the CD or DVD.

2. Right-click the guest session name, and choose Settings.

3. Click DVD Drive and choose Physical CD/DVD Drive if you want to mount a disc in the physical drive of the host system, or click Image File and browse for the ISO image file you want to mount as a disc image.

4. Click OK when you have finished.

Other Settings to Modify for a Guest Session Configuration

Other settings can be changed for a guest session. These options can be modified by going into the Settings option of the guest session and making changes. These other settings include the following:

▶ **BIOS**—This setting allows for the selection of boot order on the guest machine to boot in an order that can include floppy, CD, IDE (disk), or network boot.

▶ **Processor**—Hyper-V provides the ability to allocate core processors to the guest image, so a guest image can have up to four core processors allocated for each session. In addition, resource control can be weighted between guest sessions by allocating system resource priority to key guest server sessions versus other guest sessions.

▶ **IDE Controller**—The guest session initially has a single virtual hard drive associated with it. Additional virtual hard drives can be added to a virtual guest session.

▶ **SCSI Controller**—A virtual SCSI controller can be associated with a virtual guest session, too, providing different drive configuration options for the different drive configurations.

▶ **COM Ports**—Virtual communication ports such as COM1 or COM2 can be associated with specific named pipes for input and output of information.

Launching a Hyper-V Guest Session

After a Hyper-V guest session has been created, and the settings have been properly modified to meet the expected needs of the organization, the virtual guest session can now be launched and run. Decisions need to be made whether you want the guest session to automatically launch as soon as the server is booted, or whether you want to manually launch a guest session. In addition, a decision needs to be made on the sequence in which guest sessions should be launched so that systems that are prerequisites to other sessions come up first. As an example, you'd want a global catalog server session and DHCP server session to come up before an application server that logs on and authenticates to Active Directory comes online and needs to authenticate to Active Directory before the server service begins.

Automatically Launching a Guest Session

One option for launching and loading guest sessions is to have the guest session boot right after the physical server completes the boot cycle. This is typically the preferred option if a guest session is core to the network infrastructure of a network (such as a domain controller or host server system) so that in the event of a physical server reboot, the virtual guest sessions boot up automatically, too. It would not be convenient to have to manually boot each virtual server session every time the physical server is rebooted.

The option for setting the boot option for a virtual session is in the configuration settings for each guest session.

To change the boot action, do the following:

1. From the Server Manager console or from the Hyper-V MMC snap-in, right-click the virtual machine for which you want to change the setup option, and select Settings.

2. In the Management section of the settings, click Automatic Start Action.

3. You are provided three options, as shown in Figure 5.4, of what to do with this virtual guest session upon boot of the physical server. Either click Nothing (which would require a manual boot of the guest session), click Automatically Start If It Was Running When the Service Stopped, or click Always Start This Virtual Machine Automatically. To set the virtual session to automatically start after the physical server comes up, choose the Always Start This Virtual Machine Automatically option.

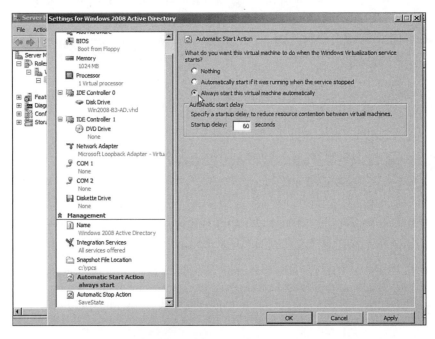

FIGURE 5.4   Automatic start actions.

4. Also on this setting is the ability to have an *automatic start delay*. This allows you to sequence the boot of image files by having some images take longer to automatically start than others. Click OK to save these settings.

Manually Launching a Guest Session

Another option for guest session boot is to not have a guest session automatically start after a physical server boots. This is typically the preferred option if a guest session will be part of a demonstration or test server where the administrator of the system wants to control which guest sessions are automatically launched, and which sessions need to be manually launched. It would not be convenient to have a series of demo or test sessions automatically boot every time the system is booted. The administrator of the system would typically want to choose to boot guest sessions.

To set the boot action to manually launch a guest session, do the following:

1. From the Server Manager console or from the Hyper-V MMC snap-in, right-click the virtual machine for which you want to change the setup option, and select Settings.
2. In the Management section of the settings, click Automatic Start Action.
3. When provided the three options of what to do with this virtual guest session upon boot of the physical server, either click Nothing (which would require a manual boot of the guest session), click Automatically Start If It Was Running When the Service Stopped, or click Always Start This Virtual Machine Automatically. Choose the Nothing option and the session will need to be manually started.

Save State of a Guest Session

In Windows 2008 Hyper-V, there are two concepts for saving guest images, one being snapshots and the other being a saved state. At any time, an administrator can select a guest session and choose Action, Save State. This Save State function is similar to a Hibernate mode on a desktop client system. It saves the image into a file with the option of bringing the saved state image file back to the state the image was in before being saved.

Installing the Windows Guest Session Integration Tools

Hyper-V provides integration tools that are components and drivers that get added into the guest session of the operating system. For Linux-based guest sessions, the Linux integration components were installed as part of the installation of the operating system. However, for Windows server and client guest sessions, the integration tools are installed after the operating system has been installed. The Windows integration tools include specific drivers for the network adapter, hard drive controller drivers, sound drivers, and the like. Instead of using legacy drivers, the drivers with the integration tools are optimized to provide better performance and better integration of the guest operating system as a virtual guest session.

Microsoft provides integration tools for the core operating systems they support as guest sessions. Additional integration tools will be released by Microsoft as they add support for other guest sessions.

Installing the Windows Integration Tools

The integration tools for Windows are installed from a virtual CD that is mounted when you select to install the integration tools on the guest session. The Windows integration tools require the following operating systems:

▶ Windows Server 2008 x86 and x64

▶ Windows Server 2003 SP2 or later x86 and x64

▶ Windows Vista x86

▶ Windows XP SP3 or later x86

To install the Windows integration tools, do the following:

1. Start the virtual Windows guest session that you want to install the integration tools onto.

2. Log on as an administrator to the guest session, effectively an administrator that has the security rights to install drivers and applications onto the guest session (typically a local or domain administrator).

3. On the guest session window, choose Action, Install Integration Services Setup Disk, as shown in Figure 5.5.

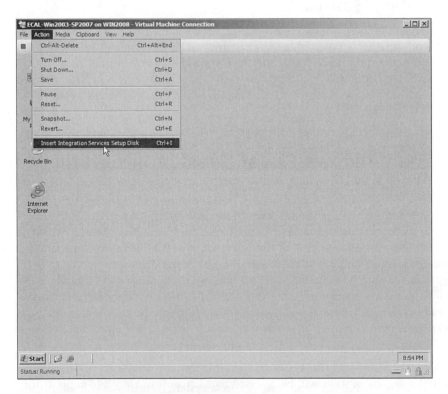

FIGURE 5.5   Adding the integration tools.

4. Within the Windows guest session, you will be prompted to launch the integration tools installation utility. Click the installation utility to begin the installation.

5. Reboot the guest session, and the integration tools will now be activated.

What you'll find with the integration tools is that the mouse no longer gets "captured," nor does it have to be "released" as required before the integration tools were installed. With the integration tools installed, the mouse will have control of the guest session when the mouse is within the guest session window, and the mouse will control host session screens when the mouse is outside of a guest session window.

Using Snapshots of Guest Operating System Sessions

A highly versatile function in Windows 2008 Hyper-V is the option to create a snapshot of a guest session. A snapshot in Windows Hyper-V uses Microsoft Volume Shadow Copy Service (VSS) technology, which captures an image of a file on a server—in this case, the file is the VHD image of the virtual server itself. At any point in time in the future, the snapshot can be used for recovery.

Snapshots for Image Rollback

One common use of a guest image snapshot is to roll back an image to a previous state. This is frequently done with guest images used for demonstration purposes, or test labs where a scenario is tested to see the results and compared with identical tests of other scenarios, or for the purpose of preparing for a software upgrade or migration.

For the case of a guest image used for demonstration purposes, a user might run through a demo of a software program where he adds information, deletes information, makes software changes, or otherwise modifies information in the software on the guest image. Instead of having to go back and delete the changes, or rebuilding the image from scratch to do the demo again, with a snapshot the user can just roll the image back to the snapshot that was available before the changes were made to the image.

Image rollback has been successfully used for training purposes where an employee runs through a process, then rolls back the image so that he can run through the same process all over again, repeating the process on the same base image but without previous installations or configurations.

In network infrastructures, a snapshot is helpful when an organization applies a patch or update to a server, or a software upgrade is performed and problems occur; the administrator can simply roll the image back to the point prior to the start of the upgrade or migration.

Snapshots for Guest Session Server Fault Tolerance

Snapshots are commonly used in business environments for the purpose of fault tolerance or disaster recovery. A well-timed snapshot right before a system failure can help an organization roll their server back to the point right before the server failed or problem occurred. Instead of waiting hours to restore a server from tape, the activation of a snapshot image is nothing more than choosing the snapshot and selecting to start the guest image. When the guest image starts up, it is in the state that the image was at the time the snapshot was created.

Creating a Snapshot of a Guest Image

Snapshots are easy to create. To create a snapshot, do the following:

1. From the Server Manager console or from the Hyper-V MMC snap-in, click to select the guest session for which you want to create a snapshot.

2. Right-click the guest session name, and choose Snapshot. A snapshot of the image will immediately be taken of the guest image, and the snapshot will show up in the Snapshots pane, as shown in Figure 5.6.

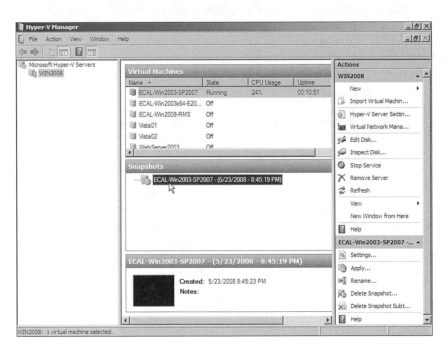

FIGURE 5.6   Viewing snapshots of a guest server.

Rolling Back a Guest Image to a Previous Snapshot Image

The term used in Windows 2008 Hyper-V to roll back an image is *applying* a snapshot to an existing image. When an image is rolled back, the image currently running has the snapshot information applied to the image, thus bringing the image back to an earlier configuration state. To apply a snapshot, do the following:

1. From the Server Manager console or from the Hyper-V MMC snap-in, click the snapshot to which you want to revert the running guest image.

2. Right-click the snapshot image and choose Apply. The configuration state of the image will immediately be reverted to the state of the image when the snapshot was taken.

> **NOTE**
>
> By default, the name of the snapshot image takes on the date and time the image was created. As an example, if the image is called Windows 2008 IIS, an image taken on April 26, 2008 at 6:19 a.m. will show up as Windows 2008 IIS-20080426-061900.

Reverting a Snapshot Session

When working with snapshots, if you snapshot a session and then apply an older session snapshot to the current session, to effectively undo the rollback choose Action, Revert to bring the server back to the state it was in before the rollback had occurred.

Summary

The installation of a guest session in Windows 2008 Hyper-V is nothing more than running an Installation Wizard that provides prompts to specify memory, processor, disk, and other resources that'll be allocated for the guest session. Then you just insert the guest session operating system and walk through the installation procedure of the operating system.

Hyper-V supports the installation of Windows 2003 Server, Windows 2008 Server, Windows Vista, Windows XP, and non-Windows clients such as SUSE Linux Enterprise Server 10.

The process of installing guest sessions, whether Windows or non-Windows, is the same. After a guest session has been installed, the integration tools for the operating system can be installed on the system. These provide better drivers for disk, network, audio, and the like. The integration tools are available for the supported guest operating systems and provide better mouse control and switching between guest and host sessions on keyboard and the mouse.

This chapter focused on the new installation of a guest operating system. For the conversion of existing physical or virtual sessions to a Hyper-V virtual guest session, see Chapter 10, "Creating Guest Images from Existing Production and Virtual Systems."

Best Practices

The following are best practices from this chapter:

▶ Select the guest operating system you want to install on Hyper-V from the list of operating systems supported by Microsoft on Hyper-V.

▶ Refer to Chapter 3 to properly size the Hyper-V host server to accept the amount of resources required for the guest sessions.

▶ Refer to Chapter 4 to properly install the Hyper-V host role on a Windows Server 2008 system, whether that is a full server configuration or a server running Windows 200 Server Core.

▶ Have the installation media and license keys needed for the installation of the guest operating system handy when you are about to install the guest operating system session.

▶ Apply all patches and updates on guest sessions soon after installing the guest operating system, just as you would for the installation of updates on physical systems.

▶ For Microsoft Windows guest sessions, install the Windows integration tools to improve the use and operation of the guest session.

▶ For SUSE Linux guest sessions, install the Linux integration tools to improve the use and operation of the guest session.

▶ After installing the guest session and its associated applications, confirm whether the memory of the guest session is enough, and adjust the memory of the guest session accordingly to optimize the performance of the guest session.

▶ Allocate enough disk space to perform snapshots of images so that the disk subsystem can handle both the required guest image and the associated snapshots of the guest session.

▶ Consider using snapshots before applying major patches, updates, or upgrades to an image session to allow for a rollback to the original image.

▶ Set a guest session to automatically launch if the guest session is a live server on the network; that way, the Hyper-V host reboots, and the guest session will start soon after the Hyper-V host has restarted.

PART III

Administering and Maintaining Hyper-V Host Services

IN THIS PART

6

Managing, Administering, and Maintaining a Hyper-V Host Server

Hyper-V host systems are the heart of an IT infrastructure that supports several other virtual guest sessions running on the hosts. These host servers need to be managed and maintained to keep businesses application running optimally. Hyper-V host server management and maintenance help maximize investment in infrastructure and productivity. It also keep the IT infrastructure running effectively and efficiently to boost availability and reliability of the guest sessions.

Windows Server 2008 and Hyper-V bring many new tools and features to help keep the servers managed and maintained. These tools include the Hyper-V Administration console and Windows 2008 Server Manager that provide improved configuration and better auditing of servers through the isolation of roles and features. In addition, they provide better remote management and a slew of other capabilities.

Server management entails many different tasks, including administering and supervising servers based on functional roles, proactively monitoring the network environment, keeping track of activity, and implementing solid change-control practices. These management functions for Windows 2008 and Hyper-V can be performed both locally and remotely.

As system workloads, capacities, and usage change in the environment, Hyper-V host systems and guest sessions need to be maintained so that they operate as efficiently as possible. Without such maintenance, the systems become more susceptible to causing slower response times and decreased reliability. Efforts to maintain those systems should be made periodically to avoid any inefficiency. This chapter covers best practices to maintain and manage a Windows 2008 environment.

Becoming Familiar with the Hyper-V Administration Console

After Hyper-V has been installed on a Windows 2008 host server, the Hyper-V Administration console is added to the Administrative Tools on the server. The Hyper-V Administration console has several configuration options and settings available to be configured that can be applied to a single guest session or applied to all guest sessions on the server.

Launching the Hyper-V Administration Console

To open the Hyper-V Administration console, there are two ways to access the configuration options. One way is to the use the Server Manager tool and administer the host server through Server Manager. The other option is to launch the freestanding Microsoft Management Console (MMC) to perform administrative tasks for the host system.

> **NOTE**
>
> The functions and settings between the Server Manager console and the standalone MMC application are the same. Administrators who manage several server roles tend to use the Server Manager console because they have access to more than just the Virtualization role to manage. They can also manage DNS, Terminal Services, Network Policy Server, and other roles that might apply to their job. For those who do nothing but administer Windows virtualization systems, they might choose the freestanding Hyper-V Administration console application for administering and managing just Windows virtual server systems.

Using the Server Manager Tool to Manage Hyper-V Systems

For administrators who want to manage their Hyper-V systems from a centralized console, the Server Manager tool provides a common administrative interface for all the server roles installed on a particular system. To start the Server Manager tool to view and edit Hyper-V settings, complete the following steps:

1. Click Start and then click Run.

2. In the Run dialog box, enter **ServerManager.msc**, and click OK. This will start the Server Manager application if it is not already running on the system.

3. Expand the Roles section of the tree by clicking the plus sign (+).

4. Expand the Hyper-V branch of the tree, and expand the Virtualization Services branch of the tree, as shown in Figure 6.1.

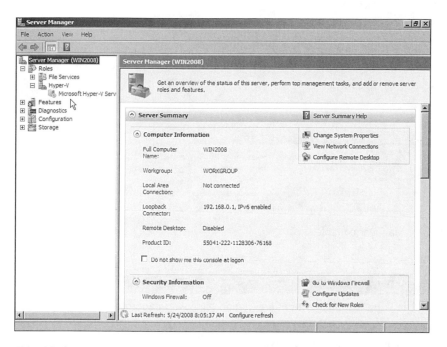

FIGURE 6.1   Windows 2008 Server Manager console.

Using the Hyper-V MMC Tool to Manage Hyper-V Systems

Administrators who want to manage their Hyper-V systems from a dedicated console just for Hyper-V administration should use the Hyper-V Administration tool. To start the Hyper-V Administration tool, follow these steps:

1. Click Start, All Programs, Administrative Tools, and then choose Hyper-V Manager for the tool to launch.

2. Click Microsoft Hyper-V Servers to see the virtual servers to which you are connected.

3. Click the name of one of the virtual servers listed to see the virtual machines and actions available for the confirmation of the server system. By default, the Hyper-V MMC will have the local virtual server system listed, as shown in Figure 6.2.

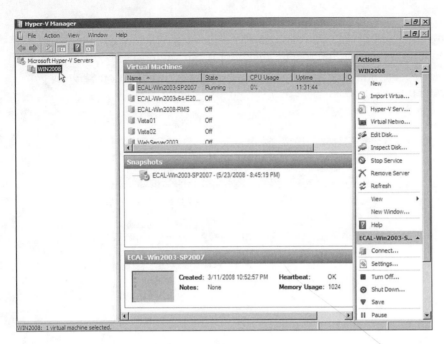

FIGURE 6.2   Hyper-V Manager console.

NOTE

If you want to run the Hyper-V Manager from a command line, you can enter the following:

```
c:\Program Files\Hyper-V\vmconnect.exe
```

You can also launch the Hyper-V Manager and note a specific Hyper-V host server you want to manage from the command line plus start monitoring a specific guest session by entering the following:

```
c:\Program Files\Hyper-V\vmconnect.exe {hostname} "Guest Name"
```

In this case, {hostname} is the name of the Hyper-V host, and "Guest Name" (within quotes) is the name of the guest session you want to launch to monitor.

Connecting to a Different Virtual Server System

If you want to administer or manage a different virtual server system, you need to log on and connect to another server. To connect to a different virtual server, complete these steps:

1. From within the Hyper-V Manager console, click the Microsoft Hyper-V Servers option in the leftmost pane.

2. Select Action, Connect to Server.

3. Select Another Computer and either enter the name of the server and click OK or click Browse to search Active Directory for the name of the server you want to remotely monitor and administer.

4. When the server appears in the Hyper-V Manager Console, click to select the server to see the actions available for administering and managing that server.

Managing Windows Server 2008 Remotely

Windows 2008's built-in feature set allows it to be easily managed remotely. This capability eases administration time, expenses, and energy by allowing administrators to manage systems from remote locations, instead of having to be physically at the system. For organizations that deploy Hyper-V on Server Core that has no graphical user interface (GUI) to install the Hyper-V Manager tool, the administration must be done remotely. *Remote administration* in this section covers both the process of remotely accessing a full Hyper-V host server to take control of the Hyper-V host servers console session and the process of remotely accessing a Hyper-V host server that does not have the administration tools installed on the local host system.

Remote Server Administration Tools

The remote server administration tools in Windows Server 2008 include a number of tools to manage Windows 2008 remotely. This set of tools replaced the Adminpack.msi set of tools that shipped with earlier versions of Windows.

There are different tools for the roles (see Table 6.1) and for the features (see Table 6.2).

TABLE 6.1   Remote Server Administration Tools for Roles

Tool	Description
Active Directory Certificate Services tools	Active Directory Certificate Services tools include the Certification Authority, Certificate Templates, Enterprise PKI, and Online Responder Management snap-ins.
Active Directory Domain Services (AD DS) tools	Active Directory Domain Services tools include Active Directory Users and Computers, Active Directory Domains and Trusts, Active Directory Sites and Services, and other snap-ins and command-line tools for remotely managing Active Directory Domain Services.

TABLE 6.1   Remote Server Administration Tools for Roles

Tool	Description
Active Directory Lightweight Directory Services (AD LDS) tools	Active Directory Lightweight Directory Services tools include Active Directory Sites and Services, ADSI Edit, Schema Manager, and other snap-ins and command-line tools for managing Active Directory Lightweight Directory Services.
Active Directory Rights Management Services (AD RMS) tools	Active Directory Rights Management Services (AD RMS) tools include the Active Directory Rights Management Services (AD RMS) snap-in.
DHCP Server tools	DHCP Server tools include the DHCP snap-in.
DNS Server tools	DNS Server tools include the DNS Manager snap-in and dnscmd.exe command-line tool.
Fax Server tools	Fax Server tools include the Fax Service Manager snap-in.
File Services tools	File Services tools include Distributed File System tools, File Server Resource Manager tools, and Services for Network File System tools.
	Distributed File System tools include the DFS Management snap-in, and the dfsradmin.exe, dfscmd.exe, dfsdiag.exe, and dfsutil.exe command-line tools.
	File Server Resource Manager tools includes the File Server Resource Manager snap-in, and the filescrn.exe and storrept.exe command-line tools.
	Services for Network File System tools includes the Network File System snap-in and the nfsadmin.exe, showmount.exe, and rpcinfo.exe command-line tools.
Hyper-V Server tools	Hyper-V Server tools is the component that allows a system to log on and access a Hyper-V host server for the purpose of administering and managing the host server for both host and guest session configuration.
Network Policy and Access Services tools	Network Policy and Access Services tools include the Routing and Remote Access and Health Registration Authority snap-ins.
Print Services tools	Print Services tools include the Print Management snap-in.

TABLE 6.1   Remote Server Administration Tools for Roles

Tool	Description
Terminal Services tools	Terminal Services tools include the TS RemoteApp Manager, TS Gateway Manager, and TS Licensing Manager snap-ins.
Universal Description, Discovery, and Integration (UDDI) Services tools	UDDI Services tools include the UDDI Services snap-in.
Web Server (IIS) tools	Web Server (IIS) tools include the Internet Information Services (IIS) 6.0 Manager and IIS Manager snap-ins.
Windows Deployment Services tools	Windows Deployment Services tools include the Windows Deployment Services snap-in, wdsutil.exe command-line tool, and Remote Install extension for the Active Directory Users and Computers snap-in.

TABLE 6.2   Remote Server Administration Tools for Features

Tool	Description
BitLocker Drive Encryption tools	BitLocker Drive Encryption tools include the manage-bde.wsf script.
BITS Server Extensions tools	BITS Server Extensions tools include the Internet Information Services (IIS) 6.0 Manager and IIS Manager snap-ins.
Failover Clustering tools	Failover Clustering tools include the Failover Cluster Manager snap-in and the cluster.exe command-line tool.
Network Load Balancing tools	Network Load Balancing tools include the Network Load Balancing Manager snap-in and the nlb.exe and wlbs.exe command-line tools.
SMTP Server tools	SMTP Server tools include the Internet Information Services (IIS) 6.0 Manager snap-in.
WINS Server tools	Windows Internet Naming Service (WINS) Server tools include the WINS snap-in.

The tools are installed as a feature. You can install all the tools or only the specific ones that you need. Even if the Hyper-V Server role is not installed on a server system, you can still install the Hyper-V Server tool to remotely manage a remote Hyper-V host. This allows an administrator to load up the various administrative tools on a single system and manage several different host systems from a central location.

To install the remote server administration tools, follow these steps:

1. Launch Server Manager.

2. Select the Features folder.

3. Click the Add Features link.

4. Locate the Remote Server Administration Tools feature.

5. Select the desired tools (such as the Hyper-V tools), as shown in Figure 6.3.

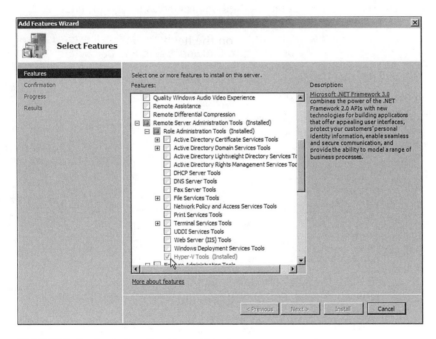

FIGURE 6.3   Installing the Hyper-V tools.

6. Click Next to accept the selected tools.

7. Click Install to install the selected tools.

8. Click Close to exit the wizard.

9. Close the Server Manager window.

After the tools are installed, you can manage remote computers by selecting the Connect to Another Computer command from the Action menu. This tool can be used to remotely administer a Hyper-V host even if the Hyper-V does not have the administrative tools loaded on the system itself, such as in the case of a Hyper-V host running on Windows 2008 Server Core.

Remote Desktop

A common method to remotely access a host system has been to use Windows Terminal Services, which effectively enables an administrator to take control of the keyboard and mouse of a remote system and perform tasks just as if the administrator were on the remote system. Unlike running the Remote Server Administration tool that enables an administrator to manage a host system that may not have the Administration tool on the host server itself (for example, Server Core), Terminal Services takes control of the host system and thus all administration tools need to be on the host system being accessed.

With Windows Server 2008, although Microsoft still provides Terminal Services as a add-in to the server for remote access, they have enhanced Remote Desktop on server systems for remote administration and management. Instead of installing the full Terminal Services server role that is intended to provide many users access to a single host server for thin client application and desktop virtualization, the Remote Desktop uses the same security and technology, but is focused at allowing an administrator to take control of the console of the host system. This drastically minimizes the overhead of the host system because it does not need a licensing server to track guest session connections, and it doesn't need to load up application publishing components or gateway components. Remote Desktop merely enables an administrator to remotely take control of the console of a host system.

To install Remote Desktop on a host server, complete the following steps:

1. Launch Server Manager.
2. Click the Server Manager (*hostname*) in the leftmost pane
3. In the Server Summary section under Computer Information in the rightmost pane, there is a Configure Remote Desktop option on the far right of the screen. Click that option.
4. On the System Properties page that displays, click the Remote tab.
5. Choose the Allow Connections Only from Computers Running Remote Desktop with Network Level Authentication (More Secure), as shown in Figure 6.4.
6. You will get a warning that notes that a Firewall exception will need to be enabled on the server to allow remote access to this host system. Click OK.
7. Click OK when prompted. The server is now configured for remote desktop access.

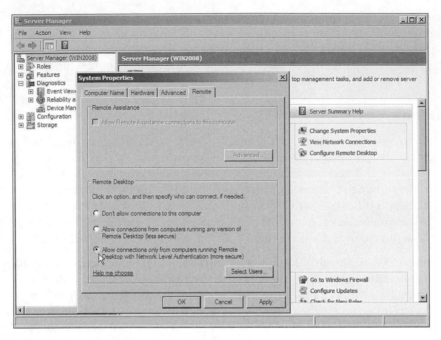

FIGURE 6.4   Enabling Remote Desktop on a host system.

NOTE

In step 5, you could choose to Allow Connections from Computers Running Any Version Of Remote Desktop (Less Secure). This option allows the use of the Remote Desktop Connection (RDC) earlier than version 6.0, which is the RDC software that came by default with Windows 2000, Windows 2003, and Windows XP. Because you are accessing a host server in your network environment, however, and you can likely control what RDC client software you, as the administrator, can choose to use, it is recommended to use the latest RDC client (version 6.1 or later).

The latest RDC client provides a significantly higher level of security for remote connection. Windows Vista SP1 and Windows Server 2008 come with the latest RDC client, and older versions can be easily upgraded to the latest release by going to www.microsoft.com/downloads. When there, search for "Remote Desktop Connection" to download and install the most current version of the client. With the latest RDC client installed, choose to use the "more secure" network-level authentication method of connecting to the host server.

To access the host server from a remote system, you need to run the RDC client software. This software is the same application used to remotely access a Windows Terminal Services system. The location of the RDC software varies from system to system based on the operating system that you are running. In general, you can launch the RDC as follows:

1. Click Start, All Programs, Accessories and choose Remote Desktop Connection.

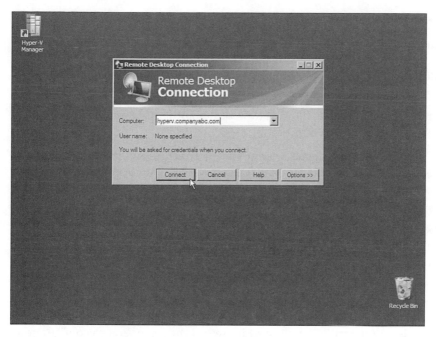

FIGURE 6.5   Using the RDC application.

2. Enter the name of the host server you want to remotely access, similar to what is shown in Figure 6.5.

3. Click Connect to access the host server.

4. When prompted for your credentials, enter a valid logon name and password that you would normally use to log on to the remote host system from the system's console screen. (If the host is connected to a domain, for the username, enter the domain and username, such as administrator@companyabc.com.) Enter the password for the account and click OK.

Once logged on to the host server, you can do whatever you would normally do on a host system, such as administer the system, change system settings, and even restart the system.

CAUTION

Be careful what you do on the remote system. If you "shut down" the system and no one is there to power the system back up, you will need to physically go to the system and power it back on.

When you are done remotely administering the system, you can just click Start, Log Off, and that will log you out of the system and terminate your remote session (yet keep the server operational and running).

Windows Remote Management

Windows Remote Management (WinRM) enables an administrator to run command lines remotely on a target server. When WinRM is used to execute the command remotely, the command executes on the target server, and the output of the command is piped to the local server. This allows administrators to see the output of those commands.

The commands run securely, because the WinRM requires authentication and also encrypts the network traffic in both directions.

WinRM is both a service and a command-line interface for remote and local management of servers. The service implements the WS-Management protocol on Windows 2008. WS-Management protocol is a standard web services protocol for management of software and hardware remotely.

In Windows 2008, the WinRM service establishes a listener on the HTTP and HTTPS ports. It can coexist with IIS and share the ports, but uses the /wsman URL to avoid conflicts. The IIS role does not have to be installed for this to work.

The WinRM service must be configured to allow remote management of the target server, and the Windows Firewall must be configured to allow WinRM traffic inbound. The WinRM service can be configured through GPO or via the WinRM command line. To have the WinRM service listen on port 80 for all IP addresses on the server and to configure the Windows Firewall, execute the following commands on the target server:

1. Select Start, Run.
2. Enter the command `winrm quickconfig`.
3. Click OK to run the command.
4. Read the output from WinRM. Answer **y** to the prompt that asks, "Make These Changes [y/n]?."

Now the target server is ready to accept commands. For example, suppose an administrator is logged on to a server win2008.companyabc.com and needs to remotely execute a command on remote Hyper-V host server HyperV-01.companyabc.com. These steps assume that WinRM has been configured and the firewall rule has been enabled. Use the following steps to remotely execute the command:

1. Open a command prompt on the server win2008.
2. Enter the command `winrs -r:http://hyperV-01.companyabc.com ipconfig /all`.

The output of the command will be shown on the local server (win2008)—in this case, the IP configuration of the target server (hyperv-01).

This proves particularly useful when executing a command or a set of commands on numerous servers. You no longer have to log on to a remote host server using Terminal Services or the like for each server. Instead, if you want to run a command, you can execute the command remotely using a command line or even include the command in a batch file against a series of target servers.

Managing Host Server, Virtual Switch, and Disk Settings

In the Hyper-V Manager console, a number of critical configuration options are important to understand. These configuration settings and options relate to virtual network switch settings, host server configuration settings, and management of guest session disk images. These options enable you to compress or expand disk image files or create virtual local area networks (VLANs) to better optimize communications between guest sessions or from guest sessions to the physical network backbone.

Configuring Host Server Settings

Basic settings in the Hyper-V Manager console enable you to set default host server settings, such as default path of where guest image files are stored, how guest sessions are administered, and the keyboard command used to switch keyboard and mouse control between a guest session and a host session.

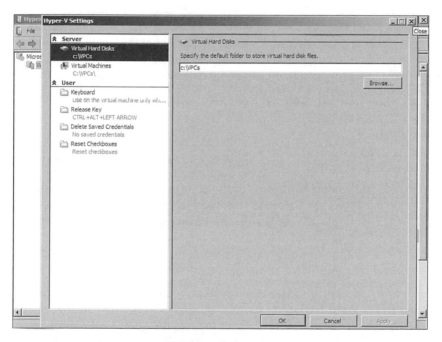

FIGURE 6.6   Hyper-V Settings options.

Regardless of whether you have chosen to use Server Manager or the Hyper-V Manager tool, or whether you are accessing the host server on the system itself or remotely, the configuration options and settings are the same. When you click the virtual server system you want to administer, action settings become available. You have the Actions menu on the right side of the console screen, and the Action menu option at the top of the screen exposes the same list of configuration options.

These action settings enable you to configure the host server settings for the system you have chosen to administer. When you click Hyper-V Server Settings from the Action menu, you see a screen similar to the one shown in Figure 6.6.

The settings you can modify in the Hyper-V Settings page are as follows:

▸ **Virtual Hard Disks**—This option enables you to set the drive path for the location where virtual hard disks (VHDs) are stored. This might be on the local C: drive of the server system or an external storage area network (SAN) or storage system.

▸ **Virtual Machines**—This option enables you to set the drive path for the location where virtual machine snapshots are stored. Snapshots are incremental image files that store the content of the image at a point where you take a snapshot of an image. At a point in time when you want to roll back to the state of the image when you took the snapshot, these image files have the data needed to roll back the guest session.

NOTE

Although you are given only a single directory name for the storage of VHDs and virtual machine snapshot images, the data for each guest session and snapshot is named differently, and Hyper-V has the ability of acknowledging the different image files and snapshots stored in these folders.

▸ **Keyboard**—This option sets a preference whether key commands are by default recognized by the physical host server, or whether the key commands are to be recognized by the virtual guest session. As an example, if you press Ctrl-Esc, are you going to pop up the Start menu of the host or the Start menu of the guest session? If you choose Use on the Physical Computer, Ctrl+Esc will pop up the Start menu on the physical host server. If you choose Use on the Virtual Machine, Ctrl+Esc will pop up the Start menu on the virtual guest session you are managing. If you choose Use on the Virtual Machine Only When Running Full-Screen, Ctrl+Esc will pop up the Start menu if you are running the guest management console in full screen.

▸ **Release Key**—When you manage a virtual guest session, all keyboard and mouse control is passed to the guest session. To switch keyboard and mouse control back to the host server, by default the key sequence that releases the guest session back to host console is Ctrl+Alt+left arrow. The Remote Control/Release Key option allows for the selection of other key combinations.

NOTE

If you installed the Windows Integration tools on the guest session, keyboard and mouse control seamlessly passes between the guest and host depending on whether your mouse is clicking the guest session or if you move the mouse outside the guest session and click it somewhere outside the guest session to let control pass back to the host. You typically will not need to do the Ctrl+Alt+left arrow after the Integration tools have been installed.

▶ **Delete Saved Credentials**—Because the access from a host server to a guest session for administration is done through an encrypted Secure Sockets Layer (SSL) session, each guest session maintains security during logon by forcing the entry of credentials to access different guest sessions. These credentials can be stored so that administrators do not need to enter their credentials to access a guest session. This option allows an administrator to delete (or flush) saved credentials so that anyone at the console who needs to access a guest session must enter credentials to do so.

▶ **Reset Checkboxes**—This option clears the Don't Ask Me This Again check box so that if an administrator does not want to be prompted again, select this option.

Stopping the Hyper-V Service

The Stop Service option in the Virtual Network Manager action item menu provides enables you to stop the Windows Hyper-V service on the machine being managed. You might choose to stop the service if you need to perform maintenance or begin the shutdown of an administered system.

NOTE

A common use of the Stop Service function is to stop the Hyper-V service to flat file (xcopy) Hyper-V guest images. With the Hyper-V service running, all the guest sessions are locked and flagged as "in use" so that Hyper-V can control the state of the images. In this state, however, the image files cannot be easily copied because they show as being in use. If you stop the service, Hyper-V releases control of the images files, and then the files can be copied off and then the Hyper-V service started again.

Managing Virtual Network Segments with the Virtual Switch

The Actions settings in the Hyper-V Manager console contain a Virtual Network Manager option. By selecting the Virtual Network Manager action item, you have access to configure the virtual network switches, as shown in Figure 6.7. You can configure the LAN and WAN connections available for the guest sessions of the virtual server host.

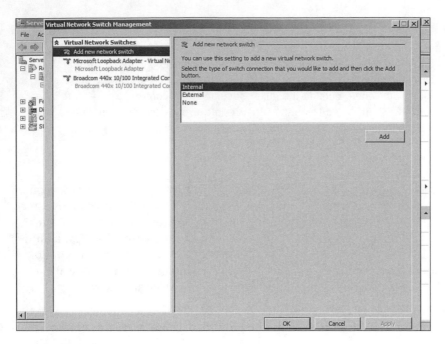

FIGURE 6.7   Virtual network switch management.

Configuring the Virtual Network Manager is more than just providing a way for guest sessions to connect to a physical network backbone. Doing so also enables administrators to control how virtual guest sessions communicate among themselves or on the network backup. As an example, if an organization has a protected VLAN network segment for key business applications, and then a general network segment for general business email servers and file servers, the Virtual Network Manager can set up a connection between the protected business applications through a dedicated network adapter in the host to a protected network segment. A separate connection can be set from the other virtual guest sessions through a different network adapter to a different network segment.

Because Hyper-V host systems can host 4, 8, 15, 20, or more guest sessions, the guest sessions are frequently applications that should be available to different groups of users. Network segmentation for application access can be achieved by setting up different network switch configurations to different network adapters in a Hyper-V host server.

Specific options include the following:

▶ **Add New Virtual Network**—This configuration option allows for the addition of a new internal or external network segment available to the guest sessions. An external network segment would be a connection to a LAN adapter in the host server so that a guest session could gain access out of the virtual server. An internal network segment would be a connection that is solely within the virtual server system where you might want to set up a virtual LAN so that the virtual server guests within a system can talk to each other and with the host server. There is also a private session for a virtual network where the guest sessions on a host system can communicate only with themselves and the private network segment does not connect to any external network adapter and not even to the host server itself. Private network segments are commonly used by application developers and IT personnel who want to test (typically for security purposes) an application to ensure the session is not accidentally connected outside of the virtual guest session.

▶ **Existing virtual network switches**—If the system you are managing already has virtual network switches configured, they will be listed individually in the leftmost pane of the Virtual Network Switch Management dialog box. By selecting an existing virtual network switch, you can change the name of the virtual switch, change the internal or external connection that the switch has access to, or remove the network switch altogether.

Modifying Disk Settings and Configurations

Another action option on the Hyper-V Manager console is the Edit Disk option. The Edit Disk option enables an administrator to modify an existing VHD image. For instance, an administrator could compress the disk image so that it uses the least amount of disk space possible. Alternatively, the administrator could expand the disk image to make more disk space available for the guest session. For any guest image session you want to make modifications to, the guest image must be shut down and off. The image cannot be in a paused or saved state, and you want to confirm that the last time you shut down the image that it was shut down cleanly.

The Edit Disk option launches a wizard. You are prompted as follows:

1. At the Before You Begin screen, read the description of what the wizard will do, and then click Next.

2. Browse or enter the filename of the virtual guest image you are looking to modify, and then click Next.

3. Choose to compact, convert, or expand the image:

   ▶ **Compact**—This option allows you to shrink a VHD to remove portions of the disk image file that is unused. This is commonly used when a disk image will be archived and stored and having the smallest disk image file possible is preferred. You would also use this option if you had a lot of files in your guest image and then deleted the files and are therefore using significantly less of the allocated space than the image file is taking. In this scenario, compression will bring the file back to the size that the image is currently using.

   ▶ **Convert**—This option enables you to convert a VHD file from a dynamic virtual disk to a fixed virtual disk. A dynamic virtual disk allows the disk image to grow based on the needs of the guest session. A fixed virtual disk establishes a maximum disk size; when the guest image reaches that limit, the guest session, just like a physical hard drive, runs out of disk space. A dynamic virtual disk provides proves more flexible. The administrator doesn't have to worry about the guest image running out of space; the image file just keeps growing as it needs the space (or when the host server runs out of disk space). When a dynamic virtual disk expands, however, it slows down the guest image. Therefore, many organizations looking for high performance choose a fixed virtual disk size, and the administrators monitor disk space on the guest image to make sure the system doesn't run out of space, just as organizations have done for years with physical hard drive disk space availability.

▶ **Expand**—This option enables you grow the size of a dynamic disk image. For example, you might have initially created the disk image to be only 8GB maximum in size. Now that you've added a lot of applications to the guest image, however, you are running out of space in the image file. By expanding the image file, you effectively enable yourself to add more applications and data to the guest session without having to re-create the guest session all over again. Even with a dynamic virtual disk, although it will grow as the guest session requires disk space, you do set a maximum size for the image, and the guest image grows up to that limit. The Expand option enables you to extend the image beyond the maximum size limit set for the image.

4. Click Next, and then click Finished to execute the disk maintenance command your requested.

Inspect Disk

The Inspect Disk option in the Virtual Network Manager action item menu enables you to view the settings of an existing virtual image file. For the example shown in Figure 6.8, the disk image is currently 8GB in size, can dynamically grow up to the maximum limit of 2040GB, and is located on the local hard drive in the directory C:\VPCs.

Using Common Practices for Securing and Managing a Hyper-V Host Server

There are a handful of practices used to secure and manage a Windows 2008 Hyper-V host server. The first is to identify security risks to determine what the organization needs to be concerned about when applying a security policy. The second is that the organization can implement a tool such as Microsoft Operations Manager to monitor the server and simplify management tasks on a day-to-day basis. And the third is to use maintenance practices to enhance your ability to keep the host server stable and operational.

Identifying Security Risks

A network's security is only as good as the security mechanisms put into place and the review and identification process. Strong security entails using Windows 2008 security measures, such as authentication, auditing, and authorization controls, but it also means that security information is properly and promptly reviewed. Information that can be reviewed includes Event Viewer logs, service-specific logs, application logs, and performance data.

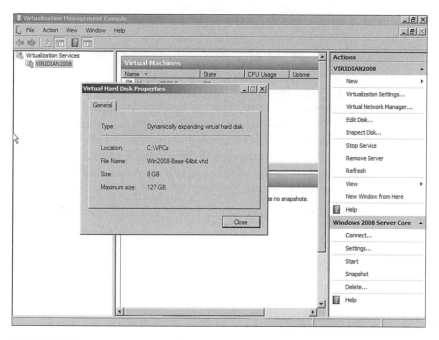

FIGURE 6.8   Viewing the VHD properties of a guest image.

All the security information for a Windows 2008 Hyper-V host can be logged, but without a formal review and identification process the information is useless. Also, security-related information can be complex and unwieldy, depending on what information is being recorded. For this reason, manually reviewing the security information might be tedious; however, doing so can prevent system or network compromise.

The formal review and identification process should be performed daily. Any identified activity that is suspicious or that could be potentially risky should be reported and dealt with appropriately. For instance, an administrator reviewing a particular security log might run across some data that alerts him to suspicious activity. This incident should be reported to the security administrator to take the appropriate action. Whatever the ultimate course of action might be in the organization, there should be points of escalation and remediation.

Using System Center Operations Manager 2007 to Simplify Management

Many of the recommendations in this chapter focus on reviewing event logs, monitoring the configuration, and monitoring the operations of the Hyper-V system. For an administrator who has several Hyper-V host servers to monitor, with each host server potentially having several virtual guest sessions running on it, such vigilance can prove to be difficult on a day-to-day basis. The challenge is proportional to the number of servers that an administrator is responsible for (and organizations with virtualized servers typically have many virtual servers they are overseeing and managing). Microsoft has developed a product to make these tasks easier and more manageable: System Center Operations Manager 2007.

System Center Operations Manager 2007 is an enterprise-class monitoring and management solution for Windows environments. It is designed to simplify Windows management by consolidating events, performance data, alerts, and more into a centralized repository. Reports on this information can then be tailored depending on the environment and on the level of detail that is needed and extrapolated. This information can assist administrators and decision makers in proactively addressing Windows 2008 operation and any problems that exist or might occur.

Many other intrinsic benefits are gained by using System Center Operation Manager 2007, including the following:

- Event log monitoring and consolidation

- Monitoring of various applications, including those provided by third parties

- Enhanced alerting capabilities

- Assistance with capacity-planning efforts

- A customizable knowledge base of Microsoft product knowledge and best practices

- Web-based interfaces for reporting and monitoring

Leveraging Windows Server 2008 Maintenance Practices

Administrators face the often-daunting task of maintaining the Windows 2008 environment and specifically Hyper-V host servers in the midst of daily administration and firefighting. Little time is spent identifying and then organizing maintenance processes and procedures.

To decrease the number of administrative inefficiencies and the amount of firefighting an administrator must go through, it's important to identify those tasks that are important to the system's overall health and security. After they've been identified, routines should be set to ensure that the Windows 2008 environment is stable and reliable. Many of the maintenance processes and procedures described in the following sections are the most opportune areas to target.

Specific Security Practices for Hyper-V Host Servers

In a network environment, specific practices can be implemented to improve the security of a Hyper-V host server. Security practices include protecting image files, establishing network security zones for secured access, and implementing Hyper-V on a Server Core host.

Protecting Hyper-V Guest Image Files

It is important that the image files of a Hyper-V host or any virtualized server environment be protected. Someone who has access to the VHD image file can boot the image file and gain access to the contents of the server, just as if someone were to physically steal a server and start hacking away at the server to gain access to the data on it. However unlike a physical server that would be noticed if it were physically stolen and missing, virtualized guest image files are nothing more than "files." Administrators have been known to copy the files onto USB hard drives or back up the guest image files to other servers for disaster-recovery purposes. The problem with that is if the files are not protected, someone can copy the files off the disk share and thus effectively obtain the full server.

Maintain good control of the VHD image files. If you do copy the image files as a backup or disaster-recovery procedure, make sure the location where you store the files is secure and properly protected. Just as your physical servers are typically locked up in a rack, digitally lock up the location where you store your virtual server image files to protect their contents.

> **NOTE**
>
> Hyper-V protects the location where the Hyper-V guest images are stored (for instance, C:\VPC\ or the like) by making the directory accessible only by the local Hyper-V service. Unless you change the file access permissions on a Hyper-V host system, the directory where the images are stored cannot be mounted or shared.
>
> Likewise, if you delete the folder where your Hyper-V images were stored and then create a new folder with the exact same name, when you try to launch your guest images, you will get an error that the guest images cannot start. You need to go into Windows Explorer, go to the folder you just created, and give the LOCALSERVICE account access to the folder. You can read more about this in Chapter 13, "Debugging and Problem Solving the Hyper-V Host and Guest OS."

Separate Network Adapters for Host and Guests

In the section "Managing Virtual Network Segments with the Virtual Switch," network segmentation was tied to noting which guest sessions needed to communicate with which network adapter in the host server. With Hyper-V and security in mind, it is best to consider having a separate network adapter just for the management of the Hyper-V host server that none of the guest sessions communicate on.

The advantage of having a separate network adapter for the host server is that internal remote administration and management of the host can be done on one network adapter, and all other communications for guest sessions will occur over a different network adapter or adapters. This setup provides isolated administrative control of the host server from the direct access, communications, and control of the guest sessions. Remember, a person who has access to a Hyper-V host server has access to all the guest sessions running on the system. If there are a dozen virtual guest sessions running on a host, the individual accessing the host has direct access to all 12 virtual guest sessions.

Splitting up the physical network communications and using a monitoring or management tool to monitor communications over the host server network adapter can provide better security for the guest sessions running on the host system.

Running Hyper-V on Windows 2008 Server Core

As noted in Chapter 3, "Planning, Sizing, and Architecting a Hyper-V Environment," Hyper-V can be installed on either a full version of Windows Server 2008 or on the GUI-less version of Windows 2008 called Server Core. Because Server Core does not have the traditional Windows GUI, the attack surface of the host system is greatly diminished. Because guest sessions need to be remotely accessed using either the Hyper-V Manager or using Remote Desktop, there's no need to have a full host operating system.

Windows 2008 Server Core is one of the better ways of providing security and protection of a host server for virtualization.

Keeping Up with Service Packs and Updates

Another major way to maintain a server for security protection is to make sure the appropriate service packs and updates are regularly applied on the Hyper-V host servers and guest sessions. Service packs (SPs) and updates for both hosts and guests, and for the operating system and applications, are vital parts to maintaining availability, reliability, performance, and security. Microsoft packages these updates into SPs or individually.

An administrator can update a system with the latest SP or update in several ways: Automatic Windows Updates, CD-ROM, manually entered commands, or Microsoft Windows Server Update Services (WSUS).

> **NOTE**
>
> Thoroughly test and evaluate SPs and updates in a lab environment before installing them on production servers and guest sessions. A good use of the snapshot feature in Hyper-V is to snapshot a guest session, apply a patch or update, and then if the system has problems with the update you can easily roll back to the state of the server from the snapshot. Installing the appropriate SPs and updates on each host server and guest session keeps all systems consistent.

Manual Update or CD-ROM Update

Manual updating is typically done when applying SPs, rather than hotfixes. SPs tend to be significantly larger than updates or hotfixes, so many administrators will download the SP once and then apply it manually to their servers. Or the SP will be obtained on CD-ROM.

When an SP CD-ROM is inserted into the drive of the server, it typically launches an interface to install the SP.

In the case of downloaded SPs or of CD-ROM-based SPs, the SP can also be applied manually via a command line. This allows greater control over the install (see Table 6.3), such as by preventing a reboot or by not backing up files to conserve space.

TABLE 6.3   Update.exe Command-Line Parameters

Update.exe Parameter	Description
-f	Forces applications to close at shutdown.
-n	Prevents the system files from being backed up. This keeps SPs from being uninstalled.
-o	Overwrites OEM files.
-q	Indicates Quiet mode; no user interaction is required.
-s	Integrates the SP in a Windows 2008 share.
-u	Installs SP in Unattended mode.
-z	Keeps the system from rebooting after installation.

Hotfixes can also be controlled in a similar manner by downloading them and then using the command-line parameters shown in Table 6.4.

TABLE 6.4   Hotfix.exe Command-Line Parameters

Hotfix.exe Parameters	Description
-f	Forces applications to close at shutdown.
-l	Lists installed updates.
-m	Indicates Unattended mode.
n	Prevents the system files from being backed up. This keeps updates from being uninstalled.
-q	Indicates Quiet mode; no interaction is required.
-y	Uninstalls the update.
-z	Keeps the system from rebooting after installation.

Automatic Updates

Windows 2008 can be configured to download and install updates automatically using Automatic Windows Updates. With this option enabled, Windows 2008 checks for updates, downloads them, and applies them automatically on a schedule. The administrator can just have the updates downloaded but not installed (to exercise more control over when they are installed). Windows Update can also download and install recommended updates, which is new for Windows 2008.

When the Windows 2008 operating system is installed, Windows Update is not configured and a message is displayed on logon, as shown in Figure 6.9. The Server Manager Security Information section shows the Windows Update as Not Configured. This can be an unsecure configuration, because security updates will not be applied.

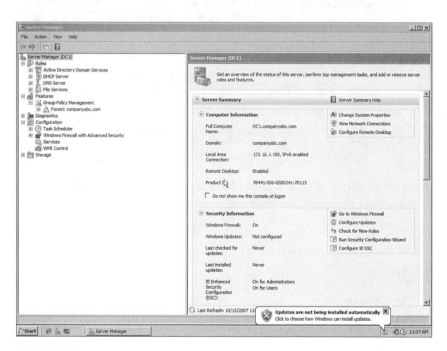

FIGURE 6.9   Windows Updates "not configured" error.

Windows Updates can be configured as follows:

1. Launch Server Manager.
2. Click the Configure Updates link in the Security Information section.
3. Click the Have Windows Install Updates Automatically to have the updates downloaded and installed.
4. The Windows Updates status will change to Install Updates Automatically Using Windows Updates.

The configuration of Windows Updates can be reviewed by clicking the Configure Updates link again. The Windows Update console appears (shown in Figure 6.10). The figure shows that updates will be installed automatically at 3:00 a.m. every day. The console also shows when updates were checked for last. In the console, the administrator can also complete the following tasks:

▶ Manually check for updates

▶ Change the Windows Updates settings

▶ View the update history

▶ See installed updates

▶ Get updates for more products

The link to get updates for more products enables the administrator to check for updates not just for the Windows 2008 platform, but also for other products such as Microsoft Exchange and Microsoft SQL. Clicking the link launches a web page to authorize the server to check for the broader range of updates.

Clicking the Change Settings link allows the Windows Update setting to be changed. The Change Settings window, shown in Figure 6.11, enables the administrator to adjust the time of installs, to install or just download, and to install (or not) recommended updates.

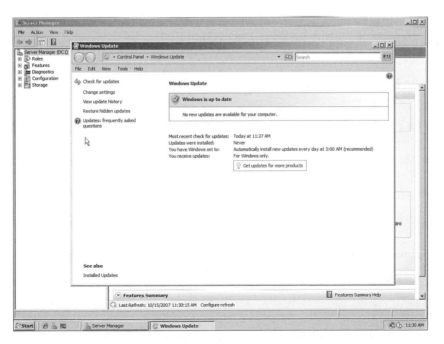

FIGURE 6.10   Windows Update console.

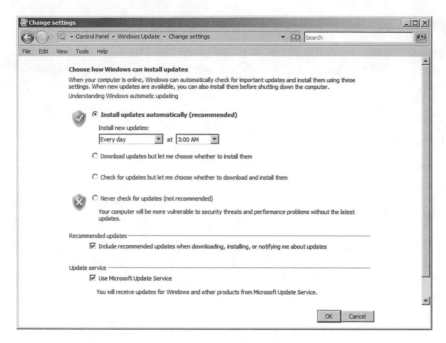

FIGURE 6.11   Windows Update Change Settings window.

The Windows Updates functionality is a great tool for keeping servers updated with very little administrative overhead, albeit with some loss of control.

Windows Server Update Services

Microsoft understands the increased administration and management efforts administrators face when using Windows Update to remain current with SPs and updates in anything other than small environments. Therefore, Microsoft has created the Windows Server Update Services (WSUS) client and server versions to minimize administration, management, and maintenance of mid- to large-sized organizations. WSUS 3.0 SP1 communicates directly and securely with Microsoft to gather the latest SPs and updates.

Microsoft WSUS provides a number of features to support organizations, such as the following:

▶ Support for a broad range of products such as Windows operating system family, Exchange messaging, SQL Server, Office, System Center family, and Windows Defender.

▶ Automatic download of updates.

▶ Administrative control over which updates are approved, removed, or declined. The Remove option permits updates to be rolled back.

▶ Email notification of updates and deployment status reports.

▶ Targeting of updates to specific groups of computers for testing and for control of the update process.

▶ Scalability to multiple WSUS servers controlled from a single console.

▶ Reporting on all aspects of the WSUS operations and status.

▶ Integration with Automatic Windows Updates.

The SPs and updates downloaded onto WSUS can then be distributed to either a lab server for testing (recommended) or to a production server for distribution. After these updates are tested, WSUS can automatically update systems inside the network.

The following steps install the Windows Server Update Services role:

1. Open the Server Manager console.
2. Select the Roles folder and click Add Roles.
3. In the Add Roles Wizard, select Windows Server Update Services and follow the instructions onscreen. The wizard will install WSUS 3.0 SP1 and any required components, including Web Server (IIS), if needed.

Unlike other server roles, the binaries for WSUS 3.0 SP1 are downloaded from Microsoft. This ensures that anytime WSUS is installed, you will always be installing the most current version.

Offline Virtual Machine Servicing Tool

As much as patching and update Hyper-V host sessions and running guest sessions is important to the security and ongoing reliability and support of hosts and guest systems, many organizations also have guest sessions that are offline that should be patched and updated. Frequently, these offline guest sessions are template images of base Windows 2003 or Windows 2008 server sessions that have been built and will be used as the base operating system for a future virtual guest server. Other times, offline virtual guest sessions are systems that are available just in case a primary server fails. (A copy of a physical server stored in an offline image can be started and put into production in a form of disaster recovery.)

However, just like physical production servers, the offline guest sessions get out of sync with available patches and updates, so Microsoft came out with an Offline Virtual Machine Service tool that can patch and update nonrunning guest sessions. You can download the Offline Virtual Machine Service tool from www.microsoft.com/downloads. Just search for "Offline Virtual Machine Servicing."

The tool plugs in to one of the following update applications:

▶ Microsoft System Center Virtual Machine Manager 2008 (VMM)

▶ Microsoft System Center Configuration Manager 2007 (SCCM)

▶ Microsoft Windows Server Update Services (WSUS)

The Installation and Configuration Wizard that comes with the Offline Virtual Machine Servicing tool connects the tool to VMM, SCCM, or WSUS. You can configure your offline guest sessions into machine groups where updates are applied to the offline servers in the machine group.

Jobs can then be scheduled to apply specified updates to the offline guest sessions. The jobs can run immediately or at a scheduled time.

Backing Up the Hyper-V Host and Guests

Another key task in the day-to-day management and operations of any server environment is backing up the server and the data that resides on the system. In the case of Hyper-V virtualization, the backup process involves *both* the host server and the guest sessions. There are different strategies for backing up virtual hosts and sessions, one of which involves backing up each guest session just like the process of backing up individual physical servers in the past. Another strategy is to back up the host server, which in turn backs up the guest sessions running on the host.

The key to keep in mind on a backup strategy is the state of the server when the information is being backed up. If a host server is being backed up with, for instance, eight guest sessions running on the system, the backup of the guest sessions will be at a state when the guest sessions are running and operational, effectively a snapshot in time. Applications such as Microsoft Exchange, SQL Server, SharePoint Server, and the like prefer that the backup be scheduled at the application level so that the Volume Shadow Copy Service (VSS) writer can properly interrupt the application, set a checkpoint where the database is being backed up; they will then flush the transaction logs on the server to clean up the state of the system after a backup was successfully completed.

When backing up a host server, the VSS writer is not involved in the backup, so the logs on the servers never show the guest server being successfully backed up. Therefore, for applications that have specific log tracking and backup procedures, backing up the guest session as if it were a standalone server is better than backing up the guest sessions simultaneously (at least from the host server perspective).

> **NOTE**
>
> New backup agents and technologies are continuously being developed to provide better ways to back up virtualized host and guest sessions. These new applications and agents provide for the backing up of Hyper-V host servers that then make VSS calls to guest sessions to properly back up the guest sessions.

For now, organizations are backing up the Hyper-V host server as a Windows server system, and backing up each Hyper-V guest session individually to ensure that the application backup procedures are followed in the current manner that the application expects a backup and flush of logs to occur. Microsoft provides a backup program that allows for the backup of Windows Server systems. The backup program is called Windows Server Backup and is included with Windows Server 2008.

Installing Windows Server Backup

Although the Windows Server Backup console is listed in Administrative Tools, the feature tools need to be installed. The easiest way to install the Windows Backup tools is to use the Add Features function within Server Manager. Of course, for Server Core deployments, the command-line version, ServerManagercmd.exe, must be used.

Installing Windows Server Backup Using Server Manager

On every edition of Windows 2008, except for Server Core installations, the Windows Server Backup feature can be installed using Server Manager. To install the Windows Server Backup feature, follow these steps:

1. Log on to the Windows Server 2008 system with an account with administrator privileges.

2. Click Start, All Programs, Administrative Tools, and select Server Manager.

3. In the tree pane, select the Features node, and click the Add Features link in the Tasks pane.

4. When the Add Features Wizard opens, check the boxes next to Windows PowerShell and Windows Server Backup Features, as shown in Figure 6.12. Click Next to continue.

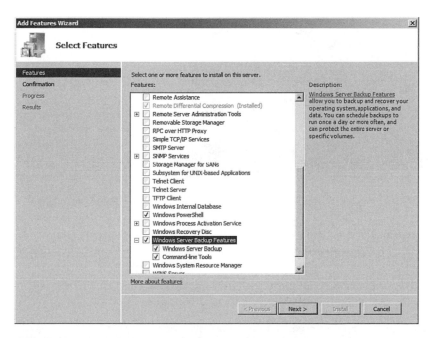

FIGURE 6.12   Selecting the Windows Server Backup features.

5. On the Confirm Installation Selections page, review the summary, and click Install to continue.

6. On the Installation Results page, review the results, and click Close to complete the installation.

Installing Windows Server Backup Using servermanagercmd.exe

In many cases, administrators might choose to use the command prompt environment as a preference when installing roles, role services, or features. When a particular feature or role is installed using the servermanagercmd.exe utility, all feature, role services, and role dependencies are also added. To install the Windows Server Backup command-line tools using servermanagercmd.exe, perform the following steps:

1. Log on to the Windows Server 2008 system with an account with administrator privileges.

2. Click Start, All Programs, All Programs, Accessories, and select Command Prompt.

3. Type **cd** \ and press Enter.

4. Type **Servermanagercmd.exe -install Backup** and press Enter.

5. After the installation completes, the results will be listed in the window, as shown in Figure 6.13.

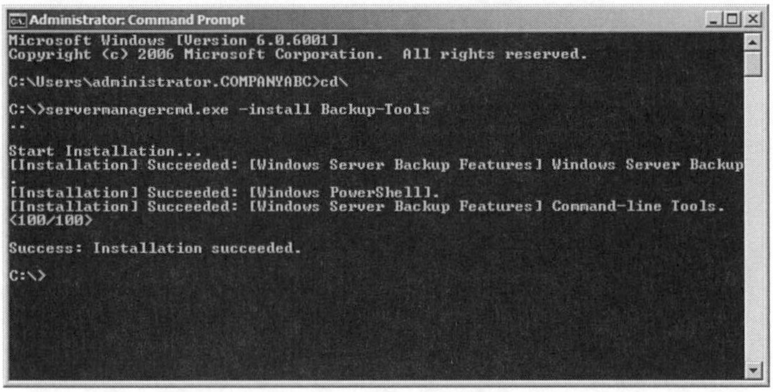

FIGURE 6.13   Installing Windows Server Backup using **servermanagercmd.exe**.

6. Type **servermanagercmd.exe -query** and press Enter to get a list of the installed roles, role services, and features. Review the list to verify that Windows PowerShell and Windows Server Backup command-line tools are now installed.

7. Type **exit** in the command prompt window and press Enter to exit the command prompt.

Installing Windows Server Backup on Server Core Installations

On a Windows 2008 Server Core deployment, if the Windows Server Backup feature is not installed, you can install it as follows:

1. Log on to the Windows Server 2008 Server Core system with an account with administrator privileges.

2. In the command prompt window, type **cd** \ and press Enter.

3. Type in **Start /w ocsetup.exe WindowsServerBackup** and press Enter. Restart if prompted to do so.

4. Log on to a different Windows Server 2008, Enterprise Edition system with an account with administrator privileges on the local system and on the Server Core system. It is assumed that both systems are part of the same domain and the Server Core system can access other resources on the network from the Server Core system.

5. Click Start, All Programs, Administrative Tools, and select Windows Server Backup.

6. In the Actions pane, click the Connect to Another Computer link.

7. In the Computer Chooser window, select the Another Computer option button, enter the name of the Server Core system, and click OK.

8. If you can connect to the Server Core system, the installation is successful. If the connection fails, either the Server Core firewall is preventing connectivity or Windows Server Backup has not been installed.

9. To determine whether the Server Core firewall is enabled, type **Netsh firewall show opmode** in the command prompt window on the Server Core system and press Enter.

10. Check to see which profile is active, domain or standard, and check to see whether the operational mode is active or inactive. Figure 6.14 shows that the domain profile is the current profile and that the firewall operational mode is disabled.

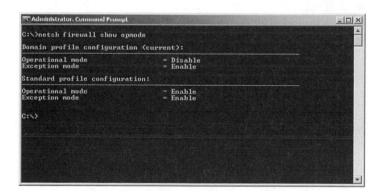

FIGURE 6.14   Using **Netsh** to verify the current firewall settings on Server Core.

11. If the current profile shows an operational state of enabled, type **Netsh firewall set opmode disable** and press Enter to disable the firewall.

NOTE

Disabling a firewall on any system is not recommended. Proper firewall configuration should be performed to only allow the necessary services, applications, and ports through the firewall.

12. After the firewall has been determined to be disabled, try to connect to the Server Core system remotely again.

13. On the Server Core system, the administrator can also verify that Windows Server Backup has been installed by typing `wbadmin.exe` in the command prompt window and pressing Enter. If the wbadmin options are listed, Windows Server Backup has been installed.

14. Enter `logoff` to log off of the Server Core system. Log off of any other system as required.

Scheduling a Backup Using Windows Server Backup and Allocating Disks

After Windows Server Backup has been installed, if local disks or scheduled backups will be used, a backup must be run to provision or allocate the disks. This can be done only by running a backup and defining which local disk or disks will be dedicated and managed by Windows Server Backup. If multiple disks will be used to provide offsite backup rotation, all the disks must be available during the creation of the backup.

The external disks that will be used by Windows Server Backup must be managed and completely available to the scheduled backup. Any volumes or data on these disks will be wiped out when the disks are assigned to the backup. This process creates a single NTFS formatted volume that spans the entire disk and sets the disk volume label to include the server name, the date and time, and the disk number for each disk. For example, if disk 1 is assigned to the backup of SERVER1 on September 19, 2008 at 12:00 p.m., the label will be SERVER1 2008_09_19 12:00 DISK_01. To allocate disks for Windows Server Backup, complete these steps:

1. Log on to the Windows Server 2008 system with an account with administrator privileges.

2. Click Start, All Programs, Administrative Tools, and select Server Manager.

3. In the tree pane, double-click the Storage node, and select Windows Server Backup.

4. In the Actions pane, click the Backup Schedule link to start the Backup Schedule Wizard. Clicking the Backup Schedule link is the only way multiple disks can be allocated to Windows Server Backup in one process.

5. Click Next on the Getting Started page.

6. Click the Full Backup (Recommended) option button, and then click Next to continue.

7. Select the time to run the scheduled backup from the Once a Day or the More Than Once a Day selections, and click Next to continue. Figure 6.15 details a backup that will run every day at 10:00 p.m.

8. On the Select Destination Disk page, click the Show All Available Disks button.

9. In the Show All Available Disks window, check each of the disks that will be dedicated to the scheduled backup, and then click OK to save the settings.

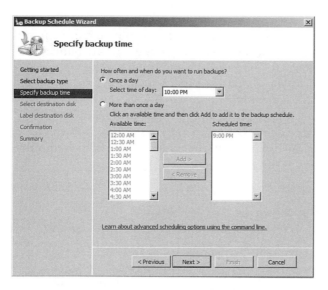

FIGURE 6.15   Setting the scheduled backup to run every day at 10:00 p.m.

NOTE

When multiple disks are assigned to a single scheduled backup, any of the disks may be used, and that is not in the control of the administrator. If a disk is removed for off-site storage, the remaining disks will be used for the next scheduled backup.

---

10. Back on the Select Destination Disk page, check all the disks that have been added, and then click Next to continue.

11. A Windows Server Backup warning window opens requiring confirmation that the selected disks will be wiped out and used by Windows Server Backup exclusively; click Yes to assign the disks for backup.

12. The Label Destination page details the actual Windows disk and the new label. Click Next to accept the labels and continue with the process.

13. On the Confirmation page, verify the settings, and then click Finish to save the new scheduled backup and backup settings and to reformat and label each of the assigned disks.

14. On the Summary page, review the results, and then click Close to complete the process.

Creating a scheduled backup using Windows Server Backup enables an administrator to automate the backup process, and with the backup and VSS managing the disk, the administrator only needs to verify that backups have been run successfully.

Manually Running a Scheduled Backup

After the scheduled backup is created for a server, an administrator can let the backup run as scheduled or can run the backup manually using the Backup Once link. To manually run a scheduled backup, just click the Backup Once link. Then, on the Backup Options page, select the option The Same Options You Used for Backup Schedule Wizard for Scheduled Backups. Follow the steps on the remaining pages to kick off the backup. Note that if multiple disks are allocated to a scheduled backup, running a manual backup does not allow the administrator to select which disk to use. The only way to control which disk is used for scheduled backup is to either remove all the other allocated disks from the system or mark the disks as offline using Disk Management or Diskpart.exe.

Running a Manual Backup to a Remote Server Share

One advantage running a manual backup has over a scheduled backup is that the backup can be directed to a remote server share. A backup stored on a remote server share enables full backups of Windows 2008 systems that do not have local disk storage suitable for backup. Also, without a locally attached disk or a full backup stored on DVD media, performing a complete PC restore can be accomplished only by using a backup stored on a remote server share. To create a manual backup to a remote server share, perform the following steps:

1. Log on to the Windows Server 2008 system with an account with administrator privileges.
2. Click Start, All Programs, Administrative Tools, and select Server Manager.
3. In the tree pane, double-click the Storage node, and select Windows Server Backup.
4. In the Actions pane, click the Backup Once link to start the Backup Once Wizard.
5. When the Backup Once Wizard opens, select the Different Options option button, and click Next, as shown in Figure 6.16. Running a manual backup and selecting the Different Options option is the only way to store a backup on DVDs or remote server shares.
6. On the Specify Backup Type page, select either the Full Backup to back up all the drives on the Windows 2008 system or select the Custom option button to select specific volumes. For this example, select Full Backup, and then click Next.
7. On the Specify Destination Type page, select Remote Shared Folder, and click Next, as shown in Figure 6.17.
8. On the Specify Remote Folder page, type in the UNC path of the remote server share, and then click the Do Not Inherit option button to set the permissions on the destination folder that will be created and will store the backup.
9. Click Next on the Specify Remote Folder page. A window opens asking for credentials to use when connecting to the share. Enter the appropriate username and password that can create subfolders and write to the share, and then click OK.

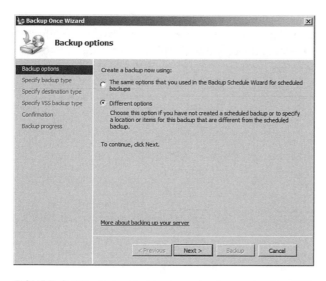

FIGURE 6.16   Selecting to run a backup using the Different Options option.

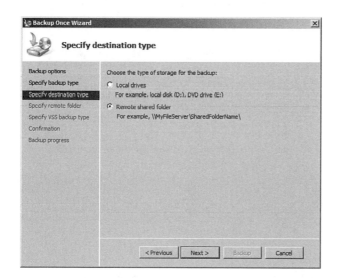

FIGURE 6.17   Selecting to store the manual backup on a remote shared folder.

NOTE

If a remote folder is specified for the backup destination, ensure that the folder does not already contain a WindowsImageBackup folder (because the permissions might be overwritten by the new backup). If the permissions are not a worry and will remain as they are, clicking the Inherit option button on the Specify Remote Folder page is preferred.

10. On the Specify VSS Backup Type page, select the Copy Backup If a Scheduled Backup Already Exists option, and then click Next to continue. If no other backup product and no scheduled backup will be created, select the VSS Full Backup option, and then click Next to continue.

11. On the Confirmation page, review the settings and click Backup to start the manual backup.

12. On the Backup Progress page, you can view the progress in real time, or you can click the Close button (in which case the progress can be tracked in the Tasks pane back in the Windows Server Backup console). Click Close when the backup completes.

Managing Backups Using the Command-Line Utility Wbadmin.exe

Windows 2008 systems running Server Core installations contain only the Windows Server Backup command-line tools. The command-line backup tool is named wbadmin.exe and can be accessed using a command prompt window. Wbadmin.exe is very functional and can be used to perform most of the functions available in the GUI.

> **NOTE**
>
> If a Standard or Enterprise Edition of Windows 2008 is deployed on the network, the Windows Server Backup console can be used to manage a Server Core backup.

Understanding and becoming familiar and fluent with the command-line options of wbadmin.exe is required for administrators who need to manage Windows 2008 Server Core systems. The following sections detail a few common tasks that can be performed using wbadmin.exe.

Viewing Backup History

To view the backup history of a system, perform the following steps:

1. Log on to the Windows Server 2008 system with an account with administrator privileges.

2. Open a command prompt.

3. Type in `wbadmin.exe Get Versions` and press Enter to list the backup history.

Running a Manual Backup to Remote Storage Using Wbadmin.exe

Using wbadmin.exe to run backups can be tedious. To understand each of the options available for a manual backup in a command prompt window, type `wbadmin.exe Start Backup /?` and press Enter. To run a manual backup and store it on a remote server share, a few options are required. The data will be stored on the remote server share

\\Server2\NetworkBackup, the C: drive will be backed up, and the companyabc\adminis-trator account will be used to connect to the remote share. To run the manual backup using the preceding criteria, perform the following steps:

1. Log on to the Windows Server 2008 system with an account with administrator privileges.

2. Open a command prompt.

3. Type in `wbadmin.exe Start Backup -backuptarget:\\Server2\NetworkBackup -include:c: -user:companyabc\administrator -password:My$3cretPW!` and press Enter to start the backup.

4. The backup will process the command and require confirmation to continue. Press Y when prompted and then press Enter to start the backup.

5. The backup progress will be detailed in the command prompt window. After the backup completes, enter `exit` to close the command prompt window.

Maintaining Windows Server 2008 Hyper-V Systems

Maintaining Windows 2008 Hyper-V host and guest systems isn't an easy task for adminis-trators. They must find time in their firefighting efforts to focus and plan for maintenance on the server systems. When maintenance tasks are commonplace in an environment, they can alleviate many of the common firefighting tasks.

The processes and procedures for maintaining Hyper-V systems can be separated based on the appropriate time to maintain a particular aspect of a server. Some maintenance proce-dures require daily attention, whereas others might require only quarterly checkups. The maintenance processes and procedures that an organization follows depend strictly on the organization; however, the categories described in the following sections and their corresponding procedures are best practices for organizations of all sizes and varying IT infrastructures.

Daily Maintenance

Certain maintenance procedures require more attention than others. The procedures that require the most attention are categorized into the daily procedures. Therefore, it is recommended that an administrator take on these procedures each day to ensure system reliability, availability, performance, and security. These procedures are examined in the following three sections.

Checking Overall Server Functionality
Although checking the overall server health and functionality might seem redundant or elementary, this procedure is critical to keeping the system environment and users working productively.

Questions that should be addressed during the checking and verification process include the following:

▶ Can users access data on guest sessions?

▶ Are guest session applications responding to client requests? Are there long queues for applications such as inbound email message queues, held or paused print queues on guest sessions running print services, and so on?

▶ Is there an exceptionally long wait to log on (that is, longer than normal)?

▶ Can users access external resources?

Verifying That Backups Are Successful

To provide a secure and fault-tolerant organization, it is imperative that a successful backup be performed each night. In the event of a host or guest server failure, the administrator might be required to perform a restore from tape. Without a backup each night, the IT organization will be forced to rely on rebuilding the server without the data. Therefore, the administrator should always back up servers so that the IT organization can restore them with minimum downtime in the event of a disaster. Because of the importance of the backups, the first priority of the administrator each day needs to be verifying and maintaining the backup sets.

If disaster ever strikes, the administrators want to be confident that a system or entire site can be recovered as quickly as possible. Successful backup mechanisms are imperative to the recovery operation; recoveries are only as good as the most recent backups.

Remember on a Hyper-V server that there's more than just one server to backup: All the guest sessions running on the host server need to be successfully backed up. At any one time, a server with 4, 8, 10, 15, or more guest sessions will require that all guest sessions are checked to confirm the backup of each guest session was successful.

Monitoring Event Viewer

Event Viewer is used to check the system, security, application, and other logs on a local or remote system. These logs are an invaluable source of information regarding the system. The Event Viewer Overview and Summary page in Server Manager is shown in Figure 6.18.

> **NOTE**
>
> Checking these logs often helps your understanding of them. There are some events that constantly appear but aren't significant. Events will begin to look familiar, so you will notice when something is new or amiss in your event logs.

All Event Viewer events are categorized either as informational, warning, or error. Some best practices for monitoring event logs include the following:

▶ Understanding the events that are being reported

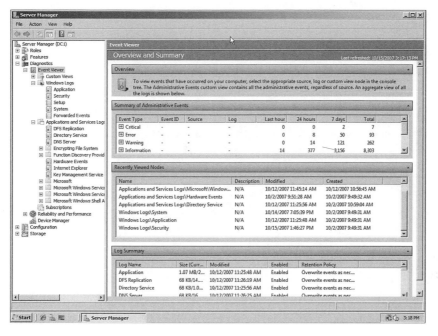

FIGURE 6.18   The Event Viewer Overview and Summary page.

► Setting up a database for archived event logs

► Archiving event logs frequently

To simplify monitoring hundreds or thousands of generated events each day, the administrator should use the filtering mechanism provided in Event Viewer. Although warnings and errors should take priority, the informational events should be reviewed to track what was happening before the problem occurred. After the administrator reviews the informational events, she can filter out the informational events and view only the warnings and errors.

To filter events, follow these steps:

1. Expand the Event View folder in Server Manager.

2. Select the log from which you want to filter events.

3. Right-click the log and select Filter Current Log.

4. In the log Properties window, select the types of events to filter. In this case, select the Critical, Error, and Warning check boxes.

5. Click OK when you've finished.

Figure 6.19 shows the results of filtering on the system log. You can see in the figure that there are a total of 7,510 events. In the message above the log, the filter is noted and also the 304 resulting number of events. The filter reduced the events by a factor of over 20 to 1. This really helps reduce the volume of data that an administrator needs to review.

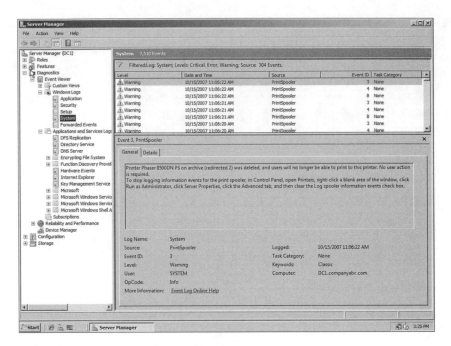

FIGURE 6.19   The Event Viewer filter.

Some warnings and errors are normal because of bandwidth constraints or other environmental issues. The more you monitor the logs, the more familiar you will become with the messages and, therefore, the more likely you will be able to spot a problem before it affects the user community.

> **TIP**
>
> You might need to increase the size of the log files in Event Viewer to accommodate an increase in logging activity. The default log sizes are larger in Windows 2008 than in earlier versions of Windows, which were notorious for running out of space.

Weekly Maintenance

Maintenance procedures that require slightly less attention than daily checking are categorized in a weekly routine and are examined in the following sections.

Checking Disk Space

Disk space is a precious commodity. Although the disk capacity of a Windows 2008 system can be nearly endless, the amount of free space on all drives should be checked at least weekly if not more frequently. Whereas a single server may grow disk space demands at a steady pace, with several virtual guest sessions running on a Hyper-V host server the use of disk space can occur exponentially. Serious problems can occur if there isn't enough disk space, so checking both guest session available disk space and the host server system will ensure an image or server won't unexpectedly run out of disk space to cache files, queue up messages, or buffer database growth required by the system.

One of the most common disk space problems occurs on data drives where end users save and modify information. Other volumes such as the system drive, and partitions with logging data can also quickly fill up.

As mentioned earlier, lack of free disk space can cause a multitude of problems including the following:

- ▶ Application failures
- ▶ System crashes
- ▶ Unsuccessful backup jobs
- ▶ Service failures
- ▶ The inability to audit
- ▶ Performance degradation

To prevent these problems from occurring, administrators should keep the amount of free space to at least 25%.

CAUTION

If you need to free disk space, you should move or delete files and folders with caution. System files are automatically protected by Windows 2008, but data is not.

Verifying Hardware

These days, hardware systems tend to be pretty reliable unlike a decade or two ago when the quality control on memory chips, hard drives, and the like dictated that a burn-in period was required for all servers to work through faulty components. However, even though reliability is much better today than years past, this doesn't mean that they'll always run continuously without failure. Hardware availability is measured in terms of mean time between failures (MTBF) and mean time to repair (MTTR). This includes downtime for both planned and unplanned events. These measurements provided by the manufacturer are good guidelines to follow; however, mechanical parts are bound to fail at one time or another. Therefore, hardware should be monitored weekly to ensure efficient operation.

Hardware can be monitored in many different ways. For example, server systems might have internal checks and logging functionality to warn against possible failure, Windows 2008's System Monitor might bring light to a hardware failure, and a physical hardware check can help to determine whether the system is about to experience a problem with the hardware.

If a failure has occurred or is about to occur, having an inventory of spare hardware can significantly improve the chances and timing of recoverability. Checking system hardware on a weekly basis provides the opportunity to correct the issue before it becomes a problem.

Monthly Maintenance

It is recommended that you perform the tasks examined in the following sections on a monthly basis.

Testing the UPS

An uninterruptible power supply (UPS) can be used to protect the system or group of systems from power failures (such as spikes and surges) and keep the system running long enough after a power outage so that an administrator can gracefully shut down the system. It is recommended that an administrator follow the UPS guidelines provided by the manufacturer at least once a month. Also, monthly scheduled battery tests should be performed.

Validating Backups

Once a month, an administrator should validate backups by restoring the backups to a server located in a lab environment. This is in addition to verifying that backups were successful from log files or the backup program's management interface. A restore gives the administrator the opportunity to verify the backups and to practice the restore procedures that would be used when recovering the server during a real disaster. In addition, this procedure tests the state of the backup media to ensure that they are in working order and builds administrator confidence for recovering from a true disaster.

Updating Documentation

An integral part of managing and maintaining any IT environment is to document the network infrastructure and procedures. The following are just a few of the documents you should consider having on hand:

- Server build guides
- Disaster-recovery guides and procedures
- Checklists
- Configuration settings
- Change configuration logs
- Historical performance data
- Special user rights assignments
- Special application settings

As systems and services are built and procedures are ascertained, document these facts to reduce learning curves, administration, and maintenance.

It is not only important to adequately document the IT environment, but it's often even more important to keep those documents up-to-date. Otherwise, documents can quickly become outdated as the environment, processes, and procedures change as the business changes.

Quarterly Maintenance

As the name implies, quarterly maintenance is performed four times a year. Areas to maintain and manage on a quarterly basis are typically fairly self-sufficient and self-sustaining. Infrequent maintenance is required to keep the system healthy. This doesn't mean, however, that the tasks are simple or that they aren't as critical as those tasks that require more frequent maintenance.

Checking Storage Limits

Storage capacity on all volumes should be checked to ensure that all volumes have ample free space. Keep approximately 25% free space on all volumes.

Running low or completely out of disk space creates unnecessary risk for any system. Services can fail, applications can stop responding, and systems can even crash if there isn't plenty of disk space.

Changing Administrator Passwords

Administrator passwords should, at a minimum, be changed every quarter (90 days). Changing these passwords strengthens security measures so that systems can't easily be compromised. In addition to changing passwords, other password requirements such as password age, history, length, and strength should be reviewed.

Performing Management Tasks with Server Manager

Server Manager is a tool that comes with Windows Server 2008 that provides a central location for managing roles and features on a Windows 2008 system. Server Manager has been used several times already in this chapter for the installation of Windows Backup features or to enable Remote Desktop connections. The balance of this chapter covers other tasks within Server Manager specific to Hyper-V and its server components.

Server Manager in general enables the administrator to complete the following steps:

- ▶ Add and remove roles and features from the server

- ▶ Monitor and manage the server

- ▶ Administer the roles and features on the server

Server Manager is a one-stop shop for all the administrator management and monitoring needs. The features of Server Manager are available via the Server Manager console.

Selecting the server name in the folder tree will show the Server Manager main window in the Details pane. This consists of several section windows. The Server Summary window (shown in Figure 6.20) shows computer information such as the computer name, networking information, and whether Remote Desktop is enabled. It also shows security information such as whether Windows Firewall is enabled and the Windows Updates status. The window also has active links that enable the administrator to launch wizards to change the configuration or get help.

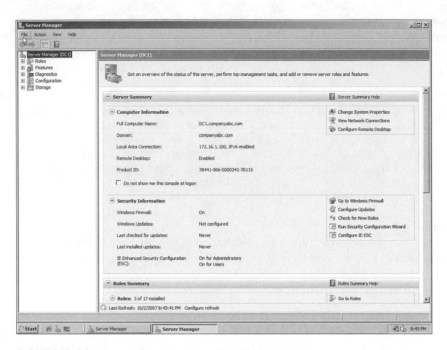

FIGURE 6.20   Server Manager Server Summary window.

Server Manager launches automatically when the Initial Configuration Wizard is closed and each time a user logs on to the server.

The next sections discuss the components and features of Server Manager.

Server Manager Roles Page

The Server Manager console has a folder tree dedicated to the roles of the server. When the Hyper-V role was installed on the host system as covered in Chapter 3 of this book, the Hyper-V Server role was added to the Roles folder in Server Manager. Selecting the Roles folder in the console tree shows a summary of the roles installed on the server (which Hyper-V will be shown) and a summary page for each of the roles. The summary page for each role shows the role status, such as the status of the system services and the events for the role.

However, selecting the folder for a specific role shows the Server Manager role-specific page for that role. The role-specific pages are dedicated to the role and contain operational information about the role. The following sections discuss the sections included in the role-specific page.

Events Section

There is a problem with going to the full Event Viewer and seeing all the events for all roles, services, and the operating system. There is usually so much information that it ends up overloading the administrator, making it difficult to see real problems. The Events section in the role-specific page addresses this by presenting only the role-specific events.

From the Events section, the administrator can see a summary of the events that pertain to the role, review the details of the events, and filter the events as needed. The default filter shows only events in the past 24 hours, but this can be adjusted via the Filter Events control.

The full Event Viewer can also be launched from this section.

System Services Section

The System Services section lists the services that the role depends on and their status. It also describes each service and includes control links to stop, start, restart, and to configure preferences.

The Preferences control allows the administrator to adjust the dependency services. For example, in Hyper-V, some of the corresponding services used for Hyper-V that may be displayed in the System Services section include the following:

- ▶ Microsoft Hyper-V Image Management Service
- ▶ Microsoft Hyper-V Networking Management
- ▶ Virtual Machine Management

Resources and Support Section

The Resources and Support section is a useful section. It provides a brief recommendation on configurations, best practices, and links to resources. The recommendations are listed in a window; highlighting the recommendation shows a brief explanation of the recommendation with a link to a more detailed explanation. This is great for researching the recommendations. The section also includes links to online resources, such as the appropriate TechCenter and Community Center for the role.

For example, the Resources and Support section for Hyper-V role (shown in Figure 6.21) includes five different recommendations on configuration optimization. One of the recommendations is "Increase the availability of your virtual machines by using clustering to configure failover for the physical computer." Highlighting this recommendation shows a brief paragraph explaining the recommendation and includes a link to get more detailed information about the recommendation.

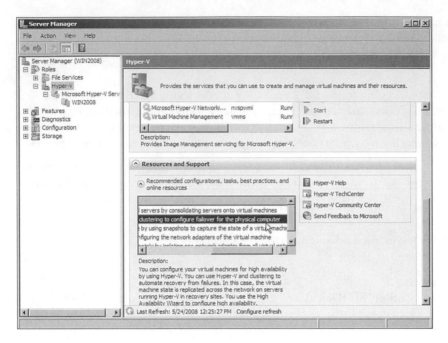

FIGURE 6.21   Resources and Support section.

An important note is that these recommendations are static and don't adjust to changes in the environment.

Server Manager Diagnostics Page

The Diagnostics page in Server Manager consolidates three different consoles into a convenient location. The three consoles are as follows:

- ▶ Event Viewer
- ▶ Reliability and Performance
- ▶ Device Manager

The next sections review the various features of the three consoles on the Diagnostics page.

Event Viewer

The Windows 2008 Event Viewer functionality has been improved over the previous version of Windows Server. The version in Windows 2008 is the version that released in Windows Vista. The event logs can contain an overwhelming volume of information, which the new Event Viewer summarizes and drills into very effectively.

Selecting the Event Viewer folder under Diagnostics shows the Overview and Summary page. The Summary of Administrative Events section on this page shows a high-level summary of the administrative events, organized by level:

▶ Critical

▶ Error

▶ Warning

▶ Information

▶ Audit Success

▶ Audit Failure

The view shows the total number of events in the past hour, 24 hours, 7 days, and the total. Each of these nodes can be expanded to show the counts of particular event IDs within each level. Double-clicking the event ID count shows a detailed list of the events with the matching event ID. This is useful for drilling on the specific events to see when they are occurring.

The Overview and Summary page also has a Log Summary section, which shows a list of all the various logs on the server. This is important because there are now more than 100 different logs in Windows 2008. In addition to the standard system, security, and application logs, there is a setup log and a forwarded events log. Then there are the numerous application and services logs, which include logs for each application, service, and a huge number of diagnostic and debugging logs. For each of the logs, the Log Summary section shows the log name, current size, maximum size, last modification, if it is enabled, and what the retention policy for the log is. This allows the administrator to quickly see the status of all the logs, which would be a daunting task otherwise.

Of course, the logs can be viewed directly by expanding the Windows Logs folder or the Applications and Services Logs folder. The Windows Logs folder contains all the standard application, security, setup, system, and forwarded events logs. The applications and services logs contain all the other ones.

Custom views can be created to filter events and combine logs into a coherent view. There is a default Administrative Events view, which combines the critical, error, and warning events from all the administrative logs. There is also a custom view created for each role that is installed on the server. New ones can be created by the administrator as needed.

Subscriptions can collect events from remote computers and store them in the forwarded events log. The events to be collected are specified in the subscription. The functionality depends on the Windows Remote Management (WinRM) and the Windows Event Collector (Wecsvc) services and they must be running on both the collecting and forwarding servers.

Server Manager Reliability and Performance Monitor

The Reliability and Performance monitor is incorporated into Server Manager, too. The Reliability and Performance Monitor was introduced with the Windows Vista platform. This diagnostic tool enables the administrator to monitor the performance of the server in real time and to save the performance data to logs for analysis.

The top-level folder of the Reliability and Performance monitor displays the Resource Overview. This gives a comprehensive overview of the CPU, disk, network, and memory utilization during the past 60 seconds (shown in Figure 6.22). The graph shows the server overall usage for each of the four categories. In addition, a Details pane for each of the categories shows the utilization by process.

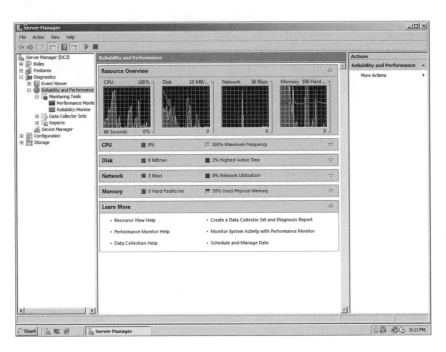

FIGURE 6.22   Resource Overview graph.

The Monitoring Tools in the Reliability and Performance monitor contain the Performance Monitor and the Reliability Monitor. These tools enable you to monitor the performance and reliability of the server.

The Performance Monitor has not really changed from earlier versions of Windows. It allows you to select performance counters and add them to a graph view for real-time monitoring. The graph can be configured to be a line graph, a bar graph, or even a simple text report of the counters being monitored. The monitor shows the last, average, minimum, maximum, and duration of the windows (1 minute 40 seconds by default).

The Reliability Monitor tracks events that could potentially affect the stability of the server, such as updates, installs, and hardware issues. It uses this information to generate a System Stability Index, which is a number between 1 (least stable) to 10 (most stable). The index tracks the following:

▶ Software Installs/Uninstalls

▶ Application Failures

▶ Hardware Failures

▶ Windows Failures

▶ Miscellaneous Failures

It plots all these events on the chart and uses them to compute the System Stability Index. This is useful for assessing the overall health of the server and for troubleshooting. You can see these events on the chart over time and see how they potentially impact the stability of the server, and then correlate the events to actual stability issues.

Finally, for longer-term tracking, the Data Collector Sets can be used. Data Collector Sets can log data from the following data sources:

▶ Performance counters

▶ Event traces

▶ Registry key values

This data can be logged over an extended period of time and then reviewed.

Device Manager

The Device Manager node shows the hardware that is installed on the server. It shows the hardware grouped by type of device, such as disk drives, display adapters, and network adapters. Each instance of the device type is listed in a node underneath the device type.

The Device Manager can be used to update the device drivers of the hardware, to change settings, and to troubleshoot issues with the hardware. Specifically, you can perform the following tasks:

▶ Scan for new hardware

▶ Identify hardware problems

▶ Adjust configurations

▶ View device driver versions

▶ Update the device drivers

▶ Roll back device driver upgrades

▶ Enable or disable hardware

For example, sometimes older video drivers or network card drivers will cause problems with the system. It is easy to check the Microsoft online driver repository using Device

Manager. To check for an update to the device driver for the network adapter, follow these steps:

1. Expand the Network Adapters node in Device Manager.
2. Select the network adapter to check.
3. Select Action, Update Driver Software from the menu.
4. Click Search Automatically for Updated Driver Software.
5. Click Yes, Always Search Online (Recommended).
6. Install the update if found.
7. Click Close to exit the wizard.

> **NOTE**
>
> Many times, the latest version of the driver will already be installed. In these cases, the message "The best driver for your device is already installed" will be shown.

Server Manager Configuration Page

The Configuration page in Server Manager is somewhat misleading. This is not the page from which you would configure the server. The Configuration node in Server Manager is just a container for the following four snap-ins:

- ▶ Task Scheduler
- ▶ Windows Firewall with Advanced Security
- ▶ Services
- ▶ WMI Control

These snap-ins allow the administrator to control some elements of the server configuration and are covered in the next four sections.

Task Scheduler

One of the greatly expanded features of Windows 2008 is the Task Scheduler. In earlier versions of Windows, this was an anemic service with limited options and auditing features. The Task Scheduler features in Windows 2008 have been expanded into a more sophisticated tool. The scheduler can start based on a variety of triggers, can take a number of predefined actions, and can even be mitigated by conditions and the settings.

> **NOTE**
>
> A creative way of using Task Scheduler in Hyper-V is to set up a task that pauses a virtual guest session, takes a snapshot of the session, copies the session image files off to an external storage system, and then restarts the session. This is a cheap and simple way to take static backups of guest images and copy images off a Hyper-V host system to an external storage system.

There are several elements to the Task Scheduler, as follows:

- ▶ **Triggers**—Tasks run when the trigger criteria are met. This could be a scheduled time, logon, startup, idle, log event, user session connect or disconnect, or workstation lock or unlock. These various triggers give the administrator a wide range of options on when to start a task.

- ▶ **Actions**—The actions are the work that the task will perform. This can be executing a program, sending an email via SMTP, or displaying a message on the desktop.

- ▶ **Conditions**—Conditions allow the task trigger criteria to be filtered. Conditions include if the computer is idle, on battery power, or connected to a network. This allows administrators to prevent tasks from running if the computer is busy, on battery, or disconnected from the network.

- ▶ **Settings**—The settings control how a task can be executed, stopped, or deleted. In the settings of a task, the administrator can control if the task can be launched manually, if it runs after a missed schedule start, if it needs to restart after a failure, if it needs to run multiple tasks in parallel, or to delete it if it is not set to run in the future.

Also included with Windows 2008 Task Scheduler is the Task Scheduler Library, which includes approximately 20 different predefined tasks. These tasks include the following:

- ▶ **ScheduledDefrag**—This task runs every week and uses the command `defrag.exe -c -i -g` to defragment all the volumes on the server. This is a major improvement of earlier versions of Windows, which required this command to be run manually. However, the trigger for this task is disabled by default, so it will not run as shipped.

- ▶ **ServerManager**—This task runs at user logon and runs the ServerManagerLauncher to launch the Server Manager console whenever a user logs on.

Both these tasks demonstrate the capabilities of the Task Scheduler to automate routine tasks or to ensure that certain tasks run at logon.

The Task Scheduler has a new feature that goes hand in hand with the library, namely the ability to create folders to store the tasks. This helps organize the tasks that are created. The scheduler includes a Microsoft folder for the tasks that ship with the operating system. Administrators can create other folders to organize and store their tasks.

Selecting the Task Scheduler folder in the System Manager configuration shows the Task Scheduler Summary (shown in Figure 6.23). This window has two sections: Task Scheduler and Active Tasks. The Task Scheduler section shows the status of tasks within a time frame, by default the past 24 hours. The time frame can be set to the last hour, last 24 hours, last 7 days, or last 30 days. For each task that has run within the time frame, it shows the Task Name, Run Result, Run Start, and Run End. The section also summarizes the task status; Figure 6.23 shows 51 total tasks have run with 1 running and 50 succeeded. The figure also shows that it is the ScheduledDefrag task that is running.

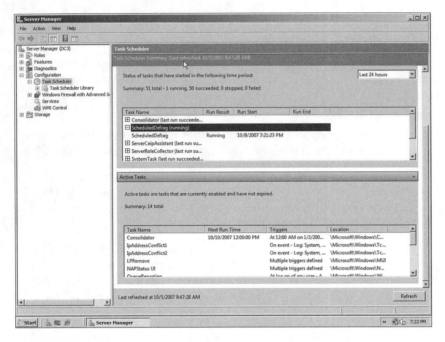

FIGURE 6.23   Task Scheduler Summary window.

The Active Tasks name is somewhat misleading because it shows tasks that are enabled and their triggers. It does not show tasks that are running. For the scheduled tasks, it shows the Next Run Time. This section is useful for seeing which tasks will run on a given server in response to a trigger, either a schedule or an event. If the task does not appear in this section, it will be run only if executed manually.

A quick review of the Active Tasks shows that the ScheduledDefrag task is not in the list. This is because the trigger for the task is disabled by default, so the task will not run and so does not show in the Active Tasks list.

To enable the ScheduledDefrag task, execute the following steps:

1. Open the Server Manager console.
2. Expand the Configuration folder.
3. Expand the Task Scheduler folder.
4. Expand the Task Scheduler Library folder.

5. Expand the Microsoft, Windows folder and select the Defrag folder.

6. Select the ScheduledDefrag task and select Action, Properties.

7. Select the Triggers tab.

8. Select the Weekly trigger and click the Edit button.

9. At the bottom of the Edit Trigger window, check the Enabled box.

10. Click OK.

11. Click OK to close the Properties of the task.

Going back to the Task Scheduler Summary window, you will now find the ScheduledDefrag task listed with a Next Run Time of the following Wednesday at 1:00 a.m.

Windows Firewall with Advanced Security

The Windows Firewall with Advanced Security feature provides access to the combined Windows Firewall and Connection Security features of Windows 2008. These technologies work in tandem to provide protection from network-based attacks to the server. The firewall rules determine what network traffic is allowed or blocked to the server. The connection security rules determine how the allowed traffic is secured.

The Windows Firewall with Advanced Security folder shows a summary of which profile is active (Domain, Private, or Public), the profile's high-level configuration, and links to the other components of the snap-in.

The other components of the Windows Firewall with Advanced Security snap-in are for configuration and monitoring the features. These components are as follows:

▶ Inbound rules

▶ Outbound rules

▶ Connection Security rules

▶ Monitoring

The inbound and outbound rules control what traffic is allowed in to an out of the server. Several hundred rules govern what traffic is allowed. These are organized into profiles for ease of application. Table 6.5 shows these profiles.

TABLE 6.5   Firewall Profiles

Profile	Description
Domain Profile	Applied when the server is connected to its Active Directory domain.
Private Profile	Applied when the server is connected to a private network but not to the Active Directory domain.
Public Profile	Applied when the server is connected to a public network.

Clearly, the vast majority of services will have the Domain Profile active, because they will likely be on a network with Active Directory. Each of the profiles has a set of rules associated with them. In addition, a number of rules apply to all profiles, which are designated as Any. Some of the rules are disabled by default.

Connection Security rules are stored in the likewise named folder. The rules specify how the computers on either side of a permitted connection authenticate and secure the network traffic. This is essentially the IPsec policy from previous versions of Windows, albeit with a much-improved interface. By default, there are no Connection Security rules created in Windows 2008. Rules can be created and reviewed in this portion of the snap-in.

The Monitoring folder is somewhat limited in scope. It has a Firewall folder and a Connection Security Rules folder. These two folders simply show what rules are active, but show no traffic details or whether the rules have blocked or allowed anything. In effect, they show the net result of the profile that is active.

More useful in monitoring is the Security Associations folder. This folder lists the security associations (shown in Figure 6.24) with the local and remote IP addresses, authentication methods, encryption, integrity, and key exchange. In the figure, you can see that the local address of the server is 172.16.1.101 and the other server is 172.16.1.100. The computers are authenticating using Kerberos, and the user is also authenticating at the connection level using Kerberos. Finally, the network traffic confidentiality is protected with the AES-128 encryption algorithm, and the network traffic is protected from modification by the SHA-1 integrity algorithm. Multiple security associations are listed, reflecting various connections that have been established between the two servers.

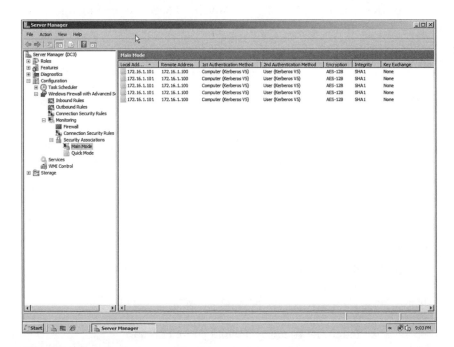

FIGURE 6.24   Security associations monitoring.

Services

The Services snap-in in the Configuration container in Server Manager is essentially unchanged from the previous version of Windows. All the services are listed, along with their status, startup type, and logon credentials.

From the Services snap-in, administrators can control services on the server, including the following:

▶ Start or stop the services

▶ Change the startup type to set the service to start automatically, be started manually, or even prevent the service from starting at all

▶ Change the account the service runs under

▶ Set up recovery actions if the service stops, such as restarting the service or even restarting the server

▶ View the configuration details of the service, such as what the executable is, what the service name is (which is shown in the Task Manager window), and what dependencies it has

A new feature is the Automatic (Delayed Start) startup type. This is a setting used to reduce the crunch of services starting all at once during boot of the server. All the services with the Automatic (Delayed Start) setting will be started after the services with the automatic setting. This allows all the services to come up automatically, but allows essential services to start first.

WMI Control

The last snap-in in the Configuration container of the Server Manager is the WMI Control tool. This is a new tool that allows administrators to maintain the Windows Management Instrumentation (WMI) configuration on the server. With this tool, an administrator can accomplish the following tasks:

▶ Back up the WMI repository

▶ Change the default scripting namespace (root\cimv2)

▶ Manage access to the WMI via the Security tab

Before the introduction of the WMI Control tool, these tasks were difficult to accomplish.

To back up the WMI repository, you just need to complete the following steps:

1. Open the Server Manager console.
2. Expand the Configuration folder.
3. Select the WMI Control folder.
4. Select the Action menu and then Properties.
5. Select the Backup/Restore tab.
6. Enter a filename with a full path. The file type will be a WMI Recovery File (REC).

7. Click Save to save the file.

8. Click OK to exit the tool.

Interestingly, the tool is not an integrated snap-in, but rather a separate tool.

Summary

Although administrators can easily get caught up in daily administration and firefighting, it's important to structure system management and maintenance of the Hyper-V host servers and guest sessions to help prevent unnecessary amounts of effort. Windows 2008 provides many tools that allow administrators to more effectively manage their servers.

The Hyper-V Manager tool provides key components in setting up virtual network switches, managing guest disk images, and configuring host services. The Windows 2008 Server Manager is a one-stop shop for the management and monitoring Hyper-V servers and is the parent operating system of the host system.

Administration of Hyper-V hosts does not need to be done at the console of each Hyper-V host because there are several different ways of connecting to a remote host server and the guest sessions running on the Hyper-V host system.

Security is also extremely important in a Hyper-V environment, being that the compromise of a single Hyper-V host server opens up the door for unauthorized access to many running host servers. Common practices can be applied to minimize the risk footprint of a Hyper-V host system.

Systems management and maintenance is not just about the cool technologies, but also about how those technologies are used. Following a management and maintenance regimen reduces administration, maintenance, and business expenses while at the same time increasing reliability, stability, and security.

The chapter covered a multitude of processes and procedures that help organizations better manage, administer, and maintain their Hyper-V host systems and the guest sessions running on the virtual host server.

Best Practices

The following are best practices from this chapter:

▶ The Hyper-V Administration console is the first tool to use in managing Hyper-V configurations and operations.

▶ Use System Manager as a centralized tool for all Windows 2008 and Hyper-V administrative tasks.

▶ Try to maintain the network environment's systems periodically to avoid any inefficiency.

► Remotely manage systems using Remote Server Administration tools, Remote Desktop for Administration, Windows Remote Management, and command-line utilities.

► Use System Center Operations Manager 2007 to proactively manage Hyper-V hosts and guest sessions.

► Identify tasks that are important to the system's overall health and security.

► Install the appropriate service packs and updates on each production server and guest sessions to keep all systems consistent.

► Use the Offline Virtual Machine Servicing tool to keep virtual guest templates and offline images up-to-date with the latest patches and updates.

► Test and evaluate service packs and updates in a lab environment before installing them on production servers.

► Use the snapshot capability in Hyper-V as a rollback strategy to recovery from a service pack or patch installation failure.

► Use Windows Software Update Services to minimize administration, management, and maintenance associated with keeping up with the latest service packs and updates.

► Categorize and document daily maintenance activities such as checking server functionality, verifying that backups were successful, and monitoring Event Viewer events.

► Categorize and document weekly maintenance processes and procedures such as checking disk space, verifying hardware operation, and archiving event logs.

► Categorize and document monthly maintenance processes and procedures such as maintaining system integrity, testing UPS functionality, validating backups, and updating documentation.

► Categorize and document quarterly maintenance processes and procedures such as checking storage limits and changing administrative passwords.

► Use Windows Server Backup to back up Hyper-V hosts and guest images, but rely on backing up guest images to take advantage of VSS recovery mechanisms and the proper flushing of application transaction logs.

► Perform management tasks such as reviewing reliability and performance monitor to ensure the Hyper-V host server and guest sessions are running properly.

## 7

Optimizing the Hyper-V Host Server and Guest Sessions

Capacity analysis and performance optimization is a critical part of deploying and managing Hyper-V host servers. Capacity analysis and performance optimization ensures that resources and applications are available, uptime is maximized, and systems scale well to meet the growing demands of business. Windows 2008 includes some new and some refreshed tools to assist IT administrators and staff with properly assessing server capacity and performance—before and after Windows 2008 is deployed on the network. If you invest time in these processes, you will spend less time troubleshooting or putting out fires, thus making your life less stressful and also reducing business costs.

Defining Capacity Analysis

The majority of capacity analysis is working to minimize unknown or immeasurable variables, such as the number of gigabytes or terabytes of storage the system will need in the next few months or years, to adequately size a system. The high number of unknown variables is largely because network environments, business policy, and people are constantly changing. As a result, capacity analysis is an art as much as it involves experience and insight.

If you've ever found yourself having to specify configuration requirements for a new server or having to estimate whether your configuration will have enough power to sustain various workloads now and in the foreseeable future, proper capacity analysis can help in the design and configuration. These capacity-analysis processes help weed out the unknowns and assist you while making decisions as accurately as possible. They do so by giving you a greater understanding of your Windows 2008 environment. This knowledge and understanding can then be used to reduce time and costs associated with supporting and designing an infrastructure. The result is that you gain more control over the environment, reduce maintenance and support costs, minimize firefighting, and make more efficient use of your time.

Business depends on network systems for a variety of different operations, such as performing transactions or providing security, so that the business functions as efficiently as possible. Systems that are underutilized are probably wasting money and are of little value. On the other hand, systems that are overworked or can't handle workloads prevent the business from completing tasks or transactions in a timely manner, might cause a loss of opportunity, or might keep the users from being productive. Either way, these systems are typically not much benefit to operating a business. To keep network systems well tuned for the given workloads, capacity analysis seeks a balance between the resources available and the workload required of the resources. The balance provides just the right amount of computing power for given and anticipated workloads.

This concept of balancing resources extends beyond the technical details of server configuration to include issues such as gauging the number of administrators who might be needed to maintain various systems in your environment. Many of these questions relate to capacity analysis, and the answers aren't readily known because they can't be predicted with complete accuracy.

To lessen the burden and dispel some of the mysteries of estimating resource requirements, capacity analysis provides the processes to guide you. These processes include vendor guidelines, industry benchmarks, analysis of present system resource utilization, and more. Through these processes, you'll gain as much understanding as possible of the network environment and step away from the compartmentalized or limited understanding of the systems. In turn, you'll also gain more control over the systems and increase your chances of successfully maintaining the reliability, serviceability, and availability of your system.

There is no set or formal way to start your capacity-analysis processes. However, a proven and effective means to begin to proactively manage your system is to first establish systemwide policies and procedures. Policies and procedures, discussed shortly, help shape service levels and user expectations. After these policies and procedures are classified and defined, you can more easily start characterizing system workloads, which will help gauge acceptable baseline performance values.

The Benefits of Capacity Analysis and Performance Optimization

The benefits of capacity analysis and performance optimization are almost inconceivable. Capacity analysis helps define and gauge overall system health by establishing baseline performance values, and then the analysis provides valuable insight into where the system is heading. Continuous performance monitoring and optimization will ensure systems are stable and perform well, reducing support calls from end users, which, in turn, reduces costs to the organization and helps employees be more productive. It can be used to uncover both current and potential bottlenecks and can also reveal how changing management activities can affect performance today and tomorrow.

Another benefit of capacity analysis is that it can be applied to small environments and scale well into enterprise-level systems. The level of effort needed to initially drive the capacity-analysis processes will vary depending on the size of your environment, geography, and political divisions. With a little up-front effort, you'll save time, expense, and gain a wealth of knowledge and control over the network environment.

Establishing Policy and Metric Baselines

As mentioned earlier, it is recommended that you first begin defining policies and procedures regarding service levels and objectives. Because each environment varies in design, you can't create cookie-cutter policies—you need to tailor them to your particular business practices and to the environment. In addition, you should strive to set policies that set user expectations and, more important, help winnow out empirical data.

Essentially, policies and procedures define how the system is supposed to be used—establishing guidelines to help users understand that the system can't be used in any way they see fit. Many benefits are derived from these policies and procedures. For example, in an environment where policies and procedures are working successfully and where network performance becomes sluggish, it would be safer to assume that groups of people weren't playing a multiuser network game, that several individuals weren't sending enormous email attachments to everyone in the global address list, or that a rogue web or FTP server wasn't placed on the network. When a host server is running several virtual guest sessions, the possibility of many various areas of performance problems can arise as guest session performance impacts the overall host server, with other guest sessions also being impacted.

The network environment is shaped by the business more so than the IT department. Therefore, it's equally important to gain an understanding of user expectations and requirements through interviews, questionnaires, surveys, and more. Examples of policies and procedures that you can implement in your environment pertaining to end users include the following:

- ▶ Email message size, including attachments, can't exceed 10MB.

- ▶ Beta software, freeware, and shareware can be installed only on test equipment (that is, not on client machines or servers in the production environment).

- ▶ All computing resources are for business use only. (In other words, no gaming or personal use of computers is allowed.)

- ▶ Only business-related and approved applications will be supported and allowed on the network.

- ▶ All home directories will be limited in size (for example, 500MB) per user.

- ▶ Users must either fill out the technical support Outlook form or request assistance through the advertised help desk phone number.

Policies and procedures, however, aren't just for end users. They can also be established and applied to IT personnel. In this scenario, policies and procedures can serve as guidelines for technical issues, rules of engagement, or an internal set of rules to abide by. The following list provides some examples of policies and procedures that might be applied to the IT department:

▶ System backups must include system state data and should be completed by 5:00 a.m. each workday and restores should be tested frequently for accuracy and disaster preparedness.

▶ Routine system maintenance should be performed only outside of normal business hours (for example, weekdays between 8:00 p.m. and 12:00 a.m. or on weekends).

▶ Basic technical support requests should be attended to within 2 business days.

▶ Priority technical support requests should be attended to within 4 hours of the request.

▶ Any planned downtime for servers should follow a change-control process and must be approved by the IT director at least 1 week in advance with a 5-day lead time provided to those impacted by the change.

Benchmark Baselines

If you've begun defining policies and procedures, you're already cutting down the number of immeasurable variables and amount of empirical data that challenge your decision-making process. The next step to prepare for capacity analysis is to begin gathering baseline performance values. The Microsoft Baseline Security Analyzer (MBSA) is an example of a tool that performs a security compliance scan against a predefined baseline.

Baselines give you a starting point with which you can compare results. For the most part, determining baseline performance levels involves working with hard numbers that represent the health of a system. On the other hand, a few variables coincide with the statistical representations, such as workload characterization, vendor requirements or recommendations, industry-recognized benchmarks, and the data that you collect.

Workload Characterization

Workloads are defined by how processes or tasks are grouped, the resources they require, and the type of work being performed. Examples of how workloads can be characterized include departmental functions, time of day, the type of processing required (such as batch or real time), companywide functions (such as payroll), volume of work, and much more.

It is unlikely that each system in your environment is a separate entity that has its own workload characterization. Most, if not all, network environments have systems that depend on other systems or are even intertwined among different workloads. This makes workload characterization difficult at best.

So, why is workload characterization so important? Identifying system workloads allows you to determine the appropriate resource requirements for each of them. This way, you can properly plan the resources according to the performance levels the workloads expect and demand.

Benchmarks

Benchmarks are a means to measure the performance of a variety of products, including operating systems, nearly all computer components, and even entire systems. Many companies rely on benchmarks to gain competitive advantage because so many professionals rely on them to help determine what's appropriate for their network environment.

As you would suspect, Sales and Marketing departments all too often exploit the benchmark results to sway IT professionals over their way. For this reason, it's important to investigate the benchmark results and the companies or organizations that produced the results. Vendors, for the most part, are honest with the results; but it's always a good idea to check with other sources, especially if the results are suspicious. For example, if a vendor has supplied benchmarks for a particular product, check to make sure that the benchmarks are consistent with other benchmarks produced by third-party organizations (such as magazines, benchmark organizations, and in-house testing labs). If none are available, try to gain insight from other IT professionals or run benchmarks on the product yourself before implementing it in production.

Although some suspicion might arise from benchmarks because of the sales and marketing techniques, the real purpose of benchmarks is to point out the performance levels that you can expect when using the product. Benchmarks can be extremely beneficial for decision making, but they shouldn't be your sole source for evaluating and measuring performance. Use the benchmark results only as a guideline or starting point when consulting benchmark results during capacity analysis. It's also recommended that you pay close attention to their interpretation.

Table 7.1 lists companies or organizations that provide benchmark statistics and benchmark-related information, and some also offer tools for evaluating product performance.

TABLE 7.1   Organizations That Provide Benchmarks

Company/Organization Name	Web Address
The Tolly Group	www.tollygroup.com
Transaction Processing	www.tpc.org/
Computer Measurement Group	www.cmg.org/

> **NOTE**
>
> New from Microsoft is the Microsoft Baseline Configuration Analyzer (MBCA) version 1.0, which is covered in more detail later in this chapter in the section "Microsoft Baseline Configuration Analyzer (MBCA)." MBCA is a tool that will deliver benchmark reports generated from baselines and system analysis. MBCA is available as a download from the Microsoft website for both 32- and 64-bit platforms.

Using Capacity-Analysis Tools

Analyzing system capacity and performance requires a handful of tools and the knowledge to use them properly to obtain valuable data. Windows 2008 includes several tools to assist with this initiative, and even more are available for download or purchase from Microsoft. In addition, several other companies also have performance and capacity-analysis solutions available. Some of these tools can even forecast system capacity, depending on the amount of information they are given.

A number of sizing tools exist from various companies. A sizing tool takes data relative to the networking environment and returns recommended hardware configurations, usually in a Microsoft Excel spreadsheet or similar reporting application. An example of one such tool is the Microsoft Exchange 2007 Sizing and Configuration tool by HP. This tool, available for download from http://h71019.www7.hp.com/activeanswers/Secure/483374-0-0-0-121.html, recommends HP servers and hardware configuration based on information about Exchange 2007, such as the number of mailboxes, volume of mail that will be migrated, and so on.

As covered in Chapter 3, "Planning, Sizing, and Architecting a Hyper-V Environment," the Microsoft Virtualization Solution Accelerator is also an excellent tool that does capacity analysis of existing physical and virtual server systems in the process of determining the proper size and capacity of the host server that will manage the guest sessions.

Microsoft also offers several useful utilities that are either inherent to Windows 2008 or are sold as separate products. Some of these utilities are included with the operating system, such as Task Manager, Network Monitor, Windows Reliability and Performance Monitor, and the enhanced Event Viewer. Data collected from these applications can be exported to other applications, such as Excel or Microsoft Access, for inventory and analysis. Other Microsoft utilities such as System Center Configuration Manager (SCCM) and System Center Operations Manager (OpsMgr) are sold separately.

Task Manager

The Windows 2008 Task Manager is similar to its Windows 2003 predecessor in that it offers multifaceted functionality. You can view and monitor processor-, memory-, application-, network-, services-, user-, and process-related information in real time for a given system. This utility is a well-known favorite among IT personnel and is great for getting a quick view of key system health indicators with the lowest performance overhead.

To begin using Task Manager, use any of the following methods:

▶ Press Ctrl+Shift+Esc.

▶ Right-click the taskbar and select Task Manager.

▶ Press Ctrl+Alt+Delete, and then click Task Manager.

When you start Task Manager, you'll see a screen similar to that shown in Figure 7.1.

FIGURE 7.1   Services tab in the Windows Server 2008 Task Manager.

The Task Manager window contains the following six tabs:

▶ **Applications**—This tab lists the applications that are currently running. You can start and end applications from this tab.

▶ **Processes**—On this tab, you can find performance metric information of the processes currently running on the system. Sorting the processes by CPU or memory usage will reveal which processes are consuming the most system resources.

▶ **Services**—New to Windows Server 2008 and Windows Vista is the Services tab in Task Manager. As shown in Figure 7.1, administrators can now see what services are running without having to load Computer Management or the Services Management Console (services.msc) separately.

▶ **Performance**—This tab can be a graphical or tabular representation of key system parameters such as kernel usage, paging, CPU cycles, and more (in real time).

> ▶ **Networking**—This tab displays the network traffic coming to and from the machine. The displayed network usage metric is a percentage of total available network capacity for a particular adapter.

> ▶ **Users**—This tab displays users who are currently logged on to the system.

In addition to the Task Manager tabs, the Task Manager is, by default, configured with a status bar at the bottom of the window. This status bar, shown in Figure 7.2, displays the number of running processes, CPU utilization percentage, and the amount of memory currently being used.

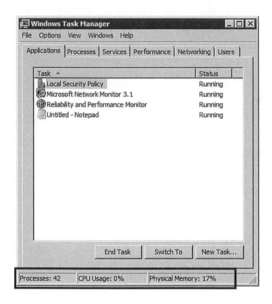

FIGURE 7.2   Windows Server 2008 Task Manager.

As you can see, Task Manager presents a variety of valuable real-time performance information. This tool proves particularly useful for determining what processes or applications are problematic and gives you an overall picture of system health with quick access to terminate applications or processes or to identify potential bottlenecks.

There are limitations, however, which prevent it from becoming a useful tool for long-term or historical analysis. For example, Task Manager can't store collected performance information for view later, it is capable of monitoring only certain aspects of the system's health, and the information that is displayed pertains only to the local machine. For these reasons alone, Task Manager doesn't make a prime candidate for capacity planning.

Network Monitor

Network Monitor is a crucial tool that system administrators should have in their arsenal. Network Monitor, now in its third version, has been overhauled to support the new networking changes introduced with both Windows 2008 and Windows Vista. Network

Monitor 3.1 includes several enhancements for capturing network traffic and parsing the captured data for use in troubleshooting, capacity analysis, and performance tuning. The next few sections cover using Network Monitor to capture network traffic between two computers, on a wireless connection, over remote-access connections, how to analyze captured data, and how to parse captured data for analysis. Network Monitor 3.1, shown in Figure 7.3, can be downloaded from the System Tools section in the Microsoft Download Center at www.microsoft.com/downloads/.

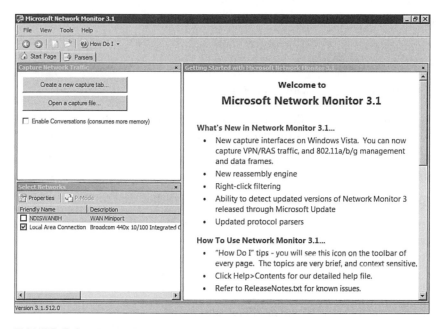

FIGURE 7.3   The Network Monitor 3.1 interface.

> **NOTE**
>
> The Network Monitor TechNet blog located at http://blogs.technet.com/netmon contains a wealth of information about Network Monitor, capturing, and analyzing data.

> **NOTE**
>
> Network Monitor 3.1 is available in 32-bit and 64-bit versions and can run on Windows Server 2008, Windows Server 2003, Windows Vista, and Windows XP systems.

What's New in Network Monitor 3.1

Network Monitor 3.1 expands on the capabilities of Network Monitor 3.0 by including several more features and fixes for issues that were discovered in the 3.0 version. Network Monitor 3.1 is very flexible and can even stop a capture based on an event log entry in Event Viewer.

Network Monitor 3.0 included the following:

▶ An optimized interface that included network conversations and an expandable tree view of frames for the conversations

▶ A real-time display and updating of captures

▶ The ability to capture traffic on multiple network cards simultaneously

▶ The ability to run multiple capture sessions simultaneously

▶ A script-based protocol parser language

▶ Support for Windows Vista, Windows Server 2008, Windows XP, and Windows Server 2003 on 32- or 64-bit platforms

Network Monitor 3.1 includes the following new features:

▶ The ability to capture wireless traffic, scan one or all wireless channels supported by the network card, and view signal strength and transfer speed of the connection

▶ The ability to trace traffic inside of a Windows Vista virtual private network (VPN) tunnel by capturing remote-access server (RAS) traffic

▶ The ability to right-click in the Frame Summary pane and click Add to Filter

▶ Support for the Windows Update service by periodically checking for updates to the Network Monitor program

▶ A redesigned filter toolbar

▶ A redesigned engine for supporting more protocol schemes

▶ New public parsers such as ip1394, ipcp, PPPoE, and more

▶ Multiple fixes to known issues and faster parser loading

Using Network Monitor 3.1

Before you can start using the advanced features of Network Monitor, analyzing captured data, and identifying potential issues and bottlenecks, a basic understanding of Network Monitor and how it works is necessary.

To capture network traffic, install Network Monitor 3.1 and complete the following steps:

1. Run Network Monitor (Start, All Programs, Microsoft Network Monitor 3.1, Microsoft Network Monitor 3.1).
2. Click the Create a New Capture Tab button on the left.
3. Click the Play button or press F10 to start capturing traffic.

To apply filters to a captured stream of information, complete the following steps:

1. With a capture running and the tab selected, as shown in Figure 7.4, click the Filter menu in the menu bar at the top of the Network Monitor program.

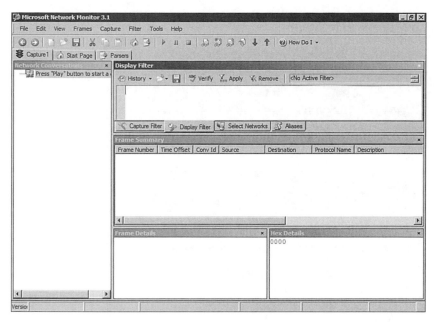

FIGURE 7.4   Capture tab in Network Monitor 3.1.

    a. **To create a capture filter**—Click Capture Filter, Load Filter, Standard Filters to select a preconfigured filter that will capture traffic relative to a specific item such as DNS.

    b. **To create a display filter**—Click Display Filter, Load Filter, Standard Filters to select a preconfigured filter that will only display information relative to a specific item such as DNS from captured data.

    c. **To create a color filter**—Click Color Filter, Load Filter, Standard Filters to apply a color effect to specific items such as DNS.

2. After a filter has been added, it must be applied. Filters can be applied by clicking the Apply button in the Capture Filter pane, pressing the Ctrl+Enter keys simultaneously, or clicking Apply in the Filter menu for the added filter.

3. Apply the filters by clicking the Filter menu at the top of the Network Monitor program.

    a. To apply a capture filter, highlight Capture Filter, and click Apply Filter.

    b. To apply a display filter, highlight Display Filter, and click Apply Filter.

    c. To add a color filter, click Color Filter, click Add, add an expression (for example, RDP or 192.168.1.5), and format the font for your preference. Click OK, and click OK again to apply the filter and close the Color Filter window.

Alternatively, a capture or display filter can be applied by right-clicking an item in the Frame Summary pane and selecting either Copy Cell as Filter or Add Cell to Display Filter, as shown in Figure 7.5. Figure 7.6 shows a sample capture with a DNS capture filter applied and all RDP packets color-coded in red using a color filter.

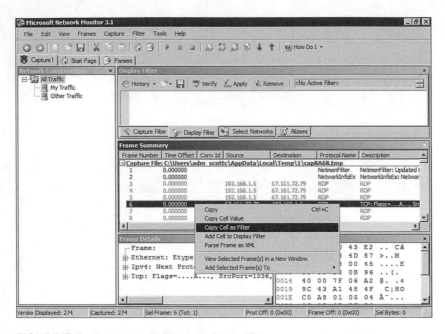

FIGURE 7.5   Choosing to copy a cell as a filter.

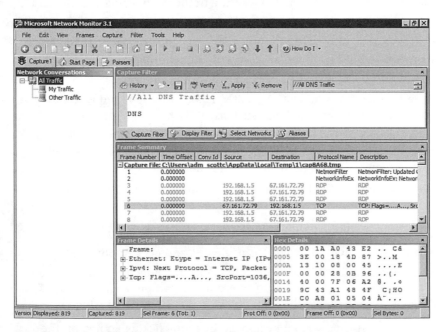

FIGURE 7.6   Sample capture with red-highlighted filtered data.

To remove a filter, just highlight the correct filter from the Filter menu and select Remove Filter, click the Remove button in the Capture Filter pane, or press the Ctrl+Shift+Enter keys simultaneously.

NOTE

Removing a filter does not remove it from the filter list. It just removes it from being applied.

Capturing Network Traffic Between Computers

As outlined previously, Network Monitor 3.1 includes the ability to capture wireless, remote, local area network (LAN), and wide area network (WAN) traffic using a remote agent. In some cases, network administrators want to diagnose or monitor a conversation between two computers. The steps necessary to monitor traffic between two different computers are outlined in the following list.

To capture network traffic between two different computers using IPv4 source and destination addresses, as shown in Figure 7.7, complete the following steps:

1. In Network Monitor, click the Create a New Capture Tab button on the left.
2. Click the Filter menu, select Capture Filter, Load Filter, Standard Filters.
3. Select IPv4SourceandDestination.
4. Edit the filter to specify the IP addresses that should be filtered in the Capture Filter window (for example, 192.168.1.5 and 192.168.1.2).

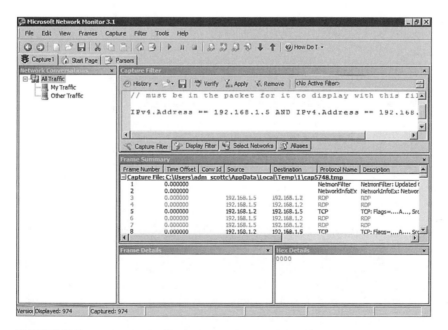

FIGURE 7.7   Network Monitor capture of network traffic between two IP addresses.

5. Click the Apply button in the Capture Filter pane.

6. Click the Play button on the main Network Monitor menu bar or press the F10 key to start the capture.

Parsing Captured Network Traffic Data

Parsing captured data allows the information to be converted into a format that is more legible to the naked eye. Parsing captured data makes analysis of the captured data easier—in fact, it's almost essential. The Network Monitor parsing engine was completely rewritten to support the new functionality of Network Monitor 3.1.

To parse captured data in Network Monitor 3.1, complete the following steps:

1. With a capture running or loaded from a saved file, select the Parsers tab in Network Monitor, as shown in Figure 7.8.

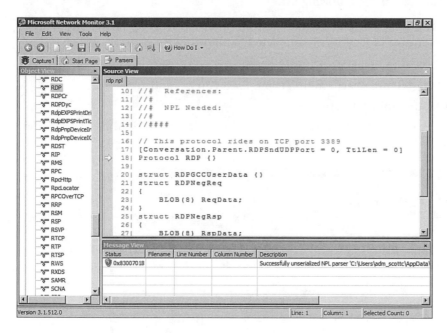

FIGURE 7.8   Parsers tab of Network Monitor 3.1.

2. Expand the appropriate parsing category and double-click the selected criteria, such as tables, data types, protocols, and so on.

For more detailed information about parsing with Network Monitor 3.1, review the online help in Network Monitor 3.1 or reference the ParserLanguage.doc file located in the C:\Program Files\Network Monitor 3.1\Help\ folder.

Windows Reliability and Performance Monitor

The Reliability and Performance Monitor in Windows 2008, shown in Figure 7.9, replaced the Performance Monitor that was included with Windows Server 2003. The Reliability and Performance Monitor bears a similarity to the Task Manager and previous Performance Monitor and highlights components that are critical to system performance. The Reliability and Performance Monitor is a combination of the previous Windows Server tools: System Monitor, Performance Monitor, and Server Performance Advisor. The Reliability and Performance Monitor is composed of four main components: Performance Monitor, Reliability Monitor, Data Collector Sets, and a reporting component. The Reliability and Performance Monitor can be launched from within the Windows 2008 Server Manager or from Start, All Programs, Administrative Tools.

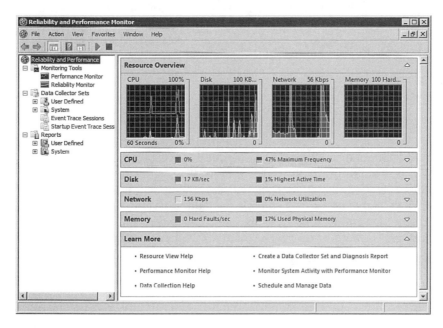

FIGURE 7.9   Reliability and Performance Monitor.

Using the Reliability and Performance Monitor, administrators can identify bottlenecks and pinpoint resource issues with applications, processes, or hardware. Monitoring these items can help to identify and resolve issues, to plan for capacity changes, and to establish baselines for use in future analysis. Upon launching the Reliability and Performance Monitor, a summary of system performance displays, showing current memory, disk, processor, and network loads.

Reliability and Performance Monitor includes the following new features:

▶ **Reliability Monitor**—The Reliability Monitor establishes and monitors a baseline of system performance and marks any errors, failures, and other problems for analysis by the administrator.

▶ **Resource Overview**—Similar to the Task Manager program is the Resource Overview window, which is presented when launching the Reliability and Performance Monitor. The Resource Overview displays real-time status of processor usage, disk usage, network throughput, and memory status.

▶ **Data Collector Sets**—Data Collector Sets are a collective grouping of items to be monitored. You can use one of the predefined sets or create your own to group together items that you want to monitor.

▶ **Diagnosis reports**—The Reliability and Performance Monitor includes an updated reporting mechanism and several template performance and diagnosis reports for use. In addition, reports can also be created manually or generated from Data Collector Sets.

Performance Monitor

Many IT professionals rely on the Performance Monitor because it is bundled with the operating system, and it allows you to capture and monitor every measurable system object within Windows 2008. The tool involves little effort to become familiar with it. You can find and start the Performance Monitor from within the Reliability and Performance Monitor program under Monitoring Tools in the console view. The Performance Monitor, shown in Figure 7.10, is by far the best utility provided in the operating system for capacity-analysis purposes. With this utility, you can analyze data from virtually all aspects of the system both in real time and historically. This data analysis can be viewed through charts, reports, and logs. The log format can be stored for use later so that you can scrutinize data from succinct periods of time.

Reliability Monitor

As mentioned previously, the Reliability Monitor establishes and monitors a baseline of system performance and marks any errors, failures, and other problems for analysis by the administrator. The Reliability Monitor is quite useful for identifying how a new application, update, or system change might behave and to correlate any errors or failures with possible causes that occurred around the same time. The Reliability Monitor is shown in Figure 7.11.

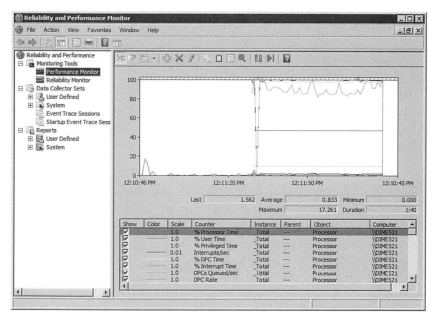

FIGURE 7.10   The Performance Monitor.

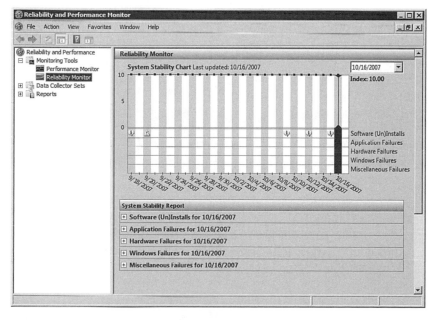

FIGURE 7.11   The Reliability Monitor.

Data Collector Sets

As mentioned previously, Data Collector Sets are a collective grouping of items to be monitored. You can use one of the predefined sets or create your own to group together items that you want to monitor. Data Collector Sets are useful for several reasons. First, data collectors can be a common theme or a mix of items. For example, you could have one Data Collector Set that monitors only memory or a Data Collector Set that contains myriad items such as memory, disk usage, processor time, and more. Data Collector Sets can also be scheduled to run when needed. The Data Collector Sets section of the Reliability and Performance Monitor is shown in Figure 7.12.

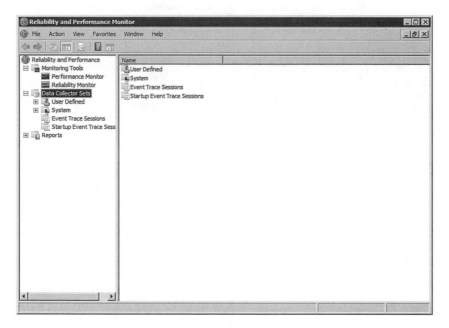

FIGURE 7.12   Data Collector Sets in the Reliability and Performance Monitor.

Reports

As previously discussed, the Reliability and Performance Monitor includes an updated reporting mechanism and several template performance and diagnosis reports for use. In addition, reports can be created manually or generated from Data Collector Sets. Three system reports are included for diagnosing and assessing system performance: LAN Diagnostics, System Diagnostics, and System Performance. The following steps outline the process to view a System Diagnostics report. Figure 7.13 shows a sample System Diagnostics report.

To create and view reports in the Reliability and Performance Monitor, complete the following steps:

1. Expand Data Collector Sets and System in the console tree of the Reliability and Performance Monitor.

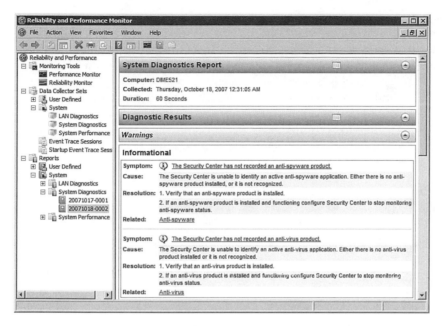

FIGURE 7.13   System Diagnostics report in the Reliability and Performance Monitor.

2. Right-click the LAN Diagnostics, System Diagnostics, or System Performance sets and select Start. Windows will begin collecting data for the report.

3. When you have collected enough data, right-click the collection set again and select Stop.

4. Expand Reports, System and click the collection set you chose earlier. Double-click the report listed under that performance set.

5. The report will be compiled and displayed.

Other Microsoft Assessment and Planning Tools

Several other products and tools are available from Microsoft to assist with proper capacity analysis and performance monitoring. Some of these tools are available for purchase separately or can be downloaded for free. Selecting the right tool or product depends on the goal you are trying to accomplish. For example, the Windows System Resource Manager would be used if you want to implement thresholds for the amount of resources an application or process is allowed to consume, and System Center Operations Manager might be deployed if you want to be notified when critical processes behave abnormally on production servers.

Discussing each of these tools in depth is beyond the scope of this book; however, a basic understanding and overview of their purposes will help you make an informed decision when selecting the right technologies for analyzing system resources, availability, and performance.

Windows System Resource Manager

Windows System Resource Manager (WSRM) is included in the feature set of Windows 2008 and provides an interface that enables you to configure how processor and memory resources are allocated among applications, services, and processes. Having the ability to control these items at such a granular level can help ensure system stability, thus improving system availability and enhancing the user experience. Assigning thresholds to services, applications, and processes can prevent issues such as high CPU consumption. WSRM is installed as a feature in Server Manager. WSRM can manage multiple items on the local system and remote computers (if Terminal Services is installed). The WSRM interface is shown in Figure 7.14.

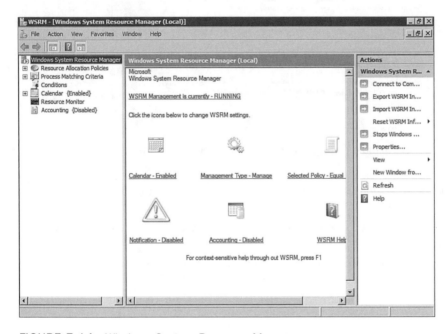

FIGURE 7.14   Windows System Resource Manager.

To install WSRM, complete the following steps:

1. Launch Server Manager by choosing it in the Administrative Tools folder.
2. Click Features in the Scope pane on the left.
3. Click Add Features in the central Details pane; the Select Features window opens.
4. Scroll down and select Windows System Resource Manager.
5. If it isn't already installed, a notification window opens stating that the Windows Internal Database feature must also be installed. Click the Add Required Features button to accept the addition of the feature.
6. Click Next.

7. Click Install to install WSRM and required components.

8. Click Close when the installation completes.

> **NOTE**
>
> A warning appears in Server Manager if the WSRM service is not started. This service must be running to use WSRM.

After WSRM is installed, you can start fine-tuning the Windows 2008 server's processes, services, applications, and other items to ensure CPU cycles and memory usage are allocated appropriately. WSRM provides administrators with a means of adjusting the system to meet the demands of those accessing it. WSRM can allocate CPU time and memory usage through the use of the included resource allocation policies or a customized one. Observed system usage and data obtained from tools such as the Reliability and Performance Monitor can be applied directly to WSRM policies. For example, if system monitoring reveals that a particular application is in high demand but the same server is busy providing other services, making the application sluggish, the WSRM can allocate enough resources to both items to ensure that neither the system nor the items being used are negatively impacted.

Resource-allocation policies are used in WSRM to divide processor and memory usage among applications, services, processes, and users. Resource-allocation policies can be in effect at all times, or they can run on a scheduled basis. If certain events occur or the system behaves differently, WSRM can switch to a different policy to ensure system stability and availability. Resource-allocation policies can be exported and imported between Windows 2008 servers, and the policies can also contain exclusions when something doesn't require specific resource assignments.

When accounting is enabled in WSRM, administrators of the servers can review data collected to determine when and why resource allocation policies were too restrictive or too loose. Accounting can also help identify problems with the items in the policy and peak access times. Administrators can use the information obtained by the accounting component of WSRM to make adjustments to the policies. WSRM resource-allocation policies can manage local and remote computers as well as Terminal Services sessions.

WSRM comes packaged with four predefined policies. These templates provide administrators with a way to quickly allocate resources, leaving room for fine-tuning later. The predefined resource allocation policy templates are as follows:

▶ **Equal per Process**—Allocates resources equally among all running processes, preventing one process from consuming all available CPU and memory resources.

▶ **Equal per User**—Allocates resources equally among all users, preventing one user from consuming all available CPU and memory resources.

▶ **Equal per Session**—Allocates resources equally among all Terminal Services sessions, preventing one session from consuming all available CPU and memory resources.

▶ **Equal per IIS Application Pool**—Allocates resources equally among all Internet Information Services (IIS) application pools, preventing one session from consuming all available CPU and memory resources.

> **NOTE**
>
> WSRM policies are only enforced when CPU usage climbs above 70%. The WSRM policies are never active on processes owned by the core operating system or any items in the exclusion list.

> **TIP**
>
> Memory limits should be applied in policies only when the application, service, or process is having issues or not allocating memory usage properly on its own.

A common task performed in WSRM is to create matching criteria rules. Matching criteria rules allow an administrator to define (or exclude) processes, services, or applications that should be monitored by WSRM. This definition is used later in the WSRM management process. To create a matching criteria rule, complete the following steps:

1. Launch Windows System Resource Manager by clicking Start, All Programs, Administrative Tools, Windows System Resource Manager.

2. Right-click the Process Matching Criteria item in the WSRM console and select New Process Matching Criteria.

3. Enter a unique name for the matching criteria in the Criteria Name box at the top and click Add under the Rules section.

   a. Enter the processes, services, or applications in the Included Files or Command Lines section of the Files or Command Lines tab.

Or

   b. Select the object type (process, service application, or IIS application pool) from the drop-down list, and click the Select button and select the policy to apply.

4. To exclude items from the policy, check the Excluded Files or Command Lines check box.

   a. Enter the processes, services, or applications in the Included Files or Command Lines section of the Files or Command Lines tab.

Or

   b. Select the object type (process, service application, or IIS application pool) from the drop-down list, and click the Select button and select the policy to apply.

5. Repeat the preceding steps to add all the exclusions and items that should be managed by or excluded from a WSRM policy.

Another task that is commonly performed is creating custom resource-allocation policies. Similar to "matching criteria rules" that look for specific process, service, and application criteria, the custom resource-allocation policy enables the administrator to define how much of a resource should be allocated to a specific process, service, or application. As an example, if only 20% of the system processing should be allocated to a print process, the resource allocation would be defined to limit the allocation of resources to that process. To create a custom resource allocation policy, complete the following steps:

1. Launch Windows System Resource Manager by clicking Start, All Programs, Administrative Tools, Windows System Resource Manager.

2. Right-click the Resource Allocation Policies option in the WSRM console, and select New Resource Allocation Policy.

3. Provide a name for the policy, and click the Add button in the Allocate These Resources section.

4. On the General tab, select the Process Matching Criteria and specify the percentage of processor time that will apply.

5. On the Memory tab, specify the maximum committed memory and working set limits.

6. The Advanced tab allows you to select which processors the policy should be assigned to and to suballocate processor resources. If you want to edit these parameters, make the changes and click OK.

7. Click OK when you have finished.

The calendar component of WSRM can be used to schedule policy enforcement on a reglar basis and by one-time or recurring events. For example, policy enforcement might be necessary only during normal business hours. Calendar control is disabled by default and can be activated by right-clicking the Calendar item in the WSRM console and selecting the Enable or Disable option. To create calendar items based on scheduled times, complete the following steps:

1. Launch Windows System Resource Manager by clicking Start, All Programs, Administrative Tools, Windows System Resource Manager.

2. Expand the calendar item in the WSRM console by clicking the plus sign.

3. Right-click the Schedule option and select New Schedule.

4. Enter a name and description for the schedule.

5. Double-click a time slot in the New Schedule window, specify the policy, start time, and stop time, and then click OK.

Instead of creating a calendar item based on scheduled times, you can create the calendar item based on a specific triggered event. To create calendar items based on specific events, complete the following steps:

1. Launch Windows System Resource Manager by clicking Start, All Programs, Administrative Tools, Windows System Resource Manager.

2. Expand the calendar item in the WSRM console by clicking the plus sign.

3. Right-click the Calendar Event option, and select New One Time Event.

4. Enter a name for the event.

5. Select Policy Name or Schedule Name, and select the appropriate policy.

6. Specify a start and end date and time (not available if associated with a schedule), and then click OK.

For calendar events that you want to trigger based on recurring events, a rule can be created for this to happen. To create recurring events, complete the following steps:

1. Launch Windows System Resource Manager by clicking Start, All Programs, Administrative Tools, Windows System Resource Manager.

2. Expand the calendar item in the WSRM console by clicking the plus sign.

3. Right-click the Calendar Event option, and select New Recurring Event.

4. Enter a name for the event.

5. Select Policy Name or Schedule Name, and select the appropriate policy.

6. Specify a start and end time and specify a recurrence schedule, such as every Monday (not available if associated with a schedule), and then click OK.

One example of where WSRM is useful is when an administrator wants to allocate system resources to sessions or users who are active on a Hyper-V host system. Configuring a WSRM policy for Hyper-V can ensure the sessions will not behave erratically and system availability will be stabilized for all the guest sessions hosted by the Hyper-V server. This is accomplished using the Equal per Session policy templates provided with WSRM or specifically allocating performance for each guest session, as covered in the "Accessing Hyper-V Resource Control" section of this chapter. To allocate resources to a Windows 2008 Terminal Services system, complete the following steps:

1. Launch Windows System Resource Manager by clicking Start, All Programs, Administrative Tools, Windows System Resource Manager.

2. Expand the Resource Allocation Policies option in the WSRM console, and select New Resource Allocation Policy.

3. Right-click Equal per Session or Equal per User, and select Set as Managing Policy.

4. A dialog box opens indicating that the calendar function will be disabled; click OK.

5. Click OK.

Microsoft Baseline Configuration Analyzer (MBCA)

The Microsoft Baseline Configuration Analyzer (MBCA) is a tool that uses a preestablished baseline to analyze a system. The MBCA is run from a command line and includes several switches to further customize its use. The gathered data is output into a report that can be reviewed to identify which baselines match and do not match. Baseline values are typically based on best practices for system configuration, security, and so on. Systems will automatically download new baseline models as they are made available on the Microsoft Update site. You can download the MBCA from the System Tools section of the Microsoft download site at www.microsoft.com/downloads/.

Assessment and Planning Solution Tool

The Assessment and Planning Solution tool provides a solution to IT personnel when faced with questions such as "Which product should we buy or deploy?" or "Are we ready for Windows 2008?." Granted, there are multiple approaches to tackling questions like this; however, Microsoft has again developed a tool that will do most of the work for you. The Assessment and Planning Solution tool inventories and assesses systems, hardware, and software and makes product and technology recommendations based on those results. You can download the Assessment and Planning Solution tool from the Microsoft download site at www.microsoft.com/downloads/.

System Center Capacity Planner (SCCP) 2007

System Center Capacity Planner 2007 is a tool for IT staff to plan their migration or deployment of System Center Operations Manager (OpsMgr) 2007 and Exchange 2007. SCCP can determine and recommend the necessary changes for deploying Exchange 2007 and OpsMgr 2007. This includes in-depth analysis of hardware, network architecture, placement of servers, and much more. SCCP 2007 can even advise on changes after deployment, whether they are planned or unplanned such as the addition of new users, new features such as Outlook Web Access (OWA), or changes to the network. You can find more information about SCCP 2007 at www.microsoft.com/systemcenter/sccp/default. mspx.

System Center Operations Manager 2007

OpsMgr 2007 has replaced its popular predecessor, Microsoft Operations Manager (MOM). OpsMgr 2007 is a comprehensive monitoring and reporting solution that reports on conditions related to services, system, and network performance. In addition, it alerts administrators when problems arise, (for example, when critical services have failed to start, when CPU usage consistently stays above a designated threshold, or when excessive paging is observed by the OpsMgr agent). OpsMgr integrates directly with Active Directory, Windows 2008, and most other Microsoft technologies to provide an overall solution to help automate monitoring of critical systems and processes. OpsMgr uses management packs specific to the technology, such as Exchange 2007 or IIS 7.0, so little configuration is needed out of the box.

Third-Party Toolset

Without a doubt, many third-party utilities are excellent for capacity-analysis and performance-monitoring purposes. Most of them provide additional functionality not found in Windows 2008 Performance Monitor and other tools, but they have a cost and might have special requirements for deployment and integration into the organization's network. You might want to evaluate some third-party utilities to get a more thorough understanding of how they might offer more features than Microsoft solutions. Generally speaking, these utilities enhance the functionality inherent to Microsoft monitoring solutions, such as scheduling, an enhanced level of reporting functionality, superior storage capabilities, the ability to monitor non-Windows systems, or algorithms for future trend analysis. Table 7.2 lists some of these third-party tools.

TABLE 7.2 Third-Party Capacity-Planning and Monitoring Tools

Utility Name	Company	Website
AppManager Suite	NetIQ Corporation	www.netiq.com/products/performancemgmt/
BMC Performance Manager	BMC Software	www.bmc.com/
HP OpenView	HP	www.openview.hp.com/
Robomon	Heroix	www.robomon.com/
UniCenter NetCenter	CA	www.ca.com/

Although it might be true that most third-party capacity-analysis and performance-monitoring products might add more or different functionality to your capacity-analysis and performance-monitoring procedures or goals, there are still pros and cons to using them over the free tools included with Windows 2008 or other solutions available from Microsoft. The key is to decide what you need to adequately and efficiently perform capacity-analysis and performance-monitoring procedures in your environment. Taking the time to research and experiment with the different solutions available today, from Microsoft and others, will only benefit you in making an informed decision for managing your Windows 2008 environment.

Optimizing the Performance of Hyper-V Host Servers and Guest Sessions

With the various tools covered in the section "Using Capacity-Analysis Tools," baseline system performance and capacity analysis will have been identified. The next step is to get into the Hyper-V host and guest sessions and tune the guest sessions so that performance can be directly managed and optimized. The two key areas of resource management that come in focus are guest session resource allocation and guest session disk image optimization.

Resource Allocation to Hyper-V Guest Sessions

For each Hyper-V guest session, a setting allows the allocation of Hyper-V host resources to the guest session. The more resources allocated to a guest session, the more resource demands the session can make on the resource pool (and thus the more scalable impact one session could have on another session).

Accessing Hyper-V Resource Control

Resource Control in Hyper-V is allocated in the Virtual Processor section of the settings for each guest session. To go to the Virtual Processor section of a guest session, complete the following steps:

1. Launch the Hyper-V Manager tool.

2. Right-click a virtual machine that you want to view or edit the Resource Control of and choose Settings.

3. In the leftmost pane, click Processor. Notice the Virtual Processor screen on the right side, and note the Resource Control section, as shown in Figure 7.15.

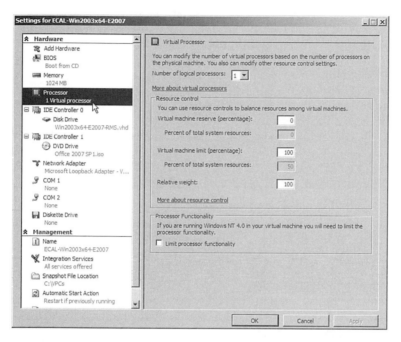

FIGURE 7.15   Resource Control settings.

Identifying Hyper-V Resource Control Settings

In the Virtual Processor settings, three settings are available to configure resource allocation for the guest session:

▶ **Virtual Machine Reserve (Percentage)**—This number (default = 0, but can range from 0 to 100) is how much of the host server's available resources the guest session should be guaranteed. If the machine reserve is set to 100, this guest session will get 100% of the resources of the server, and thus no other guest session will be able to run on this server. Consider this number as a "minimum" amount of resources the guest session should receive, whether it needs that much or not.

▶ **Virtual Machine Limit (Percentage)**—This number (default = 100, but can vary from 0 to 100) is the percentage maximum that this guest image will take of system resources. When set to 100, it is possible for this guest image to take up 100% of the resources of the system. If you want a guest image to take up no more than 25% of the resources of the host system at maximum, you should change this number to 25. Remember, however, if you set the limit at 25 and the host server is underutilized and this guest session can use extra resources, the guest session will max out at 25% despite the guest session's need or the host server's capacity to provide the resources required.

▶ **Relative Weight**—The relative weight (default = 100) is used when a contention exists between guest sessions on resource control. If three guest sessions are all trying to utilize 100% of the host server resources, based on the relative weight (where the higher number is given preference over a guest session with a lower number), the server with the highest number will take a higher priority in resource allocation than a guest session with a lower relative weight number.

Setting Hyper-V Resource Control Options

After deciding how you want to allocate resources to each guest session on the host system, you configure the settings one by one for each guest session. This includes keying in the requested value for each of the three settings, and then clicking OK to set the sessions for the guest session. Repeat this process for all guest sessions running on the host server system.

Optimizing Disk Configuration for Hyper-V Guest Sessions

Hyper-V guest session disk configurations can significantly impact performance of the guest session and how that guest session impacts the overall performance of the host server. Two factors should be considered relative to disk configuration: the type of disk selected, and where the disk image is stored.

Choosing Disk Type for Performance Considerations

There are two major differences in disk types in Hyper-V, one is a dynamically expanding disk, and the other is a fixed-size disk. (I note a third in the following bulleted list.) This disk type is selected at the time the guest image is created; by default, the image type selected is a dynamically expanding image type. After selecting a disk type and installing the OS on the image, you cannot easily switch to a different disk type. However, it is not impossible to convert a dynamically expanding to fixed or vice versa.

At the time of installation, when you are creating a new virtual hard disk (VHD), you are given the option (as shown in Figure 7.16) to choose a dynamically expanding disk type, fixed-size disk type, or a differencing disk type. The differences are as follows:

▶ **Dynamically Expanding**—A dynamically expanding disk type allows a disk image to start off as small as possible, and the image grows (up to a maximum size defined at the time of configuration; default = 127GB). The advantage of a dynamically expanding disk type is that it takes up little room on the disk (because the image may take up only 2GB or 4GB of space to start). As the image demand grows, the size of the image file grows.

▶ **Fixed Size**—The fixed-size disk is one where the size of the disk image is selected at the time of installation, whether that is 10GB or 20GB or 100GB. The disk space is immediately allocated regardless of whether the guest session uses that amount of space. So, if 100GB is allocated to the fixed size of a guest image, the guest image will take up 100GB of disk space.

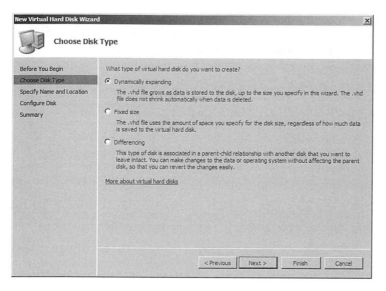

FIGURE 7.16   Choosing the disk type.

▶ **Differencing**—The differencing disk type is one where an existing image already exists, and only changes specific to this guest session image are stored for the guest session. This option is used for servers that are pretty much identical and not likely change much. The organization can reduce the amount of disk space taken up by having multiple servers each taking up 2GB or 4GB of space when a single image of, say, 2GB can be shared by multiple guest sessions.

NOTE

This VHD Configuration Wizard comes up only when creating a new VHD, not when creating a new guest image. When creating a new guest image, the default disk image type is set to dynamic if you choose New Disk. If you choose an existing virtual disk, you can choose a fixed disk that has already been created via the VHD Configuration Wizard.

As stated previously, a dynamically expanding disk type allows for a guest image to start off small and grow as needed. From a performance perspective, however, every time the image needs to grow, it has a drastic impact on the guest session and the host server. Fixed-size disks images take up a static amount of disk space whether the space is needed or not. And even though the space might not be needed, at least the image will not grow during the production day and cause performance impact on the server. So, for the best performance, choose the fixed-size disk type.

Choosing the Location for Disk Images for Performance Considerations

The other key factor when considering performance on a Hyper-V host system is the storage location of disk images. If disk images are stored all on the C: drive of the host server, and the disk is not a fast disk, all the guest images shairng a single slow disk are impacted. If the guest images are stored on a remote disk subsystem, such as an iSCSI storage area newtork (SAN) server, the communication speed between the Hyper-V host and the iSCSI SAN is not that fast, and so again, there is a performance impact on guest session operation.

If the guest sessions are stored on a high-speed FibreChannel SAN with extremely high read/write performance (both on the disk and the connectivity between the host and the high-speed SAN), however, the performance of the guest images is enhanced.

Take great care when considering where to store disk images. Your decision will impact the overall performance of the guest images and the host server managing the guest image sessions.

Monitoring System Performance

Capacity analysis is not about how much information you can collect; it is about collecting the appropriate system health indicators and the right amount of information. Without a doubt, you can capture and monitor an overwhelming amount of information from performance counters. There are more than 1,000 counters, so you'll want to carefully choose what to monitor. Otherwise, you might collect so much information that the data will be hard to manage and difficult to decipher. Keep in mind that more is not necessarily better with regard to capacity analysis. This process is more about efficiency. Therefore, you need to tailor your capacity-analysis monitoring as accurately as possible to how the server is configured.

Every Windows 2008 server has a common set of resources that can affect performance, reliability, stability, and availability. For this reason, it's important that you monitor this common set of resources, namely CPU, memory, disk, and network utilization.

In addition to the common set of resources, the functions that the Windows 2008 server performs can influence what you should consider monitoring. So, for example, you would monitor certain aspects of system performance on file servers differently than you would for a domain controller (DC). Windows 2008 can perform many functional roles (such as file and print sharing, application sharing, database functions, web server duties, domain controller roles, and more), and it is important to understand all those roles that pertain to each server system. By identifying these functions and monitoring them along with the common set of resources, you gain much greater control and understanding of the system.

The following sections go more in depth on what specific items you should monitor for the different components that constitute the common set of resources. It's important to realize, however, that several other items should be considered regarding monitoring in addition to the ones described in this chapter. Consider the following material as just a baseline of the minimum number of things to begin your capacity-analysis and performance-optimization procedures.

Key Elements to Monitor for Bottlenecks

As mentioned, four resources compose the common set of resources: memory and pagefile usage, processor, disk subsystem, and network subsystem. They are also the most common contributors to performance *bottlenecks*. A bottleneck can be defined in two ways. The most common perception of a bottleneck is that it is the slowest part of your system. It can either be hardware or software, but generally speaking, hardware is usually faster than software. When a resource is overburdened or just not equipped to handle higher workload capacities, the system might experience a slowdown in performance. For any system, the slowest component of the system is, by definition, considered the bottleneck. For example, a web server might be equipped with ample RAM, disk space, and a high-speed network interface card (NIC), but if the disk subsystem has older drives that are relatively slow, the web server might not be able to effectively handle requests. The bottleneck (that is, the antiquated disk subsystem) can drag the other resources down.

A less common, but equally important form of bottleneck, is one where a system has significantly more RAM, processors, or other system resources than the application requires. In these cases, the system creates extremely large pagefiles and has to manage very large sets of disk or memory sets, yet never uses the resources. When an application needs to access memory, processors, or disks, the system might be busy managing the idle resource, thus creating an unnecessary bottleneck caused by having too many resources allocated to a system. Thus, performance optimization not only means having too few resources, but also means not having too many resources allocated to a system.

Monitoring System Memory and Pagefile Usage

Available system memory is usually the most common source of performance problems on a system. The reason is simply that incorrect amounts of memory are usually installed on a Windows 2008 system. Windows 2008 tends to consume a lot of memory. Fortunately, the easiest and most economical way to resolve the performance issue is to configure the system with additional memory. This can significantly boost performance and upgrade reliability.

Many significant counters in the memory object can help you determine system memory requirements. Most network environments shouldn't need to consistently monitor every single counter to get accurate representations of performance. For long-term monitoring, two very important counters can give you a fairly accurate picture of memory pressure: Page Faults/sec and Pages/sec memory. These two memory counters alone can indicate whether the system is properly configured with the proper amount of memory. Table 7.3

outlines the counters necessary to monitor memory and pagefile usage, along with a description of each.

TABLE 7.3   Important Counters and Descriptions Related to Memory Behavior

Object	Counter	Description
Memory	Committed Bytes	Monitors how much memory (in bytes) has been allocated by the processes. As this number increases above available RAM, so does the size of the pagefile as paging has increased.
Memory	Pages/sec	Displays the amount of pages that are read from or written to the disk.
Memory	Pages Output/sec	Displays virtual memory pages written to the pagefile per second. Monitor this counter to identify paging as a bottleneck.
Memory	Page Faults/sec	Reports both soft and hard faults.
Process	Working Set, _Total	Displays the amount of virtual memory that is actually in use.
Paging file	%pagefile in use	Reports the percentage of the paging file that is actually in use. This counter is used to determine whether the Windows pagefile is a potential bottleneck. If this counter remains above 50% or 75% consistently, consider increasing the pagefile size or moving the pagefile to a different disk.

By default, the Memory section of the Resource Overview in the Reliability and Performance Monitor, shown in Figure 7.17, provides a good high-level view of current memory activity. For more advanced monitoring of memory and pagefile activity, use the Performance Monitor component of the Reliability and Performance Monitor.

Systems experience page faults when a process requires code or data that it can't find in its *working set*. A working set is the amount of memory that is committed to a particular process. When this happens, the process has to retrieve the code or data in another part of physical memory (referred to as a *soft fault*) or, in the worst case, has to retrieve it from the disk subsystem (a *hard fault*). Systems today can handle a large number of soft faults without significant performance hits. However, because hard faults require disk subsystem access, they can cause the process to wait significantly, which can drag performance to a crawl. The difference between memory and disk subsystem access speeds is exponential even with the fastest hard drives available. The Memory section of the Resource Overview in the Reliability and Performance Monitor includes columns that display *working sets* and *hard faults* by default.

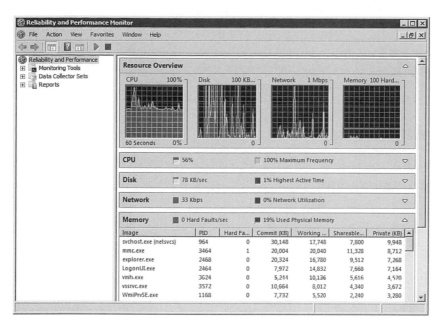

FIGURE 7.17   Memory section of the Resource Overview.

The Page Faults/sec counter reports both soft and hard faults. It's not uncommon to see this counter displaying rather large numbers. Depending on the workload placed on the system, this counter can display several hundred faults per second. When it gets beyond several hundred page faults per second for long durations, begin checking other memory counters to identify whether a bottleneck exists.

Probably the most important memory counter is Pages/sec. It reveals the number of pages read from or written to disk and is, therefore, a direct representation of the number of hard page faults the system is experiencing. Microsoft recommends upgrading the amount of memory in systems that are seeing Pages/sec values consistently averaging more than five pages per second. In actuality, you'll begin noticing slower performance when this value is consistently higher than 20. So, it's important to carefully watch this counter as it nudges higher than 10 pages per second.

> **NOTE**
>
> The Pages/sec counter is also particularly useful in determining whether a system is thrashing. *Thrashing* is a term used to describe systems experiencing more than 100 pages per second. Thrashing should never be allowed to occur on Windows 2008 systems because the reliance on the disk subsystem to resolve memory faults greatly affects how efficiently the system can sustain workloads.

System memory (RAM) is limited in size, and Windows supplements the use of RAM with virtual memory, which is not as limited. Windows will begin paging to disk when all RAM is being consumed, which, in turn, frees RAM for new applications and processes. Virtual memory resides in the pagefile.sys file, which is usually located in the root of the system drive. Each disk can contain a pagefile. The location and size of the pagefile is configured under the Virtual Memory section, shown in Figure 7.18.

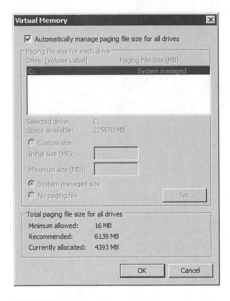

FIGURE 7.18   Virtual Memory configuration options.

To access the Performance Options window, complete the following steps:

1. Click Start.
2. Right-click Computer and select Properties.
3. Click the Advanced Settings link on the left.
4. When the System Properties window opens, click the Settings button under the Performance section.
5. Select the Advanced tab.
6. Click Change under Virtual Memory.

TIP

Windows will normally automatically handle and increase the size of pagefile.sys as needed. In some cases, however, you might want to increase performance and manage virtual memory settings yourself. Keeping the default pagefile on the system drive and adding a second pagefile to another hard disk can significantly improve performance.

Spanning virtual memory across multiple disks or just placing the pagefile.sys on another, less-used disk, will also allow Windows to run faster. Just ensure that the other disk isn't slower than the disk pagefile.sys is currently on. The more physical memory a system has, the more virtual memory will be allocated.

Analyzing Processor Usage

Most often, the processor resource is the first one analyzed when a noticeable decrease occurs in system performance. For capacity-analysis purposes, you should monitor two counters: % Processor Time and Interrupts/sec.

The % Processor Time counter indicates the percentage of overall processor utilization. If more than one processor resides on the system, an instance for each one is included along with a total (combined) value counter. If this counter averages a usage rate of 50% or greater for long durations, first consult other system counters to identify any processes that might be improperly using the processors or consider upgrading the processor or processors. Generally speaking, consistent utilization in the 50% range doesn't necessarily adversely affect how the system handles given workloads. When the average processor utilization spills over the 65% or higher range, performance might become intolerable. If you have multiple processors installed in the system, use the % Total Processor Time counter to determine the average usage of all processors.

The Interrupts/sec counter is also a good guide of processor health. It indicates the number of device interrupts that the processor (either hardware or software driven) is handling per second. Like the Page Faults/sec counter mentioned in the section "Monitoring System Memory and Pagefile Usage," this counter might display very high numbers (in the thousands) without significantly impacting how the system handles workloads.

Conditions that could indicate a processor bottleneck include the following:

▶ Average of % Processor Time is consistently more than 60% to 70%. In addition, spikes that occur frequently at 90% or greater could also indicate a bottleneck even if the average drops below the 60% to 70% mark.

▶ Maximum of % Processor Time is consistently more than 90%.

▶ Average of the System Performance Counter; Context Switches/second is consistently over 20,000.

▶ The System Performance counter Processor Queue Length is consistently greater than 2.

By default, the CPU section of the Resource Overview in the Reliability and Performance Monitor, shown in Figure 7.19, provides a good high-level view of current processor activity. For more advanced monitoring of processors, use the Performance Monitor component with the counters discussed previously.

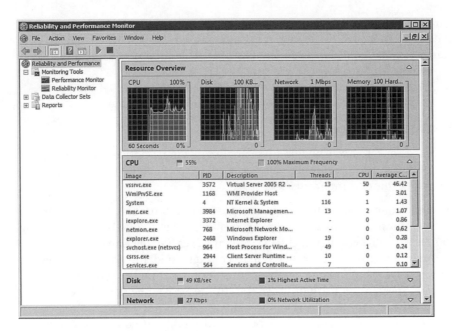

FIGURE 7.19 CPU section of the Resource Overview.

Evaluating the Disk Subsystem

Hard disk drives and hard disk controllers are the two main components of the disk subsystem. The two objects that gauge hard disk performance are the physical disk and the logical disk. Although the disk subsystem components are becoming more and more powerful, they are often a common bottleneck because their speeds are exponentially slower than other resources. The effects, however, can be minimal and maybe even unnoticeable, depending on the system configuration.

To support the Resource Overview's Disk section, the physical and logical disk counters are enabled by default in Windows 2008. The Disk section of the Resource Overview in the Reliability and Performance Monitor, shown in Figure 7.20, provides a good high-level view of current physical and logical disk activity (combined). For more advanced monitoring of disk activity, use the Performance Monitor component with the desired counters found in the Physical Disk and Logical Disk sections.

Monitoring with the physical and logical disk objects does come with a small price. Each object requires a little resource overhead when you use them for monitoring. As a result, you might want to keep them disabled unless you are going to use them for monitoring purposes.

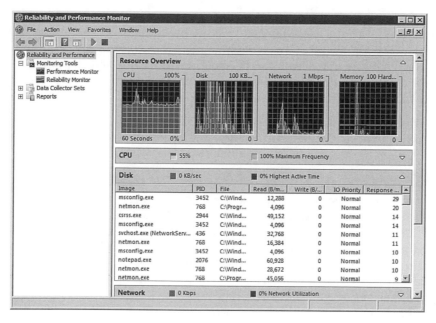

FIGURE 7.20   Disk section of the Resource Overview.

So, what specific disk subsystem counters should be monitored? The most informative counters for the disk subsystem are % Disk Time and Avg. Disk Queue Length. The % Disk Time counter monitors the time that the selected physical or logical drive spends servicing read and write requests. The Avg. Disk Queue Length monitors the number of requests not yet serviced on the physical or logical drive. The Avg. Disk Queue length value is an interval average; it is a mathematical representation of the number of delays the drive is experiencing. If the delay is frequently greater than 2, the disks are not equipped to service the workload, and delays in performance might occur.

Monitoring the Network Subsystem

The network subsystem is by far one of the most difficult subsystems to monitor because of the many different variables. The number of protocols used in the network, NICs, network-based applications, topologies, subnetting, and more play vital roles in the network, but they also add to its complexity when you're trying to determine bottlenecks. Each network environment has different variables; therefore, the counters that you'll want to monitor will vary.

The information that you'll want to gain from monitoring the network pertains to network activity and throughput. You can find this information with the Performance Monitor alone, but it will be difficult at best. Instead, it's important to use other tools, such as Network Monitor, discussed earlier in this chapter in the section "Network Monitor," in conjunction with the Reliability and Performance Monitor to get the best representation of network performance as possible. You might also consider using third-party network analysis tools such as network sniffers to ease monitoring and analysis efforts. Using these tools simultaneously can broaden the scope of monitoring and more accurately depict what is happening on the wire.

Because the TCP/IP suite is the underlying set of protocols for a Windows 2008 network subsystem, this discussion of capacity analysis focuses on this protocol.

NOTE

Windows 2008 and Windows Vista deliver enhancement to the existing quality of service (QoS) network traffic–shaping solution that is available for XP and Windows Server 2003. QoS uses Group Policy to shape and give priority to network traffic without recoding applications or making major changes to the network. Network traffic can be "shaped" based on the application sending the data, TCP or UDP addresses (source or destination), TCP or UDP protocols, and the ports used by TCP or UDP or any combination thereof. You can find more information about QoS at Microsoft TechNet: http://technet.microsoft.com/en-us/network/bb530836.aspx.

Several different network performance objects relate to TCP/IP, including ICMP, IPv4, IPv6, Network Interface, TCPv4, UDPv6, and more. Other counters such as FTP Server and WINS Server are added after these services are installed. Because entire books are dedicated to optimizing TCP/IP, this section focuses on a few important counters that you should monitor for capacity-analysis purposes.

First, examining error counters, such as Network Interface: Packets Received Errors or Packets Outbound Errors, is extremely useful in determining whether traffic is easily traversing the network. The greater the number of errors indicates that packets must be present, causing more network traffic. If a high number of errors are persistent on the network, throughput will suffer. This can be caused by a bad NIC, unreliable links, and so on.

If network throughput appears to be slowing because of excessive traffic, keep a close watch on the traffic being generated from network-based services such as the ones described in Table 7.4. Figure 7.21 shows these items being recorded in Performance Monitor.

TABLE 7.4   Network-Based Service Counters Used to Monitor Network Traffic

Object	Counter	Description
Network Interface	Current Bandwidth	Displays used bandwidth for the selected network adapter
Server	Bytes Total/sec	Monitors the network traffic generated by the Server service

| Redirector | Bytes Total/sec | Processes data bytes received for statistical calculations |
| NBT Connection | Bytes Total/sec | Monitors the network traffic generated by NetBIOS over TCP connections |

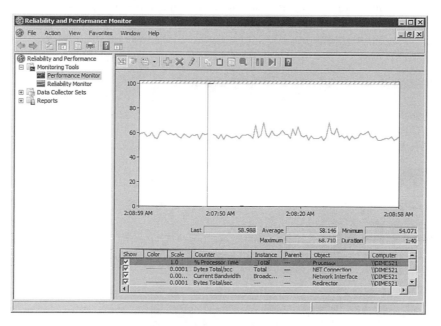

FIGURE 7.21   Network-based counters in Performance Monitor.

Optimizing Performance by Server Roles

In addition to monitoring the common bottlenecks (memory, processor, disk subsystem, and network subsystem), be aware that functional roles of the server influence what other counters you should monitor. The following sections outline some of the most common roles for Windows 2008 that require the use of additional performance counters for analyzing system behavior, establishing baselines, and ensuring system availability and scalability.

Microsoft also makes several other tools available that will analyze systems and recommend changes. For example, the Microsoft Baseline Configuration Analyzer (MBCA) identifies configuration issues, overtaxed hardware, and other items that would have a direct impact on system performance and makes recommendations to rectify those issues. Ensuring a system is properly configured to deliver services for the role it supports is essential before performance monitoring and capacity planning can be taken seriously.

Virtual Servers

Deployment of virtual servers and consolidation of hardware is becoming more and more prevalent in the business world. When multiple servers are running in a virtual environment on a single physical hardware platform, performance monitoring and tuning becomes essential to maximize the density of the virtual systems. If three or four virtual servers are running on a system and the memory and processors aren't allocated to the virtual guest session that could use the resources, virtual host resources aren't being utilized efficiently. In addition to monitoring the common items of memory, disk, network, and CPU, two performance counters related to virtual sessions are added when virtualization is running on the Windows 2008 host. Figure 7.22 shows these counters.

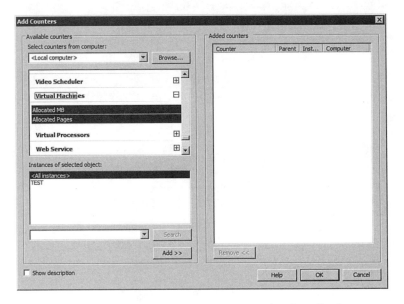

FIGURE 7.22   Performance Monitor counters for virtualization.

The performance counters related to virtualization are as follows:

▶ **Allocated MB**—Displays the amount of physical memory (RAM) allocated to each virtual server.

▶ **Allocated Pages**—Displays the number of memory pages per virtual machine.

The virtual session object and its counters are available only when a virtual machine is running. Counters can be applied to all running virtual sessions or to a specific virtual session.

Summary

Capacity planning and performance analysis are critical tasks in ensuring that systems are running efficiently and effectively in the network environment. Too much capacity being allocated to systems indicates resources are being wasted and not used efficiently, which in the long run can cause an organization to overspend in their IT budgets and not get the value out of IT spending. Too little capacity in system operations, and performance suffers in serving users and creates a hardship on servers that can ultimately cause system failure.

By properly analyzing the operational functions of a network, a network administrator can consolidate servers or virtualize servers to gain more density in system resources. This consolidation may result in additional physical servers that can ultimately be used for other purposes to provide high availability of IT resources, such as for disaster recovery, as failover servers, or as cluster servers.

Although it's easy to get caught up in daily administration and firefighting, it's important to step back and begin capacity-analysis and performance-optimization processes and procedures. These processes and procedures can minimize the environment's complexity, help IT personnel gain control over the environment, assist in anticipating future resource requirements, and ultimately, reduce costs and keep users of the network happy.

Best Practices

The following are best practices from this chapter:

- ▶ Spend time performing capacity analysis to save time troubleshooting and firefighting.
- ▶ Use capacity-analysis processes to help weed out the unknowns.
- ▶ Establish systemwide policies and procedures to begin to proactively manage your system.
- ▶ After establishing systemwide policies and procedures, start characterizing system workloads.
- ▶ Use performance metrics and other variables such as workload characterization, vendor requirements or recommendations, industry-recognized benchmarks, and the data that you collect to establish a baseline.
- ▶ Use the benchmark results only as a guideline or starting point.
- ▶ Use the Task Manager or the Resource Overview in the Reliability and Performance Monitor to quickly view performance.
- ▶ Use the Reliability and Performance Monitor to capture performance data on a regular basis.
- ▶ Consider using System Center Operations Manager or Microsoft and third-party products to assist with performance monitoring, capacity and data analysis, and reporting.
- ▶ Carefully choose what to monitor so that the information doesn't become unwieldy.

▶ At a minimum, monitor the most common contributors to performance bottlenecks: memory and pagefile usage, processor, disk subsystem, and network subsystem.

▶ Identify and monitor server functions and roles along with the common set of resources.

▶ When monitoring specific roles such as virtual servers, include the common performance counters such as memory, CPU, disk, and network and counters specific to the role of the server.

▶ Allocate process memory and resources to guest sessions that balance the requested amount of memory for a guest session without over allocating resources that may go unused.

▶ When configuring disk types, for the fastest performance choose a fixed-size disk type so that the dynamic expansion of the image file does not impact the performance of the host server or guest session.

▶ When placing guest images on a storage system, pick a storage system that has relatively high-speed access and throughput. If you don't, the performance of the guest session will be slowed because the Hyper-V host server will have slow communications with the guest session image files.

▶ Examine network-related error counters.

PART IV

System Center Virtual Machine Manager 2008 in a Hyper-V Environment

IN THIS PART

## 8

System Center Virtual Machine Manager Technology Primer

What Is Virtual Machine Manager?

Up to now, we have discussed what Hyper-V provides to the data center and how to deploy and configure single virtual machines. Once the organization understands and adopts the value of system virtualization, IT administrators look for improved ways to deploy, control, and administer the virtual infrastructure.

Enter Microsoft System Center Virtual Machine Manager 2008. Virtual Machine Manager 2008 (VMM 2008) provides a System Center common management interface for the virtualized data center that allows increased server utilization and dynamic resource allocation. It also works across multiple virtualization platforms, including those from Microsoft and VMware. Third-party add-ons for XenSource, XenWorks, and others will be available in the near future.

VMM 2008 takes a holistic approach to managing the virtual infrastructure by examining and rating the virtualization hosts. It compares these hosts against a set of criteria and rates the suitability of the virtual machine (VM) to be deployed on the hosts where it can be deployed. This is important because a single physical host server can host tens of virtual machines.

History of Virtualization and Virtualization Management

Despite Microsoft having a major release of both Windows server virtualization and Virtual Machine Management in

2008, their history in virtualization is less than six years old, with virtualization management being less than year or two.

Microsoft History of Virtualization

Microsoft obtained its role in virtualization by acquiring the technology and then developing it over time. They first purchased virtualization technology and then developed the technology into both a server and client product.

Microsoft's Introduction to Virtualization by Acquisition

Microsoft first entered the operating system virtualization market when it purchased Connectix in 2003. Microsoft's first VM product was Microsoft Virtual PC, which they released as a free product in 2004. Virtual PC was meant to allow administrators to create VMs on a desktop-class computer for testing purposes.

Microsoft's First Release of Server Virtualization

About the same time, they released Microsoft Virtual Server 2005, which was designed to run on server-class equipment and offered more robust features. In Q2 2006, Microsoft made Virtual Server 2005 R2 Enterprise Edition a free download to better compete with the free virtualization offerings from VMware and Xen. Virtual machines are created and managed through a Windows client application tool called VMRCplus or through an Internet Information Services (IIS) web-based interface. Virtual Server 2005 provides more features than Virtual PC and is designed to run in the data center.

Microsoft's Client Virtualization

In Q1 2007, Microsoft released Virtual PC 2007. The main advantages over Virtual PC 2004 were support for hardware virtualization, viewing virtual machines on multiple monitors, and support for Windows Vista as both host and guest. The following year Virtual PC 2007 SP1 was released.

Microsoft's History on Virtualization Management

While virtual servers and clients have helped organizations minimize the number of physical systems they have, the challenge has been to manage these virtual systems. It wasn't until 2007 that Microsoft finally had a product dedicated to VM management, which has then led to the current release covered in this book, Virtual Machine Manager 2008.

Early Virtualization Management Techniques

Up to this point, VM management was performed by the system administrator using the standard Windows monitoring and management techniques: viewing event logs, performance counters, and system properties of both the VM and the host that runs it. With the proliferation of VMs in the data center, there grew a need to centralize VM management and to manage the placement and provide disaster-recovery options for these guests.

Release of Virtualization Machine Manager 2007

Microsoft's answer to this need was Microsoft System Center Virtual Machine Manager 2007 (VMM 2007). VMM 2007 was available in three versions: System Center Virtual Machine Manager 2007, System Center Virtual Machine Manager 2007 Workgroup Edition (VMM WGE 2007), and System Center Essentials 2007 (Essentials 2007). VMM 2007 provides comprehensive support for consolidating 32-bit physical servers onto virtual infrastructures and rapid provisioning and deployment of new 32-bit virtual machines. To help IT administrators keep organized, VMM features a library to centrally manage the building blocks of the virtual data center, including virtual hard drives, VMM templates, and P2V conversions.

Release of Virtualization Machine Manager 2008

Microsoft System Center VMM 2008 is the latest version of the VMM product line. It replaces System Center VMM 2007 and adds many new features, including full Hyper-V support, 64-bit VM support, the ability to manage both Microsoft and VMware virtual infrastructures, and more.

What Is Virtual Machine Manager 2008?

Microsoft System Center VMM is a server application that administrators can use to manage a large number of VMs across the virtual infrastructure.

Components of VMM

VMM is a series of components that include Windows Server, SQL Server, a local agent, an Administrative console, and a self-service console. The components that make up VMM include

- ▶ A Microsoft Windows Server 2003 SP1 or later server on which the VMM service (server component) is installed.

- ▶ A Microsoft SQL Server 2005 database. This database contains all VMM objects.

- ▶ Servers on which the VMM local agent is installed. These servers act as hosts on which to deploy VMs using VMM. A host computer runs Microsoft Virtual Server 2005 R2, Virtual Server 2005 R2 Service Pack 1 (SP1), or Windows Server 2008 with Hyper-V. Be sure to read the Windows Server 2008 Hyper-V requirements in Chapter 4, "Installing Windows 2008 Server and the Hyper-V Role."

▶ Servers on which the VMM local agent is installed that act as library servers. Library servers store resources for the VMM environment.

▶ Computers on which the VMM Administrative console is installed. These computers or servers provide the administrative GUI and command shell to manage the physical and virtual infrastructure.

▶ Web servers that act as self-service portals. Self-service portals allow designated users to create/manage their own VMs.

NOTE

VMM components can be combined on the same server. Please see Chapter 4, "Installing Windows 2008 Server and the Hyper-V Role," for details.

VMM on Top of PowerShell

The VMM command shell is built on Microsoft Windows PowerShell, an administrator-focused interactive command-line shell and scripting platform that is integrated into the Windows platform. Windows PowerShell and the VMM command shell are installed with VMM.

Administrators can use the VMM command shell as an alternative to (or in addition to) the VMM Administrative console for centralized management of the physical and virtual system infrastructure. Anything that can be done in the Administrative console can be done using the VMM command shell. The Administrative console even enables you to view the command shell commands that the console will run before actually executing them.

Windows PowerShell and VMM both provide commands (called cmdlets, shown in Figure 8.1) that administrators can use alone to perform simple administrative tasks or in combination with other cmdlets or command-line elements to perform more complex tasks.

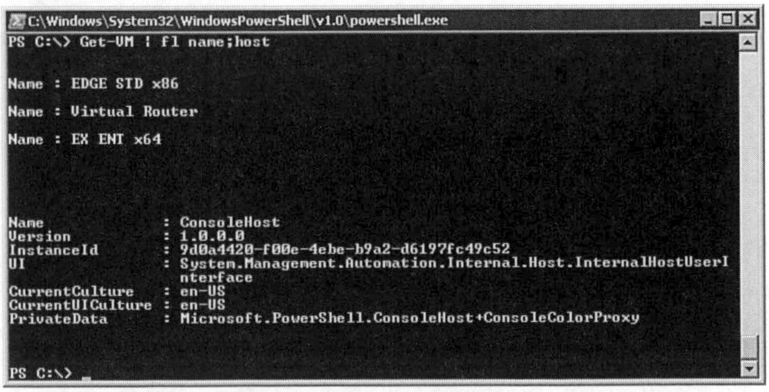

FIGURE 8.1   The VMM 2008 command shell.

PowerShell Support in VMM 2008

Like Microsoft Exchange Server 2007, VMM 2008 is written completely on top of Windows PowerShell. Anything that can be done in the Administrative console or the self-service portal user interfaces can be done in PowerShell. As a matter of fact, everything done in these consoles is done in PowerShell. When the administrator performs an action from a console, that command, shown in Figure 8.2, is passed down to the PowerShell for execution.

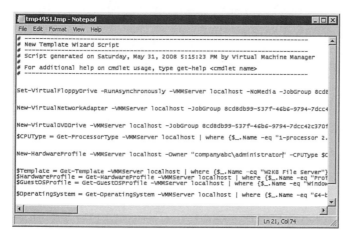

FIGURE 8.2   PowerShell command sequence.

The Administrative console offers a button at the execution of an action that displays the PowerShell commands that will be run. This allows the administrator to copy, modify, and save a collection of cmdlets for easy automation of tasks. They can then be run directly from the command line.

Consoles in VMM

The VMM server component manages the different components that make up the VMM system. Through the Administrative console, administrators manage the objects, templates, and scripts stored in the VMM library server. The self-service portal component provides a way for designated users to provision/save their own VMs in the VMM library. The VMM server component recommends the best physical host server to host the VM or best library server to store the VM image.

VMM Self-Service Portal

The self-service portal, as shown in Figure 8.3, is a web console that provides a way for self-service users to access any VM, regardless of whether it is VMware or Hyper-V. Using this console, users with appropriate rights can create, manage, and store VMs.

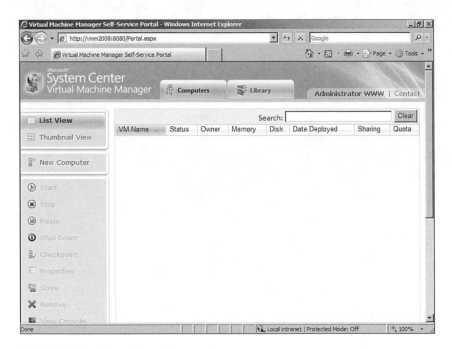

FIGURE 8.3   The self-service portal.

VMM Administrative Console

The VMM Administrative console is the main console with which VMM administrators and delegated administrators manage the virtual infrastructure components. This includes physical servers, virtual servers, virtual networks (VLANs), and the VMM library and all its objects.

Administrative Console in VMM

VMM 2008 provides a heterogeneous centralized management platform for VM management. The administrator can manage hosts running on Windows Server 2008 Hyper-V, VMware ESX, and Microsoft Virtual Server using the same familiar System Center console. The VMM 2008 console, shown in Figure 8.4, offers the same consistent look, feel, and behavior as other System Center products, including System Center Configuration Manager 2007 (SCCM 2007) and System Center Operations Manager 2007 (SCOM 2007).

Like other System Center products, the VMM Administrative console offers a Navigation pane, Views pane, Details pane, and Actions pane.

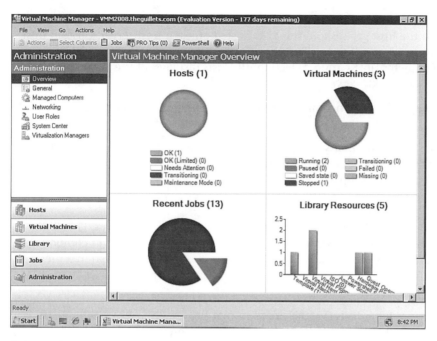

FIGURE 8.4   The VMM 2008 console.

The Navigation Pane

The VMM has in the Administrative console a Navigation pane. The Navigation pane enables the administrator to select which collection of objects the administrator wants to work with. The Navigation pane contains the following buttons:

- ▶ Hosts
- ▶ Virtual Machines
- ▶ Library
- ▶ Jobs
- ▶ Administration

Hosts

Provides access to the Virtual Machine Overview, which displays a graphical dashboard of hosts, VMs, recent jobs, and library resources in multicolor pie and bar charts. Here you can get a visual representation of the health of the hosts, the state of the VMs (running, paused, stopped, and so on), status on recent jobs (running, canceled, failed, and so forth), and the number of library resources (templates, virtual hard drives, answer scripts, and the like). Clicking any one of the graphs will drill down to the corresponding navigation item.

Virtual Machines

Provides access to the host groups and the VMs hosted on each host server. Custom host groups can be created depending on administrative requirements—for example, Domain Host Group or Perimeter Host Group. Selecting All Hosts displays all the hosts that are managed by this VMM 2008 server.

Information displayed for each host includes the VM hostname, status (running, stopped, failed, and so on), job status, host server name, and the owner of the VM.

The Details pane shows a summary of the VM and the current CPU usage and real-time system display; Storage and Networking, which shows network and drive usage information; and Latest Job information and status.

Library

Provides access to information and components stored on the library server. The library server role may be hosted on the same VMM server as the VMM 2008 server component or a separate VMM library server. Each VMM 2008 library server is displayed in a hierarchical tree structure.

Each library server displays the contents of its MSSCVMMLibrary share, which holds folders containing the virtual hard disks (VHDs) stored in that library. The MSSCVMMLibrary is a network share managed by the VMM server component. These VHDs can be used to provision new servers with identical hard disk configurations. The standard VHDs installed with VMM 2008 include Blank Disk - Large and Blank Disk - Small VHDs.

Templates

Each library server also displays the VMs and templates stored on that server. VMs created on other virtualization technologies, VMware ESX for example, can be converted to VMs compatible with Microsoft virtualization and stored in the VM library. Templates are built upon the selection of a source machine, hardware profile, and guest operating system profile. Administrators can then easily deploy identical virtual servers with these settings to the appropriate host servers.

Hardware and Guest OS Profiles

The Profiles section holds hardware and guest OS profiles. Hardware profiles are used to define common hardware characteristics the administrator can use in template creation. Guest OS profiles are used to define the operating system characteristics, properties, and answer files. These are also used in template creation.

Jobs

Provides access to the completed, running, and failed jobs run within VMM 2008. Jobs are the actions or steps performed in VMM 2008 to do work. Sample jobs include Create Virtual Machine, Update Library, and Create Hardware Profile.

Administration

Provides access to the settings used in the VMM Administrative console. Here the administrator can configure general settings, such as database connections and library settings. This location is used to configure user roles, networking, and System Center Operations

Manager 2007 integration. It is also the area to configure virtualization managers (servers that manage VMs and the physical computers that host them on non-Microsoft virtualization products).

Administrator Console Layout

The VMM 2008 Administrative console itself uses the common Microsoft System Center layout. Users of any System Center product, such as Operations Manager or Configuration Manager, will recognize the familiar and easy-to-use interface. The VMM Administrative console uses the Microsoft Management Console (MMC) 3.0 for administration.

Heterogeneous VM Management

Microsoft designed VMM 2008 to be the best virtualization deployment platform available. It does this by providing a heterogeneous management system that significantly reduces the complexity of managing different physical and virtual systems in the enterprise.

VMs Managed by VMM 2008

With Microsoft's investment in virtualization technologies, it is almost a given that Hyper-V virtualization will be leveraged by IT departments. A large number of companies have already invested in VMware virtualization, using VMware ESX server and proprietary VMware VirtualCenter for management. Adding Hyper-V to the virtual landscape can increase the complexity and time required to manage the physical and virtual infrastructure for these companies. VMM 2008 reduces this complexity by presenting a common management interface to administrators and a common self-service portal to developers and end users.

VMM 2008 provides the ability to manage the following host systems.

Hyper-V Hosts

VMM 2008 supports hosts running Windows Server 2008 that run the Hyper-V server role. If the administrator adds a Windows Server 2008 to VMM 2008 and the server does not have the Hyper-V server role enabled yet, VMM 2008 will enable the Hyper-V server role automatically as it adds the server as a host managed by VMM.

VMM 2008 can also import a Windows Server 2008 computer that is already configured as a Hyper-V host and will import any Hyper-V VMs that are already deployed on that host. The hosts and VMs can be managed from the VMM Administrative console or from the VMM command shell.

Virtual Server Hosts

VMM 2008 supports Microsoft Virtual Server 2005 R2 host servers running a Windows Server operating system (typically, Windows Server 2003). This provides the backward compatibility needed by companies that have already deployed VMM 2007.

VMware Hosts

VMM 2008 supports connecting to a VMware virtualization manager server. It will import its data (including the host servers that it manages and the VMs deployed on those hosts) into the VMM library database. VMM then integrates the imported VMware objects into its set of Windows-based objects.

From the server administrator's point of view, the Windows-based and VMware-based objects are managed in the same way using the same VMM Administrative console.

Virtualization Manager Support

VMM 2008 supports the following VMware virtualization managers and hosts:

- ▶ VMware VirtualCenter 2.0
- ▶ VMware VirtualCenter 2.5

Both of these versions of VirtualCenter are capable of managing hosts running VMware ESX Server 3.0 or ESX Server 3.5.

Backward Compatibility and Enhancements in VMM 2008

VMM 2008 is backward compatible with the earlier version of Microsoft Virtual Machine Manager, VMM 2007. This means that administrators familiar with VMM 2007 can leverage existing skills.

Command Console Cmdlets

More than 30 VMM 2007 cmdlets have been improved to work with Hyper-V, and another 30+ new cmdlets have been introduced in VMM 2008. Most of these cmdlet changes provide Hyper-V and roles-based access control support.

Enhancements in VMM 2008

VMM 2008 extends the capabilities of VMM 2007 for managing the physical and virtual enterprise by adding the following new features and capabilities:

- ▶ Extended support for VM hosts to both Hyper-V and VMware hosts
- ▶ Integrated native support for Windows Server 2008 failover clusters
- ▶ Increased options for securing access to VMM resources using roles-based access control (RBAC)
- ▶ Improved integration with Operations Manager 2007 to optimize physical resources
- ▶ Enhanced networking support, including VLANs, for virtual networking and isolation
- ▶ Improved disk and DVD management for VMs
- ▶ Expanded VMM library functionality

Cluster Support in VMM 2008

VMM 2008 supports both Windows Server 2008 failover clusters and VMware ESX host clusters. This ability reduces costs by consolidating different clustered host systems into a common managed collection of resources.

The Importance of Clusters in the Virtual Environment

Clusters are an important resource in the virtual enterprise because they offer a highly available platform to host mission-critical VMs. After all, if a single system hosts multiple mission-critical VMs, that host system is a single point of failure.

High Availability with Clustered Hosts

VMM 2008 provides the capability to move a VM from one physical node of a cluster to another, either manually or automatically. This enables the administrator to patch the active node or bring it down for maintenance without impacting the mission-critical VMs hosted on the server. It also provides automatic fault tolerance in the event of an unexpected server failure.

VMM 2008 can manage up to 16 node host clusters that are configured using the Windows Failover Cluster management console. VMM takes advantage of the many cluster management improvements available in Windows Server 2008, making cluster configuration and management much easier for the administrator. Because of this tight integration, VMM can automatically detect the addition or removal of a node within the host cluster.

Moving VMs Between Clustered Hosts

Failover clusters of two or more hosts are configured by the administrator. If one host in the host cluster becomes unavailable, the VMs on that host are automatically moved to another host in the same host cluster. VMM support for host clusters ensures the VMs deployed on hosts in that cluster are highly available. VMs deployed on host clusters are called highly available VMs, or HA VMs.

Highly Available VMs

When a VM's hardware profile is configured in VMM, an option is available to make this VM highly available. If that check box is selected, the VM can be placed only on an available host cluster, ensuring that the high availability of the VM resource.

The VMM Library

The VMM centralized library is the repository for all Windows-based and VMware-based VM objects. These objects are the building blocks of the VMs that will be created. They include hardware profiles, operating system profiles, virtual disks and ISOs, and VM templates.

Hardware Profiles

These profiles make up the virtual hardware components of a VM. BIOS boot order (CD-ROM, hard drive, floppy, and so on), CPU count and type, physical RAM, floppy drive, and serial (COM) ports are all part of the hardware profile. IDE and SCSI adapters and virtual DVD drives are part of the bus configuration. One or more network adapters can be added and the network type (external, internal, or private) or VLAN can be specified.

The Advanced settings allow the administrator to configure the priority of the VM and whether the VM is a highly available (HA) VM. Priority is a weight assigned to each VM, ranging from low to normal to high. When CPU utilization is high on the host, the host allocates more CPU cycles to VMs with a higher relative weight. As mentioned earlier, VMs marked as highly available can be placed only on host clusters. Likewise, VMM 2008 will not place VMs that are not marked as highly available on host clusters.

Guest OS Profiles

Guest operating system profiles are used to configure the name, administrator password, Windows product key, time zone, and Windows operating system type of the VM. Networking allows the administrator to choose which Windows workgroup or domain to join. To join a domain, the VM must have at least one virtual network adapter attached to a virtual network.

The guest OS profile may also include a Sysprep answer file or GUIRunOnce commands. A Sysprep answer file is used to configure additional settings in the VM not specified in the guest OS profile, such as assigning regional settings or languages. Sysprep scripts must be stored on a VMM library share.

GUIRunOnce commands are commands that run automatically the first time the user logs on to the VM. Both of these options reduce the number of possible errors created during installation and provide greater consistency in the VMs.

Disk Images and ISO Image Files

The VMM 2008 library also stores Hyper-V and Virtual Server virtual hard disks (VHD files) and VMware virtual hard disks (VMDK files). Virtual disks can be either blank or contain data, such as a preconfigured operating system or generic data used by applications.

Operating system disks must be generalized using the Windows Sysprep utility so that VMM 2008 can deploy the VM. The Windows miniprep process will configure the new VM to be unique by generating a new security identifier (SID) for each VM based on this generalized disk image.

CD-ROM and DVD-ROM disks can also be stored in the VMM 2008 library share. This is achieved by creating a single file image (ISO image) of the optical disk and copying it to the VMM library share. ISOs can be mounted by a VM in the hardware profile at VM creation or at any time after the VM is deployed by the administrator in the VM settings. ISOs can also be configured to run from directly from the VMM library or copied to the local VM folder on the host.

VM Templates

Templates are used to create new VMs. They usually consist of a VHD (one that is either stored in the library or from a VM currently located on a host), a hardware profile, and an OS profile.

After a VM template has been created, it can be deployed to a host server. The host server must be a standalone server for non-HA VMs or a host cluster for HA VMs.

Roles-Based Access Control

VMM 2008 offers a new RBAC model. Permissions in VMM 2008 are based on "user roles," which can be scoped to increase or limit the objects that a user role can access, as shown in Figure 8.5.

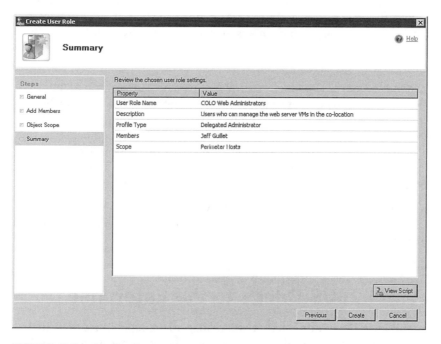

FIGURE 8.5   Configuring a user role.

NOTE

The only exception to this is the Administrator role, which cannot be limited.

User Roles in VMM 2008

User roles are similar to security groups in Active Directory. They are made up of domain accounts or groups and have a particular set of permissions granted to them. There are three basic user role types in VMM 2008.

VMM Administrator

This user role has complete unlimited access to VMM 2008 and the objects in the VMM library. Members are Active Directory users or groups. VMM administrators can add or remove members to this role, but because only one VMM Administrator role exists, they cannot create or delete the VMM Administrator role. Members of the VMM Administrator role can use the Administrative console and the VMM command shell, but cannot access the self-service portal unless they are also members of a Self-Service User role.

VMM Delegated Administrator

This user role is scoped to a particular set of VMM objects. Members are Active Directory users or groups. VMM delegated administrators cannot add themselves to the VMM Administrator role or configure global settings across the VMM environment. They can perform all operations on all VMM objects within the specified scope. Scopes are made up of one or more host groups or library servers. Members of a VMM Delegated Administrator role can use the Administrative console and the VMM command shell, but cannot access the self-service portal unless they are also members of a Self-Service User role.

Self-Service User

This user role is made up of Active Directory users or groups who can perform all allowed operations on a specific set of VMs deployed on one or more hosts within the specified scope. Scopes are made up of one or more host groups. Users can be granted the right to store their own VMs on a VMM library server. Administrators can limit their access to one or more specified library shares on a server. Members can access the self-service portal interface and the VMM command shell, but cannot access the Administrative console unless they are also a member of at least one of the Administrator roles listed previously.

VMM 2008 allows self-service users to work with any VM in either Hyper-V or VMware to check out or deploy VMs to the proper host, without having to know which host to use. It is completely transparent to the end user.

The Value VMM 2008 Brings to the Enterprise

VMM 2008 greatly enhances the administration and management capabilities of virtual guest sessions over the built-in Hyper-V management console that comes with Hyper-V. VMM 2008 allows organizations to more easily manage centralized servers and organize their servers in a manner that helps the administrators delegate access and administration rights to those that need access to specific servers or groups of servers.

Centralized Management

VMM 2008 offers a centralized management solution for the entire virtual network. Using one tool, the administrator can manage, create, deploy, move, copy, or delete any VM in the enterprise. It makes no difference whether the host or VM is running Microsoft Hyper-V or VMware ESX.

Decreases Server Sprawl

VMM 2008 prevents VM server sprawl by managing all the host servers in the enterprise. Due to the ease of VM deployment, virtual server sprawl can be a real issue. VMs may be deployed to the wrong host servers, and precious network resources can be squandered. VMM 2008 provides a way to take control of the virtual infrastructure and deploy VMs in the best way, based on resource and performance needs.

Integration with System Center Operations Manager 2007

Tight integration with Microsoft System Center Operations Manager 2007 (SCOM 2007) provides the capability to monitor and manage the virtual network like never before. SCOM 2007 offers VMM 2008 and Hyper-V management packs to provide real-time monitoring of host and virtual servers. It provides both alerting and built-in knowledge that aids the administrator in troubleshooting and recovery.

PRO (Performance and Resource Optimization) is an enhanced monitoring and management feature that is enabled when VMM 2008 is paired with SCOM 2007. It helps guide administrators by outlining ways to more efficiently deploy and run both physical and virtual resources. PRO can even move a VM from a problem host to another or perform a specified action on a VM or host in response to an error condition.

Profiles and Templates Make Provisioning Easier

VMM 2008 provides the administrator with the most complete, yet simple, server provisioning tools available. Multiple hardware and operating system profiles can be stored in the VMM library. Hundreds of VM templates can be stored and grouped together for easy deployment. Templates also aid in server standardization, an important aspect in any environment. Troubleshooting is minimized when the administrator can be sure that each VM based on the same template will be configured the same way.

Self-Service Provisioning

Self-service users can deploy the VMs they have access to without the need to understand the underlying physical infrastructure. VMware VMs and Hyper-V VMs will automatically be deployed to the most suitable server, based on the criteria set by the administrator.

Self-service users provision their own VMs using the self-service portal. This makes building or rebuilding test servers for developers a snap. Developers can spend more time testing and developing and less time worrying about the infrastructure.

Disaster Recovery and Business Continuity

One of the most important promises of virtualization is disaster recovery. VMM 2008 offers several features that increase server uptime and provide business-continuity protection. Because VMM 2008 is highly cluster aware, it can automatically move HA VMs from one cluster node to another, without the administrator having to worry which host is appropriate for the particular VMs. The administrator can define the suitability criteria of each host to help guide other administrators or self-service users to use the correct host.

Optimized Resource Allocation

By knowing and understanding the resource requirements and constraints of each physical host and VM server, VMM 2008 can make the best use of the hardware available. With this knowledge, more VMs can be placed on existing host servers, realizing an even greater value from the virtual environment.

Physical and Virtual Server Conversions

VMM 2008 provides both physical to virtual (P2V) and virtual to virtual (V2V) conversion capabilities. The P2V process, as shown in Figure 8.6, is used to rapidly convert a physical server to a Hyper-V or VMware virtual server, preserving the existing operating system, applications, and data. This is useful when the administrator needs to virtualize an existing physical server, but the configuration is too complex or the application software is no longer available. In some instances, this conversion can even occur while the server is online, reducing downtime during the conversion process.

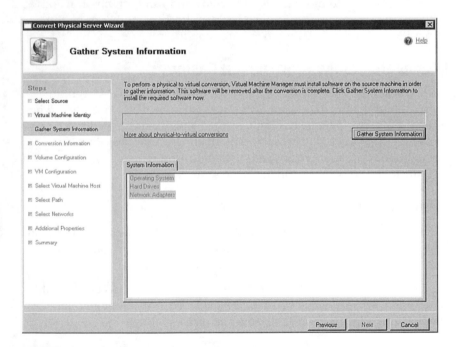

FIGURE 8.6   Performing a P2V conversion.

V2V conversion is used to convert a VMware VM to a Microsoft Hyper-V or Virtual Server VM. This is useful when the organization chooses to standardize on the Hyper-V virtualization platform and reduce its VMware footprint and associated licensing costs.

Roles-Based Access Control

VMM 2008's RBAC model, along with administrator delegation, allows VMM administrators to provide more autonomy and less administrative overhead in managing and working with the virtual network. Department VMM administrators can be granted the appropriate rights to manage and deploy the VMs needed, without the need to engage a higher administrator.

Who Needs VMM 2008?

As this chapter explains, VMM 2008 offers many advanced VM management features while emphasizing ease of use and automation. The three management interfaces (the Administrative console, the command console, and the self-service portal) offer a variety of ways for VMM administrators and users to create, deploy, and manage their VMs.

For these reasons, VMM 2008 is a good fit for the following types of IT organizations.

VMM 2008 for Delegated Administration Environments

IT environments with delegated administration/permissions models require a flexible and granular management solution to manage and control their virtual environment. VMM 2008 offers this flexibility via its RBAC model, which provides better control and granularity in administration and user delegation.

VMM 2008 for Structure ITIL-Based Organizations

Enterprises that utilize Information Technology Infrastructure Library (ITIL) concepts and techniques will benefit from the service-based management that VMM provides. The VMM administrator can provide a high level of service to other departments and users. The self-service portal provides a controlled way for users to deploy their own VMs without having to worry about VM placement.

VMM 2008 for Disaster Recovery and Business Continuity

Any IT environment with a need for server disaster recovery or line-of-business continuity will appreciate the high-availability features built in to VMM 2008. VMM 2008's native awareness of Windows and VMware clusters makes it an ideal management solution that can automatically move HA VMs from one host cluster node to another when the situation warrants.

VMM 2008 for Dynamically Adjusting Environments

Every IT environment has finite resources. VMM 2008 provides dynamic virtual server placement based on physical constraints. Administrators define scores for physical hosts that define the suitability of a VM for each host. VMM 2008 displays the score of each potential host in an easy-to-understand five-star rating. As resources change on these hosts, the rating changes.

VMM 2008 for Highly Leveraged Virtual Environments

Enterprises with a need for rapid deployment and virtualization can take full advantage of the tremendous cost savings that virtualization provides. For companies beginning to incorporate Hyper-V servers into their VMware environment, VMM 2008 provides the perfect management platform for managing both environments. For companies entering into the virtual network environment, VMM 2008 provides the advanced management capabilities that ensure rapid, controlled deployment of VMs into the physical environment.

VMM 2008 for VM Conversion Requirements

IT environments that require physical or virtual server conversions will enjoy VMM 2008's conversion capabilities. VMM 2008 can convert physical servers to virtual servers (P2V) and VMware ESX virtual servers to Microsoft Hyper-V virtual servers (V2V). P2V conversions allow organizations to get rid of old hardware running on legacy systems and provides a way to rapidly convert a physical network to a virtual one. V2V conversions allow organizations to rapidly convert expensive VMware ESX VMs to Hyper-V VMs.

VMM 2008 for Heterogeneous Environments

Current VMware ESX and VirtualCenter customers who want to use Hyper-V can use VMM 2008 to manage both environments. This heterogeneous management solution reduces administrative overhead and complexity. VMM 2008 provides the same functionality as VMware VirtualCenter and VMotion for both VMware and Hyper-V environments, all in the same VM management solution. Self-service users spend less time worrying about the host platform and more time developing.

Summary

Microsoft VMM is new to the Microsoft virtualization platform, with the first version coming out in 2007 and quickly revised to the current VMM 2008 product. VMM 2008 provides the ability for organizations to manage VMs across multiple hosts and to delegate the administration and management of the VMs on the same host or on other virtual hosts in the organization.

VMM 2008 not only supports the management of Microsoft-based virtual images, but it also provides connectivity and support for management of VMs running on other platforms such as VMware.

Best Practices

The following are best practices from this chapter:

- Organizations using Hyper-V should use the Virtual Machine Manager 2008 product, not VMM 2007.

- Install VMM 2008 on a Windows 2008 server or a Windows 2003 server with at least SP1 applied.

- Ensure the system that VMM 2008 is being installed on is attached to a Windows domain.

- For most organizations, VMM 2008 can be installed on the same system as the SQL database that stores the virtual server management information.

- View, copy, and save the commands that will be run by the VMM 2008 console when performing a task.

- Build a collection of PowerShell cmdlets for common administrative tasks.

- Use the self-service portal to allow end users or developers to create their own VMs.

- Use the VMM Administrative console to manage Microsoft Hyper-V, VMware ESX, and Microsoft Virtual Server hosts.

- Browse the VMM Administrative console to understand its capabilities and functions.

- Add Hyper-V, VMware, and Virtual Server physical hosts to the Administrative console to manage them with VMM 2008.

- Examine the Details pane of each VM in the Administrative console to ensure the VM settings are correct.

- For organizations where the VMM components are installed on separate servers, VMM libraries should be on separate servers, too.

- VMM libraries should be placed on clustered file servers where fault tolerance of the library is required.

- Multiple VMM library servers should be configured for organizations with multiple VM hosts in different sites.

- Create hardware profiles to define the hardware used in common VMs (for example, a dual processor server with 2GB of RAM and a DVD ROM).

- Create guest OS profiles to define the operating system profile used in common VMs (for example, Windows Server 2008 Standard x64).

- Review the Jobs pane to examine running, successful, or failed jobs.

- Configure user roles for VMM administrators, delegated administrators, and self-service users.

▶ Use the Filters section of the Navigation pane to reduce the number of results displayed in the Details pane.

▶ Use VMM 2008 to reduce the complexity of managing multiple virtualization platforms.

▶ Import host computers into VMM 2008 that are already running Hyper-V or VMware virtualization.

▶ Learn the new and improved VMM 2008 command console cmdlets for command-line management of the virtual environment.

▶ Use host clusters to host mission-critical virtual servers and provide a high level of fault tolerance.

▶ Store common CD images (ISOs) in the VMM library for easy access from the VMM Administrative console.

▶ Ensure that only highly available VMs are marked as such in the VM's settings. Doing so will configure the VM to be placed only on host clusters.

▶ The VMM administrator cannot be limited. Therefore, create Delegated Administrator roles for this purpose.

## 9

Installing and Getting Familiar with Virtual Machine Manager 2008

This chapter covers the installation and setup of the Virtual Machine Manager (VMM) 2008 program. It includes the preparation of the server that will host the VMM server components, and the installation of the VMM server, the VMM server Administrator console, the self-service portal, and the VMM local agent.

This chapter covers the installation of the VMM 2008 Administrator console on a separate server for centralized management, and examines this basic administrative interface and the various configuration components available.

Understanding the Components of VMM 2008

Four basic components make up VMM 2008, as shown in Figure 9.1:

▶ The VMM 2008 server

▶ The Administrator console

▶ The self-service portal

▶ The local agent

The VMM 2008 Server

The VMM 2008 server component consists of the VMM management service, the VMM database, and VMM library.

The Virtual Machine Manager service, or VMMService, provides the services necessary to run VMM. It communicates with and stores its configuration in the SQL database. The VMM library share is a simple NTFS share that houses the objects that make up a virtual machine (VM)—hardware profiles, guest OS profiles, templates, virtual hard disks (VHDs), CD-ROM images (ISOs), and so on.

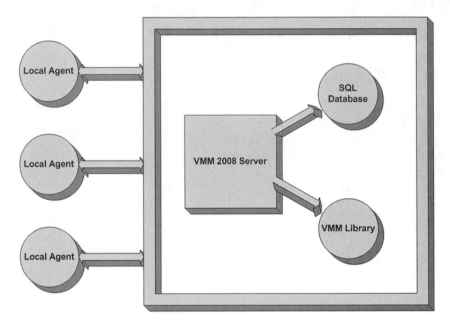

FIGURE 9.1   The basic components of VMM 2008.

Among other things, the VMM server monitors VM and host health and moves VMs, if necessary, between host servers.

The Administrator Console

The Administrator console is a Microsoft Management Console (MMC) that provides an administrative interface to the VMM 2008 server. VMM administrators can manage all VMs and the VMM organizational settings using this console, whereas VMM delegated administrators can manage only the VMs that have been delegated to them.

Even though the administrator console is very easy to use, it offers complete management of the virtual environment, including creating, managing, and deploying VMs and VLANs; managing host servers; configuring user roles; and so forth. It is built upon Windows PowerShell.

The Self-Service Portal

The VMM 2008 self-service portal provides a web-based interface that allows self-service users to provision VMs from the library. It also allows self-service users to store VMs in the library if they have sufficient rights. The most common use of the self-service portal is to provide an environment for developers and testers to use.

Multiple types of self-service user roles can be provisioned by the VMM administrator to facilitate the deployment of VMs in the virtual environment.

The Local Agent

The local agent is the agent software that allows VMM 2008 to monitor and manage Windows 2008 Hyper-V host servers. It can be installed remotely using the VMM Administrator console or manually via the VMM 2008 CD. Administrators of host servers in the perimeter (demilitarized zone, DMZ) network must install the local agent manually using the VMM 2008 CD, so that VMM 2008 can manage the host servers.

Preparing the Server for VMM 2008

Decisions should be made about how VMM 2008 will be deployed. Will VMM be installed on a single server or across multiple servers in the enterprise? Will VMM use SQL Server Express, an existing SQL server, or a new one for its configuration database?

In addition, several software and hardware prerequisites must be met before VMM 2008 can be installed on the VMM server.

Single- or Multiple-Server Deployments

VMM 2008 can be deployed on a single server that hosts the VMM server, SQL database, and Administrator console, or these components can be deployed across separate single-purpose servers. The decision about how to deploy VMM 2008 in the enterprise depends on the physical and virtual environment and, to a lesser degree, the administration of these environments.

NOTE

The computer where VMM 2008 is installed must be joined to an Active Directory Domain Services (AD DS) domain. All host servers must also be joined to domains in AD DS. A host can be in a different domain from the VMM server's domain and can be in a trusted or a nontrusted domain.

For hosts in perimeter (DMZ) networks, a VMM agent must be installed locally on that host, the firewalls must be configured, and then the host is added to VMM.

Single-Server Deployment
A single-server deployment is often used in small environments where physical resources are tight and the virtual environment is small.

In this type of deployment, a single server hosts the VMM server, SQL database (usually using SQL Express), the Administrator console, and possibly even the self-service portal. It works well when the VM environment (both the VMM server and host servers) doesn't span a wide area network (WAN).

Multiple-Server Deployment

A multiple-server deployment is usually used in larger, high-performance VMM environments or where the virtual environment spans WANs. VMM performance is improved by installing the different components on separate servers and placing these servers closest to the resources they access the most.

Typically, this involves using a dedicated (or at least separate) SQL database server and placing VMM libraries close to the host servers where the VMs will be deployed.

Often, the Administrator console is installed on separate servers or workstations to facilitate administration. The self-service console may also be deployed on its own server or on another underutilized server. It may even be virtualized itself.

Supported Operating Systems for VMM Components

Each VMM component is supported to run on different operating systems. The information in Table 9.1 will help the administrator select the proper operating system, depending on the organization's needs.

	Hyper-V Role	VMM Server	Admin Console	Self-Service Library Portal
Windows Server 2008 with Hyper-V x64 Standard, Enterprise, and Datacenter editions	X	X	X	X
Windows Server 2008 without Hyper-V x64 Standard, Enterprise, and Datacenter editions	X	X	X	X
Windows Server 2008 32-bit Standard, Enterprise, and Datacenter editions	X	X	X	X
Windows Server 2008 Server Core installation Standard, Enterprise, and Datacenter editions			X	X
Windows Server 2003 with SP2, Standard, Enterprise, and Datacenter editions		X	X	X
Windows Server 2003 x64 Edition with SP2		X	X	X
Windows Vista		X		

TABLE 9.1   SQL Server Express SP2 System Requirements

Operating System	Hyper-V Role	VMM Server	Admin Console	Self-Service Portal	Library Server
Windows Server 2008 with Hyper-V x64 Standard, Enterprise, and Datacenter editions	X	X	X	X	X
Windows Server 2008 without Hyper-V x64 Standard, Enterprise, and Datacenter editions		X	X	X	X
Windows Server 2008 32-bit Standard, Enterprise, and Datacenter editions		X	X	X	X
Windows Server 2008 Server Core installation Standard, Enterprise, and Datacenter editions				X	X
Windows Server 2003 with SP2, Standard, Enterprise, and Datacenter editions			X	X	X
Windows Server 2003 Edition with SP2 x64			X	X	X
Windows Vista			X		

Prerequisite Software

VMM 2008 requires the following software to be installed before installing the VMM server component:

- **Windows Server 2008 x64**—Standard, Enterprise, or Datacenter editions.

- **Windows PowerShell 1.0**—This software is included in Windows Server 2008 as an optional feature. If this software has not been installed or removed, the Setup Wizard automatically adds it.

- **Windows Remote Management (WinRM)**—This software is included in Windows Server 2008. The WinRM service is configured to start automatically, by default. If the WinRM service is stopped, the Setup Wizard starts the service.

- **Microsoft .Net Framework 3.0**—This software is included in Windows Server 2008 as an optional feature. If this software has not been installed or removed, the Setup Wizard automatically adds it.

- **Windows Automated Installation Kit (Windows AIK) 1.1**—If this software has not been installed previously, the Setup Wizard automatically installs it.

Windows Internet Information Services (IIS) 6.0 components must be installed before installing the self-service portal. For Windows Server 2003, the Windows Server IIS 6.0 component must be added too.

To install the self-service portal on Windows Server 2008, the administrator must add the Web Server (IIS) role and then install the following server role services:

▶ IIS 6 Metabase Compatibility

▶ IIS 6 WMI Compatibility

VMM Database Considerations

The VMM 2008 server component uses a SQL database to store and read VMM host server and guest VM configuration. VMM uses the database to correlate the individual VM objects (hardware profiles, guest OS profiles, VHDs, and so forth) into a complete VM management solution.

The SQL database can be configured on SQL Express, an existing SQL server, or on a dedicated SQL server.

SQL Server Express Installation

VMM 2008 includes an optional SQL Express installation on the VMM 2008 setup CD. SQL Express is a free version of SQL 2005 that is targeted for smaller deployments of 150 VMs or fewer.

Some technical restrictions make it unsuitable for large deployments:

▶ It has a 4GB database limit (excluding log files).

▶ It can use only one processor, even in multiple processor configurations.

▶ It can use only up to 1GB of RAM.

▶ VMM reporting is not available.

▶ The SQL Server agent service is excluded.

Table 9.2 identifies the minimum and recommended hardware requirements for a SQL Express SP2 server.

TABLE 9.2   SQL Server Express SP2 System Requirements

Hardware	Minimum	Recommended
Processor	Pentium 4, 2.8GHz	Dual core, 64 bit, 3.2GHz
RAM	2GB	4GB
Hard disk space	4GB	4GB

NOTE

SQL Server Express is SQL Express installation included on the VMM 2008 installation CD and will be installed automatically during setup if the administrator chooses to use it.

Using an Existing SQL Server 2005 Installation

VMM 2008 can create a new database on an existing SQL 2005 SP2 database server. This can save additional hardware costs if the server is currently underutilized.

Make sure that the SQL 2005 server has adequate capacity and resources to host the VMM database. It should be at least dual core with 4GB RAM and 150GB free space for the new VMM database.

Using a New SQL Server 2005 Installation

VMM 2008 will operate best with a dedicated SQL 2005 SP2 database server. VMM stores and reads a great deal of data in its operational database and will perform at its peak on a suitable SQL server without resource contention. By appropriately sizing the SQL 2005 server, the organization can count on smooth and quick database operations.

Table 9.3 identifies the minimum and recommended hardware requirements for the SQL 2005 SP2 server.

TABLE 9.3   SQL 2005 SP2 System Requirements

Hardware	Minimum	Recommended
Processor	Dual core, 64 bit, 3.2GHz	Dual core, 64 bit, 3.2GHz
RAM	4GB	8GB
Hard disk space	150GB	200GB

NOTE

If the decision is made to use SQL Server 2005 SP2, the server should be installed, running, and available before you install VMM 2008.

SQL Reporting Considerations

The administrator should be careful to install the correct version of SQL 2005, depending on the organization's reporting needs.

Table 9.4 shows the reporting capabilities of each version of SQL 2005.

TABLE 9.4   SQL 2005 Reporting Capabilities

Supported SQL Server Versions	Supports Reporting in VMM 2008
SQL Server 2005 Express Edition SP2	No
SQL Server 2005 Standard Edition SP2	Yes
SQL Server 2005 Enterprise Edition SP2	Yes

VMM 2008 Installation

Each VMM component (server, Administrator console, self-service portal, library, and local agent) can be installed on the same or different servers, depending on the organization's needs.

The following example depicts installing the VMM server component on a Windows Server 2008 x64 Standard Edition member server. SQL Express Edition will be installed, and the VMM library will be hosted on the same server.

Installing VMM Server and the SQL Server Express Database on Windows Server 2008

Begin by inserting the VMM 2008 media in the server. Setup will run and display the options for installation, as shown in Figure 9.2.

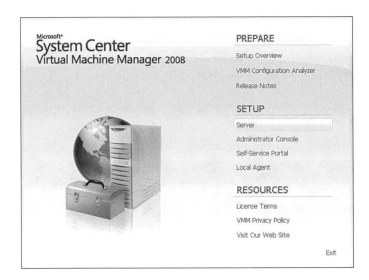

FIGURE 9.2   The VMM Setup menu.

Click Server from the Setup menu. The setup program will copy files needed during setup to the server and will prepare the Setup Wizard to run.

Read the license terms. If you agree, select to accept the agreement to install VMM server.

If Microsoft Update has not been configured on the VMM server, the Setup Wizard will recommend enabling it. Microsoft Update offers security and important updates for both Windows and VMM 2008. Make the appropriate selection and click Next.

The next screen offers to join the Customer Experience Improvement Program (CEIP). This program is used by Microsoft to help improve the quality, reliability, and performance of

Microsoft products and services; however, some anonymous data may be transmitted to Microsoft. Make the appropriate selection and click Next.

Next, enter the product registration information. Here you enter your username and company. Click Next.

The Prerequisite Checker runs to check that the software required by VMM server is installed on the server, as shown in Figure 9.3. If the server fails the Prerequisite Checker, the Setup Wizard tells you what you need to fix it. When it runs successfully, click Next.

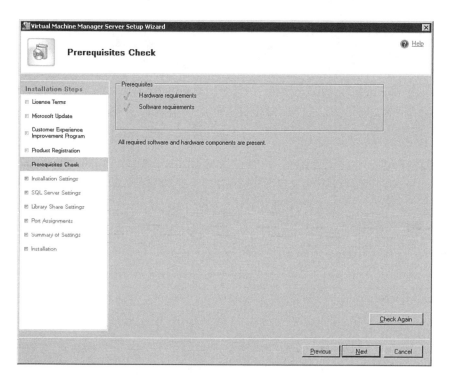

FIGURE 9.3   The Prerequisite Checker.

In the Installation Settings window, select the path where the VMM program files will be installed. The default path is C:\Program Files\Microsoft System Center Virtual Machine Manager 2008. Change the path if necessary and click Next.

The SQL Server Settings screen, shown in Figure 9.4, is where the administrator selects the database to use. The default selection is to install the VMM database on an existing SQL Server 2005 computer. If this option is chosen, the administrator must supply the following information:

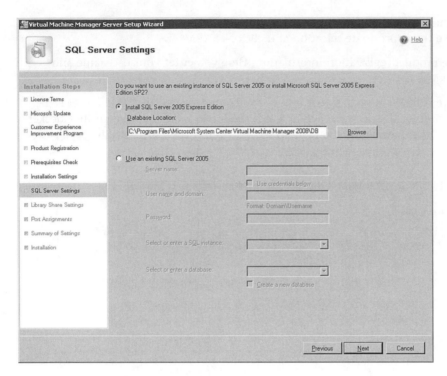

FIGURE 9.4   SQL Server settings.

- ▶ SQL server name

- ▶ Username and domain

- ▶ Password

- ▶ SQL instance (new or existing)

- ▶ SQL database (new or existing)

If the administrator chooses to use SQL Server 2005 Express Edition, select the path where the database will be installed. The default location, as shown in Figure 9.4, is C:\Program Files\Microsoft System Center Virtual Machine Manager 2008\DB. Click Next to continue.

The Library Share Settings screen allows the administrator to specify the default share for the VMM library. This is the network share that holds resources available for creating VMs.

The default library share name is MSSCVMMLibrary, and VMM will default to creating a new library share on the VMM server in C:\ProgramData\Virtual Machine Manager Library Files. Change this path if necessary.

The alternative setting is to use an existing library share. The administrator may choose to do this if there is an existing VMM library on another server or Windows cluster. Click Next to continue.

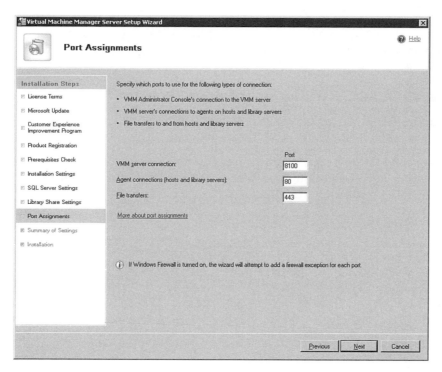

FIGURE 9.5   Port Assignments screen.

The Port Assignments screen, shown in Figure 9.5, allows the administrator to specify which ports to use for connections.

The default port assignments are as follows:

▶ VMM Server Connection: 8100

▶ Agent Connections: 80

▶ File Transfers: 443

The final screen in the Setup Wizard is the Summary of Settings. Here, the administrator can review the settings that were chosen in the Setup Wizard.

Review the settings and click Previous to go back or Install to perform the VMM server installation. Setup will install the prerequisites if necessary, and install the VMM server component. The installation may take several minutes, depending on the options that were selected.

If an error occurs during installation, click the Error tab on the Installation window to review the error and take appropriate action.

After the VMM server component is installed, two new services are installed and started. The VMMService is the heart of the VMM server, and the VMM agent service provides management services for VMM.

Besides Windows PowerShell 1.0 and the Microsoft Windows Automated Installation Kit, which are both prerequisites for VMM server, nothing is added to the Windows Start menu. To interact with the VMM server, the administrator must install the VMM Administrator console.

Installing the VMM Administrator Console

The VMM Administrator console can be installed on Windows Server 2008 (except Server Core), Windows Server 2003 SP2, Windows XP SP2, or Windows Vista.

Begin by inserting the VMM 2008 media in the server. Setup will run and display the menu for installation. Click Administrator Console under Setup, as shown in Figure 9.6. The setup program will copy files needed during setup to the server and will prepare the Setup Wizard to run.

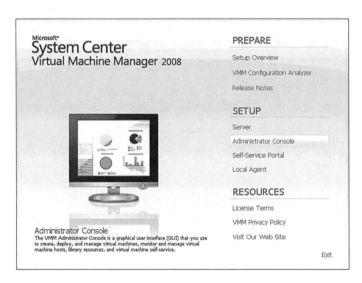

FIGURE 9.6   Selecting the Administrator Console in Setup.

Read the license terms carefully. The license agreement must be accepted to install the VMM Administrator console. Click Next.

If Microsoft Update has not been configured on the VMM server, the Setup Wizard will recommend enabling it. Microsoft Update offers security and important updates for both Windows and VMM 2008. Make the appropriate selection and click Next.

The next screen offers to join the Customer Experience Improvement Program (CEIP). If the Administrator console is being used to connect to a VMM server that is already participating in the CEIP, the administrator console will automatically be enrolled in the CEIP. Click Next to continue.

The Prerequisite Checker will run to check that the software required by the VMM Administrator console is installed on the computer. If the computer fails the Prerequisite

Checker, the Setup Wizard will tell you what you need to do to fix it. When it runs successfully, click Next.

In the Installation Settings window, select the path where the VMM program files will be installed. The default path is C:\Program Files\Microsoft System Center Virtual Machine Manager 2008. Change the path if necessary and click Next.

The Configuration Settings window allows the administrator to configure the port that the VMM Administrator console will use to connect to the VMM server. The default port is 8100. Accept or change the default port and click Next.

The final screen in the Setup Wizard is the Summary of Settings, shown in Figure 9.7. It allows the administrator to review the settings that were chosen in the Setup Wizard.

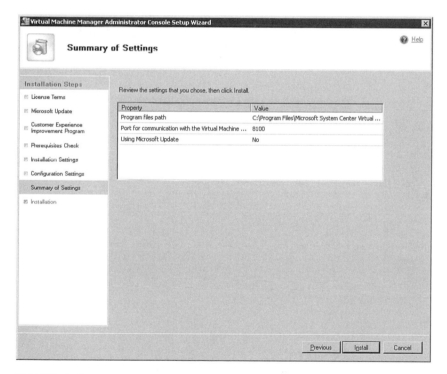

FIGURE 9.7   Summary of Settings screen.

Review the settings and click Previous to go back or Install to perform the VMM Administrator console installation. Setup will install the prerequisites if necessary, and install the VMM administrator console component. The installation may take several minutes, depending on the options that were selected.

If an error occurs during installation, click the Error tab on the Installation window to review the error and take appropriate action.

When the installation completes, the Setup Wizard will offer to create a shortcut on the desktop to the VMM Administrator console, and you can optionally open it when the wizard closes. There is also a link to check for the latest VMM updates from Microsoft.

Installing the Self-Service Portal

The VMM self-service portal can be installed on all versions of Windows Server 2008 (including Server Core) and all versions of Windows Server 2003 SP2.

The self-service portal requires IIS 6.0 or specific IIS 6.0 components, depending on the operating system the self-service portal is installed on. For Windows Server 2003, install the Windows IIS 6.0 component. For Windows Server 2008, add the Web Server (IIS) role and the IIS 6 Metabase Compatibility and IIS 6 WMI Compatibility server role services. Make sure that these prerequisites are met before installing the self-service portal.

Begin by inserting the VMM 2008 media in the server. Setup will run and display the menu for installation. Click Self-Service Portal under Setup, as shown in Figure 9.8. The setup program will copy files needed during setup to the server and will prepare the Setup Wizard to run.

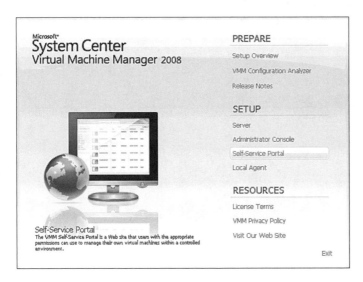

FIGURE 9.8   Selecting the Self-Service Portal in Setup.

Read the license terms carefully. The license agreement must be accepted to install the VMM self-service portal. Click Next.

If Microsoft Update has not been configured on the VMM server, the Setup Wizard will recommend enabling it. Microsoft Update offers security and important updates for both Windows and VMM 2008. Make the appropriate selection and click Next.

The Prerequisite Checker will run to check that the software required by the VMM self-service portal is installed on the computer. If the computer fails the Prerequisite Checker, the Setup Wizard will tell you what you need to do to fix it. When it runs successfully, click Next.

In the Installation Settings window, select the path where the VMM program files will be installed. The default path is C:\Program Files\Microsoft System Center Virtual Machine Manager 2008. Change the path if necessary and click Next.

The Web Server Settings screen, shown in Figure 9.9, allows the administrator to specify the VMM server that the self-service portal will connect to. The default port it will use to communicate with the VMM server is TCP port 8100. Set a new port or leave the default.

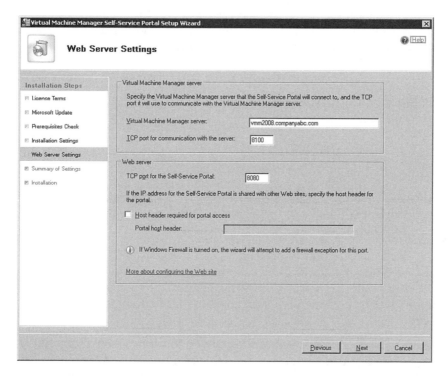

FIGURE 9.9   Web Server Settings screen.

Here the administrator can also specify the TCP port for the self-service portal and whether to use a host header for portal access.

NOTE

If the Windows firewall is turned on, the Setup Wizard will attempt to add a firewall exception for the web server port.

Click Next to continue.

The final screen in the Setup Wizard is the Summary of Settings. It allows the administrator to review the settings that were chosen in the Setup Wizard.

Review the settings and click Previous to go back or Install to perform the VMM self-service portal installation. Setup will install the prerequisites if necessary, and install the VMM self-service portal component.

Installation of the Local Agent

The VMM local agent must be installed on every Microsoft Hyper-V and Virtual Server host computer that will be managed by VMM 2008.

VMM 2008 can "push" the local agent to hosts that are members of the same domain that the VMM 2008 server belongs to using the VMM administrator console. The administrator must install the VMM local agent manually on workgroup servers in the perimeter network (DMZ) to be managed by VMM 2008.

To manually install the VMM local agent, insert the VMM 2008 media in the server to manage. Setup will run and display the menu for installation. Click Local Agent under Setup. The setup program will copy files needed during setup to the server and will prepare the Setup Wizard to run.

Read the license terms carefully. The license agreement must be accepted to install the VMM local agent. Click Next.

In the Destination Folder window, accept or change the path where the VMM program files will be installed. The default path is C:\Program Files\Microsoft System Center Virtual Machine Manager 2008. Click Next.

The Configuration Settings screen, shown in Figure 9.10, allows the administrator to configure the ports that VMM server will use to communicate to this host and the port the host will use to transfer files between the VMM server and host computers. Accept the default port of 80 for VMM server communication and 443 for file transfers, or change them and click Next.

The Security File Folder screen, shown in Figure 9.11, is used to configure a security file that will allow the VMM server to communicate and manage a nondomain host server in a perimeter network. Select the check box for This Host Is in a Perimeter Network and enter and confirm an encryption key. A security file will be placed in the C:\Program Files\Microsoft System Center Virtual Machine Manager 2008 folder that will be imported into the managing VMM server. Click Next.

In the Host Network Name screen, select how the VMM server will contact the host. You can choose either hostname or IP address. Enter the appropriate information and click Next.

Finally, click Install to install the VMM local agent software. A new VMM agent service will be installed and started on the host server. Click Finish to complete the installation.

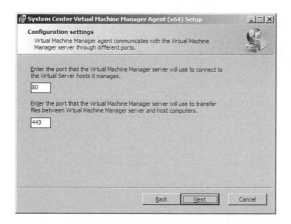

FIGURE 9.10   Configuration Settings screen.

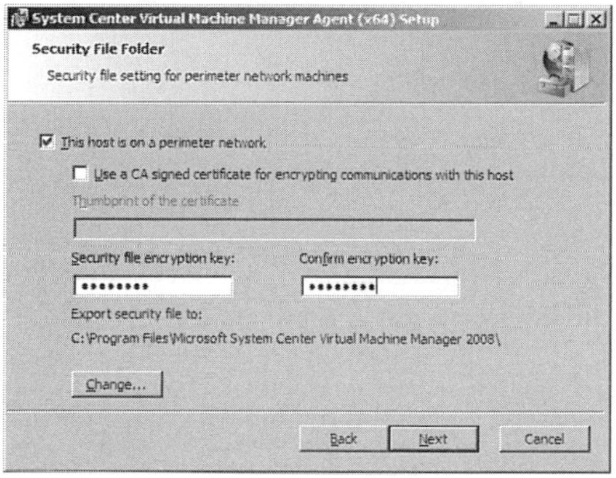

FIGURE 9.11   Security File Folder screen.

Understanding the VMM Administrator Console

The VMM Administrator console is the primary management interface for VMM 2008, host server, and VM management. It is an MMC application that runs on top of Windows PowerShell. The VMM command shell has more than 60 commandlets (cmdlets) that are specific to VMM 2008.

This section covers the basic functions of the Administrator console.

Overview of the Administrator Console

The Administrator console, shown in Figure 9.12, consists of the view buttons on the lower left, the view area above the view buttons, the Results pane in the top middle, the Detail pane below the Results pane, and the Actions pane on the right.

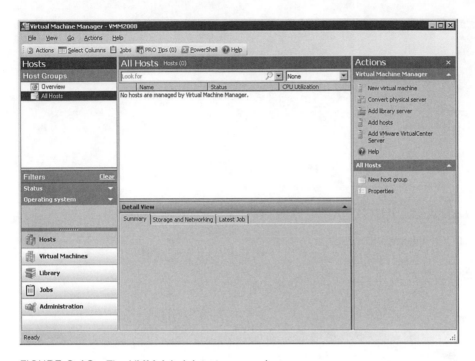

FIGURE 9.12   The VMM Administrator console.

The most common actions performed using the Administrator console include the following:

- ▶ Adding hosts

- ▶ Creating host groups

- ▶ Managing hosts

- ▶ Managing host clusters

- ▶ Configuring the VMM library

- ▶ Creating VMs

- ▶ Deploying and migrating VMs

- ▶ Managing VMs

- ▶ Configuring the self-service portal

- ▶ Monitoring and reporting

- ▶ Administering and managing roles

Adding Hosts

Hosts must be added to the VMM server to manage them from the VMM Administrator console. This section describes how to add hosts, both domain members and perimeter workgroup servers, to the VMM Administrator console.

Open the VMM Administrator console using the shortcut on the Windows desktop or via the Start menu under Microsoft System Center, Virtual Machine Manager 2008, Virtual Machine Manager Administrator Console.

A Connect to Server window may open, prompting for the VMM server to connect to. Enter the server name and connection port (the default is port 8100) using the format VMMserver:port.

NOTE

You may choose to always open a connection to this server by selecting the Make This Server My Default check box. Doing so prevents this connection window from displaying when the Administrator console is run.

Go to the Hosts view by clicking the Hosts button, then select All Hosts. The hosts managed by this VMM server will display in the Results pane. Selecting any host in the Results pane will display the details about that host in the Details pane.

To add a new host, select Add Hosts from the Actions pane or click the Actions menu, Virtual Machine Manager, Add Hosts. The Add Hosts Wizard will run.

In the Select Host Location screen, select one of the following options. The option chosen will alter the subsequent prompts in the Add Hosts Wizard.

► **Windows Domain Joined Host**—If the host to add is a member of a Windows Active Directory domain, select this option and enter the credentials for a domain account with administrative rights on the host. Click Next to continue.

On the Select Servers screen, enter the host server name and click Add or click the Host Server Name button to search for hosts. Enter a search term and click Search. Select one or more servers and click Add. Click OK to close the search window when finished. Click Next to continue.

NOTE

The administrator can also limit the scope of the search to servers with Virtual Server or Hyper-V already installed.

On the Configuration Settings screen, select the host group to add the host servers to. If any of the hosts are currently being managed by another VMM server, select the Reassociate Agent with Virtual Machine Manager Server check box. This will reassociate the local agent on the host to be managed by this VMM server.

On the Virtual Machine Paths screen, specify one or more default paths for storing the VMs deployed on these hosts. Here, you also can specify whether to enable remote connections to these hosts and which port to use. The default remote connection port is 5900. Click Next to continue.

Review the Summary screen and, if everything looks fine, click Add Hosts to add the hosts to the VMM server and the administrator console.

NOTE

The administrator can also click the View Script button to view, copy, or edit the VMM command shell that performs the same task in a script that is done in the graphical user interface.

After the hosts have been added using the Add Hosts Wizard, the VMM server will install the VMM local agent and the Hyper-V role on the hosts if it is not already installed. Then it will add the hosts to the Administrator console.

▶ **Windows Perimeter Network Host**—This option guides you through adding perimeter hosts to the VMM Administrator console. Click Next.

NOTE

For a host that is on a perimeter network, you must install the VMM local agent manually on the host before you can add the host to VMM.

On the Select a Host screen, enter the hostname or IP address, encryption key, and security file path. The encryption key was entered when the perimeter host installed the VMM local agent. The security key is located in the C:\Program Files\Microsoft System Center Virtual Machine Manager 2008 folder on the perimeter host. Copy it to the local computer and use this path for the security file. Add the hosts and click Next.

On the Configuration Settings screen, select the host group to add the host server(s) to. If any of the hosts are currently being managed by another VMM server, select the Reassociate Agent with Virtual Machine Manager Server check box. This will reassociate the local agent on the host to be managed by this VMM server.

On the Virtual Machine Paths screen, specify one or more default paths for storing the VMs deployed on these hosts. Here, you also can specify whether to enable remote connections to these hosts and which port to use. The default remote connection port is 5900. Click Next to continue.

Review the Summary screen and, if everything looks fine, click Add Hosts to add the hosts to the VMM server and the Administrator console.

NOTE

The administrator can also click the View Script button to view, copy, or edit the VMM command shell that performs the same task in a script that is done in the graphical user interface.

After the hosts have been added using the Add Hosts Wizard, the VMM server will add the hosts to the Administrator console.

▶ **Other Host**—This option allows the administrator to add non-Windows–based hosts, such as VMware ESX hosts, to the VMM server. Enter the username and password used to connect to the other host and click Next.

On the Select Hosts screen, enter the hostname or IP address of the host server to add, select the virtualization manager from the drop-down list, and select the host group to add the hosts to. Click Add and repeat for other hosts, if necessary. Click Next to continue.

Review the Summary screen and, if everything looks fine, click Add Hosts to add the hosts to the VMM server and the Administrator console.

After the hosts have been added using the Add Hosts Wizard, the VMM server will add the hosts to the Administrator console.

Creating Host Groups

Host groups allow the administrator to group together collections of similar hosts, such as perimeter hosts, domain hosts, or account servers.

Open the VMM Administrator console using the shortcut on the Windows desktop or via the Start menu under Microsoft System Center, Virtual Machine Manager 2008, Virtual Machine Manager Administrator Console.

A Connect to Server window may open, prompting for the VMM server to connect to. Enter the server name and connection port (the default is port 8100) using the format VMMserver:port.

NOTE

You may choose to always open a connection to this server by selecting the Make This Server My Default check box. Doing so prevents this connection window from displaying when the Administrator console is run.

Go to the Hosts view by clicking the Hosts button, and then select All Hosts. The hosts managed by this VMM server will display in the Results pane.

To add a new host group, select New Host Group from the Actions pane or click the Actions menu, All Hosts, New Host Group. A new host group will appear under All Hosts in the Hosts view. Rename the group as required.

Host groups can be moved or deleted using the Actions pane from the Hosts view.

Managing Hosts

Hosts can be managed from the Hosts view in the Administrator console. Select the appropriate host group or All Hosts to view all hosts.

Open the VMM Administrator console using the shortcut on the Windows desktop or via the Start menu under Microsoft System Center, Virtual Machine Manager 2008, Virtual Machine Manager Administrator Console.

A Connect to Server window may open, prompting for the VMM server to connect to. Enter the server name and connection port (the default is port 8100) using the format VMMserver:port.

NOTE

You may choose to always open a connection to this server by selecting the "Make this server my default" checkbox. Doing so prevents this connection window from displaying when the Administrator console is run.

Go to the Hosts view by clicking the Hosts button, and then select All Hosts. The hosts managed by this VMM server will display in the Results pane.

Right-click the host to manage and a choice of actions is presented. The administrator can move the host to a host group, refresh the host in the Details pane, remove the host from the VMM server, or access the host properties.

The Properties page allows the administrator to view or configure the host summary, host status, VM status, hardware reserves (for example, CPU and RAM), hardware, networking, VM placement path, remote connections, security settings, and more. The details for each of these settings are beyond the scope of this chapter; suffice to say that many more options are available to configure than are available in the standard Windows Server 2008 Hyper-V management console.

Managing Host Clusters

Host clusters are Windows cluster or VMware ESX cluster hosts that provide high availability and fault tolerance. The actions for host clusters allow the administrator to move a Hyper-V host cluster to a different host group, delete a host cluster from VMM, monitor host clusters, and modify the host cluster properties.

Open the VMM Administrator console using the shortcut on the Windows desktop or via the Start menu under Microsoft System Center, Virtual Machine Manager 2008, Virtual Machine Manager Administrator Console.

A Connect to Server window may open, prompting for the VMM server to connect to. Enter the server name and connection port (the default is port 8100) using the format VMMserver:port.

> **NOTE**
>
> You may choose to always open a connection to this server by selecting the Make This Server My Default check box. Doing so prevents this connection window from displaying when the Administrator console is run.

Go to the Hosts view by clicking the Hosts button, and then select All Hosts. The hosts managed by this VMM server will display in the Results pane.

Select the host cluster to manage in the Results pane. The actions available for managing the host cluster are listed in the Actions pane.

When Failover Cluster Node Management is used in Windows Server 2008 to add a node to a VMM-managed host cluster, the new node is discovered and added to the cluster. It will display in the Hosts view with a status of Pending Addition. Select Add Pending Hosts to add the host in VMM.

VMM 2008 also detects when a node is removed from a VMM-managed host cluster using Failover Cluster Node Management MMC. VMM sets the Clustered property of the node to False and begins managing the host as a regular, nonclustered host. VMM marks the node as Pending Removal. Select Remove to remove the host from VMM.

Configuring the VMM Library

The VMM library is a Windows share that hosts the resources used by VMM to create VMs. The library contains files contains files (VHDs, ISOs, and so on). The VMM database stores hardware profiles, guest OS profiles, and templates.

Select the appropriate host group or All Hosts to view all hosts.

Open the VMM Administrator console using the shortcut on the Windows desktop or via the Start menu under Microsoft System Center, Virtual Machine Manager 2008, Virtual Machine Manager Administrator Console.

A Connect to Server window may open, prompting for the VMM server to connect to. Enter the server name and connection port (the default is port 8100) using the format VMMserver:port.

NOTE

You may choose to always open a connection to this server by selecting the Make This Server My Default check box. Doing so prevents this connection window from displaying when the Administrator console is run.

Go to the Library view by clicking the Library button, and then select the Library Server in the View pane. The library contents will display in the Results pane.

Additional VMM libraries can be added to the Administrator console by clicking the Add Library Server action in the Actions pane. A library can be removed by right-clicking the library and selecting Remove.

If Windows PowerShell scripts are stored in the VMM library, they can be viewed, edited, and removed. The administrator can run the scripts in Library view.

Entire VMs can be stored in VMM library. From here they can be cloned, deployed, and removed. VMware VMs stored in the library can be converted to a VMM virtual machine. The VMware VM's configuration files must be stored in the library to convert them.

NOTE

VMM libraries can be stored on Windows clusters to increase the availability and fault tolerance of the library resources.

Creating VMs

The administrator can use VMM 2008 to create VMs. This is similar to creating VMs using the Windows Server 2008 Hyper-V management console, described in Chapter 6, "Managing, Administering, and Maintaining a Hyper-V Host Server," but includes many more features and options. This process is covered in detail in Chapter 11, "Using Virtual Machine Manager 2008 for Provisioning."

Deploying and Migrating VMs

One of the most impressive capabilities of VMM 2008 is deploying and migrating VMs. This process is covered in detail in Chapter 10, "Creating Guest Images from Existing Production and Virtual Systems."

Managing VMs

VMs managed by VMM 2008 can be fully managed within the VMM Administrator console.

Open the VMM Administrator console using the shortcut on the Windows desktop or via the Start menu under Microsoft System Center, Virtual Machine Manager 2008, Virtual Machine Manager Administrator Console.

A Connect to Server window may open, prompting for the VMM server to connect to. Enter the server name and connection port (the default is port 8100) using the format VMMserver:port.

> **NOTE**
>
> You may choose to always open a connection to this server by selecting the Make This Server My Default check box. Doing so prevents this connection window from displaying when the Administrator console is run.

Go to the Virtual Machine view by clicking the Virtual Machine button, and then select the host in the View pane. The VMs hosted on that host will display in the Results pane.

The administrator can start, pause, stop, save the state, shut down, or connect to any managed VM. Other actions include migrating the VM, creating and managing checkpoints, repairing the VM, installing guest services, cloning the VM, storing it in a VMM library, removing the VM, and configuring its properties.

The details for each of these settings are beyond the scope of this chapter; suffice to say, many more options are available to configure than are available in the standard Windows Server 2008 Hyper-V management console.

Monitoring and Reporting

VMM 2008 has advance monitoring and reporting capabilities. VMM operates using jobs, which can be managed. Advanced reporting capabilities are achieved when using System Center Operations Manager 2007 (SCOM 2007) and the Server Virtualization Management Pack. The reports generated by SCOM can be opened directly in the Reporting view of the VMM Administrator console.

Jobs can be managed from the Jobs view in the Administrator console. In the Results pane, the administrator can view all the jobs run by VMM. Running jobs can be canceled by right-clicking the job and selecting Cancel.

If a job fails, it can usually be restarted by right-clicking the job and choosing Restart. The job will begin again where the operation failed.

Administering and Managing Roles

The entire VM infrastructure can be administered from the VMM Administrator console or by using the VMM command console. VMM administration includes managing user roles, managing agents on managed servers, adding non-Microsoft virtualization managers to VMM, and configuring VMM settings.

Open the VMM Administrator console using the shortcut on the Windows desktop or via the Start menu under Microsoft System Center, Virtual Machine Manager 2008, Virtual Machine Manager Administrator Console.

A Connect to Server window may open, prompting for the VMM server to connect to. Enter the server name and connection port (the default is port 8100) using the format VMMserver:port.

> **NOTE**
>
> You may choose to always open a connection to this server by selecting the Make This Server My Default check box. Doing so prevents this connection window from displaying when the Administrator console is run.

Go to the Administration view by clicking the Administration button, and then select the administrative operation in the View pane.

The General settings allow the administrator to configure global settings in VMM, such as CEIP settings, the database connection, library settings, placement settings, remote control, and the self-service administrator email address.

Managed Computers returns a list of the hosts managed by this VMM server, their status, version, and role.

Networking allows the administrator to configure a static range of MAC addresses VMM should use when creating new virtual network devices.

User Roles allows the administrator to manage user roles and create new user roles, such as delegated administrator groups and self-service users. Each of these roles can be scoped to a particular set of VMs, libraries, and so on. Self-service users can be permitted to perform only certain actions, as configured by the VMM administrator.

> **NOTE**
>
> The VMM Administrator role cannot be scoped or reduced in functionality.

The System Center setting provides a way for the administrator to configure SCOM reporting and the SCOM connection to enable PRO functionality. Physical Resource Optimization (PRO) provides workload- and application-aware resource optimization for Hyper-V host clusters.

Virtualization Managers displays the name, status, version, managed hosts, and managed VMs of non-Windows virtualization managers.

Summary

Microsoft Virtual Machine Manager 2008 provides an easy installation process that installs its own prerequisite software. Only a few steps must be run on Windows Server 2008 computers before installing VMM 2008.

The Administrator console, although simple and easy to use, is full featured and offers myriad choices for deploying and managing the virtual infrastructure. Its ability to manage both Hyper-V and non-Windows hosts and VMs brings unparalleled management opportunities to organizations. It offers the fine degree of granularity needed in today's virtual environments.

Best Practices

The following are best practices from this chapter:

- ▶ Make sure the system that VMM 2008 will be installed on is connected to the domain that hosts your Hyper-V host servers.

- ▶ Use a single-server deployment for VMM 2008 and SQL 2005 for a relatively simple environment; split the roles for a large enterprise environment.

- ▶ Unless your server configuration requires configuration variations that differ from the standard requirements for VMM 2008 (for example, PowerShell 1.0, .NET Framework 3.0), just let the installation script install the add-on components for you.

- ▶ Install VMM 2008 on a Windows 2008 or a Windows 2003 SP2 or later system.

- ▶ Choose the Make This Server My Default when launching VMM 2008 so that you won't have to be prompted again to select the VMM 2008 host server you are working from.

- ▶ To provide better security and simplified access to only host servers running Hyper-V, limit the scope of the search for virtual servers that can be administered by the Hyper-V or the VMM 2008 consoles.

- ▶ Create other roles beyond the VMM administrator so that you can have a more granular set of roles for administration, because the VMM Administrator role cannot be scoped or reduced in functionality.

Creating Guest Images from Existing Production and Virtual Systems

This chapter focuses on the process of using System Center Virtual Machine Manager (VMM) 2008 to create a guest image from a production system and from another virtual guest image for the purpose of creating a static lab environment. This process is also used to create real-time replications of images for operational purposes.

Understanding Virtual Machine Conversions

VMM 2008 enables the administrator to convert existing physical computers into virtual machines (VMs). This is known as a production to virtual, or P2V, conversion. VMM simplifies P2V conversions by providing an automated wizard for much of the conversion process.

VMM 2008 can also converting VMs from other virtualization platforms, such as VMware ESX and Microsoft Virtual Server to Windows Hyper-V. This process is known as virtual to virtual, or V2V, conversion and can be performed with different processes, depending on the source virtualization platform.

Physical Computers That Can Be Converted

There are two methods for converting physical computers to VMs. Online P2V conversions are performed using the Volume Shadow Copy Service (VSS) to copy data while the server continues to service user requests. The source computer is not interrupted during a P2V online conversion.

A P2V offline conversion is performed by restarting the source computer in the Windows Preinstallation Environment (Windows PE). VMM then converts the physical disks to Virtual Hard Disks (VHDs).

The information in Table 10.1 shows the supported operating systems that VMM can convert using the P2V process.

TABLE 10.1   Supported Operating Systems for P2V Conversion

Operating System	P2V Online	P2V Offline
Windows Server 2008 with Hyper-V	No	No
Windows Server 2008 without Hyper-V	Yes	Yes
Windows Server 2003 with Service Pack 1	Yes	Yes
Windows Server 2003 x64 Edition	No	No
Windows 2000 with Service Pack 4	No	Yes
Windows XP with Service Pack 2	Yes	Yes
Windows XP x64 Edition	No	No
Windows Vista	No	No
Windows Vista x64	Yes	Yes

In both online and offline P2V conversions, VMM 2008 temporarily installs an agent on the physical source computer to be converted.

NOTE

VMM 2008 does not support P2V conversion of Windows NT Server 4.0 source computers. These computers can be migrated using the Microsoft Virtual Server 2005 Migration Toolkit (VSMT) or third-party solutions.

Additional Requirements for P2V Conversion

To perform a P2V conversion, the source computer must meet the following additional requirements.

▶ **Domain**—Source computers must be in the same domain as the VMM server or a member of a domain that has a full two-way trust with the VMM server's domain.

▶ **RAM**—Offline P2V conversions require that the source computer has a minimum of 512MB of RAM.

▶ **Updates**—Most P2V conversions will not be affected by updates. However, certain system files and drivers are replaced during the conversion and may require updates after the conversion completes. If those files are missing, the administrator must add them to the Patch Import directory on the VMM server.

Performing a P2V Conversion

During a P2V conversion, a VM configuration file is created and new VHDs are created and formatted for use by the new VM. Disk images are then created from the source computer.

To perform the conversion, the VMM administrator must provide an account and password with administrator rights on the source computer.

NOTE

The administrator should perform a disk defragmentation on the source computer's hard drives to help minimize the time required for the imaging phase. Also, ensure that a fast network connection exists between the source and VMM computers.

Performing a P2V Online Conversion

Ensure that the source computer meets the operating system and additional requirements listed at the beginning of this chapter.

The P2V online conversion process is run from the VMM 2008 Administrator console.

Running the Convert Physical Server Wizard

The process of running the physical server to virtual server configuration process requires launching a conversion wizard. The process is as follows:

1. Open the VMM Administrator console using the shortcut on the Windows desktop or via the Start menu under Microsoft System Center, Virtual Machine Manager 2008, Virtual Machine Manager Administrator Console.

    A Connect to Server window may open, prompting for the VMM server to connect to. Enter the server name and connection port (the default is port 8100) using the following format VMMserver:port.

NOTE

You may choose to always open a connection to this server by selecting the Make This Server My Default check box. Doing so prevents this connection window from displaying when the Administrator console is run.

---

2. Click Convert Physical Server on the Actions pane in any view in the Virtual Machine Manager Administrator console. The Convert Physical Server Wizard will run, as shown in Figure 10.1.

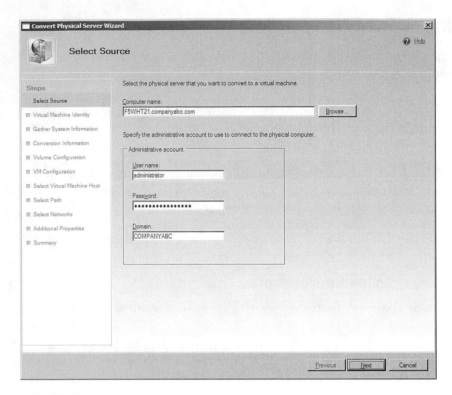

FIGURE 10.1   The Convert Physical Server Wizard.

3. Configure the following on the Select Source page:

   ▶ **Computer Name**—Enter the name of the physical computer or click the Browse button to locate the computer object to convert in the Active Directory.

   ▶ **User Name**—Enter a username of an account with local administrator rights on the source computer.

   ▶ **Password**—Enter the password for the local administrator user account.

   ▶ **Domain**—Enter the domain of the local administrator user account if it is not already populated. Click Next.

4. Configure the following on the Virtual Machine Identity page:

   ▶ **Virtual Machine Name**—Enter a new name for the VM or accept the default name, which is the same as the source computer.

NOTE

Renaming the VM name only renames the VM as it appears in the Administrator console. It does not rename the actual computer account in Active Directory.

▶ **Owner**—Accept the prepopulated domain\username value, enter a new domain\username value or click Browse to choose a new value. The owner account must be a member of Active Directory.

▶ **Description**—This optional field is used to describe the VM. Click Next.

NOTE

The owner of a VM is used to identify the owner of the new VM. It does not assign any rights to the VM itself.

---

5. On the Gather System Information page, click the Gather System Information button. By doing so, you begin a survey of the physical source computer and will display a list of operating system, hardware, and software components installed, as shown in Figure 10.2. It will also identify any missing components that are required for the P2V conversion to run. The wizard installs agent software on the source computer to gather this information and will remove it when the conversion is complete.

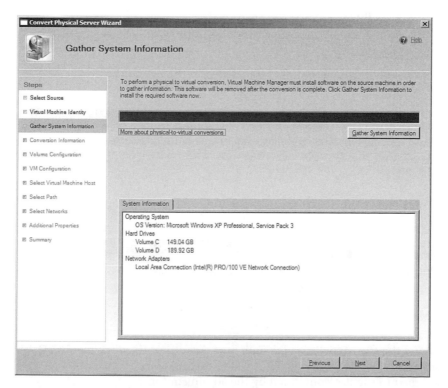

FIGURE 10.2   The Gather System Information page.

NOTE

Ensure that the WMI service is running on the source computer and that a firewall is not blocking HTTP and WMI traffic to the VMM server. A firewall exception will be created for remote administration service (RemoteAdmin) if a firewall is installed on the source computer. The administrator can remove this exception after the conversion operation is complete.

The System Information results window displays the operating system, hard drives, and network adapter information gathered from the survey. Click Next to continue the wizard.

6. The Conversion Information page displays any issues encountered while checking the source computer for suitability for P2V conversion. Do one of the following actions:

   ▶ Confirm that the message "No issues detected" is displayed.

   ▶ Review any issues that the wizard reports. These issues must be resolved before the P2V conversion can succeed. Each issue listed is accompanied by a solution that explains how to resolve it. After all issues have been resolved, click the Check Again button to rerun the survey.

   ▶ When there are no issues detected, click Next.

7. On the Volume Configuration page, review the list of disk volumes detected and make changes, if required:

   ▶ Deselect volumes that should not be included in the new VM.

NOTE

The system volume that contains the operating system cannot be deselected.

   ▶ Increase the size of the VHD for each volume.

NOTE

The size of a VHD can be increased, but not reduced. The minimum size is determined by the size of actual data on the volume.

   ▶ Configure the VHD type to be dynamic (the default) or fixed. Dynamic VHDs automatically grow as more data is saved to the disk. Fixed VHDs are constrained to the size configured by the administrator.

> **NOTE**
>
> If the VHD is configured as a fixed VHD type, ensure the VHD size is configured to allow for additional data, if necessary.

> ▶ Configure the channel that the VHD will use. Options include up to 2 IDE channels and up to 62 SCSI channels each on 4 virtual SCSI buses (providing up to 250 separate channels total). Click Next to continue.

8. On the Virtual Machine Configuration page, select the number of processors and RAM to use on the new VM. The number of processors available for selection is limited by the number of physical processors available in the source computer. The default amount of memory specified by the wizard is equal to the amount of physical RAM in the source computer.

9. On the Select Virtual Machine Host page, select the most suitable host to deploy the new VM on, as shown in Figure 10.3. Each host has a star rating (from zero to five stars) indicating its suitability to host the new VM.

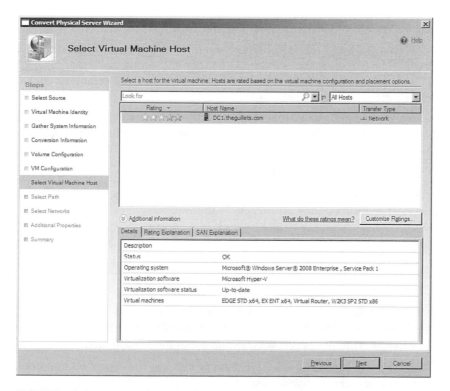

FIGURE 10.3   Selecting the VM host.

> **NOTE**
>
> If a large number of hosts are listed, the administrator can use the Host Group, Look For, or Group By fields to display a smaller set of possible hosts.

The Details tab displays the status, operating system, virtualization software platform, virtualization software status, and names of the VMs running on the selected host.

The Rating Explanation tab explains what the star rating means for the selected host and tells what requirements are met for the VM by this host.

The SAN Explanation tab describes the suitability of the host to connect to a SAN for VM storage. Items listed here include Fibre Channel host bus adapters (HBAs) installed and iSCSI initiators installed.

> **NOTE**
>
> The ratings can be customized using the Customize Ratings button. Here, the administrator can select multiple criteria and assign weights of importance for each component, such as processor load, memory used, network utilization, and so forth.

Select the host on which to deploy the new VM and click Next.

10. On the Select Path page, select the folder where the files associated with the new VM should be placed. The default folder is %SYSTEMDRIVE%\Documents and Settings\All Users\Documents\Shared Virtual Machines. Accept the default or click Browse to select a different path. Click Next.

11. On the Select Networks page, the Virtual Network drop-down list will display all the current networks available on the selected host. Select Not Connected or the appropriate virtual network for the VM to use. Click Next.

12. On the Additional Properties page, configure the following:

   ▶ **Automatic Start Action**—Select the action to perform for this VM when the physical host starts. Available actions are as follows:

      Never automatically turn on the VM.

      Always automatically turn on the VM.

      Automatically turn on the VM if it was running when the physical server stopped.

   ▶ **Automatic Stop Action**—Select the action to perform for this VM when the physical host shuts down. Available actions are as follows:

      Save state. This action is similar to the Windows Hibernate function.

      Turn off VM. This action is equivalent to turning the power off and does not provide a graceful shutdown.

      Shut down guest OS. This provides a graceful shutdown of the operating system.

13. The Summary page displays a summary of the settings selected in the Convert Physical Server Wizard. Carefully review these settings and click Create to proceed with the P2V conversion or click Previous to go back and change the configuration.

An optional check box can be selected to start the VM immediately after deploying it to the host.

As with many actions performed from the VMM Administrator console, the Convert Physical Server Wizard offers a View Script button. This option enables the administrator to view, modify, and save the PowerShell commands that the wizard will execute to perform the P2V conversion, as shown in Figure 10.4.

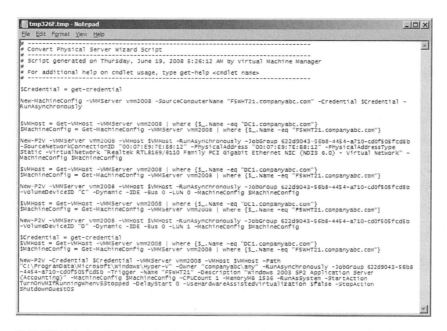

FIGURE 10.4   Convert physical server script.

14. In the Jobs view of the Administrator console, the administrator can monitor the progress of the P2V conversion and confirm that the VM is created successfully. If the job fails, read the error message in the Details pane for information about the cause of the failure and the recommended course of action to resolve the issue.

The P2V process will take several minutes and consists of the following steps:

▶ Collect the machine configuration information.

▶ Add the source machine agent.

▶ Create the VM.

- Copy the hard disk.

- Deploy the file (using Background Intelligent Transfer Service, BITS).

- Make the operating system virtualizable.

- Install the VM components.

- Start the VM to install the VM components.

- Stop the VM.

- Remove the source machine agent.

- Remove the VMM agent.

Finalizing the P2V Online Conversion

After the physical computer has been captured and deployed as a VM, the administrator can turn off the source physical computer and start the new VM.

> **NOTE**
>
> If the physical computer is using only direct attached storage, take care to copy any data that has changed since the P2V process began, if necessary. How this data is collected depends on the type of data and how it is stored. On local databases, for example, the database may have to be taken offline (quiesced), migrated to temporary storage, and copied to the newly created VM.

Performing a V2V Conversion

During a V2V conversion, an existing VMware ESX VM configuration file and its associated virtual disk files are converted to Hyper-V VM files.

The VMM administrator does not need administrator rights on the VMware VM to perform the conversion because the V2V conversion is just converting files to another type. The VMware VM is turned off, and the files are copied to the VMM library for conversion.

> **NOTE**
>
> The administrator should perform a disk defragmentation on the source computer's hard drives to help minimize the time required for the imaging phase. Also, ensure that a fast network connection exists between the source and VMM computers.

Performing a V2V Conversion

The administrator can use VMM to convert VMs that run on VMware ESX into Windows 2008 Hyper-V VMs. This is known as a virtual to virtual, or V2V, conversion.

Ensure that the source VM meets the operating system and additional requirements listed at the beginning of this chapter.

Adding VMware VM Files to the VMM Library

Before the administrator can perform a V2V operation, the VMware server-based VM files (VMX and VMDK) must be added to a VMM library, as follows:

1. Copy the VMX and VMDK files to the library share on the appropriate VMM library server.

2. Open the VMM Administrator console and display Library view.

3. In the Navigation pane, expand Library Server, and then navigate to the library share where the VMware files were copied.

4. Select the library share and in the Actions pane, and under Library Share, click Refresh Library Server.

All files on the share will be immediately indexed by VMM and will be added to the Library view.

Running the V2V Wizard

The V2V online conversion process is run from the VMM 2008 Administrator console as follows:

1. Open the VMM Administrator console using the shortcut on the Windows desktop or via the Start menu under Microsoft System Center, Virtual Machine Manager 2008, Virtual Machine Manager Administrator Console.

   A Connect to Server window may open, prompting for the VMM server to connect to. Enter the server name and connection port (the default is port 8100) using the format VMMserver:port.

> **NOTE**
>
> You may choose to always open a connection to this server by selecting the Make This Server My Default check box. Doing so prevents this connection window from display-ing when the Administrator console is run.

2. Go to the Library view by clicking the Library button, and then select the library group where the files are stored.

3. Click Convert Physical Server in the Actions pane in the Library view. The Convert Virtual Machine Wizard will run.

4. On the Select Source page, click Browse to open the Select Library Resource, as shown in Figure 10.5.

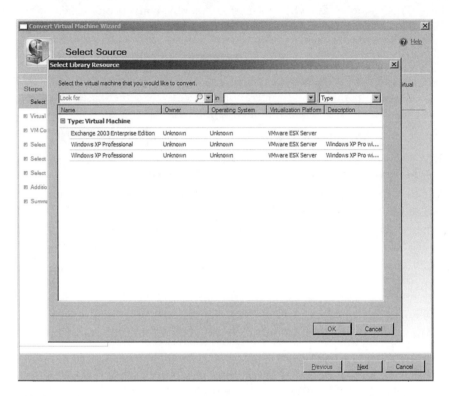

FIGURE 10.5   Selecting a resource from the Convert Virtual Machine Wizard.

▶ To search for a file, type the complete filename or the first few letters of the filename in the Look For box.

▶ In the Library Group list, select the library group where the VM files are stored.

▶ To filter the files by group, click a group type in the Group By list.

▶ Click the VMX file to convert, and then click OK. Click Next to continue.

5. On the Virtual Machine Identity page, configure the following:

▶ **Virtual Machine Name**—Enter a new name for the VM or accept the default name, which is the same as the source computer.

NOTE

Renaming the virtual machine name only renames the VM as it appears in the Administrator console. It does not rename the actual computer account in Active Directory.

▶ **Owner**—Accept the prepopulated domain\username value, enter a new domain\username value or click Browse to choose a new value. The owner account must be a member of Active Directory.

▶ **Description**—This optional field is used to describe the VM. Click Next.

> **NOTE**
>
> The owner of a VM is used to identify the owner of the new VM. It does not assign any rights to the VM itself.

6. On the Virtual Machine Configuration page, select the number of processors and the amount of RAM to use on the new VM.

7. On the Select Virtual Machine Host page, select the most suitable host to deploy the new VM on, as shown in Figure 10.6. Each host has a star rating (from zero to five stars) indicating its suitability to host the new VM.

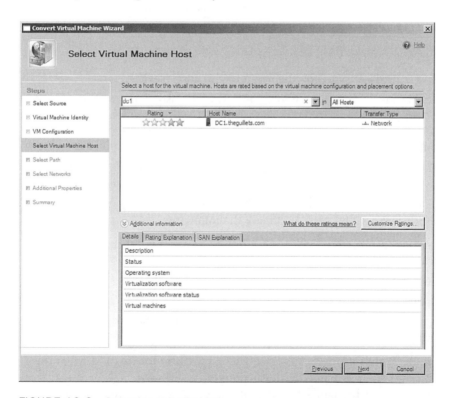

FIGURE 10.6   Selecting the VM host.

10

NOTE

If a large number of hosts are listed, the administrator can use the Host Group, Look For, or Group By fields to display a smaller set of possible hosts.

The Details tab displays the status, operating system, virtualization software platform, virtualization software status, and names of VMs running on the selected host.

The Rating Explanation tab explains what the star rating means for the selected host and tells what requirements are met for the VM by this host.

The SAN Explanation tab describes the suitability of the host to connect to a SAN for VM storage. Items listed here include Fibre Channel HBAs installed and iSCSI initiators installed.

NOTE

The ratings can be customized using the Customize Ratings button. Here, the administrator can select multiple criteria and assign weights of importance for each component, such as processor load, memory used, network utilization, and so forth.

Select the host on which to deploy the new VM and click Next.

8. On the Select Path page, select the folder where the files associated with the new VM should be placed. The default folder is %SYSTEMDRIVE%\Documents and Settings\All Users\Documents\Shared Virtual Machines. Accept the default or click Browse to select a different path. Click Next.

9. On the Select Networks page, the Virtual Network drop-down list will display all the current networks available on the selected host. Select Not Connected or the appropriate virtual network for the VM to use. Click Next.

10. On the Additional Properties page, configure the following:

  ▶ **Automatic Start Action**—Select the action to perform for this VM when the physical host starts. Available actions are as follows:

    Never automatically turn on the VM.

    Always automatically turn on the VM.

    Automatically turn on the VM if it was running when the physical server stopped.

  ▶ **Automatic Stop Action**—Select the action to perform for this VM when the physical host shuts down. Available actions are as follows:

    Save state. This action is similar to the Windows Hibernate function.

    Turn off VM. This action is equivalent to turning the power off and does not provide a graceful shutdown.

> **Shut down guest OS.** This provides a graceful shutdown of the operating system.

11. The Summary page displays a summary of the settings selected in the Convert Physical Server Wizard. Carefully review these settings and click Create to proceed with the V2V conversion or click Previous to go back and change the configuration.

    An optional check box can be selected to start the VM immediately after deploying it to the host.

    As with many actions performed from the VMM Administrator console, the Convert Physical Server Wizard offers a View Script button. This option enables the administrator to view, modify, and save the PowerShell commands that the wizard will execute to perform the V2V conversion, as shown in Figure 10.7.

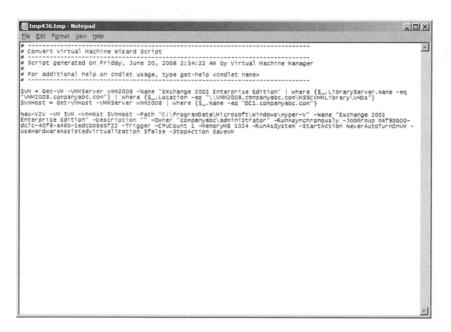

FIGURE 10.7   Convert virtual server script.

12. In the Jobs view of the Administrator console, the administrator can monitor the progress of the V2V conversion and confirm that the VM is created successfully, as shown in Figure 10.8. If the job fails, read the error message in the Details pane for information about the cause of the failure and the recommended course of action to resolve the issue.

10

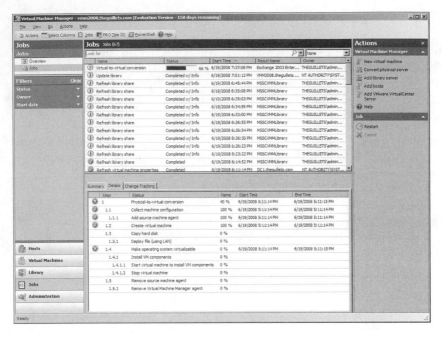

FIGURE 10.8   Monitoring the V2V conversion job.

The V2V process may take several minutes, but is significantly faster than a P2V conversion. It consists of the following steps:

▶ Collect the machine configuration information from the VMX file.

▶ Create the VM.

▶ Convert the VMDK file to a VHD file.

▶ Deploy the file (using LAN).

▶ Make the operating system virtualizable.

▶ Install the VM components.

▶ Start the VM to install the VM components.

▶ Stop the VM.

▶ Remove the source VMX machine configuration.

Finalizing the V2V Conversion

After the VMware ESX VM has been deployed as a Hyper-V VM, the administrator can start the new VM.

Further configuration and customization of the VM can be performed from the VMM Administrator console from the Virtual Machines view. Select the VM and click Properties in the Action pane.

Creating a Virtual Lab

The processes listed in this chapter can be used to create a lab environment for testing and application development.

Using P2V to Create a Virtual Copy of Production

The P2V conversion functions of VMM 2008 provide a simple, nonintrusive way to create a virtualized copy of the production environment.

Because VMM uses the VSS to make online copies of production computers, the P2V process will not disrupt the normal operation of these computers. Furthermore, the scripting functions of the VMM command shell enable the administrator to automate the P2V process, simplifying the entire lab-creation process.

Choosing What to Convert

Even complex distributed environments can be virtualized into a lab using the P2V process. For example, a large environment may include many domain controllers, Exchange 2007 servers, file and print servers, and application servers. Depending on the organization's testing needs, the administrator may be able to create a suitable testing environment with just one of each type of server.

In another scenario, the administrator may want to virtualize only the servers necessary to perform a series of tests, such as a domain controller for authentication and two or three application servers to test replication and fault tolerance.

> **CAUTION**
>
> Care must be taken to ensure that the lab environment is isolated from the production environment to prevent unintended changes to the production environment. This can be achieved by using a separate network, or even better, by physically isolating the lab from the production network.

Automating the Lab-Creation Process Using the Command Shell

Administrators can leverage the View Script button that is available on the Summary page of the P2V and V2V wizards. The entire P2V or V2V process can be configured using the wizards up to the point where the VMs are actually created. At that point, click the View Script button and save the resulting script to a scripts folder.

These scripts can be customized, duplicated, and grouped together to automate the entire lab-creation process. For example, the administrator may have a script called CreateTestDomain.ps1 that will automatically create VMs of a physical domain controller, Exchange 2007 server, and a line-of-business application server, and then deploy it to a Hyper-V host for testing. This script may even be run as a scheduled task for even further automation.

Summary

In this chapter, we have discussed the process of creating Hyper-V VMs that were converted from physical servers (P2V). This process can be performed online without disrupting the physical server by using the VSS. This process can be used to reduce the number of physical servers in the organization's environment.

VMware ESX VMs can be converted to Hyper-V VMs using the virtual to virtual (V2V) capabilities built in to VMM 2008. This is a quick and easy way to convert from VMware ESX and realize the benefits of Hyper-V.

Both of these processes can be used to create virtual labs for use in testing and application development.

Best Practices

▶ Use VMM's P2V function to convert physical computers to VMs.

▶ Use the VMM V2V function to convert VMs created on VMware ESX to Hyper-V VMs.

▶ Use the online P2V process to convert physical computers to VMs without disrupting the online server.

▶ Use the offline P2V process to convert offline physical computers to Hyper-V VMs.

▶ Know which operating systems can be converted to VMs using the P2V and V2V processes before attempting the conversion.

▶ Use the Microsoft Virtual Server 2005 Migration Toolkit (VSMT) to convert Windows NT Server 4.0 computers to VMs.

▶ Ensure that source computers are members of the same domain as the VMM server or that there is a full two-way trust with the VMM server's domain.

▶ Perform a disk defragmentation on the source computer before performing the P2V conversion.

▶ Ensure that a fast network connection exists between the source computer and the VMM server.

▶ Renaming the VM name only renames the VM as it appears in the VMM Administrator console. Be sure to also rename the computer within the operating system.

▶ Use the owner property of a VM to identify the owner or contact person for the VM.

▶ Ensure that the WMI service is running on the source computer and that a firewall is not blocking HTTP and WMI traffic to the VMM server.

▶ Remove the RemoteAdmin firewall exception, if necessary, after the conversion is complete to increase server security.

- ▶ Increase the size of a dynamic VHD to allocate more space for the VM if necessary.

- ▶ Ensure that the size of a fixed-size VHD includes enough additional space for additional data.

- ▶ When selecting which host to deploy to, use the Host Group, Look For, or Group By fields to display a smaller set of possible hosts.

- ▶ Use the Customize Ratings button to customize the importance of computer and network resources available on hosts.

- ▶ Use the Jobs view to monitor the progress of P2V and V2V conversions.

- ▶ Review the details in the Jobs view for errors and to determine the cause of failures and the recommended course of action to resolve issues.

- ▶ Pay special attention to collect any data that was changed on the source server after the conversion process was begun.

- ▶ Copy VMware ESX VMX and VMDK files to a VMM library that is closest to the host server to speed VM conversion.

- ▶ Always refresh the VMM library server after adding files to the library.

- ▶ Use the P2V process to create a virtual copy of the organization's production environment for testing.

- ▶ Create virtual labs that contain only the servers needed for testing.

- ▶ Ensure that the lab environment is isolated from the production environment to prevent unintended changes to the production environment.

- ▶ View, save, and customize the scripts that the P2V and V2V conversion wizards produce.

- ▶ Automate lab creation using the VMM command shell.

10

## 11

Using Virtual Machine Manager 2008 for Provisioning

This chapter covers the administrative provisioning and the delegated provisioning capabilities of Virtual Machine Manager (VMM) for the creation of guest images. This includes building new images from a template and building images from other image files.

Understanding Roles-Based Access and Delegation to Provision Virtual Machines

System Center Virtual Machine Manager 2008 provides a granular roles-based access control (RBAC) model for managing administrative permissions. Each user role has an administrative profile that determines which actions the user can perform. User roles are scoped to determine which VM objects the user can manage.

There are three user roles in VMM 2008: the Administrator role, the Delegated Administrator role, and the Self-Service User role.

Administrator Role in VMM 2008

Users in the Administrator role have full rights to the VMM infrastructure and can perform all actions in the VMM Administrator console. Administrators can create new Delegated Administrator and Self-Service User roles. Only members of this role can add additional members to the Administrator role.

The Administrator role is created when VMM is installed for the first time in the domain. The user who installs VMM is automatically added to the Administrator user role during installation. There is only one Administrator user role in each domain.

> **NOTE**
>
> Because the Administrator role encompasses the entire VMM infrastructure, this role cannot be scoped.

Delegated Administrator Within VMM 2008

Users who are members of the Delegated Administrator role can perform all actions in the VMM Administrator console that apply, or are scoped, to them. The scope of objects is defined during the creation of the role.

The Delegated Administrator user role does not exist by default. There can be zero or more Delegated Administrator roles in each domain. Delegated Administrator roles are created by users who are members of the Administrator user role.

Members of this user role can create new Delegated Administrator and Self-Service User roles, but only within the scope of objects that applies to them.

Self-Service User as a Role in VMM 2008

Members of the Self-Service User role can use the VMM self-service portal to perform actions on their VMs. This role is scoped by a member of the Administrator or Delegate Administrator role to pertain to a specific set of VM objects.

Members of this role cannot manage their role or any other role in VMM. They also cannot create new user roles.

> **NOTE**
>
> Members of the Administrator or Delegated Administrator roles cannot access the self-service portal unless they are members of one or more Self-Service User roles.

Managing User Roles

User roles are managed by users in the Administrator or Delegated Administrator role using the VMM Administrator console. User roles are granted access to manage objects in a defined scope.

Managing the Administrator User Role

The administrator role can be used to manage user roles. To manage the user roles, do the following:

1. Open the VMM Administrator console using the shortcut on the Windows desktop or via the Start menu under Microsoft System Center, VMM 2008, VMM Administrator console.

A Connect to Server window may open, prompting for the VMM server to connect to. Enter the server name and connection port (the default is port 8100) using the format VMMserver:port.

2. Go to the Administration view by clicking the Administration button. Then select User Roles from the view area.

3. Select the Administrator user role in the Results pane. The current members of the Administrator user role are displayed in the Results pane below.

4. Click Properties in the Actions pane to display the properties of the role.

5. The General tab displays the description for the Administrators role. Modify it if desired.

6. Click the Members tab. The current members are listed, as shown in Figure 11.1.

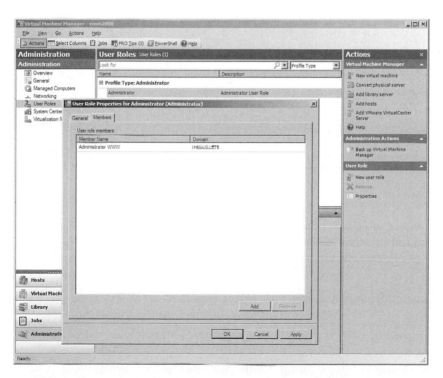

FIGURE 11.1   Managing members of the Administrator user role.

7. To remove members from the Administrator user role, select the user to remove and click the Remove button.

There must be at least one member in the Administrator user role at all times. VMM will not allow you to remove all members of the Administrator user role.

8. To add members to the Administrator user role, click the Add button and enter the name or names of the users or security groups to add. Click the Check Names button to resolve the users or groups. Members must be users or security groups in the Active Directory where the VMM server is a member or in a domain where a full two-way trust exists.

9. Click OK to close the Administrator Properties window.

Creating a Delegated Administrator User Role

The delegated administrator role can be used to manage user roles. To manage the user roles, do the following:

1. Open the VMM Administrator console using the shortcut on the Windows desktop or via the Start menu under Microsoft System Center, VMM 2008, VMM Administrator console.

   A Connect to Server window may open, prompting for the VMM server to connect to. Enter the server name and connection port (the default is port 8100) using the format VMMserver:port.

You may choose to always open a connection to this server by selecting the Make This Server My Default check box. Doing so prevents this connection window from displaying when the Administrator console is run.

2. Go to the Administration view by clicking the Administration button. Then select User Roles from the view area.

3. Click New User Role in the Actions pane.

4. On the General page, enter the following information:

   a. **User Role Name**—Type a name for the Delegated Administrator role.

   b. **Description**—Type a useful description for the Delegated Administrator role.

   c. **Profile**—Select Delegated Administrator from the Profile drop-down list. Click Next to continue.

5. On the Add Members page, click Add to add new members to the role. Enter the name or names of the users or security groups to add. Click the Check Names button to resolve the users or groups.

   Members must be users or security groups in the Active Directory where the VMM server is a member or in a domain where a full two-way trust exists.

NOTE

The administrator may choose to not populate the members of the Delegated Administrator user role at this time. Members may be populated after the role is created.

   Click Next to continue.

6. On the Object Scope page, select the objects that members of this group can monitor. The delegated administrator will not be able to view or monitor objects from the Administrator console that are not selected in this page. Click Next to continue (see Figure 11.2).

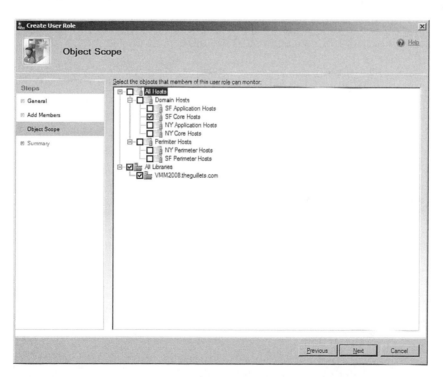

FIGURE 11.2   Scoping the objects for the Delegated Administrator user role.

7. On the Summary page, carefully review the settings and click Create to proceed with the creation of the Delegated Administrator role or click Previous to go back and change the configuration.

The Create User Role Wizard offers a View Script button. This option allows the administrator to view, modify, and save the PowerShell commands that the wizard will execute to create the Delegated Administrator role, as shown in the following example:

```
$AddMember = companyabc\amy
$hostGroup1 = Get-VMHostGroup -VMMServer vmm2008 ¦ where {$_.Path -eq "All
Hosts\Domain Hosts\SF Core Hosts"}
$libServer2 = Get-LibraryServer -VMMServer vmm2008 ¦ where {$_.Name -eq
"VMM2008.companyabc.com"}
$AddScope = $hostGroup1, $libServer2
Set-VMMUserRole -AddMember $AddMember -AddScope $AddScope -VMMServer vmm2008 -Job-
Group 06fb48f5-96c7-4133-acc4-cbf58f5fb2e4
New-VMMUserRole -Name "SF Core Server Delegated Administrators" -Description "" -
UserRoleProfile DelegatedAdmin -JobGroup 06fb48f5-96c7-4133-acc4-cbf58f5fb2e4
```

This code can be saved and edited to facilitate creating other Delegated Administrator groups from the VMM command shell.

Creating a Self-Service User Role

The Self-Service User role grants users permissions to operate, create, manage, store, create checkpoints for, and connect to virtual machines (VMs) in their scope using the VMM self-service portal.

1. Open the VMM Administrator console using the shortcut on the Windows desktop or via the Start menu under Microsoft System Center, VMM 2008, VMM Administrator console.

   A Connect to Server window may open, prompting for the VMM server to connect to. Enter the server name and connection port (the default is port 8100) using the format VMMserver:port.

> **NOTE**
>
> You may choose to always open a connection to this server by selecting the Make This Server My Default check box. Doing so prevents this connection window from displaying when the Administrator console is run.

2. Go to the Administration view by clicking the Administration button. Then select User Roles from the view area.

3. Click New User Role in the Actions pane.

4. On the General page, enter the following information:

   a. **User Role Name—** Type a name for the Delegated Administrator role.

   b. **Description**—Type a useful description for the Delegated Administrator role.

   c. **Profile**—Select Self-Service User from the Profile drop-down list, as shown in Figure 11.3. Click Next to continue.

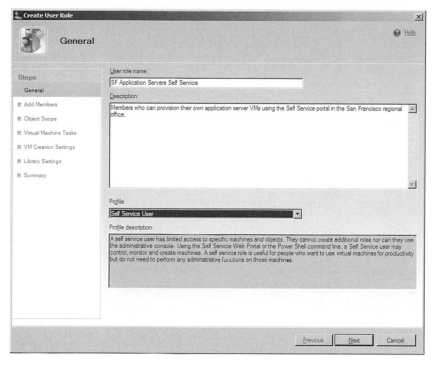

FIGURE 11.3   Creating the Self-Service User role.

5. On the Add Members page, click Add to add new members to the Self-Service User role. Enter the name or names of the users or security groups to add. Click the Check Names button to resolve the users or groups.

Members must be users or security groups in the Active Directory where the VMM server is a member or in a domain where a full two-way trust exists.

Click Next to continue.

NOTE

The administrator may choose to not populate the members of the Delegated Administrator user role at this time. Members may be populated after the role is created.

6. On the Object Scope page, select the objects that members of this Self-Service User role can monitor. Click Next to continue.

7. On the Virtual Machine Tasks page, configure one of the following:

   a. Select All Tasks to permit this Self-Service User role to perform all VMM tasks, as shown in Figure 11.4.

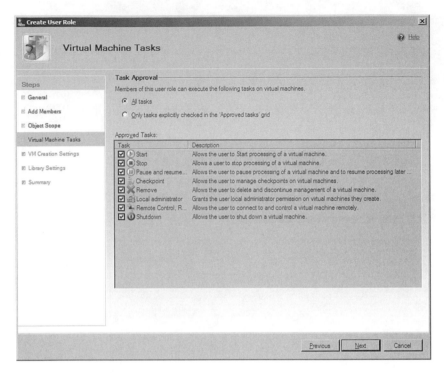

FIGURE 11.4   Configuring the tasks the Self-Service User role can run.

b. Select Only Tasks Explicitly Checked in the "Approved Tasks" Grid. Table 11.1 lists all the tasks available for the Self-Service User to run.

TABLE 11.1   Self-Service User Virtual Machine Tasks

Task	Description
Start	Allows the user to start processing of a VM.
Stop	Allows the user to stop processing of a VM.
Pause & Resume	Allows the user to pause processing of a VM and resume processing after the VM has been paused.
Checkpoint	Allows the user to manage checkpoints on a VM.
Remove	Allows the user to delete and discontinue management of a VM from VMM.
Local Administrator	Grants the user local administrator permission on VMs they create.
Remote Control	Allows the user to connect to and control a VM remotely. This is also known as Virtual Machine Remote Control (VMRC) access.

8. The VM Creation Settings page provides the option to allow users to create their own VMs. If this right will not be granted, click Next; otherwise, configure the following:

a. Check the Allow Users to Create New Virtual Machines check box to allow self-service users to do so.

b. In the Templates pane, click Add to add a new template that the self-service user can deploy.

NOTE

To search for a template, type the complete filename or the first few letters of the template name in the Look For box. In the Library group list, select the library group where the VM files are stored. To filter the files by group, click a group type in the Group By list.

c. Optionally, the administrator can set a quota for deploying VMs. Quotas are used to limit the number of VMs the users can deploy at one time.

9. On the Library Settings page, the administrator can grant members of this self-service user group access to a library share to store their own VMs. To configure this setting:

a. Check the Allow Users to Store Virtual Machines in a Library check box.

b. Select the VMM Library server to allow users to access. If a large number of library servers are listed, the administrator can type the first few characters of the library server name in the Look For box to limit the results.

NOTE

Stored VMs do not count against the VM quota that may have been set when allowing self-service users to create a VM.

c. To specify the Library Path, click Browse and select the share path to allow access to the Self-service user.

NOTE

The library path entered can exist at any point under the MSSCVMMLibrary share. For example, if the Library Path is specified as \\VMM2008.companyabc.com\ MSSCVMMLibrary\VHDs, the self-service user can access that folder and any subfolders, but cannot access the higher-level \\VMM2008.companyabc.com\ MSSCVMMLibrary folder itself.

d. Click Next to continue.

10. On the Summary page, carefully review the settings and click Create to proceed with the creation of the Self-Service User role or click Previous to go back and change the configuration.

The Create User Role Wizard offers a View Script button. This option allows the administrator to view, modify, and save the PowerShell commands that the wizard will execute to create the Self-Service User role, as shown in the following example:

```
$VMPermission = 1023
$AddMember = COMPANYABC\Administrator, COMPANYABC\amy
$hostGroup1 = Get-VMHostGroup -VMMServer vmm2008 ¦ where {$_.Path -eq "All
Hosts\Domain Hosts\SF Application Hosts"}
$hostGroup2 = Get-VMHostGroup -VMMServer vmm2008 ¦ where {$_.Path -eq "All
Hosts\Perimiter Hosts\SF Perimeter Hosts"}
$AddScope = $hostGroup1, $hostGroup2
Set-VMMUserRole -VMPermission $VMPermission -AddMember $AddMember -RemoveQuo-
taPoint -AddScope $AddScope -LibraryStoreSharePath "\\VMM2008.companyabc.com\
MSSCVMMLibrary\VHDs" -VMMServer vmm2008 -JobGroup 3dcd2c05-3271-4fbd-b905-
e42a4295aadb
New-VMMUserRole -Name "SF Application Servers Self-service" -Description "Mem-
bers who can provision their own application server VMs using the Self-service
portal in the San Francisco regional office." -UserRoleProfile SelfServiceUser
-JobGroup 3dcd2c05-3271-4fbd-b905-e42a4295aadb
```

This code can be saved and edited to facilitate creating other Self-Service User roles from the VMM command shell.

Modifying User Roles

The administrator of a user role can modify an existing user role by modifying its properties in the Administrator console. To modify a user role, follow these steps:

1. Open the VMM Administrator console using the shortcut on the Windows desktop or via the Start menu under Microsoft System Center, VMM 2008, VMM Administrator console.

A Connect to Server window may open, prompting for the VMM server to connect to. Enter the server name and connection port (the default is port 8100) using the format VMMserver:port.

> **NOTE**
>
> You may choose to always open a connection to this server by selecting the Make This Server My Default check box. Doing so prevents this connection window from displaying when the Administrator console is run.

2. Go to the Administration view by clicking the Administration button. Then select User Roles from the view area.

3. Select the user role to modify and click Properties in the Actions pane.

4. On the General tab, modify the settings as needed.

5. On the Members tab, add or remove members as needed.

6. For Delegated Administrators and Self-Service User roles, click the Object Scope tab and modify the settings as needed.

7. For Self-Service User roles, click the VM Tasks tab and modify the settings as needed.

8. For Self-Service User roles, click the Create VM tab and modify the settings as needed.

9. For Self-Service User roles, click the Store VM tab and modify the settings as needed.

10. Click OK to save the new settings.

Removing User Roles

The administrator of a user role can remove an existing user role by removing it from the Administrator console. To remove a user role, follow these steps:

1. Open the VMM Administrator console using the shortcut on the Windows desktop or via the Start menu under Microsoft System Center, VMM 2008, VMM Administrator console.

   A Connect to Server window may open, prompting for the VMM server to connect to. Enter the server name and connection port (the default is port 8100) using the format VMMserver:port.

> **NOTE**
>
> You may choose to always open a connection to this server by selecting the Make This Server My Default check box. Doing so prevents this connection window from displaying when the Administrator console is run.

2. Go to the Administration view by clicking the Administration button. Then select User Roles from the view area.

3. Select the user role to remove and click Remove in the Actions pane.

4. Click Yes to the confirmation prompt to remove the user role.

Deploying Virtual Machines

This section describes how to deploy VMs on managed hosts using VMM. In this section, the process of VM placement is discussed, and you learn how to customize host ratings during placement, and we examine the procedures for deploying and migrating VMs to another host.

Virtual Machine Placement

The process of selecting the most suitable host upon which to deploy a VM is called VM placement. When the administrator deploys a VM, a list is created in VMM of all the managed hosts where the VM can be placed. Each host is given a start rating, from zero to five stars, indicating its suitability for the given VM.

This star rating is based on the VM's hardware and resource requirements and each host's ability to fulfill these requirements. Host ratings also take resource maximization, fault tolerance, and load balancing into consideration.

> **NOTE**
>
> If a VM has been configured by the administrator with the Make This VM Highly Available option, the VM can only be placed on Hyper-V host clusters. Hosts that are not clusters cannot host highly available VMs (HA VMs).

Automatic VM Placement

Automatic VM placement occurs during deployment of a VM in the following situations:

▶ When VMs are deployed by self-service users from the self-service portal, the VM is deployed to the most suitable host server in the specified host group.

▶ When the drag-and-drop method of migration within the VMM Administrator console is used, the VM is deployed to the most suitable host server in the target group.

When Automatic Placement occurs, the configuration files and virtual hard disks (VHDs) for the VM are moved to the most suitable host.

> **NOTE**
>
> For Automatic Placement to succeed, a VM path must be configured on the recommended host's VMM volume.

Customizing Host Ratings

The default criteria used to create host ratings can be customized by the VMM administrator, as follows:

1. Open the VMM Administrator console using the shortcut on the Windows desktop or via the Start menu under Microsoft System Center, VMM 2008, VMM Administrator console.

   A Connect to Server window may open, prompting for the VMM server to connect to. Enter the server name and connection port (the default is port 8100) using the format VMMserver:port.

> **NOTE**
>
> You may choose to always open a connection to this server by selecting the Make This Server My Default check box. Doing so prevents this connection window from displaying when the Administrator console is run.

2. Go to the Administration view by clicking the Administration button. Then select General from the view area.

3. Select Placement Settings in the results pane and click Modify in the Actions pane.

4. In the Placement Settings dialog box, select the placement goal for determining the most suitable host for a VM from one of the following choices:

    a. Load balancing—Hosts with the most free resources receive the highest rating. This setting provides the best VM performance.

    b. Resource maximization—Hosts that meet the VM's required resources and have the least free resources receive the highest rating. This setting provides the highest VM density on hosts.

5. Under Resource Importance, use the sliding scales to select the relative importance of the following resources to VMs, from not important to very important:

- CPU utilization

- Free memory

- Disk I/O

- Network utilization

NOTE

By default, CPU utilization and free memory are given more importance than disk I/O and network utilization.

---

6. Click OK to change the default placement settings.

Customizing Host Ratings for a Virtual Machine

The host ratings can be configured for specific VMs that override the systemwide VM placement settings.

The override settings can be specified whenever the administrator runs any of the following VMM wizards:

- New Virtual Machine Wizard

- Clone Virtual Machine Wizard

- Convert Virtual Machine Wizard

- Deploy Virtual Machine Wizard

- Migrate Virtual Machine Wizard

To configure the override placement settings for a VM, follow these steps on the Select Virtual Machine Settings page of the wizard:

1. Click the Customizable Ratings button.
2. Click the appropriate Placement Goal for this VM from either Load Balancing (most free resources available) or Resource Maximization (least free resources available).
3. Use the slider controls to adjust the importance of CPU utilization, free memory, disk I/O, and network utilization.
4. On the VM Load tab, refine the workload characterization of the VM using the following settings:

    ▶ CPU: Expected CPU Utilization

    ▶ Disk: Required physical disk space (GB)

    ▶ Disk: Expected disk I/O per second (IOPS)

    ▶ Network: Expected utilization (megabits per second)

5. Click OK to continue the wizard.

Deploying Virtual Machines Using the Administrator Console

The following steps detail how to deploy a new VM using the VMM Administrator console.

1. Open the VMM Administrator console using the shortcut on the Windows desktop or via the Start menu under Microsoft System Center, VMM 2008, VMM Administrator console.

   A Connect to Server window may open, prompting for the VMM server to connect to. Enter the server name and connection port (the default is port 8100) using the format VMMserver:port.

> **NOTE**
>
> You may choose to always open a connection to this server by selecting the Make This Server My Default check box. Doing so prevents this connection window from displaying when the Administrator console is run.

2. Go to the Library view by selecting the Library button.
3. In the navigation pane, expand Library Server and the appropriate library server that holds the VM to deploy.
4. Expand VMs and Templates to display the available VMs, as shown in Figure 11.5.

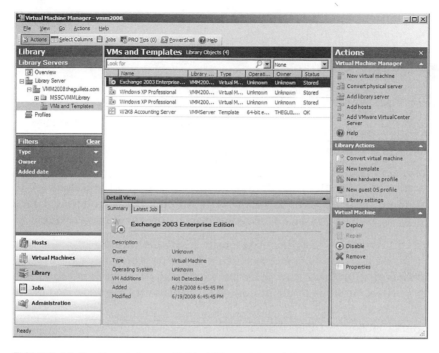

FIGURE 11.5   Examining available VMs and templates.

5. In the Results pane, select the VM to deploy to a host.

6. In the Actions pane, Click Deploy.

7. On the Select Virtual Machine Host page, select the host upon which to deploy the new VM. All hosts are given a zero- to five-star rating to gauge the suitability of the host for the given VM, but the administrator can choose any host that has enough disk space to host the VM.

NOTE

The administrator can get additional information about the selected VM by viewing the Details, Rating Explanation, and SAN Explanation tabs in the Details view. Each of these tabs display detailed information about how the rating is calculated for each host.

The administrator can customize the ratings for this VM by clicking the Customize Ratings button and adjusting the CPU, memory, disk I/O, and network criteria for the VM.

Click Next to continue.

8. In the Select Path page, type the path on the host where the VM and its associated files should be stored on the host.

Optionally, the administrator can check the Add This Path to the List of Host Default Paths check box to add the path to the default paths on the host.

If SAN transfers are enabled, the VM is transferred to the host over the SAN, by default. If the administrator does not want to perform a SAN transfer, check the Transfer over the Network Even if a SAN Transfer Is Available check box. This check box is not available if SAN transfers are not available for this deployment.

Click Next to continue.

9. On the Select Network page, select the appropriate network that exists on the selected host. If the administrator does not want to configure a network, select Not Connected. Click Next.

10. On the Additional Properties page, configure one of the following actions:

   a. Action When Physical Server Starts

      i. Never Automatically Turn on the Virtual Machine

      ii. Always Automatically Turn on the Virtual Machine

      iii. Automatically Turn on the Virtual Machine If Was Running When the Physical Server Stopped

   b. Automatic Stop Action

      i. Save State

      ii. Turn Off Virtual Machine

      iii. Shut Down Guest OS

   Click Next to continue.

11. On the Summary page, carefully review the settings. The administrator can also choose to select the Start the Virtual Machine Immediately After Deploying It to the Host check box, if desired.

The Deploy Virtual Machine Wizard offers a View Script button. This option allows the administrator to view, modify, and save the PowerShell commands that the wizard will execute to deploy the VM, as shown in the following example:

```
# ----------------------------------------------------
# Deploy Virtual Machine Script
# ----------------------------------------------------
# Script generated on Sunday, June 22, 2008 1:23:39 AM by Virtual Machine Man-
ager
#
# For additional help on cmdlet usage, type get-help <cmdlet name>
# ----------------------------------------------------
$VMHost = Get-VMHost -VMMServer vmm2008 ¦ where {$_.Name -eq "DC1.companyabc.
com"}
$VM = Get-VM -VMMServer vmm2008 -Name "Windows XP Professional" ¦ where
{$_.LibraryServer.Name -eq "VMM2008.companyabc.com"} ¦ where {$_.Location -eq
"\\VMM2008.companyabc.com\MSSCVMMLibrary\VHDs"}
$VirtualNetworkAdapter = Get-VirtualNetworkAdapter -VMMServer vmm2008 ¦ where
{$_.Name -eq "Windows XP Professional"}
New-V2V -VMMServer vmm2008 -VMHost $VMHost -RunAsynchronously -JobGroup
d710839e-c062-43ac-979a-a38315d051c0 -VM $VM -VirtualNetworkAdapter $Virtual-
NetworkAdapter -NetworkLocation "" -NetworkTag ""
$VM = Get-VM -VMMServer vmm2008 -Name "Windows XP Professional" ¦ where
{$_.LibraryServer.Name -eq "VMM2008.companyabc.com"} ¦ where {$_.Location -eq
"\\VMM2008.companyabc.com\MSSCVMMLibrary\VHDs"}
$VmHost = Get-VmHost -VMMServer vmm2008 ¦ where {$_.Name -eq "DC1.companyabc.
com"}
New-V2V -VM $VM -VmHost $VmHost -Path "C:\ProgramData\Microsoft\Windows\Hyper-
V" -RunAsynchronously -JobGroup d710839e-c062-43ac-979a-a38315d051c0 -Trigger
-RunAsSystem -StartAction TurnOnVMIfRunningWhenVSStopped -DelayStart 0 -Use-
HardwareAssistedVirtualization $false -StopAction SaveVM
```

This is useful to automate the deployment of new VMs from the command line for multiple server deployment or lab creation scenarios.

12. Click Deploy to proceed with the deployment of the VM on the host or click Previous to go back and change the deployment options.

To review the progress and results of the operation, the administrator can view the Jobs window in the VMM Administrator console.

Deploying a Virtual Machine Using the Self-Service Portal

The Virtual Machine Manage self-service portal, shown in Figure 11.6, is a website that allows self-service users to deploy, manage, and delete their own VMs. Automatic Placement is used to select the best-qualified host to host the VM, based on the default VMM placement settings or the override settings specified in a VM.

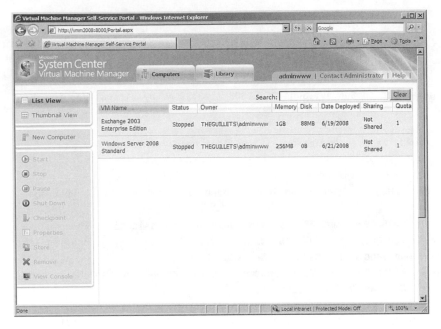

FIGURE 11.6   The VMM self-service portal.

The following steps detail how to deploy a new VM using the self-service portal:

1. The self-service user opens the self-service portal by entering the following URL in Internet Explorer:

    a. If the self-service portal website is using a dedicated port, type **http://** followed by the computer name of the web server, a colon (:), and then the port number (for example, **http://vmm2008:8000**).

    b. If the self-service portal is configured to use host headers, type **http://** followed by the host header name.

2. Enter a valid self-service user domain\username and password, and click the Log On button. The self-service portal will display in the browser.

3. Select New Computer from the Actions pane on the right. The New VM window will open.

4. Select the correct Self-Service User role to use from the Role drop-down box at the top of the New VM window.

5. On the New VM window, enter the following information:

    a. **Name**—Type a friendly name for the new VM (for example, **Windows Server 2008 x64 Accounting Server**).

    b. **Description**—Type a description for the new VM.

c. **Computer Name**—Type the computer name of the new VM (for example, **SF-ACCT03**).

d. **Administrator Password/Confirm Password**—Enter and confirm the local administrator password for the new VM.

e. **OS Product Key**—Type the Microsoft product key for the new VM.

> **NOTE**
>
> The number of quota points, if any, is displayed at the bottom of the New VM window. This indicates how many quota points the user has available. If the user does not have enough quota points available for this VM, the user will be unable to deploy it.

Figure 11.7 shows an example of the New VM window.

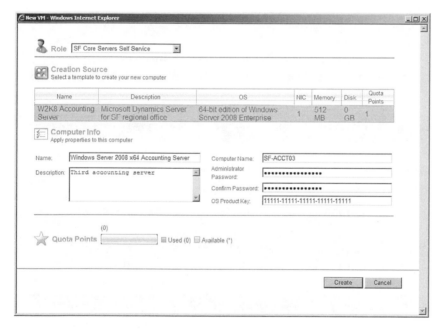

FIGURE 11.7   The self-service portal New VM Window.

6. Click the Create button to create and deploy the new VM. A pop-up window will display indicating that the VM was successfully created.

7. Click OK to the pop-up message and to close the New VM window.

The self-service portal will update to show the status of the deployment of the new VM. The deployment may take a few minutes as files are copied to the host server and the VM is configured.

NOTE

The progress of the VM deployment can be monitored by selecting the VM in the self-service portal and clicking Properties in the Actions pane. Then click the Latest Job tab.

Migrating a VM

VMM provides the capability to move, or migrate, VMs quickly and easily between hosts. There are three ways this can be accomplished in VMM.

The Migrate Virtual Machine Action

The Migrate Virtual Machine Wizard enables the administrator to migrate a VM to another host using a VMM wizard, as follows:

1. Open the VMM Administrator console using the shortcut on the Windows desktop or via the Start menu under Microsoft System Center, VMM 2008, VMM Administrator console.

   A Connect to Server window may open, prompting for the VMM server to connect to. Enter the server name and connection port (the default is port 8100) using the format VMMserver:port.

NOTE

You may choose to always open a connection to this server by selecting the Make This Server My Default check box. Doing so prevents this connection window from displaying when the Administrator console is run.

2. Go to the Virtual Machines view by clicking the Virtual Machines button.

3. Select the VM to migrate and click Migrate Virtual Machine from the Actions pane.

NOTE

If the selected VM is currently running, VMM will display a pop-up dialog warning the administrator that migrating the VM will cause the VM to be stopped, resulting in a temporary loss of service to all users of the machine. The VM is not stopped until the migration actually begins. Click Yes to continue or No to quit.

4. On the Select Virtual Machine Host page, select the host to migrate the VM to. Use the star ratings to determine a suitable host. Review the Additional Information tabs in the Results pane for further information about the host's star rating. Click Next to continue.

5. On the Select Path page, type the path on the host where the VM, and its associated files should be stored on the host.

> **NOTE**
>
> The path entered must be a valid and already exist on the host.

Optionally, the administrator can check the Add This Path to the List of Host Default Paths check box to add the path to the default paths on the host.

If SAN transfers are enabled the VM is transferred to the host over the SAN, by default. If the administrator does not want to perform a SAN transfer, check the Transfer over the Network Even if a SAN Transfer Is Available check box. This check box is not available if SAN transfers are not available for this deployment.

Click Next to continue.

6. On the Select Network page, select the appropriate network that exists on the selected host. If the administrator does not want to configure a network, select Not Connected. Click Next.

7. On the Summary page, carefully review the settings and click Move to proceed with the migration. The administrator can also choose to select the Start the Virtual Machine Immediately After Deploying It to the Host check box, if desired.

The Migrate Virtual Machine Wizard offers a View Script button. This option allows the administrator to view, modify, and save the PowerShell commands that the wizard will execute to migrate the VM, as shown in the following example:

```
# — — — — — — — — — — — — — — — — — — — — — — — — — — — — — — — — — —
# Migrate Virtual Machine Wizard Script
# — — — — — — — — — — — — — — — — — — — — — — — — — — — — — — — — — —
# Script generated on Sunday, June 22, 2008 3:18:31 AM by Virtual Machine Manager
#
# For additional help on cmdlet usage, type get-help <cmdlet name>
# — — — — — — — — — — — — — — — — — — — — — — — — — — — — — — — — — —
$VirtualNetworkAdapter = Get-VirtualNetworkAdapter -VMMServer vmm2008 ¦ where
{$_.Name -eq "EDGE STD x64"}
Set-VirtualNetworkAdapter -VirtualNetworkAdapter $VirtualNetworkAdapter -RunAsyn-
chronously -VirtualNetwork "Realtek RTL8169/8110 Family PCI Gigabit Ethernet NIC
(NDIS 6.0) - Virtual Network" -NetworkTag "" -Location "" -JobGroup 3b72ecf7-ee0a-
4d5b-b84b-844505c3a7ed -VLanEnabled $false
$VM = Get-VM -VMMServer vmm2008 -Name "EDGE STD x64" ¦ where {$_.VMHost.Name -eq
"DC1.companyabc.com"}
$VMHost = Get-VMHost -VMMServer vmm2008 ¦ where {$_.Name -eq "DC1.companyabc.com"}
Move-VM -VM $VM -VMHost $VMHost -Path "C:\ProgramData\Microsoft\Windows\Hyper-V" -
RunAsynchronously -UseLAN -JobGroup 3b72ecf7-ee0a-4d5b-b84b-844505c3a7ed
```

This code can be saved and edited to facilitate migrating other VMs using the VMM command shell.

NOTE

Running the wizard in this way is an easy way to create the PowerShell scripts necessary to perform migrations using the VMM command shell. After the scripts have been saved, the administrator can cancel the Migrate Virtual Machine Wizard.

Drag and Drop the VM onto a Host

Adding a guest virtual session onto an existing Hyper-V host server requires the process of associating the virtual session to the host. This is done by dragging and dropping the virtual guest session onto the host by doing th following:

1. Open the VMM Administrator console using the shortcut on the Windows desktop or via the Start menu under Microsoft System Center, VMM 2008, VMM Administrator console.

   A Connect to Server window may open, prompting for the VMM server to connect to. Enter the server name and connection port (the default is port 8100) using the format VMMserver:port.

NOTE

You may choose to always open a connection to this server by selecting the Make This Server My Default check box. Doing so prevents this connection window from displaying when the Administrator console is run.

2. Go to the Virtual Machines view by clicking the Virtual Machines button.
3. Expand the Host Groups in the Properties pane to display the host upon which the VM will be migrated, as shown in Figure 11.8.
4. Select the VM to migrate and drag and drop it onto the new host. The VM will be migrated to the new host.

NOTE

If the selected VM is currently running, VMM will display a pop-up dialog warning the administrator that migrating the VM will cause the VM to be stopped, resulting in a temporary loss of service to all users of the machine. The VM is not stopped until the migration actually begins. Click Yes to continue or No to quit.

Drag and Drop the VM onto a Host Group

This process is the same as dragging and dropping the VM onto a host, as described previously, with a few differences. Instead of dropping the VM onto a specific host, the VM is dropped onto a host group that contains one or more hosts.

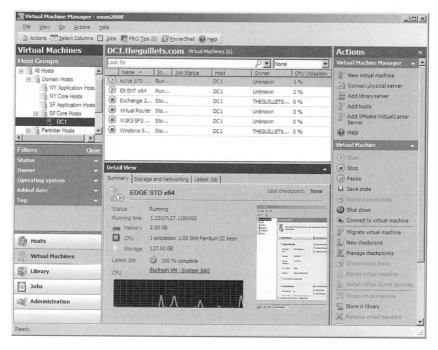

FIGURE 11.8   Selecting the host on which to migrate the VM.

Automatic Placement, explained earlier in this chapter, will automatically place the VM on the most suitable host in the selected host group. Host selection is based on the host ratings defined either through the VMM global settings or by override settings in the VM's Properties page.

Summary

In this chapter, we discussed VM placement and host ratings to help the administrator select the appropriate host for VM deployment. User roles provide a good deal of granularity of administration within the VMM Administrator console and the self-service portal.

VMs can easily be deployed using both the VMM Administrator console and the self-service portal. Migrations of VM can be performed easily using the Administrator console, via wizards, or simple drag-and-drop methods, or from the VMM command console.

Best Practices

The following are best practices from this chapter:

▶ Use roles-based access control (RBAC) to define the administrator roles in VMM.

▶ Because the Administrator user role has full access to the VMM infrastructure, limit the number of members of this group as much as possible.

▶ Use delegate administrators to scope administrators to a specific set of objects in VMM.

▶ Create a VMM Administrators group in the Active Directory and add that group to the Administrator role in VMM. This is better than adding an individual user account, in case that user account is deleted.

▶ Create security groups in the Active Directory and use these groups to define members of Delegated Administrator and Self-Service User roles in VMM.

▶ Monitor the members of Delegated Administrator groups, because delegated administrators can manage the groups they are members of.

▶ Add administrators or delegated administrators to the Self-Service User role if self-service portal access is required.

▶ Delegated Administrator and Self-Service User groups can be pre-created without members, and the members can be added later.

▶ Run wizards, such as the Create Virtual Machine Wizard, to view, customize, and save the PowerShell scripts that the wizard will run.

▶ Build a collection of PowerShell cmdlets that perform commonly used VMM administration tasks.

▶ Use the Look For box, present in many of the VMM wizards, to filter the results of collections of VMM objects.

▶ Scope the VMM library resources that self-service users can access by creating their own folders in the VMM Library share.

▶ Use Automatic Placement to automatically deploy VMs to the best-suited host.

▶ Customize the global host rating to match the organization's needs and environment.

▶ Only use the Make This VM Highly Available option on VMs you plan to deploy to host clusters.

▶ Use a common VM path on all host servers to ensure that VM migrations will succeed.

▶ Use quota points for self-service users to control the number of VMs they can deploy to hosts.

▶ Monitor the progress of VM migrations using the Jobs view in the Administrator console or the Properties page of the VM in the self-service portal.

▶ Notify users of an active VM before migrating it to a new host, because the VM will temporarily be stopped during the migration.

▶ Use Automatic Placement of migrated VMs by using the "drag and drop onto a host group" method.

11

PART V

Managing Guest Sessions with Uptime in a Hyper-V Environment

IN THIS PART

12

Application-Level Failover and Disaster Recovery in a Hyper-V Environment

Organizations have expanded their implementation of clustered servers and recovery solutions for physical server systems. But now, with virtualization and several guest sessions depending on the operation of a single host system, the interest to implement highly available host servers has grown dramatically. The failure of a single host server can simultaneously bring down the services of several systems, so the proper implementation of high-availability technologies becomes extremely important. If properly implemented, virtual servers can actually improve an organization's ability to create highly available and fault-tolerant environments, because the creation of a redundant guest session does not require the purchase of an addition physical server for each replicated server.

However, the biggest challenge most organizations have in creating a highly available virtualized environment is to choose which technology to implement. There are many ways to create fault tolerance, including the following:

▶ Clustering the host server

▶ Clustering the guest session

▶ Using native high-availability functionality of the application being protected

▶ Purchasing and using a third-party application

An administrator must choose which failover or disaster-recovery method to implement. The key is to choose the best solution to meet the needs of the organization and to try to minimize the number of methods implemented so that the recovery process is simplified and not dependent on the execution of several processes to reach the same recovery-state goal.

This chapter covers the various failover and recovery options commonly used in a Hyper-V virtualized environment, and how to choose which method is best given the end state desired by the organization.

Choosing the Best Fault-Tolerance and Recovery Method

The first thing the administrator needs to do when looking to create a highly available and protected environment is to choose the best fault-tolerance and recovery method. Be aware, however, that no single solution does everything for every application identically. High-availability and disaster-recovery protected environments use the best solution for each application server being protected.

Using Native High-Availability and Disaster-Recovery Technologies Built in to an Application

Before considering external or third-party tools for high availability and disaster recovery, administrators should investigate whether the application they are trying to protect has a native "built-in" method for protection. Interestingly, many organizations purchase expensive third-party failover and recovery tools even though an application has a free built-in recovery function that does a better job. For example, it doesn't make sense to purchase and implement a special fault-tolerance product to protect a Windows domain controller. By default, domain controllers in a Windows networking environment replicate information between domain controllers. The minute a domain controller is brought onto the network, the server replicates information from other servers. If the system is taken offline, other domains controllers, by definition, automatically take over the logon authentication for user requests.

Key examples of high-availability and disaster-recovery technologies built in to common applications include the following:

▶ **Active Directory global catalog servers**—By default, global catalog servers in Windows Active Directory are replicas of one another. To create redundancy of a global catalog server, an additional global catalog server just needs to be added to the network. Once added, the information on other global catalog servers is replicated to the new global catalog server system.

▶ **Windows domain controller servers**—By default, Microsoft Windows domain controller server systems are replicas of one another. To create redundancy of a domain controller server, an additional domain controller system just needs to be added to the network. Once added, the information on other domain controller servers is replicated to the new domain controller server system.

▶ **Load-balanced web servers**—To protect information on web servers, Microsoft provides a technology called "network load balancing" (NLB) that provides for the failover of one web server to another web server. Assuming the information on each web server is the same, when one web server fails, another web server can take on the web request of a user without interruption to the user's experience.

▶ **Domain name system (DNS) servers**—DNS servers also replicate information from one system to another. Therefore, if one DNS server fails, other DNS servers with identical replicated information are available to service DNS client requests.

▶ **Distributed File Server replication**—For the past 8+ years, Windows Server has had built-in file server replication for the protection of file shares. Distributed File Server (DFS) replication replicates information from one file server to another for redundancy of data files. With the release of Windows Server 2003 R2 and more recently Windows Server 2008, DFS has been improved to the point where organizations around the world are replicating their file shares. When a file server fails or becomes unavailable, another file server with the data becomes immediately and seamlessly available to users for retrieval and storage.

▶ **SQL mirroring and SQL replication**—With Microsoft SQL Server, systems can mirror and replicate information from one SQL server to another. The mirrored or replicated data on another SQL server means that the loss of one SQL server does not impact access to SQL data. The data is mirrored or replicated within the SQL Server application and does not require external products or technologies to maintain the integrity and operations of SQL in the environment.

▶ **Exchange Continuous Replication**—Exchange Server 2007 provides a number of different technologies to replicate information from one server to another. Continuous Replication provides such replication of data. In the event that one Exchange mailbox server fails, with Continuous Replication enabled on Exchange user requests for information will remain because the replica of the mailbox server data is stored on a second system. This is a built-in technology in Exchange 2007 and requires no additional software or hardware to provide complete redundancy of Exchange data.

All these technologies can be enabled on virtual guest sessions. Therefore, if a guest session is no longer available on the network, another guest session on another virtual host can provide the services needed to maintain both availability and data recoverability.

Many other servers have built-in native replication and data protection. Before purchasing or implementing an external technology to create a highly available or fault-tolerant server environment, confirm whether the application has a native way of protecting the system. If it does, consider using the native technology. The native technology usually works better than other options. After all, the native method was built specifically for the application. In addition, the logic, intelligence, failover process, and autorecovery of information are well tested and supported by the application vendor.

> **NOTE**
>
> This book does not cover planning and implementing these built-in technologies for redundancy and failover. However, several other Sams Publishing Unleashed books do cover these specific application technologies, such as Windows Server 2003 Unleashed, Windows Server 2008 Unleashed, Exchange Server 2007 Unleashed, and SharePoint 2007 Unleashed.

Using Guest Clustering to Protect a Virtual Guest Session

You can protect some applications better via clustering rather than simple network load balancing or replication, and Hyper-V supports virtual guest session clustering. Therefore, you can cluster an application such as an Exchange server, SQL server, or the like across multiple guest sessions. The installation and configuration of a clustered virtual guest is the same as if you were setting up and configuring clustering across two or more physical servers.

Guest clustering within a Hyper-V environment is actually easier to implement than clustering across physical servers. After all, with guest clustering, you can more easily configure the amount of memory, the disk storage, and the number of processors and drivers. For virtual guest sessions, the configuration of such is standard and dynamic. Unlike with a physical cluster server for which you must physically open the system to add memory chips or additional processors, in a virtual guest clustering scenario, you just have to change a virtual guest session parameter.

When implementing guest clustering, you should place each cluster guest session on a different Hyper-V host server. Thus, if a host server fails, you avoid the simultaneous failure of multiple clusters. By distributing guest sessions to multiple hosts, you give the remaining nodes of a cluster a better chance of surviving and being available to take on the server role for the application (in the event of a guest session or host server failure).

Traditionally, clustering is considered a high-availability strategy that keeps an application running in the event of a failure of one cluster node. It has not been considered a WAN disaster-recovery technology. With the release of Windows Server 2008, however, Microsoft has changed the traditional understanding clustering by providing native support for "stretch clusters." Stretch clusters allow cluster nodes to reside on separate subnets on a network, something that clustering in Windows 2003 did not support. For the most part, older cluster configurations required cluster servers to be in the same data center. With stretch clusters, cluster nodes can be in different data centers in completely different locations. If one node fails, another node in another location can immediately take over the application services. And because clusters can have two, four, or eight nodes, an organization can place two or three nodes of a cluster in the main data center and place the fourth node of the cluster in a remote location. In the event of a local failure, operations are maintained within the local site. In the event of a complete local server failure, the remote node or nodes are available to host the application remotely.

Windows 2008 stretch clusters now provide high availability through the implementation of clustering, with seamless failover from one node to another. In addition, stretch clusters allow nodes to reside in separate locations that provide disaster recovery. Instead of having two or more different strategies for high availability and disaster recovery, an organization can get both high availability and disaster recovery by properly implementing out-of-the-box stretch clustering with Windows Server 2008.

NOTE

Whereas failover clustering for a Hyper-V host server is covered later in this chapter in the "Failover Clustering in Windows Server 2008" section and is similar to the process of creating a failover cluster within a virtual guest session, clustering of guest sessions specific to applications such as Exchange, SQL, SharePoint, and the like is not covered in this book. Because the setup and configuration of a cluster in a virtual guest session is the same as setting up and configuring a cluster on physical servers, refer to an authoritative guide on clustering of the specific application (Exchange, SQL, Windows, and so on), such as any of the Sams Publishing *Unleashed* books. Specifically, for the implementation of stretch clusters, see *Windows Server 2008 Unleashed*.

Using Host Clustering to Protect an Entire Virtual Host System

An administrator could use the native high-availability and disaster-recovery technologies built in to application and use guest session clustering if that is a better-supported model for redundancy of the application. However, Hyper-V enables an organization to perform clustering at the host level. Host clustering in Hyper-V effectively uses shared storage, where Hyper-V host servers can be clustered to provide failover from one node to another in the event of a host server failure.

Hyper-V host server failover clustering automatically fails the Hyper-V service over to a surviving host server to continue the operation of *all* guest sessions managed by the Hyper-V host. Host server failover clustering is also a good high-availability solution for applications that do not natively have a way to replicate data at the virtual guest level (for example, a custom Java application, a specific Microsoft Access database application, or an accounting or CRM application that doesn't have built-in replication or clustering support).

With host clustering, the Hyper-V host server administrator does not need to manage each guest session individually for data replication or guest session clustering. Instead, the administrator creates and supports a failover method from one host server to another host server, rolling up the failover support of all guest sessions managed by the cluster.

> **NOTE**
>
> Organizations may implement a hybrid approach to high availability and disaster recovery. Some applications would use native replication (such as domain controllers, DNS servers, or frontend web servers). Other applications would be protected through the implementation of virtual guest clustering (such as SQL Server or Exchange). Still other applications and system configurations would be protected through Hyper-V host failover clustering to fail over all guest sessions to a redundant Hyper-V host.

Purchasing and Using Third-Party Applications for High Availability and Disaster Recovery

The fourth option, which is very much the last and final option in high availability in disaster recovery these days, is to purchase and use a third-party application to protect servers and data. With the built-in capabilities of applications to provide high availability and redundancy, plus the two clustering options that protect either the guest session application or the entire host server system, the need for organizations to purchase additional tools and solutions to meet their high-availability and disaster-recovery requirements has greatly diminished.

Strategies of the past, such as snapshotting data across a storage area network (SAN) or replicating SQL or Exchange data using a third-party add-in tool, are generally no longer necessary. Also, an organization needs to evaluate whether they want to create a separate strategy and use a separate set of tools for high availability than they do for disaster recovery, or whether having a single strategy that provides both high availability and site-to-site disaster recovery is feasible to protect the organization's data and applications.

Much has changed in the past couple of years, and now better options are built in to applications. These should be evaluated and considered as part of a strategy for the organization's high-availability and disaster-recovery plans.

Failover Clustering in Windows Server 2008

As mentioned previously, Windows Server 2008 provides a feature called failover clustering. *Clustering*, in general, refers to the grouping of independent server nodes that are accessed and viewed on the network as a single system. When a service or application is run from a cluster, the end user can connect to a single cluster node to perform his work or each request can be handled by multiple nodes in the cluster. If data is read-only, the client may request data from one server in the cluster, and the next request may be made to a different server in the cluster. The client may never know the difference. In addition, if a single node on a multiple-node cluster fails, the remaining nodes will continue to service client requests, and only clients originally connected to the failed node may notice any change. (For example, they might experience a slight interruption in service. Alternatively, their entire session might need to be restarted depending on the service or application in use and the particular clustering technology used in that cluster.)

Failover clusters provide system fault tolerance through a process called failover. When a system or node in the cluster fails or is unable to respond to client requests, the clustered services or applications that were running on that particular node are taken offline and moved to another available node where functionality and access is restored. Failover clusters in most deployments require access to shared data storage and are best suited for deployment of the following services and applications:

▸ **File servers**—File services on failover clusters provide much of the same functionality as standalone Windows Server 2008 systems. When deployed as a clustered file server, however, a single data storage repository can be presented and accessed by clients through the currently assigned and available cluster node without replicating the file data.

▸ **Print servers**—Print services deployed on failover clusters have one main advantage over standalone print servers: If the print server fails, each shared printer becomes available to clients under the same print server name. Although Group Policy–deployed printers are easily deployed and replaced (for computers and users), standalone print server failure impact can be huge, especially when servers, devices, services, and applications that cannot be managed with group policies access these printers.

▸ **Database servers**—When large organizations deploy line-of-business applications, e-commerce, or any other critical services or applications that require a backend database system that must be highly available, database server deployment on failover clusters is the preferred method. Remember that the configuration of an enterprise database server can take hours, and the size of the databases can be huge. Therefore, in the event of a single-server system failure, database server deployment on standalone systems and a system rebuild may take several hours.

▸ **Backend enterprise messaging systems**—For many of the same reasons as cited previously for deploying database servers, enterprise messaging services have become critical to many organizations and are best deployed in failover clusters.

Windows Server 2008 Cluster Terminology

Before failover clusters can be designed and implemented, the administrator deploying the solution should be familiar with the general terms used to define the clustering technologies. The following list contains many terms associated with Windows Server 2008 clustering technologies:

▸ **Cluster**—A cluster is a group of independent servers (nodes) accessed and presented to the network as a single system.

▸ **Node**—A node is an individual server that is a member of a cluster.

▸ **Cluster resource**—A cluster resource is a service, application, IP address, disk, or network name defined and managed by the cluster. Within a cluster, cluster resources are grouped and managed together using cluster resource groups, now known as service and application groups.

▶ **Service and application groups**—Cluster resources are contained within a cluster in a logical set called service or application groups or historically just as a cluster group. Service and application groups are the units of failover within the cluster. When a cluster resource fails and cannot be restarted automatically, the service or application group this resource is a part of is taken offline, moved to another node in the cluster, and the group is brought back online.

▶ **Client access point**—A client access point refers to the combination of a network name and associated IP address resource. By default, when a new service or application group is defined, a client access point is created with a name and IPv4 address. IPv6 is supported in failover clusters, but an IPv6 resource will either need to be added to an existing group or a generic service or application group will need to be created with the necessary resources and resource dependencies.

▶ **Virtual cluster server**—A virtual cluster is a service or application group that contains a client access point, a disk resource, and at least one additional service- or application-specific resource. Virtual cluster server resources are accessed either by the domain name system (DNS) name or a NetBIOS name that references an IPv4 or IPv6 address. In some cases, a virtual cluster server can also be directly accessed using the IPv4 or IPv6 address. The name and IP address remain the same regardless of which cluster node the virtual server is running on.

▶ **Active node**—An active node is a node in the cluster that is currently running at least one service or application group. A service or application group can be active on only one node at a time, and all other nodes that can host the group are considered passive for that particular group.

▶ **Passive node**—A passive node is a node in the cluster that is currently not running any service or application group.

▶ **Active/passive cluster**—An active/passive cluster is a cluster that has at least one node running a service or application group and additional nodes the group can be hosted on but that are currently in a waiting state. This is a typical configuration when only a single service or application group is deployed on a failover cluster.

▶ **Active/active cluster**—An active/active cluster is a cluster in which each node is actively hosting or running at least one service or application group. This is a typical configuration when multiple groups are deployed on a single failover cluster to maximize server or system usage. The downside is that when an active system fails, the remaining systems must host all the groups and provide the services or applications on the cluster to all necessary clients.

▶ **Cluster heartbeat**—The cluster heartbeat refers to the communication that is kept between individual cluster nodes that is used to determine node status. Heartbeat communication can occur on designated networks, but is also performed on the same network as client communication. Because of this internode communication, network monitoring software and network administrators should be forewarned of the amount of network chatter between the cluster nodes. The amount of traffic generated by heartbeat communication is not large based on the size of the data, but the frequency of the communication may ring some network alarm bells.

▶ **Cluster quorum**—The cluster quorum maintains the definitive cluster configuration data and the current state of each node, each service and application group, and each resource and network in the cluster. Furthermore, when each node reads the quorum data, depending on the information retrieved the node determines whether it should remain available, shut down the cluster, or activate any particular service or application group on the local node. To extend this even further, failover clusters can be configured to use one of four different cluster quorum models, and essentially the quorum type chosen for a cluster defines the cluster. For example, a cluster that utilizes the Node and Disk Majority Quorum can be called a Node and Disk Majority cluster.

▶ **Cluster witness disk or file share**—The cluster witness or the witness file share is used to store the cluster configuration information and is used to help determine the state of the cluster when some if not all the cluster nodes cannot be contacted (a.k.a. the cluster quorum).

▶ **Generic cluster resources**—Generic cluster resources were created to define and add new or undefined services, applications, or scripts that are not already included as available cluster resources. Adding a custom resource provides the ability for that resource to be failed over between cluster nodes when another resource in the same service or application group fails. In addition, when the group the custom resource is a member of moves to a different node, the custom resource follows. One disadvantage with custom resources is that the failover cluster feature cannot actively storage refers to the disks and volumes presented to the Windows Server 2008 cluster nodes as LUNs.

▶ **LUNs**—LUN stands for logical unit number. A LUN is used to identify a disk or a disk volume that is presented to a host server or multiple hosts by the shared-storage device. Of course, there are shared storage controllers, firmware, drivers, and physical connections between the server and the shared storage. However, the concept is that a LUN or set of LUNs is presented to the server for use as a local disk. LUNs provided by shared storage must meet many requirements before they can be used with failover clusters. When they do meet these requirements, all active nodes in the cluster must have exclusive access to these LUNs. More information about LUNs and shared storage is provided later in this chapter.

▶ **Failover**—Failover refers to a service or application group moving from the current active node to another available node in the cluster when a cluster resource fails. Failover occurs when a server becomes unavailable or when a resource in the cluster group fails and cannot recover within the failure threshold.

▶ **Failback**—Failback refers to a cluster group automatically moving back to a preferred node when the preferred node resumes cluster membership. Failback is a nondefault configuration that can be enabled within the properties of a service or application group. The cluster group must have a preferred node defined and a failback threshold configured for failback to function. A preferred node is the node you want your cluster group to be running or hosted on during regular cluster operation when all cluster nodes are available. When a group is failing back, the cluster is performing the same failover operation but is triggered by the preferred node rejoining or resuming cluster operation instead of by a resource failure on the currently active node.

Overview of Failover Clustering in a Hyper-V Host Environment

After an organization decides to cluster a Hyper-V host server, it must then decide which cluster configuration model best suits the needs of the particular deployment. Failover clusters can be deployed using four different configuration models that will accommodate most deployment scenarios and requirements. The four configuration models are the Node Majority Quorum, Node and Disk Majority Quorum, Node and File Share Majority Quorum, and the No Majority: Disk-Only Quorum. The typical and most common cluster deployment that includes two or more nodes in a single data center is the Node and Disk Majority Quorum model.

Failover Cluster Quorum Models

As previously stated, Windows Server 2008 failover clusters support four different cluster quorum models. Each model is best suited for specific configurations. However, if all the nodes and shared storage are configured, specified, and available during the installation of the failover cluster, the best-suited quorum model is automatically selected.

Node Majority Quorum

The Node Majority Quorum model has been designed for failover cluster deployments that contain an odd number of cluster nodes. When determining the quorum state of the cluster, only the number of available nodes is counted. A cluster using the Node Majority Quorum is called a Node Majority cluster. A Node Majority cluster will remain up and running if the number of available nodes exceeds the number of failed nodes. For example, in a five-node cluster, three nodes must be available for the cluster to remain online. If three nodes fail in a five-node "Node Majority" cluster, the entire cluster will be shut down. Node Majority clusters have been designed and are well suited for geographically or network-dispersed cluster nodes. For this configuration to be supported by Microsoft, however, it will take serious effort, quality hardware, a third-party mechanism to replicate any backend data, and a very reliable network. Once again, this model works well for clusters with an odd number of nodes.

Node and Disk Majority

The Node and Disk Majority Quorum model determines whether a cluster can continue to function by counting the number of available nodes and the availability of the cluster witness disk. Under this model, the cluster quorum is stored on a cluster disk that is accessible and made available to all nodes in the cluster through a shared storage device using Serial Attached SCSI (SAS), Fibre Channel, or iSCSI connections. This model is the closest to the traditional single-quorum device cluster configuration model and is composed of two or more server nodes that are all connected to a shared storage device. In this model, only one copy of the quorum data is maintained on the witness disk. This model is well suited for failover clusters using shared storage, all connected on the same network with an even number of nodes. For example, on a two-, four-, six-, or eight-node cluster using this model, the cluster will continue to function as long as half of the total nodes are available and can contact the witness disk. In the case of a witness disk failure, a majority of the nodes will need to remain up and running. To calculate this, take half of the total nodes and add one. Doing so will give you the lowest number of available nodes required to keep a cluster running. For example, on a six-node cluster using this model, if the witness disk fails the cluster will remain up and running as long as four nodes are available.

Node and File Share Majority Quorum

The Node and File Share Majority Quorum model is similar the Node and Disk Majority Quorum model, but instead of a witness disk the quorum is stored on a file share. The advantage of this model is that it can be deployed similarly to the Node Majority Quorum model. However, as long as the witness file share is available, this model can tolerate the failure of half the total nodes. This model is well suited for clusters with an even number of nodes that do not use shared storage.

No Majority: Disk Only Quorum

The No Majority: Disk Only Quorum model is best suited for testing the process and behavior of deployed built-in or custom services or applications on a Windows Server 2008 failover cluster. In this model, the cluster can sustain the failover of all nodes except one, as long as the disk containing the quorum remains available. The limitation of this model is that the disk containing the quorum becomes a single point of failure. That is why this model is not well suited for production deployments of failover clusters.

As a best practice, before deploying a failover cluster, determine whether shared storage will be used, verify that each node can communicate with each LUN presented by the shared storage device, and when the cluster is created, add all nodes to the list. Doing so will ensure that the correct recommended cluster quorum model is selected for the new failover cluster. When the recommended model uses shared storage and a witness disk, the smallest available LUN will be selected. This can be changed, if necessary, after the cluster has been created.

Shared Storage for Failover Clusters

Shared disk storage is a requirement for Hyper-V host failover clusters using the Node and Disk Majority Quorum and the Disk-Only Quorum models. Shared storage devices can be a part of any cluster configuration, and when they are used, the disks, disk volumes, or LUNs presented to the Windows systems must be presented as basic Windows disks.

All storage drivers must be digitally signed and certified for use with Windows Server 2008. Many storage devices certified for Windows Server 2003 may not work with Windows Server 2008 and either simply cannot be used for failover cluster shared storage or may require a firmware and driver upgrade to be supported. One main reason for this is the fact that all failover shared storage must comply with SCSI-3 architecture model SAM-2. This includes any and all legacy and SAS controllers, fiber host bus adapters, and iSCSI hardware- and software-based initiators and targets. If the cluster attempts to perform an action on a LUN or shared disk and the attempt causes an interruption in communication to the other nodes in the cluster or any other system connected to the shared storage device, data corruption can occur, and the entire cluster and each SAN-connected system may be lose connectivity to the storage.

When LUNS are presented to failover cluster nodes, each LUN must be presented to each node in the cluster. Also, when the shared storage is accessed by the cluster and other systems, the LUNs must be masked or presented only to the cluster nodes and the shared storage device controllers to ensure that no other systems can access or disrupt the cluster communication. There are strict requirements for shared storage support, especially with failover clusters. Storage area networks (SANs) or other types of shared storage must meet the following requirements:

▶ All fiber, SAS, and iSCSI host bus adapters (HBAs) and Ethernet cards used with iSCSI software initiators must have (or obtain) the Designed for Microsoft Windows logo for Windows Server 2008 and have suitable signed device drivers.

▶ SAS, fiber, and iSCSI HBAs must use StorPort device drivers to provide targeted LUN resets and other functions inherent to the StorPort driver specification. SCSIport was at one point supported for two-node clusters, but if a StorPort driver is available it should be used to ensure support from the hardware vendors and Microsoft.

▶ All shared-storage HBAs and backend storage devices, including iSCSI targets, fiber, and SAS storage arrays, must support SCSI-3 standards and must also support persistent bindings or reservations of LUNs.

▶ All shared-storage HBAs must be deployed with matching firmware and driver versions. Failover clusters using shared storage require a stable infrastructure, and applying the latest storage controller driver to outdated HBA firmware can cause undesirable situations and may disrupt data access.

▶ All nodes in the cluster should contain the same HBAs and use the same version of drivers and firmware. Each cluster node should be an exact duplicate of each other node when it comes to hardware selection, configuration, and driver and firmware revisions. This allows for a more reliable configuration and simplifies management and standardization.

▶ When iSCSI software initiators are used to connect to iSCSI software- or hardware-based targets, the network adapter used for iSCSI communication must be connected to a dedicated switch, cannot be used for any cluster communication, and cannot be a teamed network adapter.

In addition, for Microsoft to officially support failover clusters and shared storage, the entire configuration must be tested as a whole system before it will be considered a "Windows Server 2008 Failover Cluster Supported Configuration." The whole system includes the server brand and model, local disk configuration, HBA, and network card controller firmware and driver version (and, if applicable, iSCSI software initiator software, storage array, and storage array controller firmware or SAN operating system version).

The point to keep in mind is that if a company really wants to consider using failover clusters, they should research and find a suitable solution to meet their budget. If a tested and supported solution cannot be found within their price range, they should consider alternative solutions that can restore systems in about an hour or a few hours (if they cannot budget for a restore that takes just a few minutes). The truth is that failover clusters are not for everyone, they are not for the faint of heart, and they are not within every organization's IT budget.

Even after reading all this, some administrators will still want to deploy test failover cluster configurations to gain knowledge and experience with the features and functionality. They will want to learn how to deploy and how to manage failover clusters, and they will want to learn how to train staff and present prototype solutions to management. For those administrators, various low-cost shared-storage alternatives are available, including the Windows iSCSI initiator and a software-based iSCSI target. In case a problem is encountered or data is lost or corrupted, be aware that these are not supported by Microsoft.

SAS Storage Arrays

Serial Attached SCSI disks are one of the newest additions to the disk market. SAS storage arrays can provide organizations with affordable entry-level hardware-based direct attached storage arrays suitable for Windows Server 2008 clusters. SAS storage arrays are commonly limited to four hosts, but some models support extenders to add additional hosts as required. One of the major issues with direct attached storage (not with SAS) is that replication of the data within the storage is usually not achievable without involving one of the host systems and software.

Fiber Channel Storage Arrays

With Fiber Channel (FC) HBAs, Windows Server 2008 can access both shared and nonshared disks residing on a SAN connected to a common FC switch. This allows both the shared-storage and operating system volumes to be located on the SAN, if desired, to provide diskless servers. In many cases, however, diskless storage may not be desirable if the operating system performs many paging actions, because the cache on the storage controllers can be used up very fast and can cause delay in disk read and write operations for dedicated cluster storage. If this is desired, however, the SAN must support this option and be configured to present the OS-dedicated LUNs to only a single host exclusively. The LUNs defined for shared cluster storage must be zones and presented to every node in the cluster, and to no other systems. In many cases, the LUN zoning or masking is configured on the fiber switch that connects the cluster nodes and the shared-storage device. This is a distinct difference between direct access storage and FC or iSCSI shared storage. Both FC and iSCSI require a common fiber or Ethernet switch to establish and maintain connections between the hosts and the storage.

A properly configured FC zone for a cluster will include the World Wide Port Number (WWPN) of each cluster host's FC HBAs and the WWPN of the HBA controllers from the shared-storage device. If either the server or the storage device uses multiple HBAs to connect to a single or multiple FC switches to provide failover or load balancing functionality, this is known as multipath I/O (MPIO), and a qualified driver for MPIO management and communication must be used. Also, the function of either MPIO failover or MPIO load balancing must be verified as approved for Windows Server 2008. Consult the shared-storage vendor (including the fiber switch vendor) for documentation and supported configurations. In addition, check the cluster hardware compatibility list (HCL) on the Microsoft website to find approved configurations.

iSCSI Storage

When organizations want to use iSCSI storage for Windows Server 2008 failover clusters, security and network isolation is highly recommended. iSCSI uses an initiator or the host that requires access to the LUNs or iSCSI targets. Targets are located or hosted on iSCSI target portals. Using the target portal interface, you must configure the target to be accessed by multiple initiators in a cluster configuration. Both the iSCSI initiators and target portals come in software- and hardware-based models, but both models use IP networks for communication between the initiators and the targets. The targets will need to be presented to Windows as a basic disk. When standard network cards will be used for iSCSI communication on Windows Server 2008 systems, the built-in Windows Server 2008 iSCSI initiator can be used, as long as the iSCSI target can support the authentication and security options provided, if used.

Regardless of whether you choose the Microsoft iSCSI initiator of software-based or hardware-based initiators or targets, iSCSI communication should be deployed on isolated network segments and preferably dedicated network switches. Furthermore, the LUNs presented to the failover cluster should be masked from any systems that are not nodes participating in the cluster by using authentication and IPsec communication as possible. Within the Windows Server 2008 operating system, the iSCSI HBA or designated network card should not be used for any failover cluster configuration and cannot be deployed using network teaming software, or it will not be supported by Microsoft.

By now, you should understand that Microsoft wants to support only those organizations that deploy failover clusters on tested and approved entire systems. In many cases, however, failover clusters can still be deployed and will function; after all, you can use the Create a Cluster Wizard to deploy a cluster that is not in a supported configuration.

NOTE

When deploying a failover cluster, pay close attention to the results of the Validate a Cluster Wizard to ensure that the system has passed all storage tests to ensure a supported configuration is deployed.

Multipath I/O

Windows Server 2008 supports multipath I/O to external storage devices such as SANs and iSCSI targets when multiple HBAs are used in the local system or by the shared storage. MPIO can be used to provide failover access to disk storage in case of a controller or HBA failure, but some drivers also support load balancing across HBAs in both standalone and failover cluster deployments. Windows Server 2008 provides a built-in MPIO driver that can be leveraged when the manufacturer conforms to the necessary specifications to allow for the use of this built-in driver.

Volume Shadow Copy for Shared Storage Volume

The Volume Shadow Copy Service (VSS) is supported on shared-storage volumes. VSS can take a point-in-time snapshot of an entire volume, enabling administrators and users to recover data from a previous version. Furthermore, failover clusters and the entire Windows backup architecture use VSS to store backup data. Many of today's services and applications that are certified to work on Windows Server 2008 failover clusters are VSS compliant, and careful consideration should be made when choosing an alternative backup system, unless the system is provided by the shared-storage manufacture and certified to work in conjunction with VSS, Windows Server 2008, and the service or application running on the failover cluster.

Failover Cluster Node Operating System Selection

Hyper-V requires the 64-bit version of Windows Server 2008 to run on the host server. To do host-level failover clustering, the version of 64-bit Windows 2008 must be either the Enterprise Edition or the Datacenter Edition.

Deploying a Failover Cluster for Hyper-V Hosts

The Windows Server 2008 failover cluster feature is not installed on a Hyper-V host system by default and must be installed before failover clusters can be deployed. Alternatively, for administrative workstations, the remote server management features can be installed, which will include the Failover Cluster Management snap-in, but the feature will need to be installed on all nodes that will participate in the failover cluster. Even before installing the failover cluster features, several steps should be taken on each node of the cluster to help deploy a reliable failover cluster. Before deploying a failover cluster, perform the following steps on each node that will be a member of the failover cluster:

▶ Configure fault-tolerant volumes or LUNS using local disks or SAN attached storage for the operating system volume.

▶ Configure at least two network cards, one for client and cluster communication and one for dedicated cluster communication.

▶ For iSCSI shared storage, configure an additional, dedicated network adapter or hardware-based iSCSI HBA.

▶ Rename each network card properties for easy identification within the Cluster Management console after the failover cluster is created. For example, rename Local Area Connection to PUBLIC and Local Area Connection 2 to iSCSI and Local Area Connection 3 to HEARTBEAT, as required and possible. Also, if network teaming will be used, configure the team first, excluding teaming from iSCSI connections, and rename each physical network adapter in the team to TEAMMEMBER1 and 2. The virtual team adapter should then get the name of PUBLIC or HEARTBEAT.

▶ Configure all necessary IPv4 and IPv6 addresses as static configurations.

▶ Verify that any and all HBAs and other storage controllers are running the proper firmware and matched driver version suitable for Windows Server 2008 failover clusters.

▶ If shared storage will be used, plan to use at least two separate LUNs, one to serve as the witness disk and one to serve as the cluster disk for a high-availability service or application group.

▶ If applications or services not included with Windows Server 2008 will be deployed in the failover cluster, as a best practice, add an additional fault-tolerant array or LUN to the system to store the application installation and service files.

▶ Ensure that proper LUN masking and zoning has been configured at the FC or Ethernet switch level for FC or iSCSI shared-storage communication, suitable for failover clustering. Each node in the failover cluster, along with the HBAs of the shared storage device, should have exclusive access to the LUNs presented to the failover cluster.

▶ If multiple HBAs will be used in each failover node or in the shared-storage device, ensure that a suitable MPIO driver has been installed. The Microsoft Windows Server 2008 MPIO feature can be used to provide this function if approved by the HBA, switch, and storage device vendors and Microsoft.

▶ Shut down all nodes except one; and on that node configure the shared-storage LUNS as Windows basic disks, format as a single partition/volume for the entire span of the disk, and define an appropriate drive letter and volume label. Shut down the node used to set up the disks and bring each other node up one at a time and verify that each LUN is available. If necessary, configure the appropriate drive letter if it does not match what was configured on the first node.

▶ As required, test MPIO for load balancing and failover using the appropriate diagnostic or monitoring tool to ensure proper operation on each node one at a time.

▶ Designate a domain user account to be used for failover cluster management, and add this account to the local Administrators group on each cluster node. In the domain, grant this account the Create Computer Accounts right at the domain level to ensure that when the administrative and high-availability "service or application" groups are created, the account can create the necessary domain computer accounts.

▶ Create a spreadsheet with the network names, IP addresses, and cluster disks that will be used for the administrative cluster and the high-availability "service or application" group or groups that will be deployed in the failover cluster. Each service or application group will require a separate network name and IPv4 address. If IPv6 is used, the address can be added separately in addition to the IPv4 address or a custom or generic service or application group will need to be created.

▶ Probably most important, install the Hyper-V role on the server so that the server system is ready and configured to be a Hyper-V host server. See Chapter 4, "Installing Windows 2008 Server and the Hyper-V Role," for instructions about installing the Hyper-V role and making sure the Hyper-V host is working properly before proceeding with the cluster configuration.

After completing the tasks in the preceding list, you can install the failover cluster. Failover clusters are deployed as follows:

1. Preconfigure the nodes, as listed previously.

2. Install the failover cluster feature.

3. Run the Validate a Configuration Wizard and review the results to ensure that *all* tests pass successfully. If any tests fail, the configuration will not be supported by Microsoft and can be prone to several different types of issues and instability.

4. Run the Create a Cluster Wizard to actually deploy the administrative cluster.

5. Customize the failover cluster properties.

6. Run the High Availability Wizard to create a high-availability service or application group within the failover cluster for the Hyper-V virtualization role.

7. Test the failover cluster configuration, and back it up.

Installing the Failover Cluster Feature on a Hyper-V Host

Before a failover cluster can be deployed, the necessary feature must be installed. To install the failover cluster feature, perform the following steps:

1. Log on to the Windows Server 2008 cluster node with an account with administrator privileges.

2. Click Start, All Programs, Administrative Tools, and select Server Manager.

3. When Server Manager opens, in the tree pane select the Features node.

4. In the Tasks pane, click the Add Features link.

5. In the Add Features window, select Failover Clustering and click Next.

6. When the installation completes, click the Close button to complete the installation and return to Server Manager.

7. Close Server Manager and install the Failover Cluster feature on each of the remaining cluster nodes.

Running the Validate a Configuration Wizard

Failover cluster management is the new MMC snap-in used to administer the failover cluster feature. After the feature is installed, the next step is to run the Validate a Configuration Wizard from the Tasks pane of the Failover Cluster Management console. All nodes should be up and running when the wizard is run. To run the Validate a Configuration Wizard, perform the following steps:

1. Log on to one of the Windows Server 2008 cluster nodes with an account with administrator privileges over all nodes in the cluster.

2. Click Start, All Programs, Administrative Tools, and select Failover Cluster Management.

3. When the Failover Cluster Management console opens, click the Validate a Configuration link or the Actions Pane.

4. When the Validate a Configuration Wizard opens, click Next on the Before You Begin page.

5. In the Select Servers or a Cluster page, enter the name of a cluster node and click the Add button. Repeat this process until all nodes are added to the list, as shown in Figure 12.1, and click Next to continue.

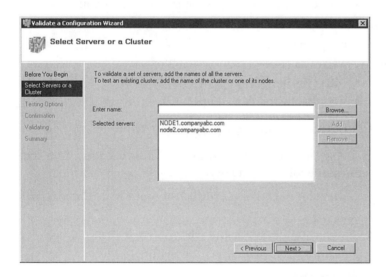

FIGURE 12.1   Adding the servers to be validated by the Validate a Configuration Wizard.

6. In the Testing Options page, read the details that explain the requirements for all tests to pass to be supported by Microsoft. Select the Run All Tests (Recommended) radio button, and then click Next to continue.

7. In the Confirmation page, review the list of servers that will be tested and the list of tests that will be performed, and then click Next to begin the testing the servers.

8. When the tests complete, the Summary window will display the results and whether the tests pass, as shown in Figure 12.2. Click Finish to complete the Validate a

Configuration Wizard. If the test failed, click the View Report button to review detailed results and determine which test failed and why.

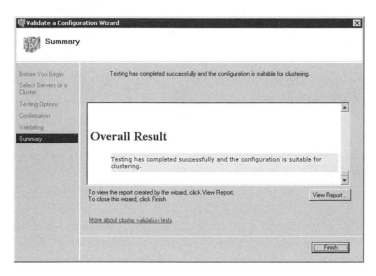

## 12

FIGURE 12.2   Successful result of the Validate a Configuration Wizard is required for Microsoft failover cluster support.

Even if the Validate a Configuration Wizard does not pass every test, you may still be able to create a cluster (depending on the test). After the Validation a Configuration Wizard is completed successfully, the cluster can be created.

Creating the Hyper-V Host Failover Cluster

When the Hyper-V host failover cluster is first created, all nodes in the cluster should be up and running. The exception to that rule is when failover clusters use direct attached storage such as SAS devices that require a process of creating the cluster on a single node and adding other nodes one at a time. For clusters that will not use shared storage or clusters that will connect to shared storage using iSCSI or Fiber Channel connections, all nodes should be powered on during cluster creation. To create the failover cluster, complete the following steps:

1. Log on to one of the Windows Server 2008 cluster nodes with an account with administrator privileges over all nodes in the cluster.

2. Click Start, All Programs, Administrative Tools, and select Failover Cluster Management.

3. When the Failover Cluster Management console opens, click the Create a Cluster link the Actions pane.

4. When the Create Cluster Wizard opens, click Next on the Before You Begin page.

5. In the Select Servers page, enter the name of each cluster node and click Add. When all the nodes are listed, click the Next button to continue.

6. In the Access Point for Administering the Cluster page, type in the name of the cluster and complete the IPv4 address and click Next, as shown in Figure 12.3.

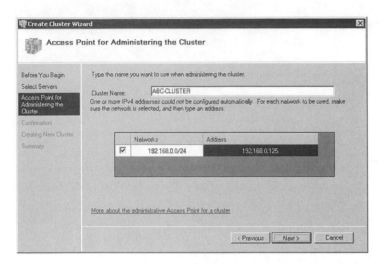

FIGURE 12.3   Defining the network name and IPv4 address for the failover cluster.

7. In the Confirmation page, review the settings, and then click Next to create the cluster.

8. In the Summary page, review the results of the cluster-creation process and click Finish to return to the Failover Cluster Management console. If there are any errors, you can click the View Report button to reveal the detailed cluster-creation report.

9. Back in the Failover Cluster Management console, select the cluster name in the tree pane. In the Tasks pane, review the configuration of the cluster.

10. In the tree pane, select and expand Nodes to list all the cluster nodes.

11. Select Storage and review the cluster storage in the Tasks pane listed under Summary of Storage, as shown in Figure 12.4.

12. Expand Networks in the tree pane to review the list of networks. Select each network and review the names of the adapters in each network.

13. After confirming that the cluster is complete, close the Failover Cluster Management console and log off of the cluster node.

After the cluster has been created, you should use the High Availability Wizard to perform additional tasks before creating any service or application groups. These tasks can include, but may not require, customizing the cluster networks, adding storage to the cluster, adding nodes to the cluster, and changing the cluster quorum model.

Configuring Cluster Networks

After the cluster has been created, you should complete several tasks to improve cluster management. One of these tasks includes customizing the cluster networks. Each node in the cluster should have the same number of network adapters, and each adapter should

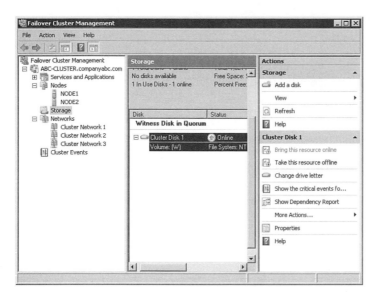

FIGURE 12.4   Displaying the dedicated cluster storage.

have already been renamed to describe a network or to easily identify which network a particular network adapter belongs to. Once the nodes are added to the failover cluster for each network card in a cluster node, there will be a corresponding cluster network. Each cluster network will be named Cluster Network 1, Cluster Network 2, and so forth for each network. Each network can be renamed and can also be configured for use by the cluster and clients, for internal cluster use only, or the network can be excluded from any cluster use. Networks and network adapters used for iSCSI communication must be excluded from cluster usage. To customize the cluster networks, complete the following steps:

1. Log on to one of the Windows Server 2008 cluster nodes with an account with administrator privileges over all nodes in the cluster.

2. Click Start, All Programs, Administrative Tools, and select Failover Cluster Management.

3. When the Failover Cluster Management console opens, if necessary type in the name of the local cluster node to connect to the cluster.

4. When the Failover Cluster Management console connects to the cluster, select and expand the cluster name.

5. Select and expand Networks in the tree pane and select Cluster Network 1 (for example).

6. In the Tasks pane, review the name of the network adapters in the network, as shown in Figure 12.5, for the iSCSI network adapters that are members of Cluster Network 1.

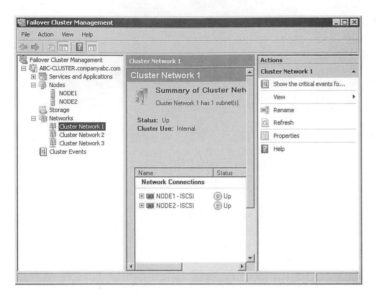

FIGURE 12.5   Displaying the network adapters in a cluster network.

7. Right-click Cluster Network 1 and select Rename. Rename the cluster to match the network adapter name.

8. For this example, right-click the renamed iSCSI network and select Properties.

9. Select the Do Not Allow the Cluster to Use This Network radio button, and then click OK, as shown in Figure 12.6.

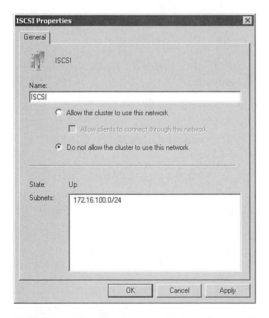

FIGURE 12.6   Configuring a network to be excluded from cluster use.

10. Back in the Failover Cluster Management console, rename the remaining cluster networks and verify that each network is configured for the proper cluster only or cluster and client communication.

11. When all the networking changes are complete, close the Failover Cluster Management console and log off of the server.

Adding Nodes to the Hyper-V Host Cluster

After the first node of a Hyper-V host cluster has been installed and configured, additional nodes need to be added to the cluster to provide the failover server for the initial node. To add additional nodes after the initial cluster creation process, follow these steps:

1. Log on to one of the Windows Server 2008 cluster nodes with an account with administrator privileges over all nodes in the cluster.

2. Click Start, All Programs, Administrative Tools, and select Failover Cluster Management.

3. When the Failover Cluster Management console opens, if necessary type in the name of the local cluster node to connect to the cluster.

4. When the Failover Cluster Management console connects to the cluster, select and expand the cluster name.

5. Select and expand Nodes in the tree pane.

6. Right-click Nodes and select Add Node.

7. When the Add Node Wizard opens, click Next on the Before You Begin page.

8. In the Select Server page, type in the name of the cluster node and click the Add button. When the node is added to the list, click Next to continue.

9. In the Confirmation page, review the names of the node or nodes that will be added and click Next to continue.

10. When the process completes, review the results in the Summary page, and then click Finish to close the wizard.

11. Close the Failover Cluster Management console and log off of the server.

Adding Storage to the Cluster

When shared storage is used with failover clusters, all the LUNs or targets presented to the cluster hosts may not have been added to the cluster during the initial configuration. When this is the case, and additional storage needs to be added to the cluster, perform the following steps:

1. Log on to one of the Windows Server 2008 cluster nodes with an account with administrator privileges over all nodes in the cluster.

2. Click Start, All Programs, Administrative Tools, and select Failover Cluster Management.

3. When the Failover Cluster Management console opens, if necessary type in the name of the local cluster node to connect to the cluster.

4. In the tree pane, select Storage, right-click Storage, and select Add a Disk.

5. If suitable storage is ready to be added to the cluster, it will be listed in the Add Disks to a Cluster window. If a disk is listed, check the box next to the desired disk or disks and click OK to add the disks to the cluster.

6. Once the process completes, if necessary change the drive letter of the new disk.

7. Close the Failover Cluster Management console.

8. Click the Start button and select Computer.

9. Review the list of disks on the cluster node and note that disks managed by the cluster are listed as clustered disks rather than local disks, as shown in Figure 12.7. This is a distinct change from server clusters in Windows Server 2003.

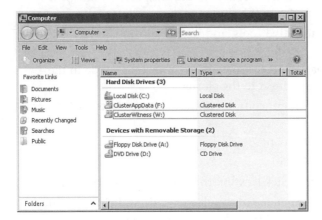

FIGURE 12.7   Displaying the local and cluster disks on a cluster node.

10. Close the Explorer windows and log off of the server.

Cluster Quorum Configuration

If all of the cluster nodes and the shared storage were available during the creation of the cluster, the best suited quorum model was automatically selected during the cluster-creation process. When the existing cluster quorum is need to be validated or changed, perform the following steps:

1. Log on to one of the Windows Server 2008 cluster nodes with an account with administrator privileges over all nodes in the cluster.

2. Click Start, All Programs, Administrative Tools, and select Failover Cluster Management.

3. When the Failover Cluster Management console opens, if necessary type in the name of the local cluster node to connect to the cluster.

4. In the tree pane, select the cluster name, and in the Tasks pane, the current quorum model will be listed.

5. Review the current quorum model. If it is correct, close the Failover Cluster Management console.

6. If the current Quorum model is not the desired model, right-click the cluster name in the tree pane, click More Actions, and select Configure Cluster Quorum Settings.

7. In the Select Quorum Configuration page, select the desired quorum model radio button or select the radio button of the recommended model, and then click Next to continue, as shown in Figure 12.8.

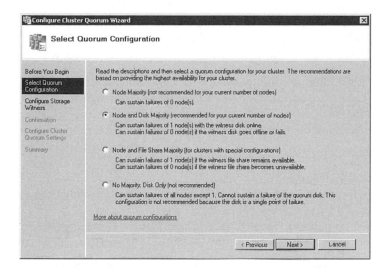

FIGURE 12.8   Configuring the cluster quorum mode for a failover cluster.

8. If a quorum model contains a witness disk or file share, select the designated disk or specify the path to the file share and click Next.

9. In the Confirmation page, review the settings and click Next to update the cluster quorum model for the failover cluster.

10. Review the results in the Summary page, and then click Finish to return to the Failover Cluster Management console.

11. Close the Failover Cluster Management console and log off of the server.

Creating a Virtual Guest Session on the Host Cluster

Once the desired cluster configuration is achieved, the cluster is ready for virtual guest sessions to be installed on the host cluster configuration. Follow the steps covered in Chapter 5, "Installing a Guest Session on Hyper-V," to build the guest session. The steps for creating the guest session on Hyper-V are identical, with the exception of the following areas to note:

▶ Make sure that when the guest session is created, the guest session image is stored on the shared storage of the Hyper-V failover cluster environment.

▶ Ensure that the network adapter chosen for the guest session is tied to a physical network adapter, not on a virtual switch specific to the host server system.

The virtual guest operating system and application can be installed, and after the guest session is booted and running, install the integration tools for the operating system to make sure the latest drivers and options specific to the operating system have been properly installed.

Configuring Start Actions and Making the Virtual Guest Highly Available

After the virtual guest session has been installed and configured to operate properly, certain settings need to be configured on the Hyper-V host server to make the virtual guest session highly available, and to set the proper start actions on the guest session.

The first step is to configure the automatic start action on the Hyper-V host. The automatic start action identifies whether a guest session will automatically start when the host server is started, or whether the guest session will wait until the guest session is manually started after a Hyper-V host server reboot. Normally, if the Hyper-V host server reboots, the administrator wants to make sure the guest sessions also automatically start so that someone does not have to manually intervene to get guest sessions running. With Hyper-V, however, the high-availability function of the Hyper-V host server configuration automatically starts managed guest sessions, because the cluster needs to choose which host node is managing the guest session. You don't want both hosts trying to turn on or manage the guest session. Therefore, in the case of Hyper-V host failover clustering, the guest session automatic start action is disabled.

To configure the automatic start action for a virtual guest session, complete the following steps:

1. Log on to one of the Windows Server 2008 cluster nodes with an account with administrator privileges over all nodes in the cluster.

2. Click Start, All Programs, Administrative Tools, and select Hyper-V Administration to launch the Hyper-V management tool.

3. In the Hyper-V management tool, under Virtual Machines, right-click Failover Test, and then click Settings.

4. In the leftmost pane, click Automatic Start Action.

5. Under What Do You Want This Virtual Machine to Do When the Physical Computer Starts?, click Nothing, and then click Apply.

The next step is to make the virtual machines highly available. This is specific to Hyper-V and is the overall failover cluster control that determines which Hyper-V host server is in control of the guest sessions. Windows Server 2008 provides several out-of-box cluster resources that can be used to deploy Windows services and applications using failover clusters for services beyond Hyper-V (including cluster high availability for DHCP servers, file servers, DFS servers, and the like, as shown in Figure 12.9).

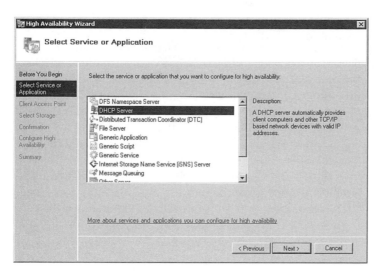

FIGURE 12.9   Windows Server 2008 built-in cluster services and applications resources.

To select and configure the services or application settings, run the High Availability Wizard as follows:

1. Log on to one of the Windows Server 2008 cluster nodes with an account with administrator privileges over all nodes in the cluster.

2. Click Start, All Programs, Administrative Tools, and select Failover Cluster Management.

3. When the Failover Cluster Management console opens, if necessary type in the name of the local cluster node to connect to the cluster.

4. In the tree pane, select the cluster name, expand it, and select Services and Applications.

5. Right-click Services and Applications and select Configure a Service or Application.

6. In the High Availability Wizard that opens, click Next in the Before You Begin page.

7. Select the Virtual Machine option from the Service or Application page, and click Next to continue. If the Hyper-V role has not been installed yet on each node prior to selecting the desired entry, an error will display, and the process cannot continue.

8. Review the settings in the Confirmation page, and then click Next to deploy the service on the failover cluster.

9. When prompted, click Finish to close the wizard.

10. In the tree pane, expand Services and Applications to reveal the new group, right-click the virtual machine name, and click Bring This Service or Application Online. Doing so brings the virtual machine online and starts the guest session.

Configuring Failover and Failback

Clusters that contain two or more nodes automatically have failover configured for each service or application group as long as each node has the Hyper-V role installed and supports running the group locally. Failback is never configured by default and needs to be manually configured for each service or application group if desired. Failback allows a designated preferred server or "preferred owner" to always run a particular cluster group when it is available. When the preferred owner fails and the affected groups fail over to an alternate node, once the preferred node is back online and functioning as desired the failback configuration options are used to determine whether the group will automatically fail back immediately or after a specified period. Also, with regard to failover and failback configuration, the failover and failback properties define how many failures in a specified number of hours will be tolerated before the group is taken offline and remains offline. To review and if necessary change the failover and failback configuration options on a particular service or application group, perform the following steps:

1. Log on to one of the Windows Server 2008 cluster nodes with an account with administrator privileges over all nodes in the cluster.

2. Click Start, All Programs, Administrative Tools, and select Failover Cluster Management.

3. When the Failover Cluster Management console opens, if necessary type in the name of the local cluster node to connect to the cluster.

4. In the tree pane, select the cluster name, expand it, and select Services and Applications.

5. Expand Services and Applications and right-click the desired group and select Properties. For this example, the ABC-CLUSTER-P5 Hyper-V cluster group is used.

6. In the ABC-CLUSTER-P5 group properties on the General tab, in the Preferred Owner section, check the box next to the desired node if failback will be configured. Do not close the group property window.

7. Select the Failover tab and review the number of allowed failures in a specified number of hours. The default is two group failures allowed in six hours.

8. In the lower section of the page, if desired enable failback and configure whether failback will be allowed and whether it will occur immediately when the preferred node is online or if the failback can occur only during after hours, such as between the hours of 9 p.m. and 6 a.m. or 17 and 6, as shown in Figure 12.10.

NOTE

To reduce the chance of having a group failing back to a node during regular business hours after a failure, configure the failback schedule to allow failback only during non-peak times or after hours using settings similar to those made in Figure 12.10 and based on the organization's work hours and automated backup schedule.

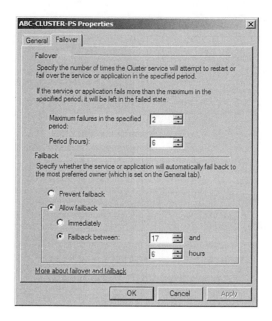

FIGURE 12.10   Configuring a services or application failover threshold and failback configuration.

Testing Failover Clusters

After all the desired cluster nodes are added to the failover cluster and failover and failback configuration options are set for each service or application group, each group should be verified for proper operation on each cluster node. For these tests to be complete, failover and, when applicable, failback of cluster groups need to be tested. They can be tested by simulating a cluster resource failure or by manually moving the service or application groups between nodes.

Testing Services and Applications Groups Using Manual Failover

To manually fail over or move a service or application group between failover cluster nodes, perform the following steps:

1. Log on to one of the Windows Server 2008 cluster nodes with an account with administrator privileges over all nodes in the cluster.

2. Click Start, All Programs, Administrative Tools, and select Failover Cluster Management.

3. When the Failover Cluster Management console opens, if necessary type in the name of the local cluster node to connect to the cluster.

4. In the tree pane, select the cluster name, expand it, and select Services and Applications.

5. Expand Services and Applications and select the desired group. For this example, the ABC-CLUSTER-PS Hyper-V server group is used.

6. In the Tasks pane, note the current owner of the group.

7. In the tree pane, right-click the desired group, select Move This Service or Application to Another Node, and select any of the desired available nodes, as shown in Figure 12.11, for use to move the group to node 2.

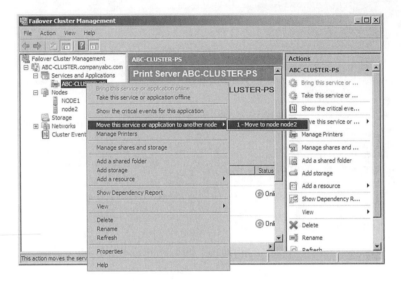

FIGURE 12.11   Moving a service or application group to another available node.

8. The group will be moved to the chosen node, and when the group is back online it will be reflected as Status: Online in the Tasks pane. Close the Failover Cluster Management console and log off of the server.

Simulating the Failure of a Cluster Resource

Simulating a cluster resource failure can be easily accomplished using the Failover Cluster Management console. Each resource will have its own properties, and simulating a failure will usually just initiate the startup or restoration of the resource back to an online state. When the failure threshold is reached, the service or application group will be taken offline, moved to another available node, and brought back online. To simulate the failure of a cluster resource and test the failover of a group, perform the following steps:

1. Log on to one of the Windows Server 2008 cluster nodes with an account with administrator privileges over all nodes in the cluster.

2. Click Start, All Programs, Administrative Tools, and select Failover Cluster Management.

3. When the Failover Cluster Management console opens, if necessary type in the name of the local cluster node to connect to the cluster.

4. In the tree pane, select the cluster name, expand it, and select Nodes.

5. Select More Actions, and then click Stop Cluster Service. Doing so stops the cluster service on the Hyper-V Host server system.

6. The virtual machine service will be moved to the other node of the Hyper-V cluster, with user services remaining operational.

Failover Cluster Maintenance

Services and applications are deployed on failover cluster based on the fact that they are critical to business operations. The reliability of each cluster node is very important, and making any changes to the software or hardware configuration of each node can compromise this reliability. Before any changes are implemented on a production failover cluster, a few premaintenance tasks should be performed.

Premaintenance Tasks

Before maintenance is run on a cluster node or the entire failover cluster, several tasks should be completed. To prepare a cluster node for maintenance, complete the following steps:

1. Whether you're planning a software or hardware upgrade, research to see whether the changes will be supported on Windows Server 2008 failover clusters.

2. Log on to one of the Windows Server 2008 cluster nodes with an account with administrator privileges over all nodes in the cluster.

3. Click Start, All Programs, Administrative Tools, and select Failover Cluster Management.

4. When the Failover Cluster Management console opens, if necessary type in the name of the local cluster node to connect to the cluster.

5. In the tree pane, select the cluster name, and in the tree pane note the current host server. If the current host server is the node that will be taken offline for maintenance, the cluster will be automatically moved to an alternate node if the maintenance node is rebooted.

6. In the tree pane, select and expand Services and Applications to reveal each of the groups.

7. Select each group, and in the Tasks pane, note which node is the current owner of the move. Manually move each group to the node that will remain online if any of the groups are currently running on the node that will be taken offline for maintenance.

8. After all the groups have been moved to a node that will remain online, in the tree pane expand Nodes to reveal all the nodes in the failover cluster.

9. Locate the node that will be taken offline for maintenance, right-click the node, and select Pause.

10. When the node is paused, resources cannot fail over and come online and the system can have the software and hardware configuration or updates applied and, if necessary, rebooted.

11. When the maintenance tasks are complete, the node can be configured to be active in the failover cluster by right-clicking the node in the Failover Cluster Management console and selecting Resume.

12. When the node resumes operation, if necessary move the groups to this node and perform the maintenance tasks on the remaining nodes in the cluster.

13. After completing the maintenance tasks on all the failover cluster nodes, close Failover Cluster Management and log off of the server.

Removing Nodes from a Failover Cluster

Cluster nodes can be removed from a cluster for a number of reasons, and this process can be accomplished quite easily.

> **NOTE**
>
> If you're removing nodes from a cluster that uses the Node Majority Quorum model, be sure that a majority of the nodes remain available; otherwise, the cluster may be shut down. If this is not possible, you might need to change the quorum model before removing a node from the failover cluster.

To remove a node from a failover cluster, follow these steps:

1. Log on to one of the Windows Server 2008 cluster nodes with an account with administrator privileges over all nodes in the cluster.

2. Click Start, All Programs, Administrative Tools, and select Failover Cluster Management.

3. When the Failover Cluster Management console opens, if necessary type in the name of the local cluster node to connect to the cluster.

4. In the tree pane, select the cluster name, expand it, and select Nodes.

5. Expand nodes to reveal all the cluster nodes.

6. Right-click the node that will be removed from the cluster, select More Actions, and click Evict.

7. A Confirmation window will open. Select the option to evict the desired node from the cluster. When the process starts, if the cluster or any service or application groups are running on this node, they will be moved to a remaining node before this node is removed from the cluster.

8. After removing the node, close Failover Cluster Management and log off of the server.

Backing Up and Restoring Failover Clusters

Windows Server 2008 contains a rebuilt backup program appropriately named Windows Server Backup. Windows Server Backup can be used to back up each cluster node and any cluster disks that are currently online on the local node. In addition, the system state of the cluster node can be backed up individually or as part of a complete system backup.

To successfully back up and restore the entire cluster or a single cluster node, the cluster administrator must first understand how to troubleshoot, back up, and restore a stand-alone Windows Server 2008 system using Windows Server Backup. The process of backing up cluster nodes is the same as for a standalone server, but restoring a cluster may require additional steps or configurations that do not apply to a standalone server. To be prepared to recover from different types of cluster failures, you must complete the following tasks on each cluster node:

▶ Back up each cluster node's local disks.

▶ Back up each cluster node's system state.

▶ Back up the cluster quorum from any node running in the cluster.

▶ For failover clusters using shared storage, back up shared cluster disks from the node the disk are currently hosted on.

Failover Cluster Node Backup Best Practices

As a backup best practice for cluster nodes, administrators should strive to back up every-thing as frequently as possible. Because cluster availability is so important, here are some recommendations for cluster node backup:

▶ Back up each cluster node's system state daily and immediately before and after a cluster configuration change is made.

▶ Back up cluster local drives and system state daily if the schedule permits or weekly if daily backups cannot be performed.

▶ Back up cluster shared drives daily if the schedule permits or weekly if daily backups cannot be performed.

▶ Using Windows Server Backup, perform a full system backup before any major changes occur and monthly if possible. If a full system backup is scheduled using Windows Server Backup, this task is already being performed.

Restoring an Entire Cluster to a Previous State

Changes to a cluster should be made with caution and, if at all possible, should be tested in a nonproduction isolated lab environment first. When cluster changes have been implemented and deliver undesirable effects, the way to roll back the cluster configuration to a previous state is to restore the cluster configuration to all nodes. This process is simpler than it sounds and is performed from only one node. There are only two caveats to this process:

▶ All the cluster nodes that were members of the cluster previously need to be currently available and operational in the cluster. For example, if Cluster1 was made up of Server1 and Server2, both of these nodes need to be active in the cluster before the previous cluster configuration can be rolled back.

▶ To restore a previous cluster configuration to all cluster nodes, the entire cluster needs to be taken offline long enough to restore the backup, reboot the node from which the backup was run, and manually start the cluster service on all remaining nodes.

To restore an entire cluster to a previous state, complete the following steps:

1. Log on to one of the Windows Server 2008 cluster nodes with an account with administrator privileges over all nodes in the cluster. This example assumes the node has a full system backup available for recovery.

2. Click Start, All Programs, Accessories, and select Command Prompt.

3. At the command prompt, enter **wbadmin get versions** to reveal the list of available backups. For this example, our back version is named 10/30/07-18:28.

4. When the correct backup version is known, type the command **wbadmin Start Recovery -version:10/30/07-18:28 -ItemType:App -Item:Cluster** and press Enter.

5. WBadmin will return a prompt stating that this command will perform an authoritative restore of the cluster, as shown in Figure 12.12. Type in **Y** and press Enter to start the authoritative cluster restore.

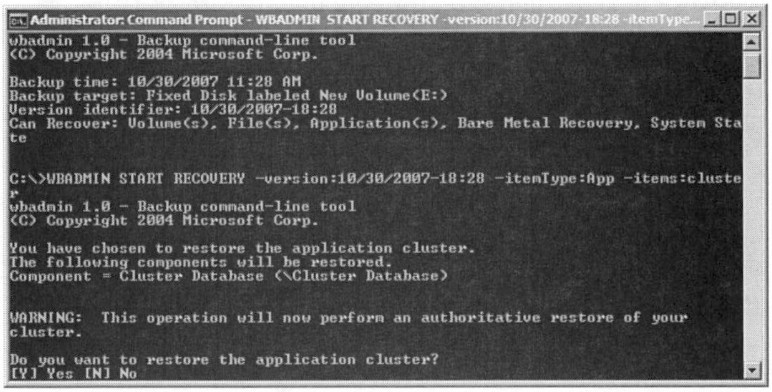

FIGURE 12.12   Performing an authoritative restore of the cluster configuration.

6. When the restore completes, each node in the cluster must have the cluster service started to complete the process. This can be performed on the local node in the command prompt window by typing the command Net **Start ClusSvc** and pressing Enter. Repeat the process on all the remaining cluster nodes.

7. Open the Failover Cluster Management console to verify that the restore has completed successfully. Close the console and log out of the server when done.

Summary

A highly available and fault-tolerant environment for virtualization is one that blends traditional application redundancy along with sophisticated clustering capabilities available for both the Hyper-V guests and hosts. When an application has built-in technologies for replication and high availability such as a domain controller, global catalog server, load-balanced web server, or even SQL Server mirroring or Exchange 2007 Continuous Replication, leveraging the built-in technology for guest sessions works extremely well in protecting the state of an application seamlessly and natively to the application.

When clustering is a better method for an application, configuring virtual guest clustering of the application can provide high availability of the application, and Windows 2008 stretch clustering can extend high availability across a WAN for combined high availability and disaster recovery in a single solution.

And for organizations that take a virtual host perspective on protecting all the guest sessions on a given host server, or for applications that do not have built-in redundancy or clustering capabilities, Hyper-V host clustering with shared storage enables an organization to fail over all the guest sessions of the host server to another cluster node on the network.

Best Practices

The following are best practices from this chapter:

- ▶ Consider using the native built-in high-availability and disaster-recovery capabilities of an application (for services such as global catalog services, domain controller services, NLB web server services, and the like) to leverage the simple managed recoverability technologies built in to the applications before implementing a more complicated clustering (host or guest) solution.

- ▶ Leverage clustering at the virtual guest session level for applications that have high availability of the application with superior support for application clustering (such as Exchange, SQL, SharePoint, and the like).

- ▶ Evaluate the use of Windows 2008 stretch clusters for virtual guest sessions where cluster nodes can be placed in multiple sites, thus providing both a high-availability clustered environment along with a redundant site model for disaster recovery.

- ▶ Use Windows Server 2008 failover clusters within a virtual guest session to provide application-level redundancy and recoverability for enterprise messaging, databases, and file and print services and other networking services.

- ▶ Purchase quality server, network hardware, and shared-storage devices and HBAs that are certified for Windows Server 2008 when deploying Hyper-V host failover clusters.

- ▶ Deploy cluster node operating systems on fault-tolerant disk arrays.

▶ If iSCSI is used for shared storage, ensure that any network adapters used for iSCSI communication are excluded from any cluster usage.

▶ Rename and clearly label all network adapters on each cluster node and configure static IPv4 and if necessary IPv6 addresses.

▶ Configure the appropriate cluster quorum model (and, hopefully, the recommended model) that is right for the deployment.

▶ Use multiple network cards in each node so that one card can be dedicated to internal cluster communication (private/heartbeat network), while the other can be used only for client connectivity and cluster communication.

▶ If failback is required, configure the failback schedule to allow failback only during nonpeak times or after hours to reduce the chance of having a group failing back to a node during regular business hours.

▶ Thoroughly test failover and failback mechanisms.

▶ Carefully consider backing up and restoring a cluster, and do not deploy any clusters until a tested and documented backup and recovery plan exists.

Debugging and Problem Solving the Hyper-V Host and Guest Operating System

Up until this chapter, this book has focused on planning and implementing the Hyper-V host and guest sessions. This chapter pays attention to the built-in management tools for monitoring, logging, debugging, and validating reliability, which help organizations identify and isolate problems in their Hyper-V and networking environments. Unlike other Windows application servers where the analysis of problems on a server is typically isolated to a specific application, whether that is SharePoint, or Exchange, or global catalog services, for Hyper-V, because the host server acts as the basis of a full network, and guest sessions can be running a variety of applications, the debugging and problem-solving efforts take on the same task of assessing problems in a full enterprise network.

Many of the tools identified in this chapter are similar to those used in Windows Server 2003; however, as with most features of the Windows Server family of products, the features and functionality of the tools have been improved and expanded upon in Windows 2008.

This chapter covers the Task Manager for logging and debugging issues, the new Event Viewer for monitoring and troubleshooting system issues, the completely redesigned Performance and Reliability Monitoring tool, and additional debugging tools available with Windows 2008.

Using the Task Manager for Logging and Debugging

The Task Manager is a familiar monitoring tool found in Windows 2008. Ultimately, the tool is similar to the Task Manager included with earlier versions of Windows such as Windows Server 2003. It still provides an instant view of system resources, such as processor activity, process activity, memory usage, networking activity, user information, and resource consumption. However, there are some noticeable changes, including the addition of a Services tab and the ability to launch the Resource Monitor directly from the Performance tab.

The Windows 2008 Task Manager is useful for an immediate view of key system operations. It comes in handy when a user notes slow response time, system problems, or other nondescript problems with the network. With just a quick glance at the Task Manager, you can see whether a server is using all available disk, processor, memory, or networking resources.

There are three ways to launch the Task Manager:

▶ **Method 1**—Right-click the taskbar and select Task Manager.

▶ **Method 2**—Press Ctrl+Shift+Esc.

▶ **Method 3**—Press Ctrl+Alt+Del, and select Start Task Manager.

When the Task Manager loads, you will notice six tabs, as shown in Figure 13.1.

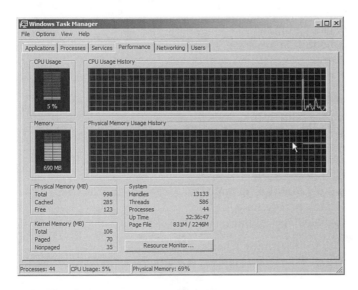

FIGURE 13.1　The Windows Task Manager.

13

> **TIP**
>
> If you are working on other applications and want to hide the Task Manager, deselect Always on Top in the Task Manager's Options menu. In addition, select Hide When Minimized to Keep the Task Manager off the taskbar when minimized.

The following sections provide a closer look at how helpful the Task Manager components can be.

Monitoring Applications

The first tab on the Task Manager is the Applications tab. The Applications tab provides a list of tasks in the left column and the status of these applications in the right column. The status information enables you to determine whether an application is running and allows you to terminate an application that is not responding. To stop such an application, highlight the particular application and click End Task at the bottom of the Task Manager. You can also switch to another application if you have several applications running. To do so, highlight the program and click Switch To at the bottom of the Task Manager. Finally, you can create a dump file that can be used when a point-in-time snapshot of every process running is needed for advanced troubleshooting. To create a dump file, right-click an application and select Create Dump File.

Monitoring Processes

The second Task Manager tab is the Processes tab. It provides a list of running processes, or image names, on the server. It also measures the performance in simple data format. This information includes CPU percent used, memory allocated to each process, and username used in initiating a process, which includes system, local, and network services.

You can sort the processes by clicking the CPU or Memory (Private Working Set) column header. The processes are then sorted in order of usage. This way, you can tell which one is using the most of these resources and is slowing down performance of your server. You can terminate a process by selecting the process and clicking the End Process button.

Many other performance or process measures can be removed or added to the Processes tab. They include, but are not limited to, process identifier (PID), CPU time, session ID, and page faults. To add these measures, select View, Select Columns to open the Select Column property page. Here, you can add process counters to the process list or remove them from the list.

Monitoring Services

The newest edition to the family of Task Manager tabs is the Services tab. When selected, you can quickly assess and troubleshoot a specific service by viewing whether it has stopped or is still running. The Services tab also offers additional key details, including the service name, service description, and service group. In addition, it is also possible to launch the Services snap-in if there is a need to make changes to a specific service. For example, if you know a given service should be running and you don't see it running on the Processes tab (a common one is spoolsvc.exe, which is the Windows Print Spooler service executable), you can just go to the Services tab and attempt to start the service from there. It's very rudimentary; but in keeping with what Task Manager is typically used for, it does offer a quick overview of system status and preliminary problem resolution.

Monitoring Performance

The Performance tab enables you to view the CPU and physical memory usage in graphical form. This information proves especially useful when you need a quick view of a performance bottleneck.

The Performance tab makes it possible to graph a percentage of processor time in Kernel mode. To show this, select View, Show Kernel Times. The kernel time is represented by the red line in the graph. The kernel time is the measure of time that applications are using operating system services. The other processor time is known as User mode. User mode processor time is spent in threads that are spawned by applications on the system.

If your server has multiple CPU processors installed, you can view multiple CPU graphs at a time by selecting View, CPU History and choosing either One Graph Per CPU or One Graph, All CPUs.

Also on the Performance tab, you will find a button labeled Resource Monitor. You can invoke Resource Monitor for additional analysis of the system.

Monitoring Network Performance

The Networking tab provides a measurement of the network traffic for each adapter on the local server in graphical form, as shown in Figure 13.2.

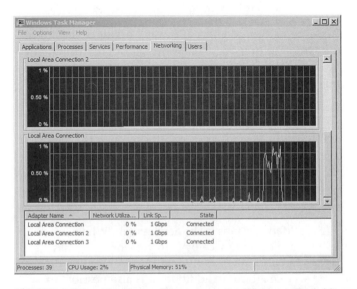

FIGURE 13.2   The Networking tab on the Windows Task Manager.

For multiple network adapters—whether they are dial-up, a local area network (LAN) connection, a wide area network (WAN) connection, a virtual private network (VPN) connection, or the like—the Networking tab displays a graphical comparison of the traffic for each connection. It provides a quick overview of the adapter, network utilization, link speed, and state of your connection.

To show a visible line on the graph for network traffic on any interface, the view automatically scales to magnify the view of traffic versus available bandwidth. The graph scales from 0% to 100% if the Auto Scale option is not enabled. The greater the percentage shown on the graph, the less is the magnified view of the current traffic. To autoscale and capture network traffic, select Options, Auto Scale.

It is possible to break down traffic on the graph into Bytes Sent, Received, and Total Bytes by selecting View, Network Adapter History and checking the selections you want graphed. This can be useful if you determine the overall throughput is high and you need to quickly determine whether inbound or outbound traffic is an issue. In this situation, the default setting is displayed in Total Bytes.

You can also add more column headings by selecting View, Select Columns. Various network measures can be added or removed; they include Bytes Throughput, Bytes Sent/Interval, Unicast Sent and Received, and so on.

TIP

If you suspect a possible network server problem, launch the Task Manager and quickly glance at the CPU utilization, memory available, process utilization, and network utilization information. When the utilization of any or all of these items exceeds 60% to 70%, there might be a bottleneck or overutilization of the resource. However, if all the utilization information shows demand being less than 5%, the problem is probably not related to server operations.

Monitoring User Activity

The final tab on the Task Manager is the Users tab, which displays a list of the users who are connected to or logged on to the server, session status, and names. The Hyper-V host typically doesn't have users logged in to the host system, but guest sessions and the applications running on the guest sessions may have users logged on to access Web services, email messages, file and print content, and the like. So this function may be more applicable to Hyper-V guests than to the Hyper-V host itself. The following five columns are available on the Users tab:

▶ **User**—Shows the users logged on the server. As long as the user is not connected via a console session, it is possible to remote control the session or send a message. Remote control can be initiated by right-clicking the user and selecting Remote Control. The level of control is dictated by the security settings configured in Remote Desktop.

▶ **ID**—Displays the numeric ID that identifies the session on the server.

▶ **Client Name**—Specifies the name of the client computer using the session, if applicable.

▶ **Status**—Displays the current status of a session. Sessions can be either Active or Disconnected.

▶ **Session**—Displays which session the user is logged on with.

Using Event Viewer for Logging and Debugging

Event Viewer is the next tool to use when debugging, problem solving, or troubleshooting to resolve a problem with a Windows 2008 system. Event Viewer, as shown in Figure 13.3, is a built-in Windows 2008 tool completely rewritten based on an Extensible Markup Language (XML) infrastructure, which is used for gathering troubleshooting information and conduction diagnostics. Event Viewer has been completely rewritten in Windows 2008, and many new features and functionality have been introduced, including a new user interface and a home page, which includes an overview and summary of the system.

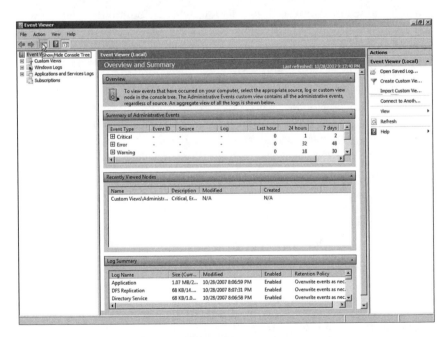

FIGURE 13.3   Event Viewer, including the Overview and Summary pane.

The upcoming sections focus on the basic elements of an event, including detailed sections covering the new features and functionality.

Microsoft defines an *event* as any significant occurrence in the operating system or an application that requires tracking of the information. An event is not always negative. A successful logon to the network, a successful transfer of messages, or replication of data can also generate an event in Windows. It is important to sift through the events to determine which are informational events and which are critical events that require attention.

When server or application failures occur, Event Viewer is one of the first places to check for information. Event Viewer can be used to monitor, track, view, and audit security of your server and network. It is used to track information of both hardware and software contained in your server. The information provided in Event Viewer can be a good starting point to identify and track down the root cause of any system errors or problems.

Event Viewer can be accessed through the Administrative Tools menu, or by right-clicking the My Computer icon on the desktop and selecting Manage, or by expanding the Diagnostics section of the new Server Manager MMC snap-in. You can also launch Event Viewer by running the Microsoft Management Console (Start, Run, **mmc.exe**, and adding the snap-in) or through a command line by running eventvwr.msc.

Each log has common properties associated with its events. The following bullets define these properties:

- ▶ **Level**—This property defines the severity of the event. An icon appears next to each type of event. It helps to quickly identify whether the event is informational, a warning, or an error.

- ▶ **Date and Time**—This property indicates the date and time that the event occurred. You can sort events by date and time by clicking this column. This information proves particularly helpful in tracing back an incident that occurred in the past, such as a hardware upgrade before your server started experiencing problems.

- ▶ **Source**—This property identifies the source of the event, which can be an application, remote access, a service, and so on. The source is useful in determining what caused the event.

- ▶ **Event ID**—Each event has an associated event ID, which is a numeral generated by the source and is unique to each type of event. You can use the event ID on the Microsoft Support website (www.microsoft.com/technet/) to find topics and solutions related to an event on your server.

- ▶ **Task Category**—This property determines the category of an event. Task Category examples from the Security log include Logon/Logoff, System, Object Access, and others.

Examining the New Event Viewer User Interface

The interface for Event Viewer in Windows 2008 has changed significantly from earlier versions. Although the information produced by logged events remains much the same, it's important to be familiar with the new interface to take advantage of the new features and functionality.

Administrators accustomed to using the latest Microsoft Management Console (MMC) 3.0 will notice similarities in the new look and feel of the Event Viewer user interface. The navigation tree on the leftmost pane of the Event Viewer window lists the events and logs available to view and also introduces new folders for creating custom event views and subscriptions from remote systems. The central Details pane, located in the center of the console, displays relevant event information based on the folder selected in the navigation tree. The central Details pane also includes a new layout to bolster the administrator's experience by summarizing administrative events by date and criticality, providing log summaries, and displaying recently viewed nodes. Finally, the Tasks pane, located on the extreme right side of the window, contains context-sensitive actions depending on the focus in the Event Viewer snap-in.

The folders residing in the leftmost pane of the Event Viewer are organized by the following elements:

▶ Custom Views

▶ Windows Logs

▶ Applications and Services Logs

▶ Subscriptions

The Custom Views Folder

Custom views are filters either created automatically by Windows 2008 when new server roles or applications such as Active Directory Certificate Services, DHCP Server, and Office 2007 are added to the system or manually by administrators. It is important for administrators to have the ability to create filters that target only the events they are interested in viewing to quickly diagnose and remediate issues on the Windows 2008 system and infrastructure. By expanding the Custom Views folder in the Event Viewer navigation tree and right-clicking Administrative Events, selecting Properties, and clicking the Edit Filter button, you can see how information from the event log is parsed into a set of filtered events. The Custom View Properties Filter tab is displayed in Figure 13.4. In the built-in Administrative Events custom views, all critical, error, and warning events are captured for all event logs. Instead of looking at the large number of informational logs captured by Windows 2008 and cycling through each Windows log, this filter gives the administrator a single place to go and quickly check for any potential problems contained on the system.

Also listed in the Custom View section of Event Viewer are predefined filters created by Windows 2008 when new roles are added to the system. These queries cannot be edited; however, they provide events related to all Windows 2008 roles and can be used to quickly drill down into issues affecting the performance of the system as it relates to specific server roles. Again, this is a way of helping an administrator find the information needed to identify and ultimately resolve server problems quickly and efficiently.

Creating a New Custom View

To create a new custom view, in Event Viewer right-click the Custom View folder and select Create Custom View. Alternatively, select Custom View from the Action menu. This results in the Custom View Properties box, as illustrated in Figure 13.4.

First, decide whether you want to filter events based on date; if so, specify the date range by using the Logged drop-down list. Options include Any Time, Custom Range, and specific time intervals. The next step is to specify the Event Level criteria to include in the custom view. Options include Critical, Error, Warning, Information, and Verbose. After the

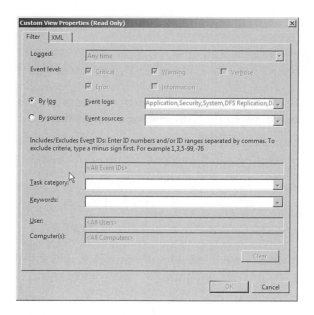

FIGURE 13.4   The Filter tab located in the Custom View Properties page.

Event Level settings are specified, the next area to focus on is the By Log and By Source sections. By leveraging the drop-down lists, specify the event log and event log sources to be included in this custom filter. To further refine the custom filter, enter specific event IDs, task categories, keywords, users, computers, and then click OK and save the filter by providing it a name, description, and the location of where to save the view.

> **TIP**
>
> Performance and memory consumption will be negatively affected if you have included too many events in the custom view.

After the custom view is defined, it can be exported as an XML file, which can then be imported into other systems. Filters can also be written or modified directly in XML, but keep in mind that after a filter has been modified using the XML tab, it can no longer be edited using the GUI described previously.

The Windows Logs Folder

The Windows Logs folder contains the traditional application, security, and system logs. Windows 2008 also introduces two new out-of-the-box logs, which can also be found under the Windows Logs folder—the Setup and Forwarded Events logs. The following is a brief description of the different types of Windows logs that are available:

▶ **Application log**—This log contains events based on applications or programs residing on the system.

▶ **Security log**—Depending on the auditing settings configured, the Security log captures events specific to authentication and object access.

▶ **Setup log**—This new log captures information tailored toward installation of applications, server roles, and features.

▶ **System log**—Failures associated with Windows system components are logged to the System log. This might include driver errors or other components failing to load.

▶ **Forwarded Events log**—Because computers can experience the same issues, this new feature consolidates and stores events captured from remote computers into a single log to facilitate problem isolation, identification, and remediation.

The Applications and Services Logs Folder

The Applications and Services Logs folder introduces a new way to logically organize, present, and store events based on a specific Windows application, component, or service instead of capturing events that affect the whole system. An administrator can easily drill into a specific item such as DFS Replication or DNS Server and easily review those events without being bombarded or overwhelmed by all the other systemwide events.

These logs include fours subtypes: Admin, Operational, Analytic, and Debug logs. The events found in Admin logs are geared toward end users, administrators, and support personnel. This log is very useful because it not only describes a problem, but also identifies ways to deal with the issues. Operational logs are also a benefit to systems administrators, but they typically require more interpretation.

Analytic and Debug logs are more complex. Analytic logs trace an issue and often a high number of events are captured. Debug logs are primarily used by developers to debug applications. Both Analytic and Debug logs are hidden and disabled by default. To view them, right-click Applications and Services Logs, and then select View, Show Analytic and Debug Logs.

The Subscriptions Folder

The final folder in the Event Viewer console tree is called Subscriptions. Subscriptions is another new feature included with the Windows 2008 Event Viewer. It allows remote computers to forward events; therefore, they can be viewed locally from a central system. For example, if you are experiencing issues between two Windows 2008 systems, diagnosing the problem becomes challenging because both systems typically log data to their respective event logs. In this case, it is possible to create a subscription on one of the servers to forward the event log data from the other server. Therefore, both system event logs can be reviewed from a central system.

Configuring Event Subscriptions   Use the following steps to configure event subscriptions between two systems.

First, each source computer must be prepared to send events to remote computers:

1. Log on to the source computer. Best practice is to log on with a domain account that has administrative permissions on the source computer.

2. From an elevated command prompt, run `winrm quickconfig`. Exit the command prompt.

3. Add the collector computer to the Local Administrators group of the source computer.

4. Log on to the collector computer following the steps outlined previously for the source system.

5. From an elevated command prompt, run `wecutil qc.`

6. If you intend to manage event delivery optimization options such as Minimize Bandwidth or Minimize Latency, also run `winrm quickconfig` on the collector computer.

After the collector and source computers are prepared, a subscription must be made identifying the events that will be pulled from the source computers. To create a new subscription, complete the following steps:

1. On the collector computer, run Event Viewer with an account with administrative permissions.

2. Click the Subscriptions folder in the console tree and select Create Subscription or right-click and select the same command from the context menu.

3. In the Subscription Name box, type a name for the subscription.

4. In the Description box, enter an optional description.

5. In the Destination Log box, select the log file where collected events will be stored. By default, these events are stored in the forwarded events log in the Windows Logs folder of the console tree.

6. Click Select Computers to select the source computers that will be forwarding events. Add the appropriate domain computers, and click OK.

7. Click Select Events and configure the event logs and types to collect. Click OK.

8. Click OK to create the subscription.

Conducting Additional Event Viewer Management Tasks

Now that we understand the functionality of each of the new folders associated with the newly improved Event Viewer included with Windows 2008, it is beneficial to review the upcoming sections for additional management tasks associated with Event Viewer. These tasks include the following:

▶ Saving event logs

▶ Organizing data

▶ Viewing logs on remote servers

▶ Archiving events

▶ Customizing the event log

▶ Understanding the Security log

Saving Event Logs

Event logs can be saved and viewed at a later time. You can save an event log by either right-clicking a specific log and choosing Save Events As or by picking individual events from within a log, right-clicking the selected events, and choosing Save Selected Items. Entire logs and selected events can also be saved by selecting the same command from the Actions pane. After being saved, these logs can be opened by right-clicking the appropriate log and selecting Open Saved Log or by clicking the same command in the Actions pane. After a log has been opened, it displays in a new top-level folder called Saved Logs from within Event Viewer.

Organizing Data

Vast numbers of logs can be collected by Windows and displayed in the central pane of Event Viewer. New tools or enhancement to old ones make finding useful information much easier than in any other iteration of Event Viewer:

▶ **Sorting**—Events can be sorted by right-clicking the folder or Custom View icon and then selecting View, Sort By. Select the column name on which to sort on in the left-most pane or clicking the column to be sorted or the heading. Right-click the View item in the Actions pane and select Sort By. Finally, select the column in which sorting is desired. This is a quick way to find items at a very high level (for example, by time, source, or event ID). The new features for finding and sorting data are more robust and well worth learning.

▶ **Selection and sorting of column headings**—Various columns can be added to or removed from any of the event logs. The order in which columns display from left to right can be altered, too, by selecting the column in the Select Column dialog box and clicking the up- or down-arrow button.

▶ **Grouping**—A new way to view event log information is through the grouping function. By right-clicking column headings, an administrator can opt to group the event log being viewed by any of the columns in view. By isolating events, desired and specific criteria trends can be spotted that can help in isolating issues and ultimately resolving problems.

▶ **Filtering**—As mentioned earlier, filtering, like grouping, provides a means to isolate and display only the data you want to see in Event Viewer. Filtering, however, gives the administrator many more options for determining which data should be displayed than grouping or sorting. Filters can be defined based on any or all of the event levels, log or source, event IDs, task category, keywords, or user or computers. After being created, filters can be exported for use on other systems.

▶ **Tasks**—By attaching tasks to events, logs, or custom views, administrators can bring some automation and notification into play when certain events occur. To create a task, just right-click the custom view, built-in log, or specific event of your choice, and then right-click Attach a Task to This Custom View, Log, or Event. The Create a Basic Task Wizard then launches. On the first tab, just select a name and description for the task. Click Next to view the criteria that will trigger the task action. (This section cannot be edited and is populated based on the custom view, log, or task selected when the wizard is initiated.) Click Next and select Start a Program, Send an E-mail, or Display a Message as desired.

Viewing Logs on Remote Servers

You can use Event Viewer to view event logs on other computers on your network. To connect to another computer from the console tree, right-click Event Viewer (Local) and click Connect to Another Computer. Select Another Computer and then enter the name of the computer or browse to it and click OK. You must be logged on as an administrator or be a member of the Administrators group to view event logs on a remote computer. If you are not logged on with adequate permissions, you can select the Connect as Another User check box and set the credentials of an account that has proper permissions to view the logs on the remote computer.

Archiving Events

Occasionally, you might need to archive an event log. Archiving a log copies the contents of the log to a file. Archiving is useful in creating benchmark records for the baseline of a server or for storing a copy of the log so that it can be viewed or accessed elsewhere. When an event log is archived, it is saved in one of four forms:

▶ **Comma-delimited text file (.csv)**—This format allows the information to be used in a program such as Microsoft Excel.

▶ **Text-file format (.txt)**—Information in this format can be used in a program such as a word processing program.

▶ **Log file (.evtx)**—This format allows the archived log to be viewed again in the Windows 2008 or Windows Vista Event Viewer. Note that the new event log format is XML, which earlier versions of Windows cannot read.

▶ **XML (.xml)**—This format saves the event log in raw XML. XML is used throughout Event Viewer for filters, tasks, and logging.

The event description is saved in all archived logs. To archive, right-click the log to be archived and click Save Log File As. In the File Name field of the resulting property page, type in a name for the archived log file, choose a file type from the file format options of .csv, .txt, .evtx, or .xml, and then click Save.

> **NOTE**
>
> You must be a member of the Backup Operators group at the minimum to archive an event log.

Logs archived in the new log-file format (.evtx) can be reopened using the Windows 2008 Event Viewer utility. Logs saved in log-file format retain the XML data for each event recorded. Event logs, by default, are stored on the server where the Event Viewer utility is being run. Data can, however, be archived to a remote server by just providing a UNC path (such as \\servername\share\) when entering a filename.

Logs archived in comma-delimited (.csv) or text (.txt) format can be reopened in other programs such as Microsoft Word or Excel. These two formats do not retain the XML data or formatting.

Customizing the Event Log

The properties of an event log can be configured. In Event Viewer, the properties of a log are defined by general characteristics: log path, current size, date created, when last modified or accessed, maximum size, and what should be done when the maximum log size is reached.

To customize the event log, access the properties of the particular log by highlighting the log and selecting Action and then Properties. Alternatively, you can right-click the log and select Properties to display the General tab of the log's property page, as shown in Figure 13.5.

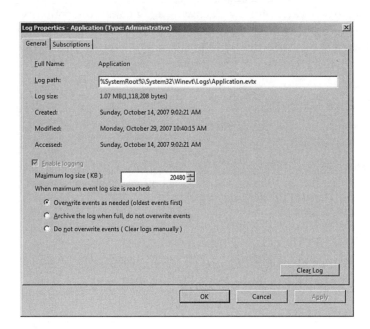

FIGURE 13.5   Selecting properties for the event log.

The Log Size section specifies the maximum size of the log and the subsequent actions to take when the maximum log size limit is reached. The three options are as follows:

▶ Overwrite Events as Needed (Oldest Events First)

▶ Archive the Log When Full, Do Not Overwrite Events

▶ Do Not Overwrite Events (Clear Logs Manually)

If you select the Do Not Overwrite Events option, Windows 2008 stops logging events when the log is full. Although Windows 2008 notifies you when the log is full, you need to monitor the log and manually clear the log periodically so that new events can be tracked and stored in the log file.

In addition, log file sizes must be specified in multiples of 64KB. If a value is not in multiples of 64KB, Event Viewer automatically sets the log file size to a multiple of 64KB.

When you need to clear the event log, click the Clear Log button in the lower right of the property page.

Understanding the Security Log

Effectively logging an accurate and wide range of security events in Event Viewer requires an understanding of auditing in Windows 2008. It is important to know events are not audited by default. You can enable auditing in the local security policy for a local server, the domain controller security policy for a domain controller machine, and the Active Directory (AD) Group Policy Object (GPO) for a domain. Through auditing, you can track Windows 2008 security events. It is possible to request that an audit entry be written to the security event log whenever certain actions are carried out or an object such as a file or printer in AD is accessed. The audit entry shows the action carried out, the user responsible for the action, and the date and time of the action.

Performance and Reliability Monitoring

Performance is a basis for measuring how fast application and system tasks are completed on a computer, and reliability is a basis for measuring system operation. How reliable a system is will be based on whether it regularly operates at the level at which it was designed to perform. Based on their descriptions, it should be easy to recognize that performance and reliability monitoring are crucial aspects in the overall availability and health of a Windows 2008 infrastructure. To ensure maximum uptime, a well thought-through process needs to be put in place to monitor, identify, diagnose, and analyze system performance. This process should invariably provide a way to quickly compare system performances at varying instances in time, thus allowing you to detect and potentially prevent a catastrophic incident before it causes system downtime.

The Reliability and Performance Monitor, which is an MMC snap-in, provides myriad new tools for administrators so that they can conduct real-time system monitoring, examine system resources, collect performance data, and create performance reports from a single console. This tool is literally a combination of three legacy Windows Server monitoring tools: System Monitor, Performance Monitor, and Server Performance Advisor. However, new features and functionalities have been introduced to shake things up, including Data Collector Sets, resource view, Reliability Monitor, scheduling, diagnosis reporting, and wizards and templates for creating logs. To launch the Reliability and Performance Monitor MMC snap-in tool, select Start, All Programs, Administrative Tools, Reliability and Performance Monitor or enter `perfmon.msc` at a command prompt.

The Reliability and Performance Monitor MMC snap-in is composed of the following elements:

- ► Resource Monitor

- ► Performance Monitor

- ► Reliability Monitor

- ► Data Collector Sets

- ► Report Generation

The upcoming sections further explore these major elements found in the Reliability and Performance Monitoring tool.

Resource Monitor

The first area of interest in the Reliability and Performance Monitor snap-in is the Resource Overview screen, also known as the Resource Monitor. It is displayed as the home page in the central details pane when the Reliability and Performance Monitoring tool is invoked. Alternatively, you can review the Resource Overview screen by selecting Reliability and Performance in the navigation tree. Resource Monitor can also be launched from within the Performance tab on the Windows Task Manager.

The Resource Monitor Overview screen presents holistic, real-time graphical illustrations of a Windows 2008 system's CPU usage, disk usage, network usage, and memory usage, as displayed in Figure 13.6.

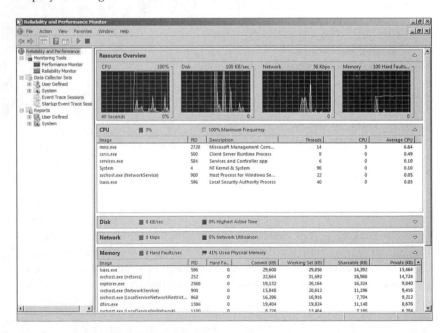

FIGURE 13.6   Viewing the Resource Monitor Overview screen.

Additional process-level details can be viewed to better understand your system's current resource usage by expanding subsections beneath the graphs. For example, when expanded, the CPU subsection includes CPU consumption by application, and the Disk subsection displays disk activity based on read and write operations. In addition, the Network subsection exhibits bytes being sent and received based on an application, and finally, the Memory subsection reveals information about the memory use of an application.

The Resource Monitor Overview screen is the first level of defense when there is a need to get a quick overview of a system's resources. If quick diagnosis of an issue cannot be achieved, an administrator should leverage the additional tools within the Reliability and Performance Monitor. These are covered in the upcoming sections.

Performance Monitor

Windows 2008 comes with two tools for performance monitoring. The first tool is called Performance Monitor, and the second tool is known as Reliability Monitor. These tools together provide performance analysis and information that can be used for bottleneck, performance, and troubleshooting analysis.

First, defining some terms used in performance monitoring will help clarify the function of Performance Monitor and how it ties in to software and system functionality. The three components noted in the Performance Monitor, Data Collector Sets, and reports are as follows:

▶ **Object**—Components contained in a system are grouped into objects. Objects are grouped according to system functionality or by association within the system. Objects can represent logical entities such as memory or a physical mechanism such as a hard disk drive. The number of objects available in a system depends on the configuration. For example, if Microsoft Exchange Server is installed on a server, some objects pertaining to Exchange would be available.

▶ **Counter**—Counters are subsets of objects. Counters typically provide more detailed information for an object such as queue length or throughput for an object. The System Monitor can collect data through the counters and display it in either a graphical format or a text log format.

▶ **Instances**—If a server has more than one similar object, each one is considered an instance. For example, a server with multiple processors has individual counters for each instance of the processor. Counters with multiple instances also have an instance for the combined data collected for the instances.

The Performance Monitor provides an interface that allows for the analysis of system data, research performance, and bottlenecks. The System Monitor displays performance counter output in line graphs, histogram (bar chart), and report format.

The histogram and line graphs can be used to view multiple counters at the same time, as shown in Figure 13.7. However, each data point displays only a single value that is independent of its object. The report view is better for displaying multiple values.

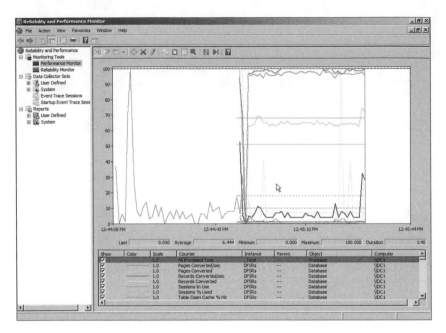

FIGURE 13.7   The graph view of the Performance Monitor.

Launching the Performance Monitor is accomplished by selecting Performance Monitor from the Monitoring Tools folder in the Reliability and Performance MMC snap-in. You can also open it from a command line by entering Perfmon.msc. When a new Performance Monitor session is started, it loads a blank system monitor graph into the console with % Processor Time as the only counter defined.

Adding Counters with Performance Monitor

Before counters can be displayed, they have to be added. The counters can be added simply by using the menu bar. The Counter button on the toolbar includes Add, Delete, and Highlight. You can use the Add Counter button to display new counters. On the other hand, use the Delete Counter button to remove unwanted counters from the display. The Highlight Counter button is helpful for highlighting a particular counter of interest; a counter can be highlighted with either a white or black color around the counter.

The following step-by-step procedures depict how to add counters to the Performance Monitor:

1. In the navigation tree of Event Viewer, first expand Reliability and Performance, Monitoring Tools, and then Performance Monitoring.
2. Either click the Add icon in the menu bar or right-click anywhere on the graph and select Add Counters.

> **NOTE**
>
> Typical baseline counters consist of Memory - Pages / Sec, PhysicalDisk - Avg. Disk Queue Length, and Processor - % Processor Time.

3. The Add Counters dialog box is invoked, as shown in Figure 13.8. In the Available Counters section, select the desired counters, and then click the Add button.

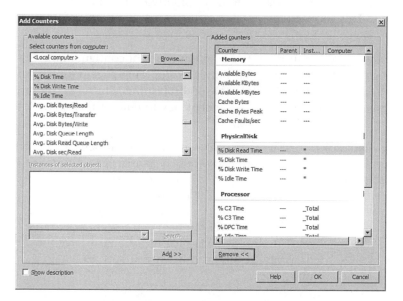

FIGURE 13.8   Adding counters to Performance Monitor.

> **NOTE**
>
> Windows 2008 includes a tremendous number of counters to choose from when conducting performance monitoring. It is challenging in this section to fully explain what each counter offers. If you want to find out more about a counter, enable the Show Description option in the Add Counters dialog box and highlight a specific counter to obtain a detailed explanation about it.

4. Review the selected counters in the Added Counters section, and then click OK.

> **NOTE**
>
> When adding counters, it is possible to conduct *remote monitoring* by selecting counters from another system. To simplify things, it is also possible to search for instances of a counter and add a group of counters.

Managing Performance Monitor Settings

While back on the Performance Monitor display, update displays by clicking the Clear Display button. Clicking the Freeze Display button or pressing Ctrl+F freezes displays, which suspends data collection. Data collection can be resumed by pressing Ctrl+F or clicking the Freeze Display button again. Click the Update Data button to display an updated data analysis.

It is also possible to export and import a display by using the Cut and Paste buttons. For example, a display can be saved to the clipboard and then imported into another instance of the Performance Monitor. This is commonly used to view or analyze system information on a different system, such as information from a production server.

The Properties page of Performance Monitor has five additional tabs of configuration: General, Source, Data, Graph, and Appearance. Generally, the Properties page provides access to settings that control the graph grid, color, style of display data, and so on. Data can be saved from the monitor in different ways. The easiest way to retain the display features is to save the control as an HTML file.

The Performance Monitor enables you to also save log files in HTML or tab-separated (.tsv) format, which you can then analyze by using third-party tools such as Seagate Crystal Reports. Alternatively, a tab-separated file can be imported into a spreadsheet or database application such as Excel or Microsoft Access. Windows 2008 also enables you to collect data in SQL database format. This is useful for performance analysis at an enterprise level rather than a per-server basis. Reports displayed in Excel can help you better understand the data and provide reports to management. And by saving log files, you can save the results from Performance Monitor as an image. This is great when you need to obtain a point-in-time depiction of a performance graph.

Reliability Monitor

The Reliability Monitor is a brand-new tool first introduced with the release of Windows Vista and now reintroduced with Windows 2008. This enhanced system management tool is the second monitoring tool available with Microsoft's Reliability and Performance Monitor MMC snap-in. Use this tool when you need help troubleshooting the root cause associated with reduced reliability of a Windows 2008 system. Reliability Monitor provides event details through system stability charts and reports that help diagnose items that might be negatively impacting the reliability of a system.

The tool uses a System Stability Index to rate the stability of a system each day over its lifetime by means of an index scorecard that identifies any reduction in reliability. An index rating of 1 represents a system in its least stable stage, whereas an index rating of 10 indicates a system in its most stable stage. Each day's index rating is displayed in a System Stability Chart graph, as illustrated in Figure 13.9. This graph typically helps administrators to identify dates when stability issues with the Windows 2008 system occurred. Additional itemized system stability information can be found in an accompanying System Stability Report section of the Reliability Monitor screen. The additional stability information further assists by identifying the root cause of the reliability issues. This information is grouped into the following categories: Software Installs and Uninstalls, Application Failures, Hardware Failures, Windows Failures, and Miscellaneous Failures.

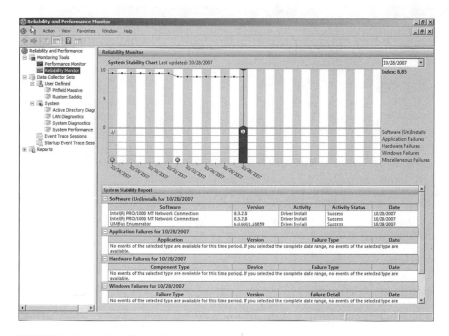

FIGURE 13.9   The Reliability Monitor screen.

Reliability Monitor is an essential tool for identifying and correlating problems with Windows 2008. With Reliability Monitor, an administrator can quickly identify changes in a system that caused a negative trend with system reliability. As such, this tool can also help administrators anticipate other problems, which ultimately leads to solving issues efficiently and effectively.

Data Collector Sets

The Data Collector Sets is a vital new feature available as a subfolder within the Reliability and Performance snap-in. The purpose of a Data Collector Set is to review or log system performance data. This is achievable through a single component that encompasses organized multiple data collection points. This information can then be analyzed to diagnose problems, correct system performance issues, or create baselines.

Performance counters, event trace data, and system configuration information are all data collector elements that can be captured and contained in a Data Collector Set. Data Collector Sets can be based on a predefined template, from a Data Collector Set that already exists, by creating it manually, with a wizard, or it can be user defined. Data Collector Sets can be exported and used for multiple systems, easing the administrative load involving the configuration of new systems producing more effective monitoring.

Wizards facilitate the creation of Data Collector Sets and enable an administrator to quickly create collections based on server roles or the type of information that is required.

> **NOTE**
>
> To create Data Collector Sets, you must be a member of the Administrators group or logged on with an account that is a member of the Performance Log Users group.

Creating Data Collector Sets

Data Collector Sets can be created manually from a template or from Performance Monitor. The following examples will help you to gain an understanding of the different ways to create Data Collector Sets.

To create a Data Collector Set from Performance Monitor, complete the following steps:

1. In the Reliability and Performance Monitor snap-in, navigate to Performance Monitor.

2. Add counters based on items you want to capture. For this example, the following counters were used: Memory - Pages / Sec, Physical Disk - Avg.Disk Queue Length, and Processor - % Processor Time.

3. After the counters are added, right-click anywhere on the Performance Monitor display screen or right-click Performance Monitor in the navigation tree, select New, and then select Data Collector Set. The Create New Data Collector Set Wizard is launched.

4. Enter a name for this new Data Collector Set on the Create New Data Collector Set page, and then click Next.

5. On the next page, specify where you want the data to be saved. The default path is the %systemdrive%\PerfLogs\. Click Finish to save the current settings and exit or click Next to enter a user account to run as.

6. Click the Change button to enter a user for this data set.

7. Select the option to Save and Close or Start This Data Collector Set Now, and then click Finish to complete the Data Collector Set creation process.

The resulting Data Collector Set can be configured to run immediately by right-clicking the new Data Collector Set and selecting Start. You can view the properties of the Data Collector Set by right-clicking and selecting Properties.

Data Collector Sets can be created, saved, or restored from templates. Many templates are built in and can be created using the Create New Data Collector Set Wizard in Windows Reliability and Performance Monitor. This wizard is invoked by right-clicking the User Defined folder, the Event Trace Sessions folder, or the Startup Event Trace Sessions folder under Data Collector Sets and selecting New, Data Collector Set.

To create a Data Collector Set from a template, complete the following steps:

1. Expand the Data Collector Sets folder and then the User Defined subfolder in the Reliability and Performance Monitor snap-in.

2. Right-click the User Defined subfolder and select New Data Collector Set to launch the Create New Data Collector Set Wizard.

3. Enter a name for this new Data Collector Set, select the Create from a Template option, and then click Next.

4. On the next page, select the desired template to use, and then click Next.

NOTE

The Create New Data Collector Set Wizard offers three templates for creating Data Collector Sets: Basic, System Diagnostics, and System Performance. Use the Basic template when there is a need to create a basic Data Collector Set. The System Diagnostics template generates a report detailing the status of local hardware resources, system response times, system information, and configuration data. The Systems Performance template is leveraged when you want to not only generate a report detailing the status of local hardware resources and system response times, but also processes on the local computers.

In summary, typically the Basic template provides basic diagnostics, whereas the Systems Diagnostics template is good for maximizing performance and streamlining system operations, and the System Performance template is a good choice when you want to identify performance issues. Regardless of which template you use to create your Data Collector Set, you can edit the Data Collector Set afterward. In addition, it is possible to select the Browse button and import templates from other servers.

---

5. On the next page, specify where you want the data to be saved. The default path is the %systemdrive%\PerfLogs\. Click Finish to save the current settings and exit or click Next to enter a user account to run as.

6. Click the Change button to enter a user for this data set.

7. Select the option to Save and Close, Start This Data Collector Set Now, or Open Properties for This Data Collector Set, and then click Finish to complete the Data Collector Set creation process.

Reports

The final folder in the Reliability and Performance Monitor snap-in is Reports. The Reports folder provides diagnostic reports to support administrators in troubleshooting and diagnosing system performance problems, including reliability. Reports are viewed in the central details pane of the Reliability and Performance Monitor snap-in.

The reports are based on Data Collector Sets that were previously defined by users or preconfigured and included with Windows 2008 Reliability and Performance Monitor. The report console's features and functionality are similar to those seen by means of the reports introduced with Server Performance Advisor in Windows Server 2003.

The Reports folder is broken into two main subfolders: User Defined reports and System reports. The default System reports typically include reports relating to LAN diagnostics, system diagnostics, and system performance. Additional system reports are automatically generated depending on the server role installed on the Windows 2008 system. For example, an Active Directory Diagnostics system report is automatically included in the console when the Active Directory Domain Services server role is installed on the Windows 2008 system.

Creating a User-Defined Report

The first step in creating a user-defined report is to create a user-defined Collector Set and define the parameters for a collection. After the user-defined Collector Set is created, data collection must be manually started or scheduled to run at a specific date. At this time, a report folder is automatically generated under the User Defined folder. After the report is created, you can review the contents by selecting it. When viewing reports, it is possible to expand specific items such as the report summary, diagnostic results, or CPU for additional information. This is depicted in the sample System Performance report in Figure 13.10.

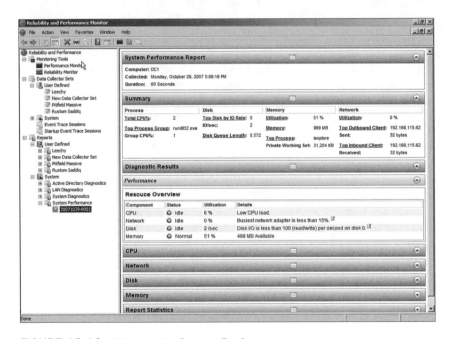

FIGURE 13.10   Viewing the System Performance report.

Viewing Predefined System Reports

Another option for assessing system health and troubleshooting system anomalies is to leverage the predefined system reports. The following steps illustrate how to view these system reports:

1. In the Reliability and Performance Monitor navigation tree, expand the Data Collector Sets folder and then System.

2. Right-click one of the predefined Data Collector Sets such as System Diagnostics, and then click Start.

   This starts the data-collection process.

3. Now expand the Reports folder, System, and then System Diagnostics.

4. Highlight the newly created report and review the contents of the report in the central Details pane.

NOTE

The report generates and appears when the data-collection process is complete. The report is automatically tagged with the current date.

Setting Baseline Values

A *baseline* is a performance level that can be used as a starting point to compare against future network performance operations. When a server is first monitored, there is little to compare the statistics against. After a baseline is created, information can be gathered at any time in the future and compared against the baseline. The difference between the current statistics and the baseline statistics is the variance caused by system load, application processing, or system performance contention.

To be able to set a baseline value, you need to gather a normal set of statistics on each system that will eventually be monitored or managed in the future. Baselines should be created for normal and stressed times. The workload on a machine at night when there are fewer users connected to it provides a poor baseline to compare real-time data in the middle of the day. Information sampled in the middle of the day should be compared with a baseline of information collected at around the same time of day during normal load prior to the sample comparison.

Creating baselines should be an ongoing process. If an application or a new service is added to a server, a new baseline should be created so that any future comparisons can be made with a baseline with the most current status of system performance.

Reducing Performance Monitoring Overhead

Performance monitoring uses system resources that can affect the performance of a system and affect the data being collected. To ensure that performance monitoring and analyzing do not affect the machines being monitored themselves, you need to decrease the impact of performance monitoring. You can take some steps to ensure that performance-monitoring overhead is kept to a minimum on the server being monitored to create as accurate of an analysis on a system as possible:

▶ Use a remote server to monitor the target server. Servers can actually be dedicated to monitoring several remote servers. Although this might also lead to an increase in network bandwidth, at least the monitoring and tracking of information do not drastically degrade CPU or disk I/O as if the monitoring tool were actually running on the server being monitored.

▶ Consider reducing the frequency of the data-collection interval, because more frequent collection can increase overhead on the server.

▶ Avoid using too many counters. Some counters are costly in terms of taxing a server for system resources and can increase system overhead. Monitoring several activities at one time also becomes difficult.

▶ Use logs instead of displaying graphs. The logs can then be imported into a database or report. Logs can be saved on hard disks not being monitored or analyzed.

Important Objects to Monitor

The numbers of system and application components, services, and threads to measure in Windows 2008 are so extensive that it is impossible to monitor thousands of processor, print queue, network, or storage usage statistics. Defining the roles a server plays in a network environment helps to narrow down what needs to be measured. Servers could be defined and categorized based on the function of the server, such as application server, file and print server, or services server such as DNS, domain controller, and so on.

Because servers perform different roles, and hence have different functions, it makes sense to monitor the essential performance objects. This helps prevent the server from being overwhelmed from the monitoring of unnecessary objects for measurement or analysis.

Overall, four major areas demand the most concern: memory, processor, disk subsystem, and network subsystem. They all tie into any role the server plays.

The following list describes objects to monitor based on the roles played by the server:

▶ **Domain controller**—Because the DC provides authentication, stores the Active Directory database, holds schema objects, and so on, it receives many requests. To be able to process all these requests, it uses up a lot of CPU resources, disks, memory, and network bandwidth. Consider monitoring memory, CPU, system, network segment, network interface, and protocol objects such as TCP, UDP, NBT, NetBIOS, and NetBEUI. Also worth monitoring are the Active Directory NTDS service and site server LDAP service objects. DNS and WINS also have applicable objects to be measured.

▶ **File and print server**—The print servers that process intensive graphics jobs can utilize extensive resources of system CPU cycles very quickly. The file server takes up a lot of storage space. Monitor the PrintQueue object to track print spooling data. Also monitor CPU, memory, network segment, and logical and physical disks for both file and print data collection.

▶ **Message collaboration server**—A messaging server such as an Exchange Server 2007 uses a lot of CPU, disk, and memory resources. Monitor memory collection, cache, processor, system, and logical and physical disks. Exchange objects are added to the list of objects after Exchange is installed, such as message queue length or name-resolution response time.

▶ **Web server**—A web server is usually much less disk intensive and more dependent on processing performance or memory space to cache web pages and page requests. Consider monitoring the cache, network interface, processor, and memory usage.

▶ **Database server**—Database servers such as Microsoft SQL Server 2008 can use a lot of CPU and disk resources. Database servers such as Microsoft SQL Server use an extensive amount of memory to cache tables and data, so RAM usage and query response times should be monitored. Monitoring objects such as system, processor, logical disk, and physical disk is helpful for overall system performance operations.

Using the Debugging Tools Available in Windows Server 2008

Several useful tools are available in Windows 2008 for troubleshooting and diagnosing various problems ranging from TCP/IP connection issues to verification and maintenance issues. These tools also make it much easier for IT professionals and administrators, allowing IT personnel to focus on business improvement tasks and functions, not on simply running specific tools in the networking environment.

TCP/IP Tools

TCP/IP forms the backbone of communication and transportation in Windows 2008. Before you can communicate between machines, TCP/IP must be configured.

In Windows 2008, TCP/IP is installed by default during the OS installation and is impossible to add or remove through the GUI.

If a TCP/IP connection fails, you need to determine the cause or point of failure. Windows 2008 includes some dependable and useful tools to troubleshoot connections and verify connectivity. The tools described in the following eight sections are useful for debugging TCP/IP connectivity problems. Most of these tools have been updated to include switches for IPv4 and IPv6.

Ping

Ping stands for *Packet Internet Groper*. It is used to send an Internet Control Message Protocol (ICMP) echo request and echo reply to verify the availability of a local or remote machine. You can think of ping as a utility that sends a message to another machine asking "Are you still there?" By default in Windows 2008, ping sends out four ICMP packages and waits for responses back in one second. However, the number of packages sent or time to wait for responses can be changed through the options available for ping.

Besides verifying the availability of a remote machine, ping can help determine a name-resolution problem.

To use ping, go to a command prompt and enter **Ping Targetname**. Different parameters can be used with ping. To display them, enter **Ping /?** or **Ping** (without parameters).

The parameters for the Ping command are as follows:

-4—Specifies that IPv4 is used to ping. This parameter is not required to identify the target host with an IPv4 address. It is required only to identify the target host by name.

-6—Specifies that IPv6 is used to ping. Just like -4, this parameter is not required to identify the target host with an IPv6 address. It is required only to identify the target host by name.

-a—Resolves the IP address to the hostname. The hostname of the target machine is displayed if this command is successful.

-f—Requests that echo back messages are sent with the Don't Fragment flag in packets. This parameter is available only in IPv4.

-i *ttl*—Increases the timeout on slow connections. The parameter also sets the value of the Time To Live (TTL). The maximum value is 255.

-j *HostList*—Routes packets using the host list, which is a series of IP addresses separated by spaces. The host can be separated by intermediate gateways (loose source route).

-k *HostList*—Similar to -j but hosts cannot be separated by intermediate gateways (strict source route).

-l *size*—Specifies the length of packets in bytes. The default is 32. The maximum size is 65,527.

-n *count*—Specifies the number of packets sent. The default is 4.

-r *count*—Specifies the route of outgoing and incoming packets. It is possible to specify a count that is equal to or greater than the number of hops between the source and destination. The count can be between 1 and 9 only.

-R—Specifies that the round-trip path is traced (available on IPv6 only).

-S *count*—Sets the time stamp for the number of hops specified by count. The count must be between 1 and 4.

-S *SrcAddr*—Specifies the source address to use (available on IPv6 only).

-t—Specifies that Ping should continue sending packets to the destination until interrupted. To stop and display statistics, press Ctrl+Break. To stop and quit ping, press Ctrl+C.

-v *TOS*—Specifies the value of the type of service in the packet sent. The default is 0. TOS is specified as a decimal value between 0 and 255.

-w *timeout*—Specifies the time in milliseconds for packet timeout. If a reply is not received within the timeout, the Request Timed Out error message is displayed. The default timeout is 4 seconds.

TargetName—Specifies the hostname or IP address of the destination to ping.

NOTE

Some remote hosts can be configured to ignore ping traffic as a method of preventing acknowledgment (and thus as a security measure). Therefore, your inability to ping a server might not necessarily mean that the server is not operational, just that the server is not responding for some reason.

Tracert

Tracert is generally used to determine the route or path taken to a destination by sending ICMP packets with varying TTL values. Each router the packet meets on the way decreases the value of the TTL by at least one; invariably, the TTL is a hop count. The path is determined by checking the ICMP Time Exceeded messages returned by intermediate routers. Some routers do not return Time Exceeded messages for expired TTL values and are not captured by Tracert. In such cases, asterisks are displayed for that hop.

To display the different parameters that can be used with Tracert, open a command prompt and enter **tracert** (without parameters) to display help or type **tracert /?**. The parameters associated with Tracert are as follows:

-4—Specifies that tracert.exe can use only IPv4 for the trace.

-6—Specifies that tracert.exe can use only IPv6 for the trace.

-d—Prevents resolution of IP addresses of routers to their hostname. This is particularly useful for speeding up results of Tracert.

-h *maximumHops*—Specifies the maximum number of hops to take before reaching the destination. The default is 30 hops.

-j *HostList*—Specifies that packets use the loose source route option. Loose source routing allows successive intermediate destinations to be separated by one or multiple routers. The maximum number of addresses in the host list is nine. This parameter is useful only when tracing IPv4 addresses.

-R—Sends packets to a destination in IPv6, using the destination as an intermediate destination and testing reverse route.

-S—Specifies the source address to use. This parameter is useful only when tracing IPv6 addresses.

> **NOTE**
>
> Tracert is a good utility to determine the number of hops and the latency of communications between two points. Even if an organization has an extremely high-speed connection to the Internet, if the Internet is congested or if the route a packet must follow requires forwarding the information between several routers along the way, the performance and, ultimately, the latency (or delay in response between servers) will cause noticeable communications delays.

Pathping

Pathping is a route-tracing tool that combines features of both Ping and Tracert commands, but with more information than either of those two commands provides. Pathping is most ideal for a network with routers or multiple routes between the source and destination hosts. The Pathping command sends packets to each router on its way to a destination, and then gets results from each packet returned from the router. Because Pathping computes the loss of packets from each hop, you can easily determine which router is causing a problem in the network.

13

To display the parameters in Pathping, open a command prompt and enter **Pathping /?**. The parameters for the Pathping command are as follows:

-4—Specifies that Pathping.exe can use only IPv4 for the trace.

-6—Specifies that Pathping.exe can use only IPv6 for the trace.

-g *Host-list*—Allows hosts to be separated by intermediate gateways.

-h *maximumHops*—Specifies the maximum number of hops before reaching the target. The default is 30 hops.

-n—Specifies that it is not necessary to resolve the address to the hostname.

-p *period*—Specifies the number of seconds to wait between pings. The default is a quarter of a second.

-q *num_queries*—Specifies the number of queries to each host along the route. The default is three seconds.

-w *timeout*—Specifies the timeout for each reply in milliseconds.

Ipconfig

Ipconfig displays all TCP/IP configuration values. It is of particular use on machines running Dynamic Host Control Protocol (DHCP). It is used to refresh DHCP settings and to determine which TCP/IP configuration values have been assigned by DHCP. If Ipconfig is used without parameters, it displays IP addresses, subnet masks, and gateways for each of the adapters on a machine. The adapters can be physical network adapters or logical adapters such as dial-up connections.

Some of the parameters for Ipconfig are as follows:

/all—Displays all TCP/IP configuration values.

/displaydns—Displays the contents of the DNS client resolver cache.

/flushdns—Resets and flushes the contents of the DNS client resolver cache. This includes entries made dynamically.

/registerdns—Sets manual dynamic registration for DNS names and IP addresses configured on a computer. This is particularly useful in troubleshooting DNS name registration or dynamic update problems between a DNS server and client.

/release *[Adapter]*—Sends a DHCP release message to the DHCP server to discard DHCP-configured settings for adapters. This parameter is available only for DHCP-enabled clients. If no adapter is specified, IP address configuration is released for all adapters.

/renew *[Adapter]*—Renews DHCP configuration for all adapters (if an adapter is not specified) and for a specific adapter if the *Adapter* parameter is included. This parameter is available only for DHCP-enabled clients.

/setclassid *Adapter [classID]*—Configures the DHCP class ID for a specific adapter. You can configure the DHCP class ID for all adapters by using the wildcard (*) character in place of *Adapter*.

/**showclassid** *Adapter*—Displays the DHCP class ID for a specific adapter.

/**allcompartments**—Displays information about all compartments.

/**allocmpartments** /**all**—Displays detailed information about all compartments.

> **NOTE**
>
> Ipconfig determines the assigned configuration for a system such as the default gateway, DNS servers, local IP address, subnet mask, and so on. When you're debugging network problems, you can use Ipconfig to validate that the proper TCP/IP settings have been set up for a system so that a server properly communicates on the network.

13

ARP

ARP stands for *Address Resolution Protocol*. ARP enables the display and modification of the ARP table on a local machine, which matches physical MAC addresses of machines to their corresponding IP addresses. ARP increases the speed of connection by eliminating the need to match MAC addresses with IP addresses for subsequent connections.

Some of the parameters for ARP are as follows:

-a *[InetAddr]* *[-N IfaceAddr]*—Displays the ARP table for all adapters on a machine. Use Arp –a with the *InetAddr (IP address)* parameter to display the ARP cache entry for a specific IP address.

-d *InetAddr* *[IfaceAddr]*—Deletes an entry with a specific IP address (*InetAddr*). Use the *IfaceAddr* parameter (IP address assigned to the interface) to delete an entry in a table for a specific interface. Use the wildcard character in place of InetAddr to delete all entries.

-g *[InetAddr]* *[-N IfaceAddr]*—Similar to the –a parameter.

-s *InetAddr EtherAddr* *[IfaceAddr]*—Adds a static entry to the ARP cache that resolves the IP address (*InetAddr*) to a physical address (EtherAddr). To add a static ARP cache entry to the table for a specific interface, use the IP address assigned to the interface *(IfaceAddr)*.

Netstat

As its name implies, Netstat (or *network statistics*) is used to display protocol statistics for any active connections, monitor connections to a remote host, and monitor IP addresses or domain names of hosts with established connections.

The parameters for Netstat are as follows:

-a—Displays all connections and listening ports by hostname.

-an—Similar to the –a parameter, but displays connections and listening ports by IP addresses.

-e—Displays Ethernet packets and bytes to and from the host.

-n—Displays address and port numbers without resolving the address to the hostname.

-o—Displays TCP connections and includes the corresponding process ID (PID). Used in combination with –a, -n, and –p. Not available in earlier Windows versions.

-P protocol—Displays statistics based on the protocol specified. Protocols that can be specified are TCP, UDP, TCPv6, or UDPv6. It can be used with –s to display TCP, UDP, ICMP, IP, TCPv6, UDPv6, ICMPv6, or IPv6.

-s—Displays statistics on a protocol-by-protocol basis. Can be used with the –p parameter to specify a set of protocols.

-r—Displays the route table. Information displayed includes network destination, netmask, gateway, interface, and metric (number of hops).

[Parameter] Interval—Displays the information at every interval specified. *Interval* is a numeral in seconds. Press Ctrl+C to stop the intervals.

Route

Route is particularly useful for troubleshooting incorrect static routes or for adding a route to a route table to temporarily bypass a problem gateway. Static routes can be used in place of implicit routes specified by a default gateway. Use Route to add static routes to forward packets going to a gateway specified by default to avoid loops, improve traffic time, and so on.

The parameters for Route are as follows:

-add—Adds a route to a table. Use –p to make the route persistent for subsequent sessions.

-Delete—Deletes a route from the table.

-Print—Prints a route.

-change—Modifies an existing route.

-destination—Specifies the host address.

-gateway—Specifies the address of gateway for Route.

IF interface—Specifies the interface for the routing table to modify.

-mask Netmask—Uses the subnet mask specified by *Netmask*. If mask is not used, it defaults to 255.255.255.255.

-METRIC Metric—Specifies the metric, or cost, for the route using the value *Metric*.

-f—Clears the routing table of all gateway entries.

-p—Used with -add to create a persistent route.

Nslookup

Nslookup is used to query DNS. You can think of Nslookup as a simple diagnostic client for DNS servers. It can operate in two modes: Interactive and Noninteractive. Use Noninteractive mode to look up a single piece of data. To look up more than one piece of data, use Interactive mode. To stop Interactive mode at any time, press Ctrl+B. To exit from the command, enter **exit.** If Nslookup is used without any parameters, it uses the default DNS name server for lookup.

The parameters for Nslookup are as follows:

> **-ComputerToFind**—Looks up information for the specified *ComputerToFind*. By default, it uses the current default DNS name server.
>
> **-Server**—Specifies the server as the DNS name server.
>
> **-SubCommand**—Specifies one or more Nslookup subcommands as a command-line option. Enter a question mark (**?**) to display a list of subcommands available.

NetDiag

The Network Connectivity Tester (NetDiag) tool is a command-line diagnostic tool to test network connectivity, configuration, and security. It's included with the Support Tools on the Windows 2008 media. The tool gathers information on and tests network configuration, network drivers, protocols, connectivity, and well-known target accessibility. This is a good tool to use right off the bat if you think there are problems with the network connectivity of a system.

One nice feature of the NetDiag.exe tool is that it does not require parameters, which makes it easy to use. Simple instructions can be given to the administrators who need to execute it, and the bulk of the time can be spent analyzing the results.

Although it doesn't require any parameters, several are available:

> **/q**—Displays quiet output (errors only).
>
> **/v**—Displays verbose output.
>
> **/l**—Logs to the NetDiag.log.
>
> **/debug**—Displays even more verbose output.
>
> **/d: DomainName**—Finds a domain controller in the domain.
>
> **/fix**—Fixes minor problems.
>
> **/DCAccountEnum**—Enumerates domain controller computer accounts.
>
> **/test: TestName**—Runs the specified tests only.
>
> **/skip: TestName**—Skips the specified tests.

When specifying tests to run or to skip, nonskippable tests will still be run.

DCDiag

The Domain Controller Diagnostic (DCDiag) tool analyzes the state of domain controllers and services in an Active Directory forest. It is installed when the Active Directory Domain Services (AD DS) role is added to a Windows 2008 installation. This is a great general-purpose test tool for checking the health of an Active Directory infrastructure.

Tests include domain controller connectivity, replication errors, permissions, proper roles, and connectivity, and other general Active Directory health checks. It can even run non-domain-controller-specific tests, such as whether a server can be promoted to a domain controller (the dcpromo test), or register its records properly in DNS (RegisterInDNS test).

DCDiag is run on domain controllers exclusively, with the exception of the dcpromo and RegisterInDNS tests.

When run without any parameters, the tests will be run against the current domain controller. This runs all the key tests and is usually sufficient for most purposes.

The parameters for DCDiag are as follows:

/s:DomainController—Uses the domain controller as the home server.

/n:NamingContext—Uses the specified naming context (NetBIOS, FQDN, or distinguished name) to test.

/u:Domain\UserName /p:{*¦Password¦""}—Uses the supplied credentials to run the tool.

/a—Tests all domain controllers in the site.

/e—Tests all domain controllers in the enterprise.

/q—Displays quiet output (errors only).

/v—Displays verbose output.

/I—Ignores minor error messages.

/fix—Fixes minor problems.

/f:LogFile—Logs to the specified log file.

/ferr:ErrorLogFile—Logs errors to the specified log file.

/c—Comprehensively runs all tests.

/test:TestName—Runs the specified tests only.

/skip:TestName—Skips the specified tests.

When specifying tests to run or to skip, nonskippable tests will still be run.

> **NOTE**
>
> DCDiag is automatically included on a Windows 2008 system when the AD DS role is added. Otherwise, on non–domain controllers, the utility can be added by adding the Remote Server Administration Tools feature in Server Manager.

System Startup and Recovery

The System Startup and Recovery utility stores system startup, system failure, and debugging information. It also controls the behavior (what to do) when a system failure occurs.

To open System Startup and Recovery, launch Control Panel, select System, Advanced System Settings, and click the Advanced tab in the Systems Settings dialog box, and then click Settings under Startup and Recovery to display a property page similar to the one shown in Figure 13.11.

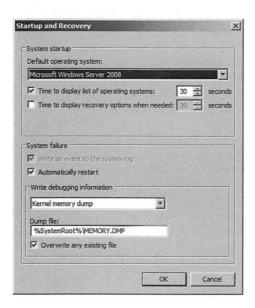

FIGURE 13.11   The Startup and Recovery page.

The Default Operating System field contains information that is displayed at startup. This information is typically the name of the operating system such as Windows Server 2008 Enterprise Edition. You can edit this information using bcdedit from a command prompt. If the machine is dual booted, there will be an entry for each operating system. The Time to Display List of Operating Systems option specifies the time the system takes to display the name of the operating system at startup. The default time is 30 seconds. This can be increased or reduced to a different time. The Time to Display Recovery Options When Needed is unchecked by default but can be selected and an interval in seconds entered.

You can set the action to be taken when system failure occurs in the System Failure section. There are two options. The first option is Write an Event to the System Log. This action is not editable in Windows 2008 because this action occurs by default every time a stop error occurs. The next option, Automatically Restart, reboots the system in the event of a system failure.

The Write Debugging Information section tells the system where to write debugging information when a system failure occurs. The options available include where the debugging information can be written to Small Memory Dump (128KB), Kernel Memory Dump, Complete Memory Dump, or (None). The Write Debugging Information To option requires a paging file on the boot volume, which should be the size of the physical RAM plus at least 1MB.

Memory resources can be saved if the Write Debugging Information To option is set to (None). The memory that would be saved depends on the server; the drivers that enable these features require about 60 to 70KB.

Windows Memory Diagnostics Tool

Many troubleshooting scenarios revolve around memory-related issues associated with a system. Typical memory issues can involve an errant application, a specific process consuming too much memory, or failing hardware such as bad RAM or the memory system on the motherboard. Thankfully, Windows 2008 has introduced a new tool for diagnosing problems associated with system memory.

By using Windows Memory Diagnostics tool, an administrator has another way to isolate root issues when a server is performing poorly or subject to crashes, or other when other abnormal behavior not caused by issues with the OS or installed applications occurs.

The Windows Memory Diagnostics tool can be launched as follows:

1. First save all work and close down open applications and utilities.

2. To invoke the tool, select Start, All Programs, Administrative Tools, Windows Memory Diagnostics Tool, or enter **MdSched** at a command prompt.

3. Select whether you want to Restart Now and Check for Problems or Check for Problems the Next Time I Start My Computer, as displayed in Figure 13.12.

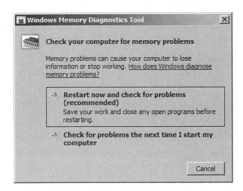

FIGURE 13.12   The options associated with running the Windows Memory Diagnostics tool.

4. When the system is rebooted, the Diagnostics tool automatically launches and conducts a Basic test by using default settings. Additional Test Mix options, Cache options, and Pass Count can be selected by pressing F1. The Test Mix options consist of Basic, Standard, and Extended, whereas the Cache option includes Default, On, or Off. In addition, set the Pass Count value. The value represents the number of times the entire test mix will be repeated. Note a value of 0 represents infinitely. Press F10 to apply the settings and start the memory tests. Status is reported throughout the test indicating results.

13

> **TIP**
>
> The Windows Memory Diagnostics tool might not detect all the problems with the system RAM. Just because no errors are reported doesn't mean the RAM or even the motherboard is working properly. Typically, the manufacturer of the hardware device will have additional diagnostics utilities that allow an administrator to conduct a deeper analysis of the root problems at the hardware level.

Resources and Support Tools

Software errors can be reported in Windows 2008. The error-reporting mechanism makes this happen. In addition, the Customer Experience Improvement Program (CEIP) enables the system to report information to Microsoft about computer hardware and usage.

The errors reported in the error-reporting mechanism and information derived from the CEIP can be sent automatically or when the user is prompted to notify Microsoft to help improve its future products.

You can manage the software error-reporting mechanism by launching Control Panel, selecting Problem Reports and Solution, and selecting the Customer Experience Improvement Settings or the Change Settings links. To change software error reporting, click the Advanced Settings link and turn problem reporting on or off by selecting the appropriate option button, as shown in Figure 13.13.

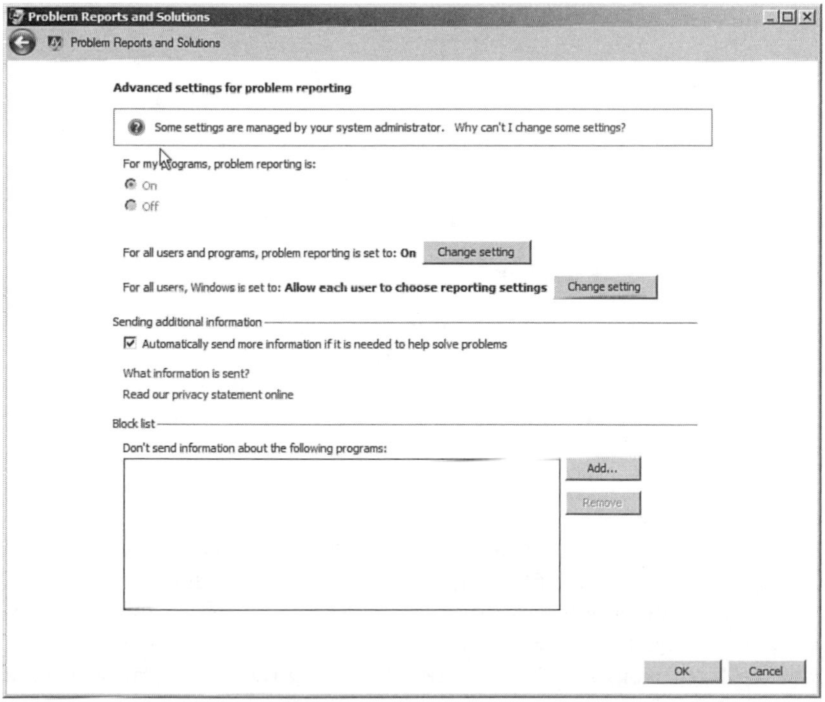

FIGURE 13.13 The Error Reporting screen.

Additional items can be configured, such as allowing each user to choose problem reporting settings, selecting the reporting settings for all users, and sending more information if it is needed to further assist in solving issues. Finally, it is possible to configure block lists, which prevents information being sent by specific programs.

This tool also helps solve problems on your computer by automatically checking online for solutions for errors logged to the system. For example, if a driver failed during installation, a fix might be presented when you check for new solutions.

The CEIP can be launched by clicking Configure CEIP, which is located in the Resources and Support section in Server Manager. When the dialog box is invoked, select whether you want to participate in the Windows Server Customer Experience Improvement Program and indicate the number of servers, desktops, and industry that best represents your organization.

The Windows Error Reporting can be launched by selecting Turn on Windows Error Reporting from the Resources and Support section in Server Manager. After selecting this option, choose whether you want to participate by sharing descriptions of problems with Microsoft. In addition, choose the level of involvement by selecting Yes, Automatically Send Detailed Reports; Yes, Automatically Send Summary Reports; or Ask Me About Sending Reports Every Time an Error Occurs.

Finally, the combination of the three resources and support tools help administrators better log, troubleshoot, and solve issues with a Windows 2008 system. At the same time, Microsoft collects this information to improve the product.

Common Problems Found in Hyper-V

Although every administrator will find something new or different that doesn't work right in an application, a handful of "issues" *have* arisen in various implementations of Windows 2008 Hyper-V. This section covers those problems and how to resolve them.

Hyper-V Installation-Related Problems

Hyper-V server installation has, for the most part, been one of those things that either works without a problem or doesn't work because of a specific (typically hardware-related) issue. The most common installation problems relate to the version of Windows 2008 that Hyper-V is being installed on and the hardware compatibility of the host server system itself.

Support for 64-Bit Windows 2008 Only

Hyper-V is supported only on the x64-bit version of Windows Server 2008 (Standard, Enterprise, and Datacenter editions). If you load up a 32-bit version of Windows Server 2008, the Hyper-V role isn't even an option to install on the server. On the topic of licensing version (Standard, Enterprise, and Datacenter), while this was covered in Chapter 1, "Windows 2008 Hyper-V Technology Primer," to repeat it here in the debugging section, a 64-bit host server regardless of the version of software installed (Standard, Enterprise, or Datacenter) will run as many guest sessions as the system has resources. From a legal licensing perspective, however, the Standard Edition of Windows 2008 x64 will allow one free guest session. The Enterprise Edition will allow four free guest sessions. The Datacenter Edition will allow an unlimited number of free guest sessions with the purchase of the host license. There's nothing wrong with an organization running the Enterprise Edition of Windows 2008 x64 with eight sessions on the server as long as the hardware has enough RAM and CPU to support the sessions. The organization just needs to buy four additional Windows server licenses beyond the four free Windows server guest session licenses received when running Hyper-V on an Enterprise Edition of the server software.

Hardware-Assisted Virtualization

The other common problem with installation of Hyper-V is that the Hyper-V server role installs properly, but when the host server is booted and a guest session is attempted to be launched, an error occurs: "The virtual machine could not be started because the hypervisor is not running." You will not find a hypervisor service to start, nor is there a hypervisor task in Task Manager to go look at. The hypervisor is loaded on system boot (hvboot.sys). If on boot Windows doesn't find hardware-assisted virtualization, the normal Windows driver is installed, and then guest sessions won't start.

This error indicates that the Windows 2008 operating system is not recognizing hardware-assisted virtualization on the system, which is required for Hyper-V to work. This typically means that the system does not have hardware-assisted virtualization or that it has hardware-assisted virtualization and it is just not enabled or working.

If you are unaware whether your system has hardware-assisted virtualization, check the process on the system. It should be an Intel EM64T chipset or an AMD64 chipset. Some of the earlier 64-bit processors (before 2005) were 64 bit, but not hardware assisted. AMD released a tool called the AMD Virtualization Technology and Microsoft Hyper-V System Compatibility Check Utility that you can download from www.amd.com/us-en/Processors/TechnicalResources/0,,30_182_871_9033,00.html.

If you know your system has a hardware-assisted virtualization processor, it is likely that hardware virtualization is not enabled. By default, most servers and definitely desktops and laptops ship with hardware virtualization disabled. The usual way to enable the hardware virtualization is to press F2 or F10 or Esc on power up of the system to run the BIOS "setup" program. In the BIOS setup program, you're typically looking for something with the word *virtualization*. Choosing to enable virtualization in the BIOS, then saving the settings and rebooting will usually solve the problem.

Hyper-V Networking-Related Problems

In virtualized environments, network communication problems between guest sessions, the host server, and servers on a backbone are common. Many times, a problem occurs because of how the network adapter is configured. Other times, guest sessions aren't connected to the physical network adapter to communicate out of the environment. To isolate network-related problems, you must confirm virtual network configuration settings on the host server.

Guest Sessions Cannot Talk Outside of the Host Server

If a guest session boots but the server cannot communicate outside the host server, or users cannot access the guest session, the isolation comes down to testing general connectivity:

1. Make sure the host server can communicate through the network adapter to other servers on the network, and vice versa (that other computers can communicate to the Hyper-V host server). You do this to confirm that the host network adapter is properly confirmed for inbound and outbound communications. If the host cannot communicate out to the network through the network adapter, check to make sure the network adapter is enabled, the network cable is plugged in, and the IP address has been properly assigned.

2. Assuming the host server can communicate externally but the guest session cannot, check the Virtual Network Manager on the Hyper-V Administrative console to make sure the guest session is connected to an external virtual network that is associated with a physical network adapter. Interestingly, even if you set the virtual network setting right, many times when you change the IP address of the physical adapter (either changing from static to DHCP or vice versa) the virtual network configuration changes, too. So even if you thought you set it right, go back and confirm you have the network setup to work properly.

Guest Sessions Cannot Talk Through Host Wireless Adapter

By design, Hyper-V does not allow binding of the virtual network to a wireless network adapter in the host server. In a real-world environment, the Hyper-V host is typically connected to a wired network or even a very fast gigabit backbone as the performance between the host and the network throttles through the network adapter. Wireless is not fast enough to handle hundreds if not thousands of connections to a handful of virtual guest sessions. There are workarounds, such as bridging a wireless and wired network adapter on the host server together to get the guest sessions to bind to a wired adapter that is bridges to a wireless adapter. Alternatively, you can install a Routing and Remote Access Server (RRAS) service to route communications between multiple adapters in the host server to link the wireless to a physical wired adapter.

Hyper-V Configuration-Related Problems

For an administrator who has Hyper-V working on a server but has the problem where the guest sessions do not automatically start up when the host server is rebooted, a configuration change needs to be made. The configuration change specifies that the guest session should be started every time the host server is started. This is the common configuration for a host server, because the presumption is that if a host server has production guests on the system, the guests should boot automatically if the host is rebooted.

To configure the guest sessions, complete the following steps:

1. Right-click the guest session in the Hyper-V Administrative console and choose Settings.

2. In the Automatic Start Actions pane within the Setting pages, shown in Figure 13.14, choose Always Start This Virtual Machine Automatically.

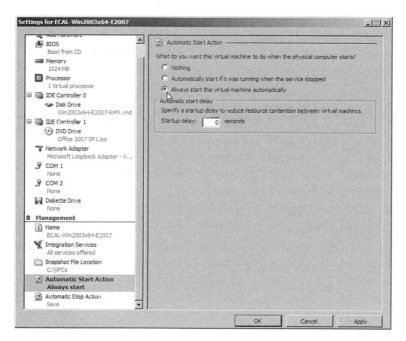

FIGURE 13.14   Automatic start action settings.

3. Click OK to save the setting.

You need to make this setting for each guest session that you want to automatically start when the host server is rebooted.

Hyper-V Miscellaneous Problems

For errors and problems that didn't fit in any of the other categories, this miscellaneous problems section covers various problems and their answers.

Cannot Cut/Paste Between Guest Sessions

By design, you generally cannot cut information from one guest session and paste that information into another guest session. In addition, you cannot drag and drop documents from one guest session into another. Although being able to do so is common on desktop virtual server applications such as Microsoft Virtual PC 2007 or Parallels for the Macintosh, these are not supported features in Hyper-V. Microsoft's explanation is that host servers are full running production systems intended to host business applications. Users are not sitting at the Hyper-V host level needing to cut and paste information between sessions; and from a security standpoint, it is better to not allow guest sessions to interact with one another at all. Therefore, if you want to get information from one guest session to another, you must log on from one guest to the other and transfer the files or information between the servers just like shuttling information from one physical server to another physical server.

Error Moving Hyper-V Guest Images to a New Folder

A task that comes up occasionally is to rename the folder on the Hyper-V host server that holds guest images and replace the folder with another folder that holds other guest images. In doing so, although the folder names are the same, the guest sessions will not start. Administrators have tried to swap folders by copying guest images into a folder and then renaming the folder to a different folder name, typically for failover reasons (for instance, images were in a folder c:\vpc, but the images got corrupt, so the administrator renames the c:\vpc to c:\vpc.old, then renames c:\vpcbackup to c:\vpc).

The images should start if the images in the c:\vpcbackup directory have the same name and configuration of the old images; however, the images do not start. The most common reason is that Hyper-V secures the folder where images are stored so that only the Hyper-V service can access the images. If the folder is replaced with a different folder, the permissions on the folder have been removed even though the folder may have the same name.

To fix the problem, complete the following steps:

1. Run Windows Explorer (Start, Run, **Explorer.exe**, OK).
2. Navigate to the folder where the guest images are being stored and right-click the folder and choose Properties.
3. Click the Security tab.
4. Click Edit, and then click Add.
5. In the Enter the Object Names to Select field, type **Virtual Machines**, and then click OK.
6. In the Permissions for Virtual Machines section, choose Allow for all permissions, as shown in Figure 13.15.
7. Click OK and then click OK again to save the setting.

Start the guest images. This time, they should begin.

Cannot Copy Guest Images

Another common challenge for administrators is to copy guest images on a Hyper-V host server. When trying to copy a guest image, the error "File is in use" appears. An administrator may attempt to copy guest images for the purpose of backing up the images or copying the images to another server for test purposes or the like. Even when the guest images are shutdown and off, the Hyper-V server still holds the files in use so that the images are ready to be booted at any time.

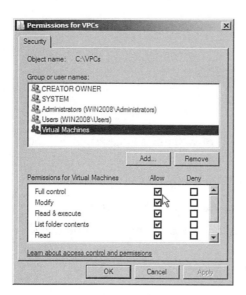

FIGURE 13.15   Giving virtual machines full control over the guest images container.

The only way to release the images from the Hyper-V server is to stop the Hyper-V service. To do so, following these steps:

1. From the Hyper-V Administrative console, click Stop Service in the Actions pane on the right side of the console. You will be prompted to confirm you want to stop the Hyper-V service. Click Yes.

2. Now that the Hyper-V service has been stopped, you can copy the Hyper-V guest images using Xcopy or Explorer or whatever you normally use to copy files.

3. After you have successfully copied the guest images you want off the server, click Start Service to restart the Hyper-V service (so that you can now restart guest images).

Summary

Logging and debugging tools help administrators monitor, manage, and problem solve errors on a Windows 2008 Hyper-V host and guest image systems and infrastructure. Many of the tools used to identify system problems in a Windows 2008 environment have been improved from previous versions of the applications in earlier releases of the Windows operating system. In addition, new tools have been introduced to enhance the administration logging and debugging experience. Key to problem solving is enabling logging and monitoring the logs to identify errors, research the errors, and perform system recovery based on problem resolution.

In addition to the tools and utilities that come with the Windows 2008 environment are resources such as the Microsoft TechNet database (www.microsoft.com/technet/). Between utility and tool improvements and online technical research databases, problem solving can be simplified in a Windows 2008 infrastructure.

Best Practices

The following are best practices from this chapter:

- ▶ Use the Task Manager to provide an instant view of system resources, such as processor activity, process activity, memory usage, and resource consumption.

- ▶ Use Event Viewer to check whether Windows 2008 is experiencing problems.

- ▶ Use filters, grouping, and sorting to help isolate and identify key events.

- ▶ Create custom filters to expedite problem identification and improve monitoring processes.

- ▶ Create alerts using triggers and actions to identify issues quickly.

- ▶ Archive security logs to a central location on your network, and then review them periodically against local security logs.

- ▶ Use subscriptions to consolidate logs from multiple systems to ensure problems are identified quickly.

- ▶ Set an auditing policy to shut down the server immediately when the security log is full. Doing so prevents generated logs from being overwritten or old logs from being erased.

- ▶ Establish a process for monitoring and analyzing system performance to promote maximum uptime and to meet service-level agreements.

- ▶ Run System Monitor from a remote computer to monitor servers.

- ▶ Use logging when monitoring a larger number of servers.

- ▶ Establish performance baselines.

- ▶ Create logging jobs based on established baselines to ensure performance data is captured during times when the system is having resource issues and to facilitate altering for proactive system management.

- ▶ Create new baselines as applications or new services are added to a server.

- ▶ Consider reducing the frequency of data collection to reduce the amount of data that must be collected and analyzed.

- ▶ Use logs to capture performance data.

- ▶ Use the Reliability Monitor to identify a timeline of system degradation to facilitate expeditious investigation of root issue causes.

- ▶ Use the Memory Diagnostics tool to facilitate hardware troubleshooting.

Index

Symbols

% Disk Time counter, 245
% Processor Time counter, 243
%pagefile in use counter, 226, 240
.txt files, creating, 83

A

actions, Task Scheduler, 201
Active Directory, 1, 16, 155-156
    Hyper-V host servers, adding, 28
Active Directory Certificate Services tools, 155
Active Directory Domain Services tools, 155
Active Directory global catalog servers, 350
Active Directory Lightweight Directory Services tools, 156
Active Directory Rights Management Services (AD RMS) tools, 156
active nodes, clusters, 356
active/active clusters, 356
active/passive clusters, 356
Add New Virtual Network option (Virtual Network Manager), 166
adding
    domains, Server Core systems, 123
    Hyper-V role, 116-117
    RAM, guest sessions, 139-140
addresses
    IP addresses, configuring, 105-106
    static IPv4 addresses, assigning, 121-123

B

C

E

F

G

I

J-L

M

N

O

Q-R

S

W

FREE Online Edition

Your purchase of **Mirosoft® Windows Server 2008 Hyper-V Unleashed** includes access to a free online edition for 120 days through the Safari Books Online subscription service. Nearly every Sams book is available online through Safari Books Online, along with over 5,000 other technical books and videos from publishers such as Addison-Wesley Professional, Cisco Press, Exam Cram, IBM Press, O'Reilly, Prentice Hall, and Que.

SAFARI BOOKS ONLINE allows you to search for a specific answer, cut and paste code, download chapters, and stay current with emerging technologies.

Activate your FREE Online Edition at www.informit.com/safarifree

> **STEP 1:** Enter the coupon code: HVXGJGA.

> **STEP 2:** New Safari users, complete the brief registration form.
> Safari subscribers, just login.

If you have difficulty registering on Safari or accessing the online edition, please e-mail customer-service@safaribooksonline.com